T0293551

Corporate Social Responsibility and Sustainability: From Values to Impact

Corporate Social Responsibility and Sustainability: From Values to Impact

Editor: Weston Clarke

MURPHY & MOORE
www.murphy-moorepublishing.com

www.murphy-moorepublishing.com

ⓂMURPHY & MOORE

Cataloging-in-Publication Data

Corporate social responsibility and sustainability : from values to impact / edited by Weston Clarke.
    p. cm.
Includes bibliographical references and index.
ISBN 978-1-63987-741-6
1. Social responsibility of business. 2. Industries--Social aspects. 3. Sustainable development--Economic aspects.
I. Clarke, Weston.
HD60 .C67 2023
658.408--dc23

Murphy & Moore Publishing
1 Rockefeller Plaza,
New York City,
NY 10020, USA

ISBN 978-1-63987-741-6

Contents

Preface

This book has been a concerted effort by a group of academicians, researchers and scientists, who have contributed their research works for the realization of the book. This book has materialized in the wake of emerging advancements and innovations in this field. Therefore, the need of the hour was to compile all the required researches and disseminate the knowledge to a broad spectrum of people comprising of students, researchers and specialists of the field.

Corporate social responsibility (CSR) refers to a business model that encourages businesses to make a concerted effort to work in ways that benefit the society and the environment instead of harming them. It is a commercial commitment that supports corporate social sustainability. It also involves businesses implementing moral and fair business practices. The four main categories of CSR are ethical responsibility, economic responsibility, environmental responsibility, and philanthropic responsibility. CSR aids in enhancing various aspects of society as well as promoting a positive brand image of businesses. CSR initiatives encourage businesses to have a beneficial impact on the environment and stakeholders such as investors, customers, communities and employees. Levi Strauss, Starbucks, and Apple are some well-known companies that practice CSR. This book elucidates the concepts and innovative studies on corporate social responsibility and sustainability. It consists of contributions made by international experts. A number of latest researches have been included to keep the readers up-to-date with the global concepts in this area of study.

At the end of the preface, I would like to thank the authors for their brilliant chapters and the publisher for guiding us all-through the making of the book till its final stage. Also, I would like to thank my family for providing the support and encouragement throughout my academic career and research projects.

Editor

Corporate Social Responsibility Influencing Sustainability within the Fashion Industry

Thorey S Thorisdottir [1],*(ID) **and Lara Johannsdottir** [2](ID)

[1] Faculty of Business, University of Iceland, 101 Reykjavik, Iceland
[2] Environment and Natural Resources, Faculty of Business, University of Iceland, 101 Reykjavik, Iceland; laraj@hi.is
* Correspondence: thth52@hi.is

Abstract: The fashion industry, one of the largest industries in the world, is a complicated phenomenon, driven by aspirations of symbolic lifestyle and the creativity of architecture and design. It pushes the use of natural resources to its limits by mass production and a low-cost structure that motivates consumerism at large. The purpose of this study is to explore corporate social responsibility and how it influences sustainability within the fashion industry. A systematic literature review was carried out. This encompassed the academic publications available in two scientific databases focusing on Corporate Social Responsibility (CSR), sustainability, and fashion, covering the period 2003–2019. The findings indicate that the CSR approach taken by managers within the fashion industry is focused on sustainability, business models, and/or supply chain innovation, with commitments undertaken concerning the economy, environment, and/or society, wherein the production of eco-friendly products and workers' safety are emphasized. Actions that tie CSR and sustainability with companies' actions are presented in a micro-meso-macro framework, where brand equity, culture, supply chain management, activism, and human rights are evident. The findings of the study are relevant for academia, practitioners, and policymakers, as they provide insight into the operations and impacts of domestic and multinational fashion companies, outlining the most relevant studies on the topic, and also highlighting research trends and gaps in the field.

Keywords: fashion industry; corporate social responsibility; sustainability; sustainable fashion

1. Introduction

Globalization of the economy has changed how companies or industries compete for consumers' attention by differentiating their products and services [1,2]. On the contrary, in the fashion industry, one of the largest industries in the world [3], and the fourth-largest in Europe after housing, food, and transport [4], standardization is critical but it has led to unsustainable actions by focusing on low-cost production at the maximum production speed [5]. The industry plays an essential role in the global economy and employs around 3384 million people, or 46% of the world's population of 7260.7 billion people, based on data from 2014 [3]. Accusations of unsafe workplaces, low salaries, violations of workers' rights [6], and low environmental performance have been constant, and these have intensified over the years, for example, the excessive use of natural resources. Over the decades, the consequences of inaction are evident [7–9] together with the resulting negative impacts on sustainable development [7,10,11].

Accusations related to the fashion industry's conduct are often linked to its ecological footprint, which is a consequence of mass production, prevalent labor abuse, and the marketing methods used in recent years, which have formed a throwaway culture [10–16]. This culture has resulted in a specific disposal problem globally, as every second, a truckload of textiles goes to landfills or is incinerated [17]. New clothes are discarded when they fall out of fashion [18,19], and often even before they do so. Despite increased consumer awareness regarding social and environmental impacts [13], the fashion industry still negatively affects the customers' sustainable future [7,10,11].

In spite of the pressure on the fashion industry to implement strategies addressing environmental and social issues, the evidence shows that the industry is still not taking corporate social responsibility (CSR) seriously, as few companies have hired CSR experts so far [20]. According to the fashion mindset and low-price policy, it is still feasible to produce by the lowest-cost methods possible, which has led to consumerism becoming a growing problem. This calls for a more explicit policy regarding pricing and the production space, and creates pressure for collaboration between fashion companies, suppliers, and other stakeholders to produce environmentally friendly products [21–23]. The long term benefit of formal CSR and sustainability practices within the fashion sector is that added value for the industry stakeholders would ultimately be created [24].

The fashion industry must face the "negative aspects of the life-cycle of their products" [25] (p. 33) by planning for the future and by conducting their business differently. This could be done by addressing, for example, "the increasing scarcity of energy, water, and their rising cost, together with the rising cost of waste and its disposal" [26] (p. 5), and their workers' rights when decisions are made on factory closures [26]. In this context, it is worth noting that companies change their behavior and take responsibility for their actions for various reasons. For example, to protect and improve their reputation, reduce stakeholder pressure, create new markets, and gain a competitive advantage [27]. Whether this involves real improvements is uncertain, since it all depends on the nature of the reasons and actions taken. Supporting diversity by donating to charity, funding volunteer programs by changing investment practices are other ways the industry will approach this. [26].

Studies have revealed an increasing number of issues related to consumerism, as consumers have not shown much interest in buying eco-friendly clothes, because the design and texture of such clothes does not appeal to them [28]. To encourage more desirable behavior, fashion designers need to add more value to eco-friendly clothing designs without damaging style or brand identity [29,30]. This is especially true in respect of consumers who use clothes to distinguish themselves from others, or see their clothes as a status symbol or as a means to show off a social position or a specific lifestyle [12]. The attention consumers give to sustainability issues is increased through education and by raising their awareness. An effective way to approach this is by utilizing marketing communication or social media [31–34], since the communication structure regarding CSR needs a new approach [35]. In order to increase consumer awareness of a sustainable product, fashion companies need to customize their marketing methods, whether these are domestically or globally focused [34,36,37].

Scholars have shown increased interest in the fashion industry in recent years, mainly with regard to fashion supply chains and their sustainability-emphasis, although some of the interest is associated with sustainability and CSR practices within the fashion industry [12,15]. CSR is a broad concept, and it is "described as an umbrella term for sustainability issues" [38] (p. 13), and in some cases, it is labeled as sustainability within the fashion industry [38,39]. This addresses the need to explore sustainability integration regarding ecological, environmental, and social responsibility within the fashion industry [40].

The purpose of this study is to explore CSR and how it influences sustainability within the fashion industry. A systematic literature review is carried out to achieve this goal, since it will help to map existing knowledge. A delimitated search was carried out through the Web of Science and EBSCOhost's databases, as these databases cover a large proportion of available studies. The results of these studies were published from 2003 to 2019. Many studies can be used as a base from which to summarize how CSR influences sustainability [41–46]. Alternatively, the micro-meso-macro framework [47] is used to describe the link between CSR and sustainability [48], as it seems to be the most suitable framework to follow in this research.

The paper is structured as follows. Section 2 explains CSR, sustainable development and sustainability, the connection between CSR and sustainability, the micro-meso-macro framework, and the sustainable fashion concepts. Section 3 begins with an explanation of the methods employed in this review. Section 4 includes the findings, illustrating differences between the years of publication; research focus by regions; the theoretical approach of studies; an overview of studies by their aim, purpose, and objective; overviews of keywords by industry sector and the frequency of keywords, key topics, and related sub-topics; a discussion of CSR; a discussion of sustainability; and contributions and suggestions for future research. Section 5 covers the discussion, and the sixth section is comprised of the conclusion.

2. Background

The review begins with a general discussion of the three main keywords this study employs: CSR, sustainability, and sustainable fashion.

2.1. Corporate Social Responsibility

The CSR concept is well known and has been around for a long time, but some forms of corporate responsibility can be traced back to the eighteenth century [14,38,49]. Latapi Agudelo et al. [50] drew attention to the evolution of CSR understanding, ranging from the discussion of businessmen's social responsibility in 1953 to the generation of sustainable values in 2016. The definition of CSR has left it unclear as to how companies should take responsibility for their actions towards the environment and society [3]. Nevertheless, as explained in the European (EU) [51] definition, the concept demonstrates how companies voluntarily participate in contributing to a cleaner environment and a better society by structuring their responsibilities [51]. Such actions affect all stakeholders, both internal and external, and influence the companies' success in the long-term [51]. While the volunteering approach is not legally binding, it influences social consent, or the license to operate, creating an obligation to ensure that operations are conducted ethically and to report cases where things go wrong or when a tragedy occurs [52]. There has been speculation as to what constitutes a socially responsible company, and it is somewhat uncertain. As Milton Friedman [53] points out, the concept entails an unclear and vague statement which indicates that a company is "an artificial person and in this sense may have an artificial responsibility" (p. 1). According to Friedman [53], companies are structured to increase profits and deliver financial benefits for their shareholders. It is the people and how they manage a company that creates responsibility for its social performance [53–55].

It is not a simple task to define CSR, as the description of the concept can differ between institutions, businesses, or countries where culture, business practice, and perceptions can affect how social issues and consequences are addressed [56]. Rasche et al. [57] drew attention to five perspectives on CSR, namely normative, integration, instrumental, political, and emergent, which show the motivation for companies to adopt CSR, and the implications if they fail to do so. A common motivation for implementing CSR stems from company leaders' "ethical obligations" (p. 8), requiring them to meet social expectations of integration by incorporating the three sustainability pillars, economic, environmental, and social, into the company structure. This is especially because CSR is still an "undisputed yet contested precondition for ongoing business development with which managers need to engage rather than respond proactively" [57] (p.10).

When defining CSR as a concept in terms of how businesses operate and what is expected, required, and desired by society, Carroll [49] summarizes the key aspects in a four-layer pyramid or a CSR framework. The layers are economic, legal, ethical, and philanthropic responsibility. The aspect of economic responsibility (the bottom layer) illustrates how society requires companies to be profitable and productive when it comes to investments, and how communications and financial structures are formed in the long-term. According to the pyramid, the legal responsibility aspect details how companies are required to be fair, for example, when it comes to products and services, ensuring the laws and regulations set by society are followed. The ethical aspect of the pyramid discusses the community expectations towards companies, pushing them to integrate moral norms and behaviors that are not defined by the legal system, thereby reflecting concepts of fairness and respect towards employees and other stakeholders. The final layer (the top layer) of the pyramid discusses how philanthropic responsibility does not reflect actual responsibility. Instead, it illustrates the nature of social expectations that can influence a company's reputation, attitudes, and willingness to support charities or give back to society in some way, and the internal and external stakeholders' roles concerning companies' responsibilities towards society [49].

2.2. Sustainable Development and Sustainability

In order to understand the history of sustainability, it is appropriate to open this discussion with the classic quotation from the Brundtland report where sustainable development (SD) is defined as "development that meets the needs of the present without compromising the ability of future generations to meet their own needs" [7] (p. 41). SD consists of four integral dimensions: economy, environment, society, and culture [58]. Other dimensions were added later: time and human [59], and time and space [60]. The Brundtland report was a milestone in raising awareness of global environmental problems [61], providing a good description of sustainability in practice [7], and creating a path to reach the goal of sustainability through its four principles [62]: (1) contributing to the ecological system by managing the use of natural resources; (2) by using environmentally friendly materials (3) practicing within an efficient ecosystem; and (4) contributing to society by meeting human needs, both globally and domestically [62] (p. 199). Sustainability is a long-term goal for the future where "environmental, societal and economic considerations are balanced in the pursuit of improved quality of life" [58] (para. 2).

Some would argue that the vision is not likely to benefit future generations as the world's ecosystems are already close to their limits, which is a matter of weak sustainability. In this instance, the focus is on new technology and market demand to support consumerism rather than limiting the overuse of natural resources [63]. This leads to a rejection of the "physical limits to economic growth" [48] (p. 269). Therefore, the goal should emphasize maintaining natural resources and supporting social equity, economic development, and environmental protection to deliver strong sustainability [63]. The discussion in Brundtland's report, nevertheless, reveals the need to develop new technology and reinforce knowledge and people skills in terms of decreasing resource consumption by developed nations [7]. Strong sustainability requires a commitment towards three pillars, economy, society, and the environment. It also discusses how businesses should deal with the problems created by their existence, such as waste and pollution [44,46,64].

Furthermore, how they plan to promote equity, to support employees' livelihoods and safety, while securing business profitability and financial performance [44,46] are components of this. Discussing a long-term vision for the economic aspects of well-being and the protection of natural resources is necessary [48,63]. The implementation of an emphasis on sustainability has been challenging for the business sector, society, and governments due to the broad structural framework encompassing negative environmental impacts and the unsustainable trends of mass resources consumption, where the wasteful use of water and land still persists [65].

Sustainability awareness among business front-runners has increased over the last decade and led to the implementation of sustainability goals to a greater extent. These leaders have used the triple bottom line (TBL) framework to analyze social, environmental, and economic impacts by measuring their results annually [66]. Despite good intentions, human welfare seems to be missing in the social equation, and natural resources are still under threat. As pointed out by Elkington, it is challenging to measure a purpose or goal, rather than "success or failure in terms of profit or loss" ([66], para. 4). Sustainability must be discussed in a broader context with the focus being placed on welfare for all human beings and the entire ecosystem [66].

A broad definition of sustainability is a research topic in White's [67] paper, in which he discusses the vision as a different perspective which varies depending on people's understanding. The paper reflects on the question of whether sustainability is a visual thing, measurable, or a tool to create a better future and if "sustainability is a vision of the future, he hopes for a shared vision among individuals and organizations" [67] (p. 218). Sustainability is more than a vision for a better future, it is a clear mission from "ecology to art, and agriculture to architecture" [68] (p. 76) as the future is unpredictable. It requires business leaders to dedicate time to creating improvements and interaction with natural resources issues [68]. "A clear, compelling mission should be at the heart of every company's effort to enhance its positive impacts on the environment and society" [69] (p. 49).

2.3. The Connection between CSR and Sustainability

There are arguments as to whether sustainability has lost its credibility or if the definition has caused misperception as the differences or the ties between CSR and sustainability seem to be unclear to business executives [61]. Examples which illustrate this can be found on the websites of many companies, where CSR is titled "sustainability" [38] (p. 11) or vice versa. The definition of sustainability within science has become more widespread over time and, in some cases, it is discussed as an outcome of CSR, or described as an element under the CSR umbrella [41] (p. 13), especially within the business sector [41].

Sustainability emerged in the early 1970s when the debate on environmental impacts intensified, becoming one of the driving forces for CSR [70]. As stated, it should be "a part of every business decision and operation" [39] (p. 131) and part of a company's DNA [70,71], guiding how the whole concept is managed [57]. Over 30 years of evolution, the concepts of CSR and sustainability have integrated the environmental, economic, and social aspects, but in different ways [48]. To show these differences, Steurer et al. [48] drew up a framework for sustainable development (SD), CSR, and corporate sustainability (CS) to illustrate the similarities between these concepts, at different levels. The framework pulls together sustainability at the macro level in combination with the economic, social, and environmental dimensions. The existence of the organization establishes corporate sustainability (CS) as a concept, while CSR sits within the management approach, which contains a specific management system, such as International Organization for Standardization (ISO), which can be used to deal with specific issues within those three dimensions at a micro level [48].

2.4. The Micro-Meso-Macro Framework

The micro-meso-macro framework consists of circles, where the innermost circle is the micro level, and the outermost circle is the macro level. The micro level describes the behavior of the economic system [47], whereas the macro level focuses on the local community, small groups, or individual organizations [72] or "refers to the individual carriers of rules and system they organize" [47] (p. 263). The meso level is next, sitting between the micro and macro levels, focusing on intermediate-sized organizations or institutions, social acceptance, integration, and equity, forming the structural architecture for efficiency and knowledge of the ecosystem [47]. The macro level consists "of the population structure of Meso" [47] (p. 263), and this discusses the social trends of everyday habits from a global perspective [72]. The macro level includes the legal aspect (law and regulations), technology, market demand, and new trends, whereas societal, cultural (norms and attitudes), and environmental aspects, such as access to natural resources, is the part that influences sustainability orientation [41]. When this framework is placed in the context of sustainability, sustainable development is seen as a societal concept at the macro level, corporate sustainability is identified as a corporate concept at the meso level, and CSR is recognized as a management approach at a micro level, including systems such as ISO standards. [73].

2.5. Sustainable Fashion

The fast-growing global fashion industry is worth over 3 trillion US dollars. It plays an essential role in the world economy as it holds around 4% of the market share or 385.7 billion dollars market value [3]. In 2015, the annual turnover in fast fashion was 1.8 trillion US dollars, and this is expected to increase by 17% or up to 2.1 US trillion dollars before 2025 [18].

Fashion is often described as a complicated phenomenon. The meaning of the word fashion can, for example, stand for apparel, clothing, footwear, garment, or textile [74]. The fashion industry is driven by aspiration, desire, and creativity [74]. It operates in the space between technology, business, and the arts [75] and is one of the "few remaining craft-based industries" [12] (p. 10) where sewing machines are still used in production [12]. It is a part of everyday activities [76], where there is the ambition and desire of consumers to use fashion products in relation to their symbolic lifestyle features, personalizing their image through textiles, clothing, garments, or apparel outfits [12,74]. Through creativity, in eco and green design, the fashion industry aligns with other creative industries such as architecture and product design. However, unlike some other businesses, the fashion industry was relatively slow to implement any sustainability emphasis [12].

The root of sustainable fashion is traceable to the eighteenth century when the first recorded instances can be found. In this case, men's waistcoats were redesigned and used as the basis for new embroidered women's vests. One such item is displayed in the Museum at the Fashion Institution of Technology (FIT) [77] in the United States (US). The ideology of reusing and recycling has, therefore, been around for quite a long time. Another good example is from the late 1960s when the fabric, which is known as paper wear, "made from a variety of nonwoven fiber rather than the actual paper", [77] (p. 46) was introduced as a disposable product. It was a part of the evolution towards reusing fabrics in the fashion industry. The development continued, and in the 1970s, the recycling of plastic bottles was developed, and they were used to create a clothing fabric, known as a fleece material [77]. Despite examples of sustainable fashion, scholars are still looking for answers as to how the fashion industry can act more responsibly towards the environment and the social impacts of its day-to-day operations [5,11,15,21]. However, because the industry's commitments are structured around the delivery of new stylish trends to stores every other week, and are still reliant on a low-cost and low-price structure, it is often less expensive to buy a plain white t-shirt than a cup of coffee in a café [5].

The disposal problem created by mass production and consumerism puts pressure on natural resources [17], as new clothes are thrown out when the expectations and perceived value of customers no longer exist [18,19]. This had led to the development of a framework by the European Commission to develop new sustainable "eco-design and other measures" [78] (p. 10) to raise consumer awareness of sustainable products by facilitating access to "re-use and repair services" [78] (p. 10), thereby conforming with circularity by improving transparency in the global production process. In addition, to deal with the disposal problem, the action plan includes an improved program to re-use, recycle, and sort fashion items overall [78].

There are several ways to highlight sustainability within the fashion industry, for instance, by emphasizing more transparency in reporting the production processes. Fashion designers work under constant pressure, where they deal with transportation miles, traceability, and waste in the design process. Therefore, it can be challenging to say whether it is time pressure or lack of interest that leads to these components not being factored into the design process [12]. Given these reasons, sustainability should be addressed as an opportunity to deliver improvements for the future of responsible fashion [12].

Concerning the issue of raising consumer awareness of sustainable products, Benedetto [31] suggests that visual merchandisers should design store plans with this in mind, or that these products should be made more visible in stores to increase their sales. Furthermore, it is suggested that labels explaining the impacts the product has on the environment should be designed so that they are more informative. If company managers implemented these suggestions, it could help firms to differentiate themselves, and gain a competitive advantage over their competitors [31,32], especially for the companies at the forefront of the development. To do so, companies must have access to information, collected through market research, about what motivates consumers in their desire for sustainable fashion [32].

3. Methods

This research follows the systematic literature review (SLR) method described in the Handbook of Organizational Research Methods authored by Denyer and Tranfield [79]. The SLR method is, in this case, used to identify the knowledge gap in the fashion industry regarding sustainability and CSR in order to establish a reliable knowledge base, which aims to serve academia, businesses, and policymakers. The value of conducting SLR is that it "provides a systematic and transparent means for gathering, synthesizing and appraising the findings of studies on a particular topic or question" [80] (p. 104), as it aims to reduce bias throughout the investigation of published literature [79,81]. The aim is also to discover how much is known or unknown about the research topic. This systematic literature review, therefore, lays the ground for empirical studies by focusing on, among other things, CSR and how it influences sustainability within the fashion industry. This will be achieved by collecting information on CSR practices and sustainability innovations to set out what is already known about the topic, which theories have been applied, and to investigate different ideas in this field. In order to do so, this research follows three stages to conduct the SLR, as proposed by Tranfield et al. [81]: (1) planning the review, (2) conducting the review, and (3) reporting and dissemination.

3.1. Planning Review

At the first stage proposed by Tranfield et al. [81], the review's planning stage consists of identifying and preparing the proposal, developing the need, and the protocol for this review. The need consists of exploring CSR integration, and establishing if or how it influences sustainability-emphasis within the fashion industry [40]. It is also important to identify what is known about the topic, something that, in some cases, is labeled as sustainability [38,39]. The focus was on articles published in peer-reviewed academic journals. Other publications, such as books and conference papers, were excluded from the review protocol. For the selection stage, two scientific databases were chosen for the search of academic papers. The Web of Science and EBSCOhost's Academic Source Premier and Business Source Premier were chosen because they include extensive coverage of relevant published papers. The selection of these two databases was based on specific inclusion criteria requiring articles to be published in peer-reviewed journals, documents, and institutional reports written in English. It was also important to have open access to full-text papers online, covering the topic of this investigation. The SLR approach is in its nature inductive, as categories were modified and classified during the review process [82].

The selection process was conducted by following the requirement of a transparent structure of selection criteria relating to each finding, as proposed by Denyer and Tranfield [79], to establish whether it fitted the study purpose. The second stage consisted of identifying, selecting, assessing quality, and the processes of extraction, monitoring, and synthesizing the data [81].

3.2. Conducting the Review

In terms of the review, the search string was defined to identify relevant academic papers serving this study purpose. The search was conducted using search tools offered by each of the selected databases with the usage of standard Boolean "AND/OR" terms, allowing the creation of a single search algorithm where the authors ran their keywords to search through titles and abstracts. The algorithm search string contained corporate social responsibility, sustainability, and fashion; it was also subdivided according to related concepts (see Table 1). Corporate social responsibility was also defined as CSR, corporate responsibility, and CR, in an attempt to capture studies from around 1970, as the social element was not included in CSR [49] until after 1970 [50]. Additionally, to cover most aspects of CSR, the stakeholders' role was included to gain a holistic view of CSR, as Carroll suggests [49].

Sustainability was also divided into three domains: economic, environmental, and social, to cover the three pillars of sustainability [41,44,46,64].

Table 1. Keywords and sub-keywords used as a search string in this SLR study.

Keywords	Sub—Keywords
Corporate Social Responsibility	Corporate Social Responsibility—CSR Corporate Responsibility—CR Stakeholder
Fashion—Fashion industry	Apparel Clothes Garments Textile
Sustainability—The three pillars	Economic Environment Social

Furthermore, to maximize the search, the fashion industry was sub-divided into apparel, clothes, garments, and textile. The final keyword search strings were as follows: (Corporate Social Responsibility or CSR or corporate responsib* or stakeholder* or economic sustainab* or environment sustainab* or social sustainab*) and (Fashion* or apparel* or clothes* or garments* or textile*). These keywords were used to cover a broad selection of CSR and sustainability papers concerning the fashion industry. The search period was from January 1970, as a starting point, to April 2019, aiming to cover as much research related to the topic from this period, and yielded 892 papers. The search and analytical processes were finalized in December 2019.

3.3. Inclusion and Exclusion Criteria

The keyword search resulted in 892 papers. Thereof, 690 papers were sourced from the Web of Science, and 202 papers were derived from Ebscohost's database (see Figure 1). In a number of cases, and to be sure that the inclusion was determined correctly, the authors read the entire articles. The process of inclusion, titles, abstracts, and the keywords of each of the 892 papers were read to determine whether they should be included in the review or not. This method was based on examples proposed by Jesson et al. [80] for SLR methods. Through this process, 574 articles were excluded since they were unrelated to the fashion industry, CSR, and sustainability, or they were not written in English. After the initial screening, 318 papers were further examined regarding CSR, sustainability, and fashion. Based on this analysis, 109 articles were excluded. The final result yielded 209 papers that fitted the purpose of the study. The full list appears in Appendix A.

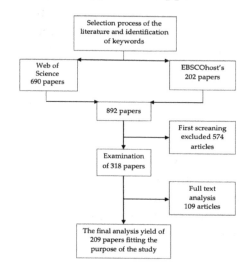

Figure 1. Flow chart of research progress.

3.4. Reporting and Dissemination

As proposed by Denyer and Tranfield [79], the final stage in conducting the SLR consists of recommendations and reporting so that evidence can be put into practice. The analytical stage was conducted using the qualitative content analysis (QCA) method, with the support of the MAXQDA 2018 software program, which was utilized to examine the text qualitatively [82,83]. During this process, "qualitative data is systematically converted to numerical data" [84] (p. 166) using the Microsoft Excel 365 software program. After reading through the 209 selected papers, the frame was combined with data-driven inductive logic for open coding to identify concepts, development, and the frame was combined with data-driven inductive logic for open coding to identify concepts, development, and implementation, by explaining and integrating each category [85]. The frame was designed for named categories based on definitions within the publications and structured based on data from the search. The QCA method and open coding allowed the researchers to go back and forth through the data collected from the search for analysis whilst finalizing the frame [82]. Thus, it is based on a "strategy for discovering concepts in the researcher's data" [82] (p. 111). This method, therefore, fits the nature of this study.

Examples of the coding frame are publication, years, markets, methods, theories, aims, purposes and objectives, topics, keywords, and future research suggestions. Topics were divided based upon themes and categorized to relate to the key topics of each study. These categories are CSR, sustainability, and a further category comprised of 12 sub-categories: social responsibility, economic, corporate sustainability, relationships, stakeholders, ethical, strategies, consumption, consumers or buyer's behavior, technology, marketing, and supply chain and management. The dissemination of the outcome is reflected in the findings section. Additionally, categorization is based on the micro-meso-macro framework [47,72], which further describes the links between CSR and sustainability [48] within the fashion industry. Thus, it is suitable for use as a theoretical framework to follow when discussing the findings of the study.

4. Findings

The findings section is structured around the following topics: (1) years of publication, (2) journals publishing the papers, and research methodology, (3) number of publication per journal in terms of the publication, (4) the geographical distribution of areas of study, (5) theories related to the researcher's topic, (6) aims, purpose, and objectives of the studies, (7) keywords used for describing the fashion industry, (8) studies by keywords and their frequency, (9) concepts found in the literature, (10) topics of CSR and sustainability in the fashion industry, and (11) contributions and suggestions for future research.

4.1. Years and Journal of Publication

The findings suggest a growing interest in sustainability and CSR issues concerning the fashion industry (see Figure 2). Of the 209 papers examined in this study, 70% (146 papers) were published within a four-year period from 2015 to 2019, 24% (50 papers) were from 2010 to 2014, 6% (13 papers) were from 2003 to 2009, and none were published before 2003. It is noteworthy that articles related to the topic did not appear until the early 21st century, around 2003, although the search criteria were based on the year 1970. One should keep in mind that papers published in 2019 were published during the first four months of the year, since the search concluded in April of that year.

Figure 2 also demonstrates an upward trend in interest in sustainability/CSR-related discussions concerning fashion since 2012, with the exceptions of the years 2013 and 2016, when the number of published papers decreased compared to the previous year.

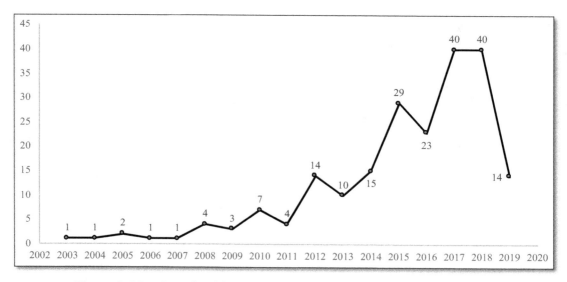

Figure 2. Number of publications about CSR, sustainability and fashion.

Table 2 shows which journals have covered most discussions regarding CSR, sustainability, and fashion, and what methods were employed in these studies. The journal, Sustainability, contained the highest number of published papers related to the topic, or 11% (23 papers), followed by the Journal of Cleaner Production 8.1% (17 papers), the International Journal of Consumer Studies 6.2% (13 papers), and the Journal of Business Ethics 5.3% (11 papers). Out of the 209 selected articles, 105 articles were published in various journals, 28 journals published two articles related to the topic, and 76 journals published one paper each in the period 2003 to 2019. Indeed, 77% (161 papers) of the 209 papers sampled were published from 2014 to 2019. Moreover, Table 2 also shows the methodology employed in the studies. Of those, qualitative methods are used in 56% of the studies (117 papers), quantitative methods in 29% of the studies (60 papers), and mixed methods in 3% of the studies (six papers). Additionally, 12% (26 papers) employed other methods, such as life cycle assessment (LCA), observation(s), and experiments. In terms of qualitative studies, five studies employed a systematic literature review method, and six consisted of other types of literature review papers. The methods employed in other papers include observation, experiments, game theory, and event studies, to name a few examples (see Table 2).

Table 2. Journals publishing papers on CSR, sustainability, and fashion, and research methods employed.

Journal	Number of Publications	Percentage	Methodology			
			Qualitative	Quantitative	Multiple	Other
Sustainability	23	11%	14	5	0	4
Journal of Cleaner Production	17	8.1%	12	5	0	0
International Journal of Consumer Studies	13	6.2%	5	6	0	2
Journal of Business Ethics	11	5.3%	8	2	1	0
Journal of Fashion Marketing and Management	9	4.3%	7	2	0	0
International Journal of Production Economics	6	2.9%	3	1	0	2
Journal of Corporate Citizenship	6	2.9%	6	0	0	0
Corporate Social Responsibility and Environmental Management	4	1.9%	1	2	1	0
Fashion and Textiles	4	1.9%	0	4	0	0
Accounting Auditing & Accountability Journal	3	1.4%	3	0	0	0
Design Journal	3	1.4%	3	0	0	0
Fibers & Textiles in Eastern Europe	3	1.4%	2	1	0	0
Transportation Research Part E-Logistics and Transportation Review	3	1.4%	2	0	0	1
Others publisher with two publication	28	13.4%	12	9	0	7
Others publisher with one publication	76	36.4%	39	23	4	10
Total	209	100%	117	60	6	26

Figure 3 illustrates publication in the top five journals, publishing most of the fashion-related articles regarding CSR and sustainability.

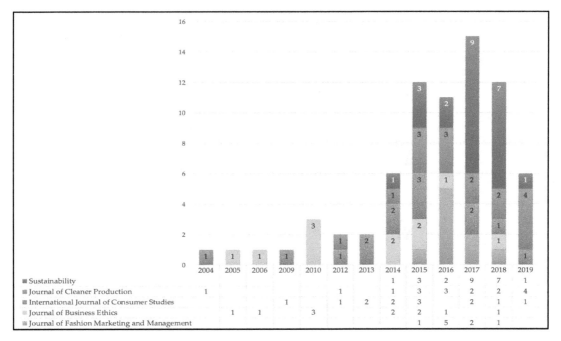

Figure 3. Journals in terms of number of publications since 2004.

Sustainability ranked first, with 23 published papers, but the first paper was published in 2014. The Journal of Cleaner Production ranked second with 17 papers published, the first one issued in 2004. International Journal of Consumer Studies ranked third with 13 published papers, the first one published in 2009. The Journal of Business Ethics ranked fourth with 11 published papers, but its first paper was published in 2005. The Journal of Fashion Marketing and Management ranked fifth with nine published papers, and its first publication related to this topic was published in 2015.

4.2. Research Focus by Regions

The 209 papers examined where the research was targeted, i.e., country, region, or the global market. The analysis shows that 137 (65%) of the articles are focused on different regions, while 72 papers (35%) approached the subject from a global perspective. The regions receiving the highest levels of attention are Asia with 24% (50 papers), and Europe with 24% (50 papers), followed by the USA with 10% (21 papers). These papers did not specify whether their focus was on the North, South or Central America. In comparison, 1% (three papers) focused on North America specifically, and 3% (seven papers) investigated the South American market. The overall focus on the US market is, therefore, 15% (31 papers). Moreover, 2.5% (five papers) focused on Africa, and just 0.5% (one paper) focused on the Australian market (see Figure 4). This reveals a research gap based on regional focus, particularly a lack of studies focusing on Africa and South America.

A more detailed analysis of the study focus reveals that most of the studies concentrated on a single country, and only 12 studies focused on more than one country. In the latter cases, the strongest focus was on comparing European countries' conditions, which were featured in a total of five papers. The coverage areas were Spain and Turkey, Italy and France, the Scandinavian countries of Norway, Denmark and Sweden, the Nordic countries of Denmark, Norway, Sweden, Finland and Iceland, and the Western European countries, namely Sweden, Norway, Germany, France, and the United Kingdom.

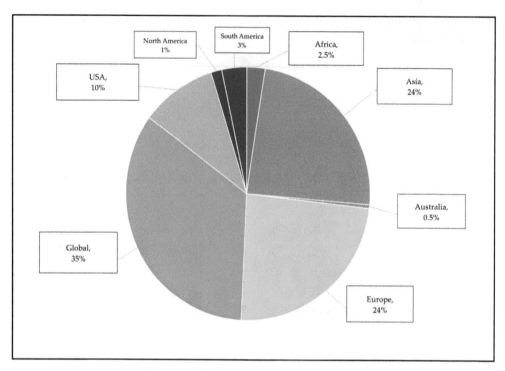

Figure 4. Research focus by region.

The analysis reveals that those who investigated CSR and sustainability in the fashion industry by focusing on the US market were also interested in comparing the US market with the markets of Honduras, El Salvador, Latin America, South Korea, and China. A total of four papers compared US fashion companies with similar firms in the UK. Those who focused on the Asian fashion market were interested in comparing China with South Korea, together with the Canadian, Sri Lankan, and US markets, respectively, in four papers.

4.3. Studies by a Theoretical Approach

As expected, the literature's theoretical approach varied for apparel, garment, clothing, and textile research regarding CSR and sustainability. The theoretical approach was specified in 63 out of 209 papers. Figure 5 shows how studies at the institutional and organizational levels comply with institutional theory, and these were the most commonly used. In this finding, various theories cover 48% (30 papers), institutional theory covers 21% (13 papers), stakeholder theory applies to 14% (nine papers), the theory of reasoned action (TRA) covers 6% (four papers), the theory of planned behavior (TPB) appears in 6% (four papers), and agency theory applies to 5% (three papers).

Of those 30 papers focusing on various theories, 13 studies concentrated on sustainability, while two studies focused on CSR. In total, nine papers out of those 30 papers covered both CSR and sustainability, where these topics were analyzed through the lenses of the value-belief-norm theory (VBN), the theory of modern slavery, transaction cost economics theory (TCE), the theory of moral responsibility, attribution theory, contingency theory, legitimacy theory, Schwartz's value theory, social cognitive theory, corporate social theory, and corporate sustainability theory. Finally, six out of those 30 papers used various theories focused on supply chain management, environmental management systems, suppliers, cultural differences, and secondhand consumption using the theory of generations, efficient market theory, and Hofstede's national cultural dimensions, and the generational cohort theory.

Concepts explored using institutional theory include the Clean Clothes Campaign, codes of conduct, CSR and sustainability reporting, communication, life cycle assessment, CSR in formal and informal practices, and environmental management strategy within the fashion industry.

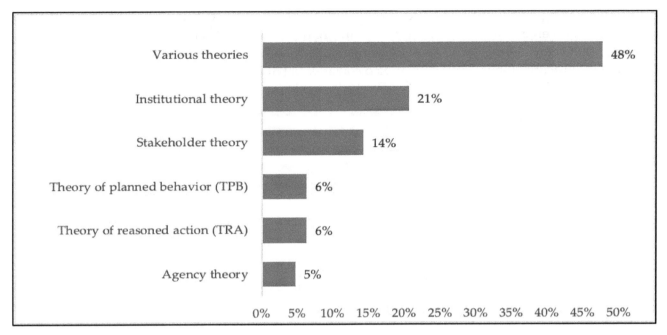

Figure 5. Overview of theoretical approach.

It is more common for scholars to utilize institutional theory by focusing on CSR rather than sustainability, as evidenced by a total of 13 papers (21%). Seven of those 13 papers focused on CSR, namely formal and informal practices and the fashion industry's communication methods. In the sustainability approach, three studies focused on life cycle assessment, sustainability impacts, and the reporting processes regarding both CSR and sustainability. In studies where stakeholder theory is used as a framework, this was featured in nine papers (14%). Three papers out of those nine discussed CSR and social responsibility, and one paper focused on sustainability through life cycle assessments. Referring to those using the theory of planned behavior (TPB), reasoned action (TRA), and agency theory, four of these studies (6%) out of 63 focused on CSR in their investigation of the fashion industry. At the same time, five papers discussed the topic from a sustainability perspective (see Figure 5).

According to publications, the stakeholder theory is the third most relevant theory, appearing in 14% (nine papers) of the papers analyzed. This theoretical approach is mostly used to examine CSR at the organizational level, and the majority of the authors discussed the influence of company conduct on the environment and the use of natural resources. They also studied how to compare and measure the advantage of implementing CSR [26,86–90] in the context of social responsibility, the return on equity (ROE), life cycle assessment, and corporate sustainability.

The fourth most commonly employed theoretical approach is the theory of planned behavior (TPB), which appears in 6% of the papers (four papers). This theory is used in relation to sustainable apparel and second-hand clothing. The theory of reasoned action (TRA) was utilized in 6% (four papers). The sixth theoretical approach employed is the agency theory, which appears in 5% (three papers) of the papers focusing on sustainable consumption and the supply chain.

4.4. Overview of Studies by Aim, Purpose, and Objective

The review reveals the aim, purpose, and objective presented by authors of the selected 209 papers. In total, 21% (43 papers) (see Figure 6) aimed to investigate fashion industry supply chains by discussing how sustainability and CSR are practiced or managed [21,91–99]. In 18% of the studies (38 papers), researchers aimed to investigate CSR and discussed, for example, the increased social expectation that organizations should employ responsible practices in terms of the environment. How CSR implementation might affect value creation or companies' competitive advantage, what barriers they have to deal with, and the influence managers have on internal and external stakeholders during the implementing process have also been analyzed. Furthermore, whether such actions might affect consumers' perceived value when buying from organizations that had integrated CSR strategies, or lead to them considering social and environmentally friendly products, and whether this influences the financial outcome for companies was also considered [20,24,31,55,86,100–114].

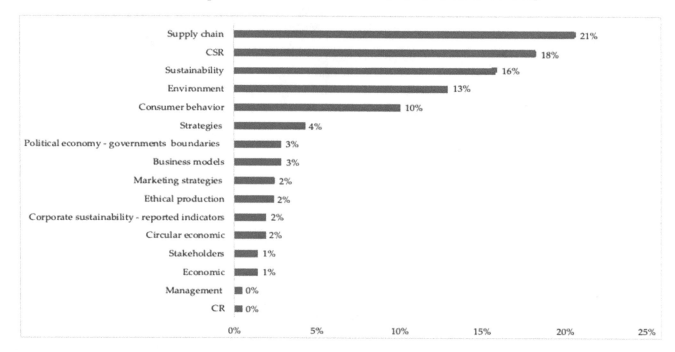

Figure 6. Result related to aims, purpose, and objectives of the studies.

A focus on sustainability was evident in 16% of the papers (33) analyzed. In these cases, researchers aimed to study fashion business models regarding innovation for sustainability, corporate sustainability, performance, and how the results are measured or defined to improve company responsibility towards environmental crises and transparency [15,115–120]. Researchers were also interested in investigating consumer knowledge of sustainability, especially younger consumers, summarized in their interest, lifestyle, and awareness regarding sustainability-related issues [121–126], in the cases of both fast and slow fashion. In addition, focus was placed on building a framework for sustainability and developing a roadmap for the main elements of sustainability, i.e., environmental, social, and economic factors [124,127–131]. Several studies focused on the production and the design process and aimed to conclude if certification related to responsible conduct results in improvements, or greater responsibility in selecting production methods that benefit ecosystems [132–134].

In total, 13% (27 of the papers analyzed) aimed to investigate the environmental impacts of fashion by evaluating company performance as well as identifying ways to improve the material usage or the lifespan of organic cotton used in production, or how to minimize pollution during the washing process [135–137].

Consumer behavior was the main focus in 10% (21 papers) of the 209 papers analyzed. In this case, the authors aimed to identify specific buying patterns related to consumers' awareness of environmental and social impacts [138], as well as their attitudes towards sustainable fashion [37,139]. Furthermore, researchers studied how companies tried to promote customer interest in buying sustainable fashion items [30], and how marketing methods affected their decisions [140]. Hence, 4% (nine papers) of the papers analyzed discussed CSR and sustainability strategies, whilst 3% (six papers) of the papers studied business models, political economy, and government boundaries, respectively. Other topics featured in 2% of the papers (five papers), focused on marketing strategies, ethical products, and the circular economy. In cases where the percentage is 1%, three papers investigated each topic in question, and in instances where there was just one paper, this is listed as 0% (see Figure 6).

4.5. Overviews of Keywords by Industry and Frequency of Keywords

The review shows that out of the 209 papers analyzed, 61 papers (29%) labeled the discussion as the fashion industry, 55 papers (26%) used the concept of the apparel industry, 43 (21%) used textile industry, whilst 19 papers (9%) used the concept of the garment industry, and 17 papers (8%) referred to the clothing industry (see Table 3). Given the nature of industry, the fashion industry is described as a "sub-sector of both the creative industries and the clothing and textiles industries and provides opportunities for innovation and creativity in the manufacturing, textiles, and apparel accessories." [141] (p. 56).

Table 3. Keywords used for describing the fashion industry.

Industry	Numbers of Studies	Percentage of Studies
Fashion industry	61	29%
Apparel industry	55	26%
Textile industry	43	21%
Garment industry	19	9%
Clothing industry	17	8%
Slow (Luxury) fashion	9	4%
Fast fashion	5	2%
Total	209	100%

The general approach regarding the fashion industry reveals, for example, the need to reform or redesign fashion business models concerning management in the supply chain in terms of performance and environmental sustainability [15,115,142]. The culture and cultural differences were discussed in few papers, which also applied to a structural framework for sustainability and eco-friendly products and marketing communication, where social media is the modern approach to gaining customers' attention [34,120,143–145]. The discussion of fashion within the apparel industry in a broader spectrum was focused on the production process, arguing how the outsourcing of production has created negative impacts within countries such as Bangladesh, Taiwan, and Sri Lanka. This was especially so regarding ethical issues such as workers' rights and welfare, to name a couple of issues [105,146]. Discussions concerning the garment industry reveal, for example, sustainable strategies to tackle sustainability-related issues such as labor welfare, environmentally friendly production processes, and trading [94], to name a few. The general discussions regarding fashion and the clothing industry focused on lack of regulations, the suppliers' criteria for defining human rights, child labor and long working hours, and increasing awareness amongst consumers regarding sustainability-related issues [89,147].

It should be noted that only nine papers (4%) focused on slow or luxury fashion and five papers (2%) on fast fashion. The general approach used in the slow/luxury fashion related papers was, for example, to investigate how customers form their values towards slow fashion or luxury fashion, the environmental or social performance of slow fashion, human rights in developing countries, and the United Nations' guiding principles. Those who studied fast fashion investigated whether attitudes towards eco-friendly products and environmental issues influenced consumers to buy sustainable products. The triple bottom line (TBL) framework for sustainability reporting was also among the keywords used in studies focusing on slow fashion.

Of the 209 selected papers, 188 (90%) provided more than one keyword that referred to their study's content. The results are shown in Tables 4 and 5 covering the frequency of the keywords researchers used to explain their topics related to CSR or sustainability, and these are categorized respectively. The total frequency of keywords related to describing CSR is 393 in the selected papers. CSR has the highest level of frequency, being used in 60 papers (15%), followed by industry, which was included in 44 papers (11%), and environment, which appeared in 30 papers (8%), countries were used in 26 papers (7%), labor in 23 papers (6%), organizations in 23 papers (6%), and ethics in 22 papers (6%), as shown in Table 4.

Table 4. Most frequently used keywords for Corporate Social Responsibility (CSR).

Corporate Social Responsibility					
Frequency of Keywords			**Frequency of Keywords**		
Keywords		**Percentage**	**Keywords**		**Percentage**
1. CSR	60	15%	14. Culture	11	3%
2. Industry	44	11%	15. Corporation	9	2%
3. Environment	30	8%	16. Management	8	2%
4. Countries	26	7%	17. Economic	7	2%
5. Labor	23	6%	18. Theories	7	2%
6. Organizations	23	6%	19. Sustainability	6	2%
7. Ethics	22	6%	20. Drivers & barriers	6	2%
8. Social factors	20	5%	21. Human rights	6	2%
9. Business	17	4%	22. Policy, strategic	5	1%
10. Communication	14	4%	23. Values	4	1%
11. Supply chain,	14	4%	24. Institutional	4	1%
12. Consumers	13	3%	25. Activism	4	1%
13. Stakeholders	11	3%			
The total frequency of keywords				393	100%

Table 5. Most frequently used keywords for Sustainability.

Sustainability					
Frequency of Keywords			**Frequency of Keywords**		
Keywords		**Percentage**	**Keywords**		**Percentage**
1. Industry	65	15%	17. Culture	5	1%
2. Sustainability	64	15%	18. Economic	4	1%
3. Business	46	11%	19. Pollution	4	1%
4. Environment	40	9%	20. Regulation	4	1%
5. Products	30	7%	21. Life cycle assessment	4	1%
6. Consumers	28	7%	22. Ethical	3	1%
7. Supply chain	26	6%	23. CSR	3	1%
8. Re-use-recycle	14	3%	24. Drivers & barriers	3	1%
9. Countries	13	3%	25. Theory of planned behavior	3	1%
10. Management	10	2%	26. Human rights	3	1%
11. Measure	8	2%	27. Technology	2	0.50%
12. Designing	8	2%	28. Entrepreneurship	2	0.50%
13. Marketing	8	2%	29. Activist	2	0.50%
14. Structural-policies	7	2%	30. Resources	1	0.20%
15. Social sustainability	6	1%	31. Employee	1	0.20%
16. Consumption	5	1%			
The total frequency of keywords				423	100%

Table 5 covers the frequency of keywords researchers used to explain their topics related to this review paper. The overall frequency of keywords related to sustainability is 423. The discussion related to the industry has the highest level of frequency, included in 65 papers (15%), followed by sustainability as a stand-alone keyword, included in 64 papers (15%), and business, included in 46 papers (11%). The fourth keyword listed in Table 5 is the environment, which appeared in 40 papers (9%).

Further analysis of keywords with a frequency of over 20 revealed consumers, included in 28 (7%), and supply chain, included in 26 papers (6%). (Further details are listed in Appendix A).

4.6. Analysis of Studies by Key Concepts

Table 6 reveals the use of key concepts in the 209 papers selected for the review. The sustainability concept is the most commonly used in 82 of the papers (39%) studied. The CSR concept was used in 74 papers (35%) analyzed, and other concepts were less frequently used, occurring in 53 of the papers (25%) analyzed.

Table 6. Breakdown by concepts found in the literature.

Categories Related to the Concepts	Number of Studies	Percentage
Sustainability	82	39%
CSR	74	35%
Other	53	25%
Total papers	209	100%

4.7. Key Topics and Related Sub-Topics

Table 7 reveals the key topics that researchers associate with CSR and sustainability. Furthermore, it shows that studies related to responsibility within the fashion industry are also labeled under other concepts: corporate responsibility, social responsibility, ethics, and supply chain. In the case of CSR, the sub-topics investigated were as follows: activities, commitments including anti-sweatshop, developing countries, and labor and workers' conditions, culture, brand equity, business models, communication, drivers and barriers, ethical fashion, financial management, frameworks, institutional pressure, the management approach, regulations, strategies, supply chain, and sustainable practices.

Table 7. Categories and topics of CSR and sustainability in the fashion industry.

Key Topic	Sub-Topics
Corporate Social Responsibility (CSR)	Activities, Commitments (including Anti-sweatshop, Developing countries, Labor and workers conditions), Culture, Brand equity, Business models, Communication, Drivers and barriers, Ethical fashion, Financial management, Framework, Institutional pressure, Management approach, Regulations, Strategies, Supply chain, Sustainability practices,
Sustainability	Business models (including Innovation), Commitment, Consumption, Drivers and barriers, Environmental practice, Environmental management system, Equity, Knowledge, Life Cycle Assessment (LCA), Lifestyle (values), Management and performance, Measurement (TBL), Slow fashion, Supply chain, Waste (reuse and recycle)
Other Key Topics	Sub-Topics
Consumers/Buyers behavior	Attitudes, Chinese/Polish consumers, Disposal intention, Life cycle assessment, Purchase intention, Secondhand clothing, Sustainable clothing, Young consumers intention attitude and behavior, Buyers behavior Community, Purchase intention for environmental and sustainable products, The role of clothing status symbol
Consumption	Apparel, Clothing, Fashion products, Slow fashion consumption
Corporate sustainability	Business models, Consumers and businesses, Environment and behavior, Employees perceptions, Low-cost, Reported indicators, Reports
Economic	Circular economy, Circular model for fashion, Creative industry, Markdown money policy, Political economy government boundaries, Social and environmental performance, Sustainability

Table 7. *Cont.*

Key Topic	Sub-Topics
Environmental	Barriers, Eco-fashion, Efficiency, Environmental practice and impacts, Entrepreneurship, Impacts of clothing. Internal motivation, Local clothes, homemade clothing, Management, Microplastic pollution, Performance, Regulation, Strategies, Sustainable solution, Technology to recycle clothes
Ethical	Codes of conducts, Ethical clothing, Ethical products, Social and eco-labeling
Marketing	Activities, Awareness for green products, Business practice, Luxury fashion strategies
Regulations	Community, Industry, Regulatory pressure, Workers rights internationally, Workers rights suppliers, Government attention towards the local economy, Rana Plaza, Policies and government approach
Relationships	Between corporate sustainability and business model innovation, Between Corporate Social responsibility (CSR) and consumer behavior in an international setting, Relationship building in fashion retail, In social media
Social Responsibility	Corporate responsibility, Civil society organizations (CSOs), Fair Labor Association (FLA), Governments and authorities' role, Human resources management (HRM), Knowledge and attitudes, Environmentally sustainable apparel (ESA), Life Cycle Assessment guidelines, Practice, Professional fashion models' reporting, Strategies, Socially sustainable practices, Supply chain orientation (SRSCO), UN guiding principles business and human rights
Stakeholders	A managerial perception, Collaboration, Innovative business strategy, Responsibility
Strategies	Cleaner production, Environmental, Management control systems (MCS) Proactive, Structural adaption
Supply chain Management	Code of conduct, Design, Environmental sustainability adaption, Global supply chain, Green drivers and practice, Human behavior, Labor network, Life Cycle Assessment (LCA), Measuring Sustainability (TBL), Modern slavery Product lifetimes and obsolescence, Product service systems (PSS) intervention Responsibility, Slow fashion definition and production, Sourcing in China foreign firms, Supply Chain management, Strategic CSR, Sustainability roadmap, Transparency, Used Intimate Apparel Collection (UIAC), Value chain, Value creation, Working conditions
Technology	Biotechnology clothes made of renewable or organic materials, Drying process technique, Self-cleaning textiles

Sub-topics related to sustainability are business models and innovation, commitment, consumption, drivers and barriers, environmental practice, equity, knowledge, life cycle assessment (LCA), and lifestyle (values), management with the main focus on performance, practice, supply chain, and environmental management systems, measurement or the triple bottom line (TBL), slow fashion, and waste to be reused and recycled in fashion items.

Other key topics listed in Table 7 are consumer behavior, consumption, corporate sustainability, economic, environmental, ethical, marketing, regulations, social responsibility, relationships, stakeholders, strategies, supply chain and management and technology. As those aspects were not expressly framed around CSR or sustainability, that discussion falls outside the scope of this paper, although these factors are included in the table to provide more information about the subject, thereby drawing attention to further research opportunities.

The discussion structure in the following two sections, featuring CSR and sustainability, includes the sub-topics identified through an analysis of the papers selected for this review.

4.8. Corporate Social Responsibility

Corporate social responsibility (CSR) activities can improve company image in cases where such actions improve social justice, thus having a positive influence on customer purchase intentions [148]. These activities also determine the company culture, reinforced through internal and external communication [145]. CSR commitments impact a company's performance, underpinning an intention to deliver value to society and establish suitable working conditions, especially in developing countries [26].

CSR relates to how the industry is managed through its activities and commitments towards the labor force and working conditions, how the industry deals with or intends to deal with sweatshops in developing countries, and the side effects of the Rana Plaza collapse building in Bangladesh. Additionally, as Yasmin [149] discusses in her paper, the responsibility lies with the state, which has a role in protecting workers, the factory owners are responsible for awful working conditions, low price and marketing practices, and the buyers in terms of their demand. The subject of CSR commitment is discussed in the context of the leveraging power that large, multi-national fashion companies have in negotiations regarding workers' welfare and wages, and how activists are diligent in reporting violations of workers' rights. This is especially so in developing countries [150], thus pushing the fashion sector to confront their environmental and social responsibilities towards workers' conditions and welfare [134,151–153]. In contrast, CSR practices and commitments do not seem to apply as a topic for workers in developing countries, and there are various shortcomings evident in how CSR is practiced [87,154,155]. As was pointed out in Tran and Jeppesen's paper, social responsibility has been practiced for a long time, and long before the concept of CSR evolved as a formal structure [156] or, as Bartley and Egels-Zanden point out, the actions of activists have motivated companies to develop a code of conduct [151].

CSR commitments are also associated with cultural differences, which can have an inhibiting effect when working conditions need to be improved, given a hierarchy where a top-down structure can affect the implementation of CSR processes [157]. A well-functioning approach, involving both multi-national and domestic stakeholders, is needed to help companies improve CSR commitments, both on the domestic and global market [87,156]. Additionally, companies can use their marketing methods to communicate about CSR, thereby increasing CSR's global value by opposing the use of sweatshops [143]. As Lee and Lee [36] discuss in their paper, humanitarian activities affect consumers if companies are willing to improve "social welfare and to develop the local community" (p. 25). Additionally, research has shown that if customer engagement is emphasized by involving them in marketing campaigns, it can result in "self-transcendence values, which can lead consumers to believe that they are practicing CSR themselves" [36] (p. 25).

Considering how vital CSR performance is in fashion operations, researchers explored how the CSR performance of a company's brand equity influences consumers. As Woo and Jin [34] explain, the only CSR that might affect consumers' awareness is how they treat workers or contribute to human rights. In contrast, responsible production, how companies tackle environmental issues, and other CSR practices, positively impact its brand equity [34].

The topic of a fashion business model demonstrates the importance of redesigning the model so that CSR forms a part of the new structure, especially if the intention is to increase consumer awareness of environmentally friendly products. In the long run, such a reshaping of the business model can result in a competitive advantage. [31].

Communication is an essential factor for companies seeking a competitive advantage. Through communication, companies' intentions to operate within society in a responsible manner is a part of their CSR structure. CSR communication is a topic in Woo and Jin's [100] paper focusing on the differences between the United States (US), Asian, and European markets. They draw attention to how the USA's fashion industry focuses on labor matters, the Asian on social issues, and those who operate on the European market focus on environmental issues. They also discuss how companies use websites to disseminate information to their customers [100]. Mann et al. [108] pointed out how CSR communication on companies' websites can express their actions or intentions to deal with social and environment-related issues. Therefore, it requires a clear and transparent expression about company achievements [108].

CSR drivers and barriers to be overcome in the implementation process were either discussed in general terms or concerning supply chain management. The Govindasamy and Suresh [114] study took a general approach to the subject, identifying the CSR structure and driving forces of CSR in the Malaysian fashion industry. These driving forces are: "customer satisfaction, sales maximization, employee satisfaction, protecting brand reputation, market access, fulfilling government requirements, leadership in CSR, top management belief in CSR, correct thing to do, and ethical orientation" (p. 2651). They point out that CSR integration within the Malaysian market is at the early stage of implementation. It seems to be based on a "halo effect" regarding competition and ethical practices, in the sense that overall knowledge and awareness of CSR seem to be missing. Therefore, Govindasamy and Suresh's argument is that lack of management awareness and support are the main barriers [114]. What drives management within the fashion supply chain to emphasize CSR is, according to Perry and Towers [113], labor intensity in production, trust in a buyer-supplier trading relationship, commitment, and cooperation (p. 19), to name a few examples. When discussing barriers within the fashion industry, Shen et al. [111] identified 12 barriers to CSR, namely "lack of stakeholder awareness, training, financial constraints, lack of consumer awareness, lack of concern for reputation, lack of knowledge, lack of regulation, standards and diversity, company culture, lack of revision, and lack of management commitment" (p. 3506).

Ethical fashion focuses on the consumer perspective and the intention to buy a product produced in accordance with ethical standards. These practices and ethical identity have a tighter relationship to slow fashion or luxury brands than to fast fashion, as the former aim to create brand awareness, incorporating their CSR efforts in terms of social impacts [107]. Reimers and Magnuson [158] studied ethical fashion from the consumer perspective. They concluded that social impacts affect consumer attitudes if such products are produced in a fair way and "with right moral intentions and are made by following the industry's ideal standards" (p. 383). However, as McNeill and Moore [159] identified, consumer attitudes towards used or second-hand clothing center around necessity rather than an interest in wearing other people's clothes. Thus, potential customers are a problematic target group for those introducing sustainable products to the market, although the ethical consumption of consumers leads to several benefits regarding the environment and social welfare [159].

The topic of financial management and financial returns relates to CSR investments and how companies measure their financial benefits by tracking both the return on investment (ROI) and the internal rate of return (IRR) of implementing CSR. Moore et al. [24] argued that if the intention is to reduce risk, it should also be a "potential source of value creation" (p.118).

Ferrell and Ferrell [99] suggest a framework that the fashion supply chain could utilize when addressing ethical and social issues, which would consequently be of benefit to their reputation. This framework outlines five ISO standards; ISO 9000, ISO 14000, ISO 26000, ISO 31000, and ISO 19600, that stand for quality management systems, environmental management, social responsibility, risk management and compliance management system, respectively [160].

Institutional pressure is a topic that Pedersen and Gwozdz [161] addressed in their study on how CSR affects the Nordic fashion industry and its behavior. The results demonstrated how pressure within stakeholder groups influences a company's strategic selections as it "stimulates opportunity-seeking at the expense of compliance" (p. 245) when companies shape their CSR initiatives. Additionally, management is essential when CSR is implemented. Cooke and He [162] examined China's pressure regarding the setting of CSR standards concerning human rights and environmentally-related issues. They concluded that the CSR focus within Chinese companies relates more to the business aspect, such as reputations, economic impacts, and regulations, rather than the social structure concerning how they intend to adopt ethical practices, such as human rights standards.

The management approach in these companies aims to respond to external stakeholder pressure by implementing a social structure, but a holistic view of CSR strategies seems to be lacking. Nevertheless, there is limited information since "most companies have not yet developed a working relationship with other companies to share experience and information related to CSR." [162] (p. 373). Despite different approaches between countries or cultures regarding how CSR is practiced or how companies carry out their social responsibilities, de Abreu et al. [102] found similarities within Brazilian companies as Cooke and He [162] had within Chinese companies. Fashion companies in neither of these countries "embedded a CSR practice in their strategic plan" [102] (p. 125). Preuss and Perschke [20] explained that the fashion industry still lacks formal approaches in terms of CSR strategies. The focus remains on the supply chain partners instead of adopting CSR in a professional manner by implementing it throughout the company.

Regulations, legal, and political perspectives. Knudsen [163] emphasized different approaches to CSR as a framework in the United States (US) and the United Kingdom (UK). These differences are reflected in how the US approach focuses more on regulations or the legal framework, while the UK approach seeks standardized solutions through "government-led processes that facilitate discussion and learning among a range of key stakeholders." (p. 179). In the latter case, CSR frameworks and strategies should reflect customer expectations towards company responsibility and standards, and how companies intend to communicate with internal and external stakeholders [25,104]. These communications need to be reliable and accountable to strengthen and preserve the relationship with stakeholders [101].

By implementing CSR strategies in line with the supply chain structure, the fashion industry can reduce its usage of natural resources and promote sustainability practices [164]. Diddi and Niehm [39] describe social responsibility within the fashion industry as a comprehensive concept to understand the interests and attitudes of consumers towards CSR activities. They also draw attention to how managers can gather information concerning the interests and behavior of customers regarding ethical choices when they buy fashion products. This information can be utilized in the development of company marketing strategies.

The fashion supply chain discussion draws attention to human rights and how the issue is especially significant in relation to workers in developing countries or where outsourcing occurs [104,165]. White et al. [104] draws further attention to how actions taken regarding workers' welfare and working conditions are more closely related to protecting a company's reputation, than they are to taking preventive measures for the sake of workers' well-being. Therefore, the focus on standards within the supply chain needs to embrace the perspective of social responsibility and ethical management, whether the company is operating on the domestic or global market (see Table 7).

4.9. Sustainability

The key topics discussed in this section concerning sustainability are business models, commitment, consumption and customer behavior, drivers and barriers, supply chain management, and textile waste (see Table 7).

The business models center on the linearity of current business models or the transformation to circular models [15]. The argument is that it is crucial to change or design new business models when companies change sustainability approaches or innovate new products or technologies. In order to monitor the success of sustainable actions, it is essential to measure performance, both environmental and social, as well as financial outcomes [15,116]. Todeschini et al. [115] compared two types of companies, new businesses and those who have gained a competitive advantage through many years of experience. Companies who have gained a competitive advantage are more willing to develop new business models for sustainability through innovation, whilst "born-sustainable startups are striving to make their business model replicable and scalable" [115] (p. 770). However, business model innovation needs to be aligned with a company's culture and values when adopting sustainability practices, as per the insights of Pedersen et al. [116].

Sustainability commitment is meant to deal with economic, social, and environmental issues, as Arrigo [127] highlighted in his study regarding sustainability communication in the slow fashion sector. As identified by Arrigo [127], managers of luxury fashion companies seem to be responsible for communications, which increases the awareness of their customers regarding sustainable products, consequently improving the brand reputation of sustainable development.

Austgulen [166] discusses the consumers' consumption of fashion clothing and speculates whether environmental responsibility "is placed on their shoulders" (p. 459) by their action and buying behavior, instead of viewing the sustainability of fashion products as a liability the industry should bear. Therefore, as suggested, it is essential to push customers towards responsible consumption by educating them about the impacts mass production has on the environment. This is done, e.g., by balancing the supply and demand of items produced and sold [166]. It has proven difficult for the fashion industry to promote environmentally friendly clothing in a way that gains sufficient consumer attention. For example, they are "struggling with understanding how to improve or at least avoid reducing consumers' receptiveness to their new green luxury models" [30] (p. 1526). Therefore, products that aim to be environmentally friendly must be marketed as other, highly fashionable products [30]. Cho et al. [167] explain how fast fashion business models have initiated consumerism over the years through mass production and a low-price strategy, and how marketing pushes consumers to use fashion garments to identify themselves. They point out that consumption is changing, and while customers are more willing to purchase fashion items with low environmental impacts, the industry has not responded to such demands as it still relies on a low-cost and low-price structure [167]. One way to influence sustainable consumption is to target fashion leaders who try to improve environmental and social welfare by becoming spokespersons for sustainable fashion [168]. Additionally, companies could use fashion bloggers and social media platforms, given that such actions can increase customer interest in more environmentally friendly products, and thereby potentially reduce excessive consumption [120].

Drivers and barriers are topics Desore and Narula [169] covered in their paper on consumers' underlying motivations for purchases, as such motivations form one of the drivers of "environmental initiatives" (p. 8). These drivers lay the ground for companies' strategies. Desore and Narula [169] developed a framework of barriers influencing consumers' decisions when buying environmentally friendly products. These include lack of information, limited knowledge and awareness, overpriced products, low quality, poorly designed or out of fashion items, and confusion regarding labels and greenwashing (p. 10). Pedersen and Andersen [170] explained the barriers hindering the fashion industry from adopting more sustainable practices and discussed opportunities to tackle social and environmental issues. They suggested issues could be solved by collaborative action between internal and external stakeholders. One of the key issues is that "sustainability challenges in the fashion industry are deeply rooted in current fast-fashion business models and consumption patterns" (p. 318). Limited regulations and the lack of support from authorities is a subject of focus in the paper by Majumdar and Sinha [91], where barriers for small and medium-sized (SMEs) clothing companies in India are explored. The authors' discussion refers to how this lack of support negatively affects sustainability outcomes and creates uncertainty regarding responsible actions. If companies are unable to respond to the pressure to enforce environmentally-friendly production, their reputation is at risk, and poor quality performance in this regard might affect their ability to gain a competitive advantage [171].

In the paper by Shubham et al. [172], environmental practices are discussed concerning how institutional pressure is used to implement corporate environmental practice (CEP) in the fashion industry. The focus is on management, particularly how managers should encourage the sharing of knowledge and employee training across company functions and departments.

An environmental management system (EMS) is a topic researched by Li and Wu [173]. This study focuses on financial performance after the adoption of an EMS system within Chinese fashion companies. Their findings indicated a negative financial result for the companies they examined, where operational efficiency was affected by increasing investment costs, such as those relating to employee training. The adoption of an EMS appeared to decrease turnover. They pointed out that companies often "adopt EMS passively due to the regulatory authority or the pressure of supply chain partners" (p. 9). The debate concerning competitive advantage by implementing sustainability throughout the supply chain is the subject of Panigrahi and Rao's [139] paper, in which they discuss the pressure from governments and stakeholders for fashion companies to participate in "environmental conservation" (p. 59) in order to gain a competitive advantage.

Equity is a topic in Norman et al.'s [121] study. It reflects on interactions between customers and suppliers within the fashion industry who carry out sustainability actions using the conduct approach's Code of Conduct. They revealed more positive experiences in customer interactions with suppliers who have advocated sustainability than non-advocates in developing countries. Suppliers within developing countries perceive "governance initiatives" (p. 383) to tackle unsustainability as an unfair means of encouraging more sustainable actions.

Knowledge is critical if business conduct is to become more sustainable. This is the focal area of Connell et al.'s [123] study, which evaluated sustainability courses and student attitudes, and whether education changed their views regarding the fashion industry. It is essential to monitor the industry know-how [123] as a lack of knowledge and awareness of sustainability has been evident, especially among students and younger consumers [125]. Management knowledge in the case of chemical consumption in the production process is lacking, according to Borjeson et al. [174]. A knowledge-based strategy within companies dealing with fabrics and textiles is required in order to "understand properties of chemicals, as well as on supplier's work and knowledge needs" (p. 135). To achieve this, responsible supply chain management is needed to improve knowledge concerning "enhanced integration of the complex worldwide actor networks and interactions of textile supply chains" (p. 136).

The life cycle assessment of products or services assesses their environmental impacts and energy consumption. Researchers used LCA as a framework to improve sustainability performance within the fashion industry [135,175–179]. The discussion relates to the sustainable practices adopted and consideration of what constitutes acceptable sustainability performance standards within the fashion industry [179], and the importance of providing a framework for managers to improve company actions towards the environment and socially related issues [135,177,178].

The impacts of consumers' lifestyles are discussed in Lee et al.'s [124] study, which investigated sustainable values, business stewardship, and consumers' lifestyles. They used a value and lifestyle (VALS) framework to identify the impacts sustainable products have on consumers' clothing consumption. The focus group were environmentalists, but the purpose was to investigate how likely this group is to buy responsibly by focusing only on environmentally friendly products and how the participants handled their clothing during usage and when the items are no longer required. Lee, Kim, and Yang [124] also discussed how companies' environmental and social structures and actions could influence consumers' decisions concerning purchases of environmentally friendly fashion items. Such actions might affect consumer values and shape their lifestyles.

The role of management concerning sustainability relates to, for example, how companies ensure access to the natural resources needed for production by involving internal and external stakeholders in the environmental and social structures, and practices of their companies [97,98,180–183]. Further, managements need to monitor and measure performance because "without measuring sustainability performance concerning targets and receiving feedback, it is impossible to control the system, and its managers, the industry sector, are like blind drivers of a car" [179] (p. 699). The management topic also relates to finding the answer to what environmental and social standards are used in the production process within the supply chain [180], and achieved by studying the reasons behind supplier decisions in the developing countries which promote responsible practices towards sustainability [184].

The Global Reporting Initiative (GRI) framework, together with the triple bottom line (TBL) approach, is used to measure the features of the environmental, economic, and social aspects of supply chain sustainability and improve company performance. These practices can increase a company's accountability and lead to more transparency across supply chains [92]. The company's efficiency improves if the employees' role, culture, and climate are considered in the context of environmentally and socially related issues, something which is often neglected.

Jung and Jin [185] emphasized the differences between slow fashion and environmentally sustainable fashion in their paper and discussed how the "conceptual distinction" (p. 510) is unclear despite a growing interest among scholars in the subject. They discussed the dimensions of slow fashion and pointed out that "slow fashion encompasses slow production, (does not exploit natural and human resources), and consumption (entails a longer product lifespan from manufacturing to discarding)" (p. 510). The discussion as to how the interest of consumers in environmentally sustainable products in slow fashion could be reinforced was the subject of De Angelis et al.'s [30] paper. Their investigation examined what type of practices slow or luxury fashion companies could embrace to lessen the burden of consumerism, and how those practices should be structured as part of a company's sustainability actions, focusing on the raising of consumer awareness concerning environmentally friendly items.

The discussion of management for sustainability highlights the fashion supply chain, the industry's environmental and social impact, and the mark it imposes on global markets through the outsourcing of production. The discussion in Khurana and Ricchetti's [181] study draws attention to the importance of transparent actions within the supply chain, both in terms of domestic and global actions, since the industry seeks to produce its products within countries where social and environmental standards are weak. Emphasis on sustainability should transform into actions that are implemented throughout the supply chain, as Macchion et al. [186] discuss in their paper, focusing on a strategic approach for sustainability. One way to achieve this goal is to gather information about consumer behavior to build a strong marketing structure and to educate them about environmentally sustainable fashion [32]. For example, sustainable practice is encouraged by emphasizing waste reduction through reuse and recycling initiatives for old garments or textile fabrics [187].

4.10. Contribution and Suggestion for Future Research

The review synthesizes the contributions of published papers and their authors' suggestions for future research regarding what is still unclear in terms of CSR and sustainability within the fashion industry (see Table 8). By analyzing the papers' contributions, it is clear that the majority intended to gain practical knowledge to inform the future direction of responsible fashion. Others aimed to fill an empirical gap with their study and contribute to the literature by framing the knowledge of the fashion supply chain's performance. The papers investigated issues related to human rights and the cultural challenges the fashion industry is dealing with by outsourcing production, for example, linked to human resource management and fashion business model specifics. Furthermore, the body of existing research has gathered information on what motivates fashion companies to implement CSR and sustainability structures, highlighting how management approaches [142], brand commitment, and commitments within the slow fashion sector concerning unsustainable actions [127] are emphasized. Moreover, the papers have sought to develop a strategic framework for sustainability by observing industry actions regarding social and environmental impacts and how the fashion industry measures and reports its performance [15,122,123,180,183]. As stated by the researchers, practical implications include information about organizations that have implemented CSR practices which operate across borders, something that requires them to adopt and adapt to new legislation so that their actions appeal to stakeholders, in both local and worldwide markets [39,87,145,161]. Research has addressed the long-term economic benefits of collecting information regarding consumer behavior and attitudes towards sustainable fashion brands. Additionally, focus has been placed on the impact marketing can have on the future direction of sustainable fashion [39,40,148,188], to name just a few examples of research contributions.

Table 8. Suggestions for future studies.

Subject	Suggestions for Future Studies
Advertisement	Advertisement and green advertisements [33]
	Anti-consumption advertisements [189]
	Social media messages, influences on subjective norms, close friends and relatives [120]
	Purchase intentions, attitudes regarding anti-consumption behavior [189]
Consumption	Second-hand clothing, other than renting and swapping clothes [190]
	Consumers' overconsumption as a motivation to increase profits [164]
	Political consumption, informal clothing exchanges, improved laundering, maintenance, mending, and disposal strategies [166]
	Hazardous waste, investment, plant closings, political support [26]
	Workplace-related CSR and intangible assets in more depth [86]
	Labor-intensive industries in developing countries [87]
	Motivations and rationales leading firms to adopt CSR initiatives [157]
	The nature of institutional pressures [161]
	Potential influences related to social desirability [191]
CSR	The pressures of growth and CSR across companies of different sizes [20]
	The dynamics of non-verbal and verbal communication [192]
	Human resource components-impacts on the product-service success [142]
	CSR drivers-aspects and dynamic effects on sustainable lifestyle [124]
	Indicator disclosures and changes over time [193]
	If executives' perception concurs with employees' perception [142]
	The views of other actors in the supply chain network [194]
	The stimulus to outsource and reduce the cost, foreign companies [195]
	Marketing strategies to enhance communication of fast fashion [40]
Cultural	Theorize relationship partners with different cultural backgrounds [196]
	Cultural differences, perceived justice, governance mechanisms [121]
	Cross-cultural differences in different countries-luxury consumers [30]
Development on existing study	Epistemological issues, absorptive capacities, and the difference between acquiring knowledge and information [172]
	Corporate sustainability performance [138]
	How actors use corporate sustainability as a risk management tool during an actual crisis [119]
	Tradeoff investigations at the tactical and operational planning levels [23]
	Distinct clusters of green consumers [140]
Environmental	Carbon emission evaluation functions, various supplies, energy, waste, and labor [118]
	To improve environmental sustainability by the use of a carbon footprint tax, examine the carbon quota issue and the corresponding probable trading mechanism in an open market for green shipment control [197]
	Corporate performance regarding human rights [198]
Performance	The productivity and financial performance of SMEs before and after the implementation of green technologies [91]
	The relationship between sustainability and performance outcomes [180]
	Whether sustainably performing companies increasingly invest in socially responsible governance [105]
	Misalignment between internal and external practices, potential implications for companies, deepening relationships between strategic approaches to sustainability and performance [186]
	Consumers' ethical decision-making and supply chain management in the apparel industry [199]
Supply chain	The impact of social compliance effectiveness, workers' rights violations in the global supply chain [200]
	Government regulation, market structure, customer pressure [201]
	Outline sophisticated managerial, academic implications at supplier level [182]
	Development of reliable systems between the three pillars of sustainability [117]
	Sustainable packaging, manufacturing processes, and the design process [31]
	Industry practitioners to achieve a sustainable competitive advantage [202]
	Design for recycling, integration and creative design process [203]
	Union, NGO relationship, workers' rights and other areas of CSR [204]
	An element of good practice, influence factor for high-performing companies [198]
	The relationship between perceptions of self and ethical purchasing behavior, and the likelihood of sustainable clothing consumption [159]
Sustainability	Sustainability strategies, elements of fashion business models, driving forces influencing actions, measurements, key performance indicators, transparency, and disclosure [15]
	Improvement and standardization of indicators, reliable systems for the three pillars [177]
	Evolution of fashion business models, driven by enlightened sustainable startups [115]
	Sustainable apparel purchasing behavior needs exploration [123]
	Association between retail price, cost of the physical return, and the impact of product return on market demand [96]
	Relationships between different types of sustainable textiles and apparel products [205]
	Income levels and attitudes, environmentally sustainable apparel, educational standards, behavioral intentions, product development, marketing and retailing strategies [206]
	Developing a sustainability stewardship framework for future studies [128]
	The moral responsibility of corporate sustainability in other countries [207]
Stakeholders	Explore brand influence, the brand's stakeholders to identify and evaluate conscientious brands [88]
	Political context, the existence of avenues for engagement and dialogue, opportunities for civic engagement and translating constituencies into stakeholders [109]
Theoretical suggestions	Employ established theories, e.g., stakeholder theory or institutional theory [184]
	Address the extent to which theorization by a central actor is picked up by other actors, the impact that it has on further change and stability in the field [208]

Regarding potential future research and some of the unanswered questions, Karaosman et al. [40] highlighted customer purchasing behavior relating to fashion companies who have adopted CSR on a global scale. They suggested investigating how cross-cultural company marketing strategies can improve communication within the fashion industry [40], together with examining the effect advertisements can have on consumer attitudes regarding consumption and purchasing behavior [189]. Battaglia et al. [86] point out that the relationship between intangible assets and the workplace-related aspects of CSR needs further investigation, suggesting that qualitative research will give new insights compared to their study on the topic. Haque and Azmat [87], studying CSR in developing countries, described the fashion industry as a labor-intensive industry. They called for more information on how CSR affects the manufacturing of ready-made garments (RDG) in low-wage areas, also pointing out the need for further exploration of the impacts of trade unions on social compliance effectiveness, and the interrelationship between "government, political leaders, factory owners, and international partners" [87] (p. 182).

Future research agendas include what determines and motivates companies to adopt CSR initiatives compared to others, specifically concerning supply chain management and the ethical decision-making of consumers [157]. In particular, the focus could be placed on the fundamental aspects of CSR issues in the fashion industry and how the industry utilizes CSR actions to increase profits, decrease costs, and conduct their business ethically [164]. Furthermore, the overconsumption of clothing has increased the trend of throwing away relatively new clothes. Therefore, research could be undertaken to explore how such behavior leads to disposal problems, and how the issue could be solved by investigating clothing swapping or renting models for new and old garments [190]. Additionally, in order to understand the motivations underlying consumption, the focus of future research could be on assessing the relationship between ethical purchasing and individual behavior [159]. See further suggestions for future studies in Table 8.

5. Discussion

The purpose of this study was to explore CSR and how it influences sustainability within the fashion industry, to identify what is already known about the topic and where research gaps exist. This paper is comprehensive as it covers an extended period (16 years) of studies from 2003 to 2019, including the basic characteristics of work in CSR and sustainable fashion covered in peer-reviewed journals publishing fashion-related articles, and evaluates research focus by region. The paper provides an overview of the research methods employed in the studies, and the main theories employed. Additionally, this study outlined the researchers' aim, purpose, objective, and the main topics and keywords used in each investigation. Moreover, it outlines the studies' core contributions in the review and states the direction for future research suggested by the various authors.

The analysis revealed topics and sub-topics related to CSR, sustainability, and the fashion industry, and how these concepts tie together in practice within the fashion industry. Also, it identified industry conduct regarding society and the environment by collecting information on CSR practices and sustainability innovations, thus revealing what is already known about the topic. Through business models, innovation is driven through commitments regarding the economic, environmental, and social pillars of sustainability. For instance, this is carried out by raising consumer awareness by educating them about the impacts of mass production, contributing to reducing consumption, and developing eco-friendly, highly fashionable sustainable products [30]. Furthermore, sharing knowledge and training employees is also a way for companies within the fashion industry to conduct their business activities more sustainably [172]. The role of managers is to ensure the company's access to natural resources, and to conduct ethical business by implementing environmental and social structures as a set of precedents for both internal and external stakeholders to adopt or participate in [97,98,184–187]. Measuring performance is also a key success factor, as this is a prerequisite for making improvements [179]. Managers, furthermore, rely on the Triple bottom line (TBL) approach to measure the environmental, economic, and social aspects of the supply chain [92], which requires transparency about their conduct. The implications of outsourcing production to countries where environmental standards are weak is also emphasized. For instance, this is evident in the lack of regulations and authority support in small and medium-sized (SMEs) clothing companies in India [91]. The discussion refers to how this lack of support negatively affects sustainability outcomes and creates uncertainty regarding responsible actions within the fashion industry. If companies cannot respond to pressure to instigate environmentally-friendly production, their reputations are at risk, and poor performance may affect their ability to gain a competitive advantage [171,181]. The importance of a strategic approach to sustainability is, therefore, also discussed [186].

Perhaps the clearest example of sustainability-related emphasis relates to the problems of sweatshops. In these cases, there is evidence of the strengthening of commitments related to workers' rights and labor conditions in factories after the Rana Plaza building collapse in Bangladesh in 2013 [149]. The fashion industry is urged to improve its CSR commitments by collaborating with multi-national and domestic stakeholders in the areas where production occurs [87,156]. Acting against the use of sweatshops would amplify the global value of CSR [146]. Lack of training, knowledge, and management commitment is also an issue, as are a lack of standards and regulations, consumer awareness, and overall concern for improving brand image and the reputation of the fashion industry [111]. As a solution, Ferrell and Ferrell [99] developed a framework where ethical and social issues are addressed, suggesting that this tool may enhance the industry's reputation by outlining a standardized way for improving practices.

In order to understand how scholars tie sustainability-related actions with CSR, key concepts can be categorized according to Steurer et al.'s [48] and Dopfer et al.'s [47] ideas. Based on keywords identified through the analysis (see Tables 4 and 5), a micro-meso-macro framework is proposed, showing how CSR influenced sustainability within the fashion industry. The analyses reveal that CSR and sustainability keywords tied to the micro level relate to consumers, drivers and barriers, employees, and managers. Keywords that tie together CSR and sustainability at the meso level are business, drivers and barriers, CSR, the supply chain, and sustainability. At the macro level, the keywords are activism, countries, culture, drivers and barriers, economic, human rights, and industry, all of which are evident regarding CSR and sustainability.

Drivers and barriers appear in all three levels, micro, meso, and macro, as motivation and hindering factors and, at the same time, as barriers in the process when companies attempt to implement CSR and sustainability in their structures or supply chain. There are also barriers related to the company's cost of implementing and measuring sustainability. These barriers relate to the pricing policy for environmentally friendly products as consumers might consider the products too expensive to buy [113,159,209]. The motivation to overcome these barriers relates to the managerial understanding of CSR activities and policies and requires employees to receive personal training to enhance CSR involvement and outcomes. Employees' knowledge and understanding of sustainability can positively influence customers' interests in environmentally friendly products, which then might see a certain value in buying such products [169,209]. The drivers and barriers at micro, meso, and macro levels relate to the organization's knowledge and visionary leadership for addressing environmental and social impacts [47].

At the Micro level, a similar discussion relates to employees, drivers and barriers, and management. However, in CSR the focus is on corporations, organizations, structure, and institutions, whilst in the case of sustainability, the focus is on consumption, design, and measures, to name a few. The focus on the meso level, both in respect of CSR and sustainability research, is on the business, drivers and barriers, and the supply chain. The CSR emphasis on the meso level relates to communication, ethics, social issues, stakeholders, and values, but if framed around sustainability, the focus is on entrepreneurship, pollution, social sustainability, and the theoretical approach. The macro level discussion involves topics such as activism, culture, and human rights, regardless of whether the discussion is framed around CSR or sustainability. The CSR framing focuses on labor, while the sustainability framing adds regulation, resources structure, and technology to the discussion (see Figure 7).

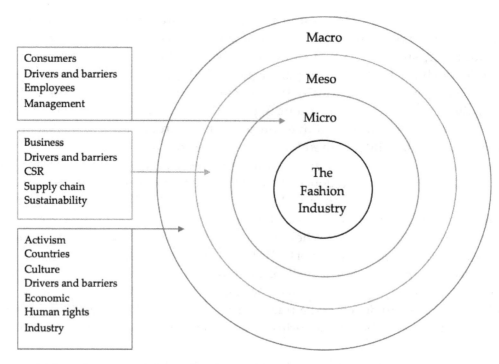

Figure 7. CSR and sustainability-related emphasis within the fashion industry presented on Micro-Meso-Macro levels.

Micro:(1) The consumers' approach in the micro dimension relates to (a) their behavior and concern for the society and environment, whether they responded to sustainable and ethical fashion [35,164,168], and whether they are (b) interested in buying from fashion brands that have implemented CSR [20]. (2) Drivers and barriers relate to, (a) Govindasamy and Suresh [114], who discussed the motivation to implement CSR structures in apparel industries due to stakeholder pressure in Malaysia, (b) the management's lack of knowledge and access to resources is one of the main barriers in the implementation process [114,169], (c) what stimulates fashion businesses to implement a sustainability structure, (d) how customers lack knowledge and awareness of green products, and (e) how highly-priced environmentally friendly products can affect buying decisions [169]. (3) Employees, (a) attitudes concerning a company's policy for CSR [20], and (b) behavior and commitments towards the company's sustainability goals [210]. (4) Management concerns (a) the company's use of a management control system to evaluate their sustainability performance [211], and (b) the history of management in an Italian family textile business [212].

Meso: (1) The business approaches in the meso dimension include discussion of (a) brand equity of CSR practices concerning positive consumer perceptions towards companies who conduct CSR practices by dealing with the environmental and economic impacts of their products [34], (b) A blue-collar worker is a focus in Chen et al.'s [213] study on the aspect of working conditions among Chinese workers in the fashion industry and how they value their work facilities now that demands for better living conditions have increased, (c) Paik and Krumwiede [26] emphasized worker conditions in their study by discussing the Bangladesh tragedy, where fashion brands outsource most of their productions, and (d) the brand image, where CSR practices lead to a more positive brand image which, in turn, affects consumers' purchasing intentions [148]. Within the focus on (2) Drivers, Wu et al. [171] discussed the drivers for green supply chain management as (a) "represent company" green management ability, (b) inter-organizational assistance, and (c) government consulting services (p. 634). In (3), CSR in the meso dimension relates to (a) the structure as part of the sustainability roadmap [129], (b) the growing interest in implementing CSR within the industry to respond to market expectations of a responsible marketing structure for ethical production [25], and (c) discussion of how responsible practices have grown over the years as the agenda and urgency to strengthen cooperation between stakeholders within the domestic and international market has focused on improving workers' facilities and welfare [156]. Within (4), the discussion of fashion supply chains reveals (a) management initiatives regarding the fashion industry by exploring execution and considering the strategic positioning of firms and trends [98], (b) environmental impacts [209], (c) the relationship between drivers and government involvement within green supply chain management [171], and (d) social issues in the sustainable supply chain [182]. In (5), sustainability discussion relates to the variance of (a) employee perceptions towards corporate sustainability and their involvement in organizational citizenship behavior within Chinese and US fashion businesses [207], and (b) the value of sustainability in a business model focusing on low-cost production [119].

Macro:(1) The activism approach in the macro dimension relates to a) anti-sweatshop movements and global labor issues [214], and (b) leading to global production networks (GPNs) and the fashion industry to adopt codes of conduct voluntarily [151]. In (2), the drivers and barriers in the discussion reveal a focus on (a) what kind of barriers firms in the fashion industry are dealing with concerning the implementation of an environmental sustainability structure, motivations, and drivers [169], and (b) what drives sustainable actions within the fashion sector [15]. Within (3), the economic aspects of studies focus on (a) the CSR dimension from economic, legal, ethical, and philanthropic perspectives regarding consumers' purchase intentions [36], (b) the economic success of organic products [215], and (c) the importance of green entrepreneurship in terms of economic development [216]. In (4), the countries' discussion is marked by (a) developing countries and the management of social sustainability between fashion companies, negotiators, and suppliers (factories) [97], and (b) if or how suppliers are implementing sustainable social practices within developing countries [184]. Within (5), environmental aspects of studies focus on (a) environment and social responsibility, commitments to engage social welfare [134,150,152,153,167], (b) responsible management and risk management [160], (c) promotion of environmentally friendly products [30,120]. In (6), the culture approach reveals (a) if cross-culture will affect brand equity by implementing CSR [34]. In item (7), the approach regarding human rights reveals (a) discussion of policies to protect social welfare and rights by using UN guiding principles on business and human rights as a guideline [198]. Within (8), the industry approach reveals (a) the diversity of the fashion industry.

The ideas set out for future CSR research in the findings suggest further investigation of the environmental impacts of production [26], the stimulus to outsource and reduce costs, especially in respect of multinational companies [195], and the impacts on the product-service success [142]. Other issues include human resource components [142], workplace-related [112], the influence of labor-intensive industries, focus on developing countries [86], plant closings, and political support [26], and the dynamics of non-verbal and verbal communication [192]. Furthermore, there needs to be more focus on CSR and intangible assets [86], investment [26], the motivations and rationales which lead firms to undertake CSR initiatives [158], the nature of institutional pressures [161], and potential influences related to social desirability [191], as well as, the pressures of growth and CSR across companies of different sizes [20]. Additionally, future research could address how CSR drives dynamic effects on sustainable lifestyles [124], indicator disclosures and changes over time [193], if and how executive perceptions concur with employee perceptions [142], and the different views of other actors in the supply chain network [194].

The suggestion for further investigation on sustainability within the fashion sector relates to the environmental impacts from fashion production through a focus on the development of reliable systems covering the three pillars of sustainability [117], sustainable packaging, manufacturing processes, and the design process [31], designing for recycling, integration and the creative design process [203], and improvement and standardization of indicators, and developing reliable systems for the three pillars [177]. Regarding workers' welfare, the suggestion for further investigation is to examine NGO relationships, unions, workers' rights, and other areas of CSR [196]. In terms of consumers and consumption, the suggestions call for further investigation of the relationship between perceptions of self and ethical purchasing behavior, the likelihood of sustainable clothing consumption [159], and sustainable apparel purchasing behavior [123]. Regarding the operational level and sustainability structure, the suggestion relates to implementing sustainability strategies, elements of fashion business models, driving forces influencing actions, measurements, key performance indicators, transparency, and disclosure [15], and aspects of good practice and influence factors for high-performing companies [198]. The evolution of fashion business models, driven by enlightened sustainable startups [115], the relationships between different types of sustainable textiles and apparel products [204], and the association between retail price, cost of the physical return, and the impact of product return on market demand [96]. The income levels and attitudes, environmentally sustainable apparel, educational standards, behavioral intentions, product development, marketing and retailing strategies [206], industry practitioners to achieve sustainable competitive advantage [202], developing a sustainability stewardship framework for future studies [128], and the moral responsibility of corporate sustainability in other countries [207].

In terms of a theoretical framework, the authors suggest an investigation to explore the employment of established theories, e.g., stakeholder theory or institutional theory [184] in order to address the extent to which other actors pick up theorization by a central actor and the impact that it has on further change and stability in the field [208].

6. Conclusions

There is an increasing interest within academia regarding CSR and sustainability actions within the fashion industry. This interest appears to be related to the expanding role of environmentally sustainable fashion and evaluating how the fashion industry handles its responsibility towards the economy, environment, and society. Although several authors have discussed CSR and sustainability within the fashion sector, most of them have studied CSR and sustainability separately.

Through a systematic literature review, this study has attempted to answer the question of how CSR influences sustainability within the fashion industry by collating information on CSR practices and sustainability innovations to establish what is already known about the topic. This study suggests that CSR studies emphasize managerial approaches to sustainability actions by innovation through the business model or supply chain. In addition to increasing a company's commitment towards the social, environmental, and economic pillars of sustainability, consumer awareness of mass consumption impacts is raised. Moreover, the company reputation is retained, when it would otherwise be is at risk, by expanding the supply of eco-friendly products, and establishing commitments and the contingencies of workers' safety and welfare. These actions are linked to CSR, as shown by the micro-meso-macro framework, (See Figure 7) which includes consumers, their behavior and concern for the society and environment, the brand equity of CSR practices, culture, and global production networks. The ties between CSR and sustainability also contribute to implementing sustainable actions within the fashion supply chain and managing social sustainability between fashion companies, negotiators, and suppliers by increasing cooperation between stakeholders within domestic and global markets. The concepts also connect via the relationship between environmental sustainability barriers and drivers, government involvement, employees' perceptions, and sustainability's overall value. Brand image is maintained via responses to environmental impacts by creating a sustainability roadmap and conducting more ethical production. The connection between CSR and sustainability also relates to the economic success of organic products, green entrepreneurship, and the legal, ethical, and philanthropic aspects of consumers' purchasing intentions. There is also a discussion of outsourcing tactics in low-cost business models and activism actions to prevent sweatshops and boost human rights to secure ethical working conditions and facilities in developing countries.

The main contributions of this study are to provide a comprehensive review of academic publications regarding CSR, sustainability, and fashion, performed by mapping existing knowledge of how the industry conducts its practices and how it intends to respond to the likelihood of more socially and environmentally friendly standards in the future. It contributes to the literature by identifying the relevant CSR and sustainability topics, as well as the research gaps and possibilities for future studies, by extending the existing knowledge on sustainability and fashion. The same applies to the CSR, and sustainability-related emphasis within the fashion industry presented on micro-meso-macro levels. Furthermore, this study may be of use for the industry, practitioners, and policymakers in gaining a deeper understanding of the critical issues and how they are addressed, and also for policymakers regulating the industry in respect of the issues that cannot be solved through industry self-regulation via CSR practices. It provides insight into the operations and impacts of domestic and multinational fashion companies, outlining the most relevant studies on the topic, highlighting research trends and gaps in the field, and determining a conclusion on how the interactions or ties between CSR and sustainability relate to their economic, environmental, and social dimensions.

This review was limited to academic papers from two databases, followed by including and excluding criteria. The selection was limited to articles written in English, focusing on CSR, sustainability, and fashion, which might have led to the omission of relevant papers that were not written in this language. These were limiting factors for the study, as they were either outside the scope of this paper, or were not specifically focused on topics such as social responsibility, environmental, economic, corporate sustainability, relationships, regulations, stakeholders, ethics, strategies, consumption, consumer behavior, technology, marketing, and supply chain and management. These limitations, however, create a basis for future research by providing a more comprehensive range of primary information, laying the groundwork for the theoretical framing of the interactions between CSR, sustainability, and fashion by providing more information about the subject. In particular, it would be interesting to study a dualistic/chameleon behavior of the industry, where it has negative environmental and social impacts, but at the same time promotes sustainable practices and CSR programs. This raises questions such as: How genuine are the sustainability and CSR practices and programs of fashion companies and is it possible to measure the real impacts weighing both the pros and cons of the fashion industry behavior? In this regard, empirical investigation is of critical importance. Moreover, the fashion industry might see a paradigm shift of relevance to explore. This paradigm shift is caused by behavioral changes of consumers that are becoming more aware of the low importance of fashion products, given the current pandemic crisis, therefore realizing the need to promote the principles of sustainable development.

The outbreak of COVID-19 in early 2020 must also be included as a limiting factor in this study. However, the growing pandemic has also opened the door for further studies. A pathway for an empirical study to investigate the impact of COVID-19 on industry behavior has clearly been established, as the fashion sector is under a continuous spotlight. Furthermore, to study the influence the crisis has had on the industry's capacity or inclination to conduct according to sustainable development principles would be illuminating, as would an investigation on how the pandemic might have influenced consumer behavior in terms of fashion trends, and impact on suppliers and their employees. Another opportunity for further research is a more in-depth analysis of another perspective on social responsibility, sustainability, regulations, stakeholders, ethics, strategies, consumption, marketing, and management within the fashion sector, before and after COVID-19.

Author Contributions: Conceptualization, T.S.T. and L.J.; methodology, T.S.T.; formal analysis, T.S.T.; investigation, T.S.T.; writing—original draft preparation, T.S.T. and L.J.; writing, review and editing, T.S.T. and L.J.; supervision, L.J. All authors have read and agreed to the published version of the manuscript.

Acknowledgments: The authors of this work would like to thank the anonymous reviewers for their valuable comments and suggestions for improving this paper.

Appendix A

Table A1. Summary of selected articles.

Author (Year)	Title	Journal	Keywords
Adam (2018)	The Role of Human Resource Management (HRM) for the Implementation of Sustainable Product-Service Systems (PSS)—An Analysis of Fashion Retailers	Sustainability	Product-service systems (PSS); Human resource management (HRM); Fashion industry; Sustainable business models; Sustainable retail
Ahlstrom (2010)	Corporate Response to CSO Criticism: Decoupling the Corporate Responsibility Discourse from Business Practice	Corporate Social Responsibility and Environmental Management	Corporate responsibility; discourse theory; New institutional theory; Civil society organizations (CSOs); Outsourced production; Garment industry; Code of conduct; Profit maximization
Albloushy et al. 2019)	Purchasing environmentally sustainable apparel: The attitudes and intentions of female Kuwaiti consumers	International Journal of Consumer Studies	Environmental concern; Environmental knowledge; Environmentally sustainable Apparel; purchasing behaviors; Kuwait
Anner (2017)	Monitoring Workers' Rights: The Limits of Voluntary Social Compliance Initiatives in Labor Repressive Regimes	Global Policy	None
Anner (2018)	CSR Participation Committees, Wildcat Strikes and the Sourcing Squeeze in Global Supply Chains	British Journal of Industrial Relations	None
Aquino (2011)	The Performance of Italian Clothing Firms for Shareholders, Workers and Public Administrations: An Econometric Analysis	Journal of Accounting Research & Audit Practices	None
Arrigo (2018)	The flagship stores as sustainability communication channels for luxury fashion retailers	Journal of Retailing and Consumer Services	Flagship store; Sustainable retailing; Luxury fashion brands; Luxury sustainability; In-store communication
Athukorala et al. (2018)	Repositioning in the global apparel value chain in the post-MFA era: Strategic issues and evidence from Sri Lanka	Development Policy Review	Apparel industry; Global value chain; Multi-Fiber Arrangement; Sri Lanka

Table A1. *Cont.*

Author (Year)	Title	Journal	Keywords
Austgulen (2016)	Environmentally Sustainable Textile Consumption-What Characterizes the Political Textile Consumers?	Journal of Consumer Policy	Sustainable consumption; Political consumption; Textiles; Clothing; Environmental regulation; Consumerism
Bair et al. (2012)	From Varieties of Capitalism to Varieties of Activism: The Antisweat shop Movement in Comparative Perspective	Social Problems	Anti-sweatshop movement; Global commodity chains; Transnational advocacy networks; Varieties of capitalism; Labor rights
Bartley (2003)	Certifying forests and factories: States, social movements, and the rise of private regulation in the apparel and forest products fields	Politics & Society	Private regulation; Certification; Sweatshops; Deforestation; Corporate Social Responsibility
Bartley et al. (2015)	Responsibility and neglect in global production networks: the uneven significance of codes of conduct in Indonesian factories	Global Networks a Journal of Transnational Affairs	Global production networks; Global value chains; Social movements; Labor standards; Code of conduct; Apparel; Electronics; Indonesia
Bartley et al. (2016)	Beyond decoupling: unions and the leveraging of corporate social responsibility in Indonesia	Socio-Economic Review	Corporate social responsibility; Globalization; Trade unions; Developing countries; Institutional theory
Baskaran et al. (2012)	Indian textile suppliers' sustainability evaluation using the grey approach	International Journal of Production Economics	Grey approach; India; Supplier evaluation; Sustainability; Textile industry
Battaglia et al. (2014)	Corporate Social Responsibility and Competitiveness within SMEs of the Fashion Industry: Evidence from Italy and France	Sustainability	Competitiveness; Corporate social responsibility; Fashion industry; SMEs; Textile
Battistoni et al. (2019)	Systemic Incubator for Local Eco entrepreneurship to Favor a Sustainable Local Development: Guidelines Definition	Design Journal	Systemic design; Eco-entrepreneurship; Local economic; Development; Zero waste; Business incubator; Textile; Piedmont Region
Benjamin et al. (2014)	An Exploratory Study to Determine Archetypes in the Trinidad and Tobago Fashion Industry Environment	West Indian Journal of Engineering	Diversification; Operant Subjectivity; Fashion industry; Q-Study

Table A1. *Cont.*

Author (Year)	Title	Journal	Keywords
Bjorquist et al. (2018)	Textile qualities of regenerated cellulose fibers from cotton waste pulp	Textile Research Journal	Cotton waste pulp; Staple fiber; Circular economy; Environmental sustainability; Spinning; Fabrication
Borjeson et al. (2015)	Knowledge challenges for responsible supply chain management of chemicals in textiles as experienced by procuring organizations	Journal of Cleaner Production	Responsible procurement; Knowledge; Corporate social responsibility; Chemical risks
Brennan et al. (2014)	Rhetoric and argument in social and environmental reporting: The Dirty Laundry case	Accounting Auditing & Accountability Journal	Environmental reporting; Stakeholder; Rhetoric; Argument; Greenpeace
Briga-Sa et al. (2013)	Textile waste as an alternative thermal insulation building material solution	Construction and Building Materials	Textile waste; Thermal conductivity; Eco-efficient; Building solution; Sustainability
Burzynska et al. (2018)	Opportunities and Conditions for the Development of Green Entrepreneurship in the Polish Textile Sector	Fibers & Textiles in Eastern Europe	Textile industry; Green entrepreneurship; Innovations; European Union
Busi et al. (2016)	Environmental sustainability evaluation of innovative self-cleaning textiles	Journal of Cleaner Production	Life Cycle Assessment; Self-cleaning textiles; Nanotechnology; Environmental sustainability
Caniato et al. (2012)	Environmental sustainability in fashion supply chains: An exploratory case-based research	International Journal of Production Economics	Environmental sustainability; Supply chain management; Fashion industry; Case studies
Carrigan et al. (2013)	From conspicuous to considered fashion: A harm-chain approach to the responsibilities of luxury-fashion businesses	Journal of Marketing Management	Harm chain; Value co-creation; Institutional theory; Luxury fashion; Corporate Social Responsibility
Chang et al. (2015)	Is fast fashion sustainable? The effect of positioning strategies on consumers' attitudes and purchase intentions	Social Responsibility Journal	Sustainability; Consumer behavior; Fast fashion; Positioning strategies
Chen et al. (2014)	Implementing a collective code of conduct-CSC9000T in Chinese textile industry	Journal of Cleaner Production	Corporate Social Responsibility (CSR); ISO 26000; China; Textile
Chen et al. (2017)	Decent Work in the Chinese Apparel Industry: Comparative Analysis of Blue-Collar and White-Collar Garment Workers	Sustainability	Decent work; Garment Manufacturing; Blue-collar workers; White-collar workers; China

Table A1. *Cont.*

Author (Year)	Title	Journal	Keywords
Cho et al. (2015)	Style consumption: its drivers and role in sustainable apparel consumption	International Journal of Consumer Studies	Consumer ethics; Guilt; Shame; Australia; Indonesia
Choi (2013)	Local sourcing and fashion quick response system: The impacts of carbon footprint tax	Transportation Research Part E-Logistics and Transportation Review	Sustainability; Local sourcing; Quick response system; Carbon footprint tax; Sustainability
Choi et al. (2018)	Used intimate apparel collection programs: A game-theoretic analytical study	Transportation Research Part E-Logistics and Transportation Review	Supply chain management; Used intimate apparel collection program; Reverse logistics; Socially responsible operations
Clarke-Sather et al. (2019)	Onshoring fashion: Worker sustainability impacts of global and local apparel production	Journal of Cleaner Production	Sustainable sourcing; Life cycle assessment; Apparel product development; Sustainability assessment; Apparel industry
Connell et al. (2012)	Sustainability knowledge and behaviors of apparel and textile undergraduates	International Journal of Sustainability in Higher Education	United States of America; Undergraduates; Clothing; Consumer behavior; Sustainability; Apparel purchasing behavior; Apparel sustainability; Sustainability knowledge
Cooke et al. (2010)	Corporate social responsibility and HRM in China: a study of textile and apparel enterprises	Asia Pacific Business Review	Business ethics; China; CSR; HRM; Private enterprises
Cortes et al. (2017)	A Triple Bottom Line Approach for Measuring Supply Chains Sustainability Using Data Envelopment Analysis	European Journal of Sustainable Development	Data Envelopment Analysis; Sustainability; Supply Chains; Triple Bottom Line; Fast Fashion
Cowan et al. (2014)	Green spirit: consumer empathies for green apparel	International Journal of Consumer Studies	Apparel; Eco; Environmentally friendly; Green; Sustainability; Theory of planned behavior
Crinis et al. (2010)	Sweat or No Sweat: Foreign Workers in the Garment Industry in Malaysia	Journal of Contemporary Asia	Corporate Social Responsibility (CSR); Codes of conduct; Contract; Foreign workers; Garment industry

Table A1. *Cont.*

Author (Year)	Title	Journal	Keywords
Crinis et al. (2019)	Corporate Social Responsibility, Human Rights and Clothing Workers in Bangladesh and Malaysia	Asian Studies Review	Fashion; Brand names; Corporate Social Responsibility (CSR); Anti-sweatshop movement; Migrant labor; Malaysia; Bangladesh
da Costa et al. (2017)	Cleaner Production Implementation in the Textile Sector: The Case of a Medium-sized Industry in Minas Gerais	Revista Eletronica Em Gestao Educacao E Tecnologia Ambiental	Cleaner production; Textile sector; Environmental management; Social Responsibility; Brazil
Da Giau et al. (2016)	Sustainability practices and web-based communication. An analysis of the Italian fashion industry	Journal of Fashion Marketing and Management	Corporate Social Responsibility; Communication; Supply chain management
Dabija et al. (2017)	Cross-cultural investigation of consumers' generations attitudes towards purchase of environmentally friendly products in apparel retail	Studies in Business and Economics	Green marketing; Consumer; purchase behavior; Environmentally friendly products; Cross-country analysis; Apparel footwear and sportswear retail
de Abreu et al. (2012)	A comparative understanding of corporate social responsibility of textile firms in Brazil and China	Journal of Cleaner Production	Sustainable development; Emerging economies; Corporate Social Responsibility; Environmental management; Stakeholder; Textile industry; Brazil; China
De Angelis (2017)	The role of design similarity in consumers' evaluation of new green products: An investigation of luxury fashion brands	Journal of Cleaner Production	Sustainability; Sustainable design; Sustainable consumption; Environmental sustainability; New green product; Design similarity; Luxury fashion brand
de Lagerie (2016)	Conflicts of Responsibility in the Globalized Textile Supply Chain. Lessons of a Tragedy	Journal of Consumer Policy	Factory collapse; Working conditions; Corporate Social Responsibility; Consumer activism; Qualitative study
de Lenne et al. (2017)	Media and sustainable apparel buying intention	Journal of Fashion Marketing and Management	Sustainability; Fast fashion; Social media; Theory of planned behavior; Sustainable apparel; Magazines

Table A1. *Cont.*

Author (Year)	Title	Journal	Keywords
Desore et al. (2018)	An overview on corporate response towards sustainability issues in textile industry	Environment Development and Sustainability	Sustainability issues; Textile industry; Textile value chain; Sustainability strategies; Drivers and barriers; Strategic response
Di Benedetto (2017)	Corporate social responsibility as an emerging business model in fashion marketing	Journal of Global Fashion Marketing	Corporate social responsibility; Fashion; Marketing; Fashion merchandising; Customer relationship management; Sustainability
Diddi et al. (2016)	Corporate Social Responsibility in the Retail Apparel Context: Exploring Consumers' Personal and Normative Influences on Patronage Intentions	Journal of Marketing Channels	Corporate Social Responsibility; Ethical behavior; Ethical Decision making; Moral norms; Retail apparel; United States; Values
Diddi et al. (2017)	Exploring the role of values and norms towards consumers' intentions to patronize retail apparel brands engaged in corporate social responsibility	Fashion and Textiles	Corporate Social Responsibility; Value norms
Dodds et al. (2016)	Willingness to pay for environmentally linked clothing at an event: visibility, environmental certification, and level of environmental concern	Tourism Recreation Research	Willingness to pay; Festival marketing; Clothing; Fair trade certification; Sustainable consumption message
Dururu et al. (2015)	Enhancing engagement with community sector organizations working in sustainable waste management: A case study	Waste Management & Research	Third sector organizations; Sustainability; England; Sustainable waste management; Resource efficiency
Egels-Zanden et al. (2006)	Exploring the effects of union-NGO relationships on corporate responsibility: The case of the Swedish clean clothes campaign	Journal of Business Ethics	Clean Clothes Campaign; Corporate responsibility; Garment industry; Labor practice; Multi-national corporation; Non-governmental organization; Transnational corporation; Supplier relation; Union
Egels-Zanden et al. (2015)	Multiple institutional logics in union–NGO relations: private labor regulation in the Swedish Clean Clothes Campaign	Business Ethics: A European Review	None

Table A1. *Cont.*

Author (Year)	Title	Journal	Keywords
Escobar-Rodriguez et al. (2017)	Facebook practices for business communication among fashion retailers	Journal of Fashion Marketing and Management	Word-of-mouth; Social networks; Marketing; Communities; Fashion retailing; E-commerce
Esmail et al. (2018)	The role of clothing in participation of persons with a physical disability: a scoping review protocol	Bmj Open	None
Fahimnia et al. (2018)	Greening versus resilience: A supply chain design perspective	Transportation Research Part E-Logistics and Transportation Review	Supply chain management; Green; Environmental sustainability; Robust; Network design; Elastic p-robust
Fang et al. (2010)	Sourcing in an Increasingly Expensive China: Four Swedish Cases	Journal of Business Ethics	China; CSR; Sourcing; Manufacturing; Price; Swedish companies; Textile and clothing industry (TCI)
Ferrell et al. (2016)	Ethics and Social Responsibility in Marketing Channels and Supply Chains: An Overview	Journal of Marketing Channels	Compliance; Corporate social responsibility; International Organization for Standardization; Marketing channels; Marketing ethics; Supply chain ethics; Supply chain management; Sustainability
Fontana (2018)	Corporate Social Responsibility as Stakeholder Engagement: Firm-NGO Collaboration in Sweden	Corporate Social Responsibility and Environmental Management	Firm–NGO collaboration; Corporate social responsibility; Stakeholder engagement; Resource-based view; Sweden; Asylum applicants
Fornasiero et al. (2017)	Proposing an integrated LCA-SCM model to evaluate the sustainability of customization strategies. International	Journal of Computer Integrated Manufacturing	Supply chain; Customization; Modular life-cycle assessment; Simulation
Fransen et al. (2014)	Privatizing or Socializing Corporate Responsibility: Business Participation in Voluntary Programs	Business & Society	Labor standards; Globalization; Corporate responsibility; Multi-stakeholder governance; NGO
Fu et al. (2018)	Blockchain Enhanced Emission Trading Framework in Fashion Apparel Manufacturing Industry	Sustainability	Blockchain; Sustainability; Fashion apparel industry; Carbon trading; Energy economics industry

Table A1. *Cont.*

Author (Year)	Title	Journal	Keywords
Garcia-Torres et al. (2017)	Effective Disclosure in the Fast-Fashion Industry: from Sustainability Reporting to Action	Sustainability	Sustainability reporting; Sustainability actions; United Nations SDGs; Fast-fashion industry; Supply chain sustainability; Sustainability scorecard
Gardas et al. (2018)	Modelling the challenges to sustainability in the textile and apparel (T&A) sector: A Delphi-DEMATEL approach	Sustainable Production and Consumption	Barriers; Sustainability; Textile and apparel supply chain; Multi-criteria decision making; India
Gardetti et al. (2013)	Entrepreneurship, Innovation and Luxury	Journal of Corporate Citizenship	Luxury; Sustainable; Cosmetics; Entrepreneurship; Latin America
Ghosh et al. (2012)	A comparative analysis of greening policies across supply chain structures	International Journal of Production Economics	Apparel industry; Green supply chains; Channel coordination; Game theory
Govindasamy et al. (2018)	Corporate Social Responsibility in Practice: The Case of Textile, Knitting and Garment Industries in Malaysia	Pertanika Journal of Social Science and Humanities	Barriers; Corporate Social Responsibility; Drivers; Malaysia; Textile
Guedes et al. (2017)	Corporate social responsibility: Competitiveness in the context of textile and fashion value chain	Environmental Engineering and Management Journal	Corporate Social Responsibility (CSR); Ethical corporate management; SMEs; Sustainable development; Textile and fashion
Guercini et al. (2013)	Sustainability and Luxury	Journal of Corporate Citizenship	Luxury; Sustainability; Fashion; Supply chain
Hale et al. (2007)	Women Working Worldwide: transnational networks, corporate social responsibility and action research	Global Networks	Commodity chains; Garment production; New Labor; Inter-nationalism; Women workers'; Organizations; Transnational networking; Corporate social responsibility
Haque et al. (2015)	Corporate social responsibility, economic globalization and developing countries A case study of the ready-made garments industry in Bangladesh	Sustainability Accounting Management and Policy Journal	Bangladesh; Developing countries; Corporate social responsibility; Economic globalization; Ready-made garments

Table A1. *Cont.*

Author (Year)	Title	Journal	Keywords
Hassan et al. (2017)	Quick dry ability of various quick drying polyester and wool fabrics assessed by a novel method	Drying Technology	Contact angle; FTIR; Quick drying; Test method; Textile fabrics
Heekang et al. (2018)	Environmentally friendly apparel products: the effects of value perceptions	Social Behavior & Personality: an international journal	Cause-effectiveness value; Monetary value; Environmentally conscious apparel products; Purchase intention
Henry et al. (2019)	Microfibers from apparel and home textiles: Prospects for including microplastics in environmental sustainability assessment	Science of the Total Environment	Plastic pollution; Synthetic fibers; Impact assessment; Marine ecosystems; Sewage sludge; Laundry
Hepburn et al. (2013)	In Patagonia (Clothing): A Complicated Greenness. Fashion Theory	The Journal of Dress, Body & Culture	Patagonia; Ethical consumption; Conservation; Sublime; Catalogue
Herva et al. (2008)	An approach for the application of the Ecological Footprint as environmental indicator in the textile sector	Journal of Hazardous Materials	Ecological Footprint; Textile sector; Environmental sustainability indicator; Simplified tool
Hischier (2018)	Car vs. Packaging-A First, Simple (Environmental) Sustainability Assessment of Our Changing Shopping Behavior	Sustainability	Sustainability assessment; Life cycle assessment; LCA; Online shopping; Packaging; Mobility; Lifestyles
Hong et al. (2019)	The impact of moral philosophy and moral intensity on purchase behavior toward sustainable textile and apparel products	Fashion and Textiles	Moral philosophy; Moral intensity; Purchase behavior; Sustainability; Organic products; Naturally dyed products
Huq et al. (2014)	Social sustainability in developing country suppliers. An exploratory study in the ready-made garments industry of Bangladesh	International Journal of Operations & Production Management	Bangladesh; Social sustainability; Developing country suppliers; Exploratory case study; Ready-made garments industry; Transaction cost economics
Hwang et al. (2016)	"Don't buy this jacket" Consumer reaction toward anti-consumption apparel advertisement	Journal of Fashion Marketing and Management	Consumer attitudes; Anti-consumption; Patagonia; CSR; Advertisement; Purchase intensions

Table A1. *Cont.*

Author (Year)	Title	Journal	Keywords
Jakhar (2015)	Performance evaluation and a flow allocation decision model for a sustainable supply chain of an apparel industry	Journal of Cleaner Production	Sustainable supply chain; Performance measures; Flow optimization; Structural equation modeling; Fuzzy analytic hierarchy process; Fuzzy multi-objective linear programming
James et al. (2019)	Bridging the double-gap in circularity. Addressing the intention-behavior disparity in fashion	Design Journal	Circular innovation; Design for longevity; Intention-behavior gap; Fashion product lifecycle
Jammulamadaka (2016)	Bombay textile mills: exploring CSR roots in colonial India	Journal of Management History	Bombay textile mills; Indian; CSR; Postcolonial
Jorgensen et al. (2012)	The shaping of environmental impacts from Danish production and consumption of clothing	Ecological Economics	Environmental management; Transnational; Supply chain; Product chain; Consumer practice; Clothing consumption
Joy et al. (2012)	Fast Fashion, Sustainability, and the Ethical Appeal of Luxury Brands	Fashion Theory-the Journal of Dress Body & Culture	Luxury brands; Fast fashion; Sustainability; Quality and consumer behavior
Jung et al. (2014)	A theoretical investigation of slow fashion: sustainable future of the apparel industry	International Journal of Consumer Studies	Slow fashion; Slow production; Slow consumption; Environmental sustainability; Small apparel business strategy; Scale development
Jung et al. (2016)	Sustainable Development of Slow Fashion Businesses: Customer Value Approach	Sustainability	Slow fashion; Fast fashion; Sustainability; Customer value; Price premium
Kang et al. (2013)	Environmentally sustainable textile and apparel consumption: the role of consumer knowledge, perceived consumer effectiveness and perceived personal relevance	International Journal of Consumer Studies	Consumer effectiveness; Consumer knowledge; Personal relevance; Sustainability; Textiles and apparel; theory of planned behavior
Karaosman et al. (2015)	Consumers' responses to CSR in a cross-cultural setting	Cogent Business & Management	Corporate social responsibility; Consumer behavior; Qualitative research; Fashion industry; Cultural differences

Table A1. *Cont.*

Author (Year)	Title	Journal	Keywords
Karaosman et al. (2017)	From a Systematic Literature Review to a Classification Framework: Sustainability Integration in Fashion Operations	Sustainability	Supply chain management; Fashion industry; Three-dimensional engineering framework; Fashion operations; Environmental sustainability; Social sustainability; Classification framework; Systematic literature review
Karell et al. (2019)	Addressing the Dialogue between Design. Sorting and Recycling in a Circular Economy	Design Journal	Circular economy; Clothing design; Design for recycling; Textile recycling; Textile sorting
Kemper et al. (2019)	Saving Water while Doing Business: Corporate Agenda-Setting and Water Sustainability	Water	Cotton; Water sustainability; Agenda setting; Water governance
Khurana et al. (2016)	Two decades of sustainable supply chain management in the fashion business, an appraisal	Journal of Fashion Marketing and Management	Fashion industry; Corporate social responsibility; Stakeholders; Supply chain management; Textile/clothing supply chains; Brands
Kim et al. (1998)	Environmental concern and apparel consumptions	Clothing and Textile Research Journal	Environmental attitude; Apparel consumption
Kim et al. (2015)	The heuristic-systemic model of sustainability stewardship: facilitating sustainability values, beliefs and practices with corporate social responsibility drives and eco-labels/indices	International Journal of Consumer Studies	Corporate social responsibility; Eco-label/index; Heuristic-systematic model; Sustainability stewardship; VBN Theory
Kim et al. (2017)	Sustainable Supply Chain Based on News Articles and Sustainability Reports: Text Mining with Leximancer and diction	Sustainability	Sustainability; Supply chain management (SCM); Triple bottom line; News articles; Sustainability report; Text mining; Leximancer
Klepp et al. (2018)	Nisseluelandet-The Impact of Local Clothes for the Survival of a Textile Industry in Norway	Fashion Practice-the Journal of Design Creative Process & the Fashion Industry	Local clothing; Home production; Textile industry; Handicrafts; Wool
Knudsen (2017)	How Do Domestic Regulatory Traditions Shape CSR in Large International US and UK Firms?	Global Policy	None

Table A1. *Cont.*

Author (Year)	Title	Journal	Keywords
Knudsen (2018)	Government Regulation of International Corporate Social Responsibility in the US and the UK: How Domestic Institutions Shape Mandatory and Supportive Initiatives	British Journal of Industrial Relations	None
Koksal et al. (2017)	Social Sustainable Supply Chain Management in the Textile and Apparel Industry-A Literature Review	Sustainability	SSCM; Supply chain management; Sourcing intermediary; Social sustainability; Apparel/clothing industry; Developing country suppliers
Koksal et al. (2018)	Social Sustainability in Apparel Supply Chains-The Role of the Sourcing Intermediary in a Developing Country	Sustainability	Sustainable supply chain management; Social sustainability; Textile/apparel industry
Kolstad et al. (2018)	Content-Based Recommendations for Sustainable Wardrobes Using Linked Open Data	Mobile Networks & Applications	Internet of things; Recommender systems; Content-based; Recommendation; Textile recycling; Linked open data; Bag of concepts; Purchase intention
Koszewska (2010)	CSR Standards as a Significant Factor Differentiating Textile and Clothing Goods	Fibers & Textiles in Eastern Europe	Corporate social responsibility; Textile & clothing goods; Consumer evaluation; Norms; Standards
Koszewska (2011)	Social and Eco-labelling of Textile and Clothing Goods as Means of Communication and Product Differentiation	Fibers & Textiles in Eastern Europe	Social labelling; Eco-labelling; Corporate social responsibility; Textile and clothing market; Fast fashion; Consumer behavior
Koszewska (2013)	A typology of Polish consumers and their behaviors in the market for sustainable textiles and clothing	International Journal of Consumer Studies	Socially responsible consumption; Typology; Textiles; Clothing; Consumer behavior; Sustainable
Kozlowski et al. (2012)	Environmental Impacts in the Fashion Industry: A Lifecycle and Stakeholder Framework	Journal of Corporate Citizenship	Fashion industry; Apparel; Environmental impacts; Life-cycle assessment; Stakeholder analysis; Corporate social responsibility; Supply chain management

Table A1. *Cont.*

Author (Year)	Title	Journal	Keywords
Kozlowski et al. (2015)	Corporate sustainability reporting in the apparel industry. An analysis of indicators disclosed	International Journal of Productivity and Performance Management	CSR reporting; Sustainability reporting; Global reporting initiative; Sustainability indicators; Sustainable fashion
Lagoudis et al. (2015)	A framework for measuring carbon emissions for inbound transportation and distribution networks	Research in Transportation Business and Management	Carbon emissions; Green supply chain; Inbound logistics; Apparel industry
Laitala et al. (2018)	Does Use Matter? Comparison of Environmental Impacts of Clothing Based on Fiber Type	Sustainability	Sustainable clothing; Fiber properties; Clothing production; Fashion consumption; Maintenance; LCA; Environmental sustainability tools; Fiber ranking; Material selection
Lee et al. (2015)	The interactions of CSR, self-congruity and purchase intention among Chinese consumers	Australasian Marketing Journal	Corporate social responsibility; China; Fashion industry; Self-congruity; Purchase intention; Collectivism
Lee et al. (2015)	Impacts of sustainable value and business stewardship on lifestyle practices in clothing consumption.	Fashion and Textiles	Business stewardship; Sustainable lifestyle; Value; VALS framework
Lee et al. (2018)	Consumer responses to company disclosure of socially responsible efforts	Fashion and Textiles	California; Transparency in Supply Chains; Act; Socially responsible consumption; Consumer response; Website; Experiment
Lee et al. (2018)	Effects of multi-brand company's CSR activities on purchase intention through a mediating role of corporate image and brand image	Journal of Fashion Marketing and Management	Brand image; Reciprocity; Corporate social responsibility; Corporate image; Multi-brand
Lee et al. (2018)	The effect of ethical climate and employees' organizational citizenship behavior on US fashion retail organizations' sustainability performance	Corporate Social Responsibility and Environmental Management	Corporate social responsibility; Ethical climate; Organizational; Citizenship behavior; Sustainability; Performance

Table A1. *Cont.*

Author (Year)	Title	Journal	Keywords
Lee et al. (2018)	The moral responsibility of corporate sustainability as perceived by fashion retail employees: a USA-China cross-cultural comparison study	Business Strategy and the Environment	Corporate sustainability; Cross-cultural studies; Fashion retail businesses; Moral responsibility; Organizational; Citizenship behavior
Lenzo et al. (2017)	Social Life Cycle Assessment in the Textile Sector: An Italian Case Study	Sustainability	Textile product; Social Life Cycle Assessment; Workers; Local communities; Social performances
Leoni (2017)	Social responsibility in practice: an Italian case from the early 20th century	Journal of Management History	Case studies; Corporate social responsibility; Italy; Family business; Management history; Accounting history
Li et al. (2014)	Governance of sustainable supply chains in the fast fashion industry	European Management Journal	Fast fashion; Sustainability; Corporate social responsibility; Supply chain governance
Li et al. (2017)	Environmental Management System Adoption and the Operational Performance of Firm in the Textile and Apparel Industry of China	Sustainability	Social sustainable performance; Operations; Event study; Textile and apparel industry
Liang et al. (2018)	Second-hand clothing consumption: A generational cohort analysis of the Chinese market	International Journal of Consumer Studies	Chinese consumers; Descriptive norm; Generational cohorts; Perceived concern; Perceived value; second-hand clothing
Lo et al. (2012)	The impact of environmental management systems on financial performance in fashion and textiles industries	International Journal of Production Economics	Environmental management systems; ISO 14000; Financial performance; Event study; Fashion and textiles industries
Lock et al. (2019)	Credible corporate social responsibility (CSR) communication predicts legitimacy Evidence from an experimental study	Corporate Communications	Legitimacy; Corporate social responsibility; Credibility; Experiment; Website
Lueg et al. (2015)	The Role of Corporate Sustainability in a Low-Cost Business Model-A Case Study in the Scandinavian Fashion Industry	Business Strategy and the Environment	Business model; Corporate social responsibility; Corporate sustainability; Sustainable development; CSR policies; Information disclosure; Labor practices; Public policy

Table A1. *Cont.*

Author (Year)	Title	Journal	Keywords
Macchion et al. (2017)	Improving innovation performance through environmental practices in the fashion industry: the moderating effect of internationalization and the influence of collaboration	Production Planning & Control	Supply chain management; Environmental sustainability; Collaboration; Innovation management; Internationalization
Macchion et al. (2018)	Strategic approaches to sustainability in fashion supply chain management	Production Planning & Control	Supply chain management; Sustainability; Fashion; Environmental sustainability; Social sustainability
Majumdar et al. (2018)	Modeling the barriers of green supply chain management in small and medium enterprises A case of Indian clothing industry	Management of Environmental Quality	Interpretive structural modelling; Green supply chain; Clothing industry; Barriers; Indian SME
Maldini et al. (2019)	Assessing the impact of design strategies on clothing lifetimes, usage and volumes: The case of product personalization	Journal of Cleaner Production	Circular/sustainable design strategies; Clothing lifetimes; Clothing usage; Clothing volumes; Wardrobe studies; Personalized products
Mamic (2005)	Managing global supply chain: The sports footwear, apparel and retail sectors	Journal of Business Ethics	Code of Conduct; Supply chain management; Compliance; Corporate social responsibility; Management systems; Multinational enterprises
Mann et al. (2014)	Assessment of Leading Apparel Specialty Retailers' CSR Practices as Communicated on Corporate Websites: Problems and Opportunities	Journal of Business Ethics	Corporate social responsibility; Apparel specialty retailer; Labor issues; Environmental issues
McNeill et al. (2015)	Sustainable fashion consumption and the fast fashion conundrum: fashionable consumers and attitudes to sustainability in clothing choice	International Journal of Consumer Studies	Behavior; Clothing; Consumers; Eco; Fashion; Sustainable
McQueen et al. (2017)	Reducing laundering frequency to prolong the life of denim jeans	International Journal of Consumer Studies	Consumer habits; Denim jeans; Laundering; Textile degradation; Wear

Table A1. *Cont.*

Author (Year)	Title	Journal	Keywords
Mena et al. (2016)	Theorization as institutional work: The dynamics of roles and practices	Human Relations	Corporate social responsibility; Institutional change; Institutional maintenance; Institutional transition; Private regulation; Private regulatory; Initiative
Merk (2009)	Jumping Scale and Bridging Space in the Era of Corporate Social Responsibility: cross-border labor struggles in the global garment industry	Third World Quarterly	None
Mezzadri (2014)	Back shoring, Local Sweatshop Regimes and CSR in India	Competition & Change	Garment commodity chain; Back shoring; Pan-Indian buyer exporters; Local sweatshop regime; Corporate social responsibility; India
Mezzadri (2014)	Indian Garment Clusters and CSR Norms: Incompatible Agendas at the Bottom of the Garment Commodity Chain	Oxford Development Studies	None
Micheletti et al. (2008)	Fashioning social justice through political consumerism, capitalism, and the internet	Cultural Studies	Political consumerism; Anti-sweatshop; Anti-slavery; Culture jamming; Market vulnerabilities; Social justice
Milne et al. (2013)	Small Business Implementation of CSR for Fair Labor Association Accreditation	Journal of Corporate Citizenship	Multi stakeholder initiative; Apparel industry; Corporate social responsibility; Labor compliance
Moon et al. (2018)	Environmentally friendly apparel products: the effects of value perceptions	Social Behavior and Personality	Cause-effectiveness value; Monetary value; Environmentally conscious; Apparel products; Purchase intention
Moore et al. (2004)	Systems thinking and green chemistry in the textile industry: concepts, technologies and benefits	Journal of Cleaner Production	Textile industry; Aquatic toxicity; Dyeing; Finishing; Systems thinking; Sustainable development; Globalization

Table A1. *Cont.*

Author (Year)	Title	Journal	Keywords
Moore et al. (2012)	An Investigation into the Financial Return on Corporate Social Responsibility in the Apparel Industry	Journal of Corporate Citizenship	Corporate social responsibility; Financial return; Apparel industry
Moreira et al. (2015)	A conceptual framework to develop green textiles in the aeronautic completion industry: a case study in a large manufacturing company	Journal of Cleaner Production	Aircraft completion industry; Textiles; Sustainable products development; Eco-design
Moretto et al. (2018)	Designing a roadmap towards a sustainable supply chain: A focus on the fashion industry	Journal of Cleaner Production	Sustainability; Supply chain; Roadmap; Fashion; Luxury; CSR
Morgan et al. (2009)	An investigation of young fashion consumers' disposal habits	International Journal of Consumer Studies	Fashion; Textile; Recycling; Consumers; Sustainable; Disposition
Na et al. (2015)	Investigating the sustainability of the Korean textile and fashion industry	International Journal of Clothing Science and Technology	Apparel reuse; Eco-materials; Eco-promotion
Nassivera et al. (2017)	Willingness to pay for organic cotton Consumer responsiveness to a corporate social responsibility initiative	British Food Journal	Consumer behavior; Corporate social responsibility; Organic cotton; Organic production; LISREL
Nayak et al. (2019)	Recent sustainable trends in Vietnam's fashion supply chain	Journal of Cleaner Production	Sustainable supply chain management; Fashion sustainability; Textiles and garment; Emerging economy; Third-party logistics; Vietnam
Niu et al. (2018)	Outsource to an OEM or an ODM? Profitability and Sustainability Analysis of a Fashion Supply Chain	Journal of Systems Science and Systems Engineering	Outsourcing; Buy-back contract; Fashion supply chain; Nash bargaining
Normann et al. (2017)	Supplier perceptions of distributive justice in sustainable apparel sourcing	International Journal of Physical Distribution & Logistics Management	Code of conduct; Apparel industry; Sustainable sourcing; Qualitative study; Distributive justice; Assessment governance
O'Rourke et al. (2017)	Patagonia: Driving sustainable innovation by embracing tensions	California Management Review	Sustainability; Innovation; Supply chain; Environmental responsibility
Olsen et al. (2011)	Conscientious brand criteria: A framework and a case example from the clothing industry	Journal of Brand Management	Brand; Conscientious; CSR; Altruistic

Table A1. *Cont.*

Author (Year)	Title	Journal	Keywords
Oncioiu et al. (2015)	White biotechnology—a fundamental factor for a sustainable development in Romanian SMEs	Romanian Biotechnological Letters	Green clothes; White biotechnology; Organic materials; SME's; Environmental sustainability; Green clothes; White biotechnology; Organic materials; SME's; Environmental sustainability
Paik et al. (2017)	Corporate Social Responsibility Performance and Outsourcing: The Case of the Bangladesh Tragedy	Journal of International Accounting Research	Corporate social responsibility; Worker safety agreement; Outsourcing; Bangladesh tragedy
Pal (2016)	Extended responsibility through servitization in PSS. An exploratory study of used-clothing sector	Journal of Fashion Marketing and Management	Clothing; Servitization; Textile/ clothing supply chains; PSS; Product-service system; Extended responsibility
Pangsapa et al. (2008)	Political economy of Southeast Asian borderlands: Migration, environment, and developing country firms	Journal of Contemporary Asia	Developing country companies; Environmental sustainability; Corporate responsibility; Labor unions; Migration; Global Compact
Panigrahi et al. (2018)	A stakeholders' perspective on barriers to adopt sustainable practices in MSME supply chain: Issues and challenges in the textile sector	Research Journal of Textile and Apparel	Interpretive structural modeling; Sustainable supply chain management; Barriers to sustainable supply chain management; Sustainable supply chain practices
Park-Poaps et al. (2010)	Stakeholder Forces of Socially Responsible Supply Chain Management Orientation	Journal of Business Ethics	Supply chain; Clothing; Sweatshop; Social responsibility
Pather (2015)	Entrepreneurship and regional development: case of fashion industry growth in south Africa	Entrepreneurship and Sustainability Issues	Creative Industries; Fashion; Clusters; Local context
Pedersen et al. (2014)	From Resistance to Opportunity-Seeking: Strategic Responses to Institutional Pressures for Corporate Social Responsibility in the Nordic Fashion Industry	Journal of Business Ethics	Corporate social responsibility; Sustainability; Institutional pressures; Strategic responses
Pedersen et al. (2015)	Sustainability innovators and anchor draggers: a global expert study on sustainable fashion	Business Strategy and the Environment	Consumer behavior; Sustainability; Organizational change; Partnerships; Business models; Accountability

Table A1. *Cont.*

Author (Year)	Title	Journal	Keywords
Pedersen et al. (2017)	The Role of Corporate Sustainability in a Low-Cost Business Model-A Case Study in the Scandinavian Fashion Industry	Social Responsibility Journal	Business model; Corporate social responsibility; Corporate sustainability; Sustainable development; CSR policies; Information disclosure; Labor practice; Public policy; Environmental policy; Risk management; Shareholder value; Stakeholder engagements; Supply chain
Pedersen et al. (2018)	Exploring the Relationship Between Business Model Innovation, Corporate Sustainability, and Organizational Values within the Fashion Industry	Journal of Business Ethics	Business model innovation; Corporate sustainability; Corporate social responsibility; Organizational values; Financial performance
Perry et al. (2013)	Conceptual framework development CSR implementation in fashion supply chains	International Journal of Physical Distribution & Logistics Management	Corporate Social Responsibility; Fashion; Supply chain management; Ethical sourcing
Perry et al. (2015)	Corporate Social Responsibility in Garment Sourcing Networks: Factory Management Perspectives on Ethical Trade in Sri Lanka	Journal of Business Ethics	Corporate social responsibility; Ethical sourcing; Retailing; Supply chain management; Sri Lanka
Pinheiro et al. (2019)	How to identify opportunities for improvement in the use of reverse logistics in clothing industries? A case study in a Brazilian cluster	Journal of Cleaner Production	Textile waste; Reverse logistics; Clothing industry; Cluster
Preuss et al. (2010)	Slipstreaming the Larger Boats: Social Responsibility in Medium-Sized Businesses	Journal of Business Ethics	Corporate social responsibility; Small and medium-sized enterprises; Owner–manager values; Consumer perceptions of CSR; Employee perceptions of CSR
Priyankara et al. (2018)	How Does Leader's Support for Environment Promote Organizational Citizenship Behavior for Environment? A Multi-Theory Perspective	Sustainability	Autonomous motivation for environment; Employee green behavior; Leader's support for environment; organizational citizenship behavior for environment; Perceived group's green climate

Table A1. *Cont.*

Author (Year)	Title	Journal	Keywords
Reilly et al. (2018)	External Communication About Sustainability: Corporate Social Responsibility Reports and Social Media Activity	Environmental Communication-a Journal of Nature and Culture	External communication; Corporate social responsibility; Sustainability; Social media
Reimers et al. (2016)	The academic conceptualization of ethical clothing Could it account for the attitude behavior gap?	Journal of Fashion Marketing and Management	Ethics; Social responsibility; Fashion; Clothing
Resta et al. (2016)	Enhancing environmental management in the textile sector: An Organizational-Life Cycle Assessment approach	Journal of Cleaner Production	Organizational Life Cycle Assessment (O-LCA); Environmental sustainability; Textile; Decision-making process; Environmental management
Ritch et al. (2012)	Accessing and affording sustainability: the experience of fashion consumption within young families	International Journal of Consumer Studies	Fashion consumption; Sustainability; Consumer behavior; Ethical retailing
Rodgers et al. (2017)	Results of a strategic science study to inform policies targeting extreme thinness standards in the fashion industry	International Journal of Eating Disorders	Eating disorders; Fashion; Models; Policy; Strategic
Roos et al. (2016)	A life cycle assessment (LCA)-based approach to guiding an industry sector towards sustainability: the case of the Swedish apparel sector	Journal of Cleaner Production	Life cycle assessment; Social assessment; Life cycle interpretation; Planetary boundaries; Actor-oriented advice; Textile
Ruwanpura (2016)	Garments without guilt? Uneven labor geographies and ethical trading-Sri Lankan labor perspectives	Journal of Economic Geography	Labor geography; Ethical trading; Sri Lanka; Corporate governance; Ethnography
Salcito et al. (2015)	Corporate human rights commitments and the psychology of business acceptance of human rights duties: a multi-industry analysis	International Journal of Human Rights	Corporate social responsibility; Human rights due diligence; Human rights; Policy; Protect; Respect; Remedy framework; UN Guiding Principles on Business and Human Rights
Savino et al. (2018)	An extensive study to assess the sustainability drivers of production performances using a resource-based view and contingency analysis	Journal of Cleaner Production	Production performances; Environment; Safety; Social issues: Sustainability; Resource based view; Contingency perspective; Structural equation modelling; Quality management

Table A1. *Cont.*

Author (Year)	Title	Journal	Keywords
Scheiber (2015)	Dressing up for Diffusion: Codes of Conduct in the German Textile and Apparel Industry, 1997–2010	Journal of Business Ethics	Corporate code of ethics; Code of conduct; Diffusion; Discourse; Institutional theory; Infomediaries
Scheper (2017)	Labor Networks under Supply Chain Capitalism: The Politics of the Bangladesh Accord	Development & Change	None
Schmitt et al. (2012)	How to Earn Money by Doing Good! Shared Value in the Apparel Industry	Journal of Corporate Citizenship	Shared value; Value creation; Innovation; Sustainability; Apparel industry; Fair-trade; Value creation; Tree; Corporate social responsibility
Schuessler et al. (2019)	Governance of Labor Standards in Australian and German Garment Supply Chains: The Impact of Rana Plaza	ILR Review	Labor standards; Garment lead firms; Global supply chains; Focusing events; Rana Plaza
Shen et al. (2014)	Perception of fashion sustainability in online community	Journal of the Textile Institute	Sustainable fashion; Online forums; Consumer perception; Cross-time approach
Shen et al. (2015)	Impacts of Returning Unsold Products in Retail Outsourcing Fashion Supply Chain: A Sustainability Analysis	Sustainability	Return policy; Cost of physical return; Supply chain coordination; Sustainability analysis
Shen et al. (2015)	Evaluation of Barriers of Corporate Social Responsibility Using an Analytical Hierarchy Process under a Fuzzy Environment-A Textile Case	Sustainability	Barriers of CSR; Fuzzy AHP; Indian textiles
Shen et al. (2016)	Enhancing Economic Sustainability by Markdown Money Supply Contracts in the Fashion Industry: China vs USA	Sustainability	Markdown money policy; Fashion industry; Supply chain management; Cross-cultural study
Shubham et al. (2018)	Institutional pressure and the implementation of corporate environment practices: examining the mediating role of absorptive capacity	Journal of Knowledge Management	Environmental management strategy; Resource-based view; Absorptive capacity; Organizational capability; Corporate environmental practices; Partial least square-structural equation modelling

Table A1. *Cont.*

Author (Year)	Title	Journal	Keywords
Siddiqui et al. (2016)	Human rights disasters, corporate accountability and the state Lessons learned from Rana Plaza	Accounting Auditing & Accountability Journal	Bangladesh; Human rights; State; Corporate accountability
Song et al. (2017)	Perceptions, attitudes, and behaviors toward sustainable fashion: Application of Q and Q-R methodologies	International Journal of Consumer Studies	Q methodology; Q-R methodology; Sustainable consumer; Sustainable consumption; Sustainable fashion
Song et al. (2018)	A Human-Centered Approach to Green Apparel Advertising: Decision Tree Predictive Modeling of Consumer Choice	Sustainability	Decision tree; Green advertising; Green apparel; Green marketing; Segmentation; Sustainable fashion; Sustainability
Stevenson et al. (2018)	Modern slavery in supply chains: a secondary data analysis of detection, remediation and disclosure	Supply Chain Management-an International Journal	Sustainability; Clothing industry; Information transparency; Modern slavery; Supply chain information disclosure; Secondary data
Svensson (2009)	SCM ethics: conceptual framework and empirical illustrations	Supply Chain Management-an International Journal	Supply chain management; Scandinavia; Fashion industry; Telecommunications; Ethics; Corporate social responsibility
Tama et al. (2017)	University students' attitude towards clothes in terms of environmental sustainability and slow fashion	Tekstil Ve Konfeksiyon	Environmental sustainability; Slow fashion; Fast fashion; University students; Environmental awareness
Testa et al. (2017)	Removing obstacles to the implementation of LCA among SMEs: A collective strategy for exploiting recycled wool	Journal of Cleaner Production	Small and medium enterprises; Life cycle assessment; Textile; Label; Collective action; Product; Environmental Footprint; Cluster
Thomas (2008)	From "Green Blur" to Eco fashion: Fashioning an Eco-lexicon. Fashion Theory	The Journal of Dress, Body & Culture	Eco fashion; Language; Lexicon; Ethical; Terminology
Thorisdottir et al. (2019)	Sustainability within Fashion Business Models: A Systematic Literature Review	Sustainability	Business model; Fashion; Sustainability; Measure; Driver; Report
Todeschini et al. (2017)	Innovative and sustainable business models in the fashion industry: Entrepreneurial drivers, opportunities, and challenges	Business Horizons	Business model innovation; Sustainable fashion; Born-sustainable; Startups; Social value creation; Slow fashion; Upcycling

Table A1. *Cont.*

Author (Year)	Title	Journal	Keywords
Tran et al. (2016)	SMEs in their Own Right: The Views of Managers and Workers in Vietnamese Textiles, Garment, and Footwear Companies	Journal of Business Ethics	Socialist Vietnam; SME managers and Workers; Formal and informal CSR practices; Institutional theory; Labor–management–state relations
Wang et al. (2017)	Sustainability Analysis and Buy-Back Coordination in a Fashion Supply Chain with Price Competition and Demand Uncertainty	Sustainability	Supply chain sustainability; Buy-back coordination; Demand uncertainty; Price competition; Dual channel system
White et al. (2017)	CSR research in the apparel industry: A quantitative and qualitative review of existing literature	Corporate Social Responsibility and Environmental Management	CSR in the apparel industry; CSR communication; Ethical supply chain management; Corporate social responsibility
Wijethilake et al. (2017)	Strategic responses to institutional pressures for sustainability. The role of management control systems	Accounting Auditing & Accountability Journal	Sustainability; Institutional pressures; Management control systems; Strategic responses
Wong et al. (2017)	Corporate social responsibility (CSR) for ethical corporate identity management Framing CSR as a tool for managing the CSR-luxury paradox online	Corporate Communications	Luxury industry; CSR communication; Corporate identity; Corporate social responsibility; Corporate branding; Framing
Woo et al. (2016)	Apparel firms' corporate social responsibility communications Cases of six firms from an institutional theory perspective	Asia Pacific Journal of Marketing and Logistics	Communications; Cross-cultural marketing; Apparel; Corporate social responsibility; Institutional theory
Woo et al. (2016)	Culture Doesn't Matter? The Impact of Apparel Companies' Corporate Social Responsibility Practices on Brand Equity	Clothing and Textiles Research Journal	Corporate social responsibility; Brand equity; Apparel; Cross-cultural
Wu et al. (2012)	The effects of GSCM drivers and institutional pressures on GSCM practices in Taiwan's textile and apparel industry	International Journal of Production Economics	Green supply chain management (GSCM); Green supply chain; Management drivers; Green supply chain; Management practices; Hierarchical moderated; Regression analysis; Institutional pressures

Table A1. *Cont.*

Author (Year)	Title	Journal	Keywords
Wu et al. (2015)	The Impact of Integrated Practices of Lean, Green, and Social Management Systems on Firm Sustainability Performance-Evidence from Chinese Fashion Auto-Parts Suppliers	Sustainability	Lean; Green; Social; Sustainability; Triple Bottom Line (3BL)
Yadlapalli et al. (2018)	Socially responsible governance mechanisms for manufacturing firms in apparel supply chain	International Journal of Production Economics	Apparel supply chains; Bangladesh; Governance mechanisms; Socially responsible supply chains
Yang et al. (2017)	Analysis of the barriers in implementing environmental management system by interpretive structural modeling approach	Management Research Review	China; Environmental management system; Barriers analysis; Business ethics and sustainability; Textile and apparel industries; Interpretive structural modeling
Yang et al. (2017)	An Exploratory Study of the Mechanism of Sustainable Value Creation in the Luxury Fashion Industry	Sustainability	Sustainability; Sustainable value; Value co-creation; Supply chain; Case study
Yasmin (2014)	Burning death traps made in Bangladesh: who is to blame?	Labor Law Journal	None
Zhang et al. (2015)	Life cycle assessment of cotton T-shirts in China	International Journal of Life Cycle Assessment	Cleaner production; Clothing; Consumer behavior; Cotton textile; Environmental management; Laundry washing; Life cycle assessment; Sustainability
Zurga et al. (2015)	Environmentally sustainable apparel acquisition and disposal behaviors among Slovenian consumers	Autex Research Journal	Environmentally sustainable; Consumer behavior; Apparel consumption; Apparel acquisition; Apparel disposal; Environment; Slovenia

References

1. Levitt, T. The Globalization of Markets. *Harv. Bus. Rev.* **1983**, 24, 1–11.
2. Gronroos, C. *Service Management and Marketing: Managing the Service Profit Logic*, 4th ed.; John Wiley & Sons Inc.: New York, NY, USA, 2016; pp. 1–522.
3. Fashion United. Global Fashion. Available online: https://fashionunited.com/global-fashion-industry-statistics (accessed on 29 September 2020).
4. European Environment Agency. News, Private Consumptions; Textile. Available online: https://www.eea.europa.eu/highlights/private-consumption-textiles-eus-fourth-1 (accessed on 10 January 2020).

5.   Foroohar, R. Newsweek Fabulous Fashion. Available online: https://www.newsweek.com/fabulous-fashion-121093 (accessed on 20 November 2018).
6.   Clean Clothes Campaign. Improving Working Conditions in the Global Garment Industry. Available online: https://cleanclothes.org/fashions-problems (accessed on 21 March 2020).
7.   World Commission on Environment and Development Report. Our Common Future. Available online: https://sustainabledevelopment.un.org/content/documents/5987our-common-future.pdf (accessed on 14 January 2017).
8.   Lash, W. Competitive Advantage on a Warming Planet. *Harward Bus. Rev.* **2007**, *85*, 1–12.
9.   European Environment Agency. State and Outlook 2015 Assessment of Global Megatrend. 2015, pp. 1–140. Available online: https://www.eea.europa.eu/soer/2015/global/action-download-pdf (accessed on 27 October 2016).
10.   Nordic Fashion Association. Background. Available online: www.nordicfashionassociation.com/background (accessed on 10 December 2016).
11.   de Brito, M.P.; Carbone, V.; Blanquart, C.M. Towards a sustainable fashion retail supply chain in Europe: Organisation and Performance. *Int. J. Prod. Econ.* **2008**, *114*, 534–553. [CrossRef]
12.   Black, S. *The Sustainable Fashion Handbook*; Thames & Hudson Inc.: New York, NY, USA, 2012.
13.   Fashion Revolution. Consumer Survey Report. 2018, pp. 1–45. Available online: https://www.fashionrevolution.org/wp-content/uploads/2018/11/201118_FashRev_ConsumerSurvey_2018.pdf (accessed on 30 November 2018).
14.   Kruse, E. Copenhagen Fashion Summit The Magazine Global Fashion Agenda: 2018. Available online: https://www.globalfashionagenda.com/publications-and-policy/pulse-of-the-industry/ (accessed on 20 May 2018).
15.   Thorisdottir, T.S.; Johannsdottir, L. Sustainability within Fashion Business Models: A Systematic Literature Review. *Sustainability* **2019**, *11*, 2233. [CrossRef]
16.   Remy, N.; Speelman, E.; Swartz, S. Style That's Sustainable: A new Fast-Fashion Formula. Available online: https://www.mckinsey.com/business-functions/sustainability/our-insights/style-thats-sustainable-a-new-fast-fashion-formula (accessed on 2 February 2020).
17.   Ellen MacArthur Foundation. A New Textiles Economy: Redesigning Fashion's Future. 2017.Available online: https://www.ellenmacarthurfoundation.org/publications/a-new-textiles-economy-redesigning-fashions-future (accessed on 4 February 2018).
18.   Cobbing, M.; Vicaire, Y. *Timeout for Fashion*; Greenpeace: Hamburg, Germany, 2016; pp. 1–12.
19.   Claudio, L. Waste Couture. *Environ. Health Perspect.* **2007**, *115*, 448–454. [CrossRef]
20.   Preuss, L.; Perschke, J. Slipstreaming the Larger Boats: Social Responsibility in Medium-Sized Businesses. *J. Bus. Ethics* **2010**, *92*, 531–551. [CrossRef]
21.   Ghosh, D.; Shah, J. A comparative analysis of greening policies across supply chain structures. *Int. J. Prod. Econ.* **2012**, *135*, 568–583. [CrossRef]
22.   da Costa, N.P.; Prado, J.F.; Fonseca, A. Cleaner Production Implementation in the Textile Sector: The Case of a Medium-sized Industry in Minas Gerais. *Rev. Eletron. Gest. Educ. E Tecnol. Ambient.* **2017**, *21*, 222–231. [CrossRef]
23.   Fahimnia, B.; Jabbarzadeh, A.; Sarkis, J. Greening versus resilience: A supply chain design perspective. *Transp. Res. Part E-Logist. Transp. Rev.* **2018**, *119*, 129–148. [CrossRef]
24.   Moore, L.L.; De Silva, I.; Hartmann, S. An Investigation into the Financial Return on Corporate Social Responsibility in the Apparel Industry. *J. Corp. Citizsh.* **2012**, 105–122. [CrossRef]
25.   Kozlowski, A.; Bardecki, M.; Searcy, C. Environmental Impacts in the Fashion Industry: A Life-cycle and Stakeholder Framework. *J. Corp. Citizsh.* **2012**, 17–36. [CrossRef]
26.   Paik, G.H.; Lee, B.; Krumwiede, K.R. Corporate Social Responsibility Performance and Outsourcing: The Case of the Bangladesh Tragedy. *J. Int. Account. Res.* **2017**, *16*, 59–79. [CrossRef]
27.   Chouinard, Y.; Stanley, V. *The Responsible Company What We've Learned from Patagonia's First 40 Years*; Bell, S., Ed.; Patagonia Books: Ventura, CA, USA, 2012.
28.   Gam, H.J. Are fashion-conscious consumers more likely to adopt eco-friendly clothing? *J. Fash. Mark. Manag.* **2011**, *15*, 178–193. [CrossRef]
29.   Niinimäki, K. Eco-clothing, Consumer Identity and Ideology. *Sustain. Dev.* **2010**, *18*, 150–162. [CrossRef]
30.   De Angelis, M.A.; Amatulli, C. The role of design similarity in consumers´evaluation of new green products. *J. Clean. Prod.* **2017**, *141*, 1515–1527. [CrossRef]

31. Di Benedetto, C.A. Corporate social responsibility as an emerging business model in fashion marketing. *J. Glob. Fash. Mark.* **2017**, *8*, 251–265. [CrossRef]

32. Shen, B.; Zheng, J.H.; Chow, P.S.; Chow, K.Y. Perception of fashion sustainability in online community. *J. Text. Inst.* **2014**, *105*, 971–979. [CrossRef]

33. Cowan, K.; Kinley, T. Green spirit: Consumer empathies for green apparel. *Int. J. Consum. Stud.* **2014**, *38*, 493–499. [CrossRef]

34. Woo, H.; Jin, B.H. Culture Doesn't Matter? The Impact of Apparel Companies' Corporate Social Responsibility Practices on Brand Equity. *Cloth. Text. Res. J.* **2016**, *34*, 20–36. [CrossRef]

35. Koszewska, M. Social and Eco-labelling of Textile and Clothing Goods as Means of Communication and Product Differentiation. *Fibrestext. East. Eur.* **2011**, *19*, 20–26.

36. Lee, J.; Lee, Y. The interactions of CSR, self-congruity and purchase intention among Chinese consumers. *Australas. Mark. J.* **2015**, *23*, 19–26. [CrossRef]

37. Ritch, E.L.; Schröder, M.J. Accessing and affording sustainability: The experience of fashion consumption within young families. *Int. J. Consum. Stud.* **2012**, *36*, 203–210. [CrossRef]

38. Haski- Leventhal, D. *Strategic Corporate Social Responsibility*; SAGE: London, UK, 2018.

39. Diddi, S.; Niehm, L.S. Exploring the role of values and norms towards consumers' intentions to patronize retail apparel brands engaged in corporate social responsibility (CSR). *Fashion Text.* **2017**, *4*, 5. [CrossRef]

40. Karaosman, H.; Morales-Alonso, G.; Grijalvo, M. Consumers' responses to CSR in a cross-cultural setting. *Cogent Bus. Manag.* **2015**, *2*. [CrossRef]

41. Ebner, D.; Baumgartner, R.J. The relationship between Sustainable Development and Corporate Social Responsibility. In Proceedings of the Corporate Responsibility Research Conference, Dublin, Ireland, 4–5 September 2006; pp. 1–17.

42. Carroll, A.B. Carroll's pyramid of CSR: Taking another look. *Int. J. Corp. Soc. Responsib.* **2016**, *1*, 1–8. [CrossRef]

43. Carroll, A.B.; Shabana, K.M. The Business Case for Corporate Social Responsibility: A Review of Concepts, Research and Practice. *Int. J. Manag. Rev.* **2010**, *12*, 85–105. [CrossRef]

44. Evans, S.; Vladimirova, D.; Holgado, M.; Fossen, K.; Yang, M.; Silva, E.A.; Barlow, C.Y. Business Model Innovation for sustainability: Towards a Unified perspective for Creation of Sustainable Business Models. *Bus. Strategy Environ.* **2017**, *26*, 597–608. [CrossRef]

45. Hristov, I.; Chirico, A. The role of sustainability key performance indicators (KPIs) in implementing sustainable strategies. *Sustainability* **2019**, *11*, 5742. [CrossRef]

46. Lozano, R. Envisioning sustainability three-dimensionally. *J. Clean. Prod.* **2008**, *16*, 1838–1846. [CrossRef]

47. Dopfer, K.; Foster, J.; Puts, J. Micro-Meso-Macro. *Evol. Econ.* **2014**, *14*, 263–279. [CrossRef]

48. Steurer, R.; Langer, M.; Konrad, A.; Martinuzzi, A. Corporations, Stakeholders and Sustainable Development I: A Theoretical Exploration of Business-Society Relations. *J. Bus. Ethics* **2005**, *61*, 263–281. [CrossRef]

49. Carroll, A. The Pyramid of Corporate Social Responsibility: Toward the Moral Management of Organizational Stakeholders. *Bus. Horiz.* **1991**, *34*, 39–48. [CrossRef]

50. Latapí Agudelo, M.; Jóhannsdóttir, L.; Davídsdóttir, B. A literature review of the history and evolution of corporate social responsibility. *Int. J. Corp. Soc. Responsib.* **2019**, *4*, 1–23. [CrossRef]

51. European Commission. Green Paper Promoting a European Framework for Corporate Social Responsibility; Corner, P., Ed.; European Union An official website of the European Union. 2001, pp. 1–26. Available online: https://ec.europa.eu/commission/presscorner/detail/en/DOC_01_9 (accessed on 7 July 2020).

52. Blowfield, M.; Murray, A. *Corporate Responsibility*, 3rd ed.; United States of America by Oxford University Press: Oxford, UK, 2008; pp. 1–143.

53. Friedman, M. The Social Responsibility of Business is to Increase its Profits. *Corp. Ethics Corp. Gov.* **2007**, 173–178. [CrossRef]

54. Aquino, S. The Performance of Italian Clothing Firms for Shareholders, Workers and Public Administrations: An Econometric Analysis. *I. J. Account. Res. Audit Pract.* **2011**, *10*, 20–37.

55. Ahlstrom, J. Corporate Response to CSO Criticism: Decoupling the Corporate Responsibility Discourse from Business Practice. *Corp. Soc. Responsib. Environ. Manag.* **2010**, *17*, 70–80. [CrossRef]

56. Matten, D.; Moon, J. "Implicit and Explicit" CSR: A Conceptual Framework for a Comparative Understanding of Corporate Social responsibility. *Acad. Manag. Rev.* **2008**, *33*, 404–424. [CrossRef]

57. Rasche, A.; Morsing, M.; Moon, J. *Corporate Social Responsibility*; Cambridge University Press: Cambridge, UK, 2017.

58. UNESCO. Education for Sustainable Development. Available online: https://en.unesco.org/themes/education-sustainable-development/what-is-esd/sd#:~{}:text=Sustainability%20is%20often%20thought%20of,research%20and%20technology%20transfer%2C%20education (accessed on 11 August 2020).

59. Lucas, S. The Five Dimensions of Sustainability. *Environ. Politics* **2009**, *18*, 539–556.

60. Lafferty, W.M.; Langhelle, O. *Sustainable Development as Concept and Norm*; Palgrave Macmillan: London, UK, 1999.

61. Hopkins, M. *CSR and Sustainability*; Greenleaf Publishing Limited.: Sheffield, UK, 2016.

62. Robért, K.; Schmidt-Bleek, B.; Aloisi de Larderel, J.; Basile, G.; Jansen, J.; Kuehr, R.; Price Thomas, P.; Suzuki, M.; Hawken, P.; Wackernagel, M. Strategic sustainable development—Selection, design and synergies of applied tools. *J. Clean. Prod.* **2002**, *10*, 197–214. [CrossRef]

63. Jacques, P. *Sustainability*; Routledge: London, UK, 2014.

64. Kuhlman, T.; Farrington, J. What is Sustainability? *Sustainability* **2010**, *2*, 3436. [CrossRef]

65. Drexhage, J.; Murphy, D. *Sustainable Development: From Brundtland to Rio 2012*; International Institute for Sustainable Development (IISD): New York, NY, USA, 2010.

66. Elkington, J. 25 Years ago, I coined the phrase "The Triple Bottom Line" Here's why it's time to rethink it. *Harv. Bus. Rev.* **2018**, *6*, 2–5.

67. White, M. Sustainability: I know it when I see it. *Ecol. Econ.* **2013**, *86*, 213–217. [CrossRef]

68. Bansal, P.; DesJardine, M. Business sustainability: It is about time. *Strateg. Organ.* **2014**, *12*, 70–78. [CrossRef]

69. Eccles, R.; Johnstone-Luis, M.; Mayer, C.; Stroehle, J.C. The Board's Rolen in Sustainability. *Harv. Bus. Rev.* **2020**, *98*, 1–152.

70. Chandler, D. *Strategic Corporate Social Responsibility*, 4th ed.; Sage Publication Inc.: London, UK, 2017; p. 716.

71. United Nations Global Compact. Guide to Corporate Sustainability. Shaping A Sustainable Future. 2014. Available online: https://d306pr3pise04h.cloudfront.net/docs/publications%2FUN_Global_Compact_Guide_to_Corporate_Sustainability.pdf (accessed on 15 November 2016).

72. Sage Publication. Sociology. A Unique Way to View the World. 2017, pp. 1–24. Available online: https://us.sagepub.com/sites/default/files/upm-binaries/86855_Ch_1.pdf (accessed on 4 June 2020).

73. Baumgartner, R.J.; Ebner, D. Corporate Sustainability Strategies: Sustainability Profiles and Maturity Levels. *Sustain. Dev.* **2010**, *18*, 769–789. [CrossRef]

74. Hines, T.; Bruce, M. *Fashion Marketing Contemporary Issues*, 2nd ed.; Elsevier Ltd.: Oxford, UK, 2001.

75. European Commission. Internal Market. Industry, Entrepreneurship and SMEs. Available online: https://ec.europa.eu/growth/index_en (accessed on 18 March 2020).

76. Global Fashion Agenda. Online event: Virginijus Sinkevičius, EU Commissioner for Environment, Oceans and Fisheries. July 2020 ed.; European Commission Audiovisual Service. 2020. Available online: https://www.linkedin.com/company/globalfashionagenda/videos/native/urn:li:ugcPost:6687355661967257601/ (accessed on 8 July 2020).

77. Gordon, J.; Hill, C. *Sustainable Fashion, Past, Present and Future*; Bloomsbury Academic: London, UK, 2015; ISBN 9780857851840.

78. European Commission. A New Circular Economy Action Plan For a Cleaner and More Competitive Europe. Available online: https://eur-lex.europa.eu/resource.html?uri=cellar:9903b325-6388-11ea-b735-01aa75ed71a1.0017.02/DOC_1&format=PDF (accessed on 16 July 2020).

79. Denyer, D.; Tranfield, D. *The Sage Handbook of Organizational Research Methods*; Sage Publication Ltd.: London, UK, 2009; pp. 1–731. ISBN 978-2-4129-3118-2.

80. Jesson, J.K.; Matheson, L.; Lacey, F.M. *Doing Your Literature Review*; Sage: London, UK, 2012.

81. Tranfield, D.; Denyer, D.; Smart, P. Towards a Methodology for Developing Evidence-Informed Management Knowledge by Means of Systematic Review. *Br. J. Manag.* **2003**, *14*, 207–222. [CrossRef]

82. Schreier, M. *Qualitative Content Analysis in Practice*; Sage Publications Ltd.: London, UK, 2012; pp. 1–269. ISBN 978-1-84920-592-4.

83. Creswell, J.W.; Poth, C.N. *Qualitative Inquiry and Research Design*, 4th ed.; Sage Publication Inc: London, UK, 2018.

84. Collis, J.; Hussey, R. *Business Research*, 4th ed.; Palgrave Macmillian: New York, NY, USA, 2014; pp. 1–351.

85. Corbin, J.; Strauss, A. *Basics of Qualitative Research Techniques and Procedures for Developing Grounded Theory*, 4th ed.; Sage Publications, Inc: Thousand Oaks, CA, USA, 2015.

86. Battaglia, M.; Testa, F.; Bianchi, L.; Iraldo, F.; Frey, M. Corporate Social Responsibility and Competitiveness within SMEs of the Fashion Industry: Evidence from Italy and France. *Sustainability* **2014**, *6*, 872–893. [CrossRef]

87. Haque, M.Z.; Azmat, F. Corporate social responsibility, economic globalization and developing countries A case study of the ready-made garments industry in Bangladesh. *Sustain. Account. Manag. Policy J.* **2015**, *6*, 166–189. [CrossRef]

88. Olsen, L.E.; Peretz, A. Conscientious brand criteria: A framework and a case example from the clothing industry. *J. Brand Manag.* **2011**, *18*, 639–649. [CrossRef]

89. Park-Poaps, H.; Rees, K. Stakeholder Forces of Socially Responsible Supply Chain Management Orientation. *J. Bus. Ethics* **2010**, *92*, 305–322. [CrossRef]

90. Pedersen, E.R.G.; Lauesen, L.M.; Kourula, A. Back to basics: Exploring perceptions of stakeholders within the Swedish fashion industry. *Social Responsibility Journal* **2017**, *13*, 266–278. [CrossRef]

91. Majumdar, A.; Sinha, S. Modeling the barriers of green supply chain management in small and medium enterprises A case of Indian clothing industry. *Manag. Environ. Qual.* **2018**, *29*, 1110–1122. [CrossRef]

92. Cortes, A. A Triple Bottom Line Approach for Measuring Supply Chains Sustainability Using Data Envelopment Analysis. *Eur. J. Sustain. Dev.* **2017**, *6*, 119–128. [CrossRef]

93. Macchion, L.; Moretto, A.; Caniato, F.; Caridi, M.; Danese, P.; Spina, G.; Vinelli, A. Improving innovation performance through environmental practices in the fashion industry: The moderating effect of internationalization and the influence of collaboration. *Prod. Plan. Control* **2017**, *28*, 190–201. [CrossRef]

94. Nayak, R.; Akbari, M.; Far, S.M. Recent sustainable trends in Vietnam's fashion supply chain. *J. Clean. Prod.* **2019**, *225*, 291–303. [CrossRef]

95. Scheper, C. Labour Networks under Supply Chain Capitalism: The Politics of the Bangladesh Accord. *Dev. Chang.* **2017**, *48*, 1069–1088. [CrossRef]

96. Shen, B.; Li, Q.Y. Impacts of Returning Unsold Products in Retail Outsourcing Fashion Supply Chain: A Sustainability Analysis. *Sustainability* **2015**, *7*, 1172–1185. [CrossRef]

97. Koksal, D.; Strahle, J.; Muller, M. Social Sustainability in Apparel Supply ChainsThe Role of the Sourcing Intermediary in a Developing Country. *Sustainability* **2018**, *10*, 1039. [CrossRef]

98. Kim, D.; Kim, S. Sustainable Supply Chain Based on News Articles and Sustainability Reports: Text Mining with Leximancer and DICTION. *Sustainability* **2017**, *9*, 1008. [CrossRef]

99. Ferrell, O.C.; Ferrell, L. Ethics and Social Responsibility in Marketing Channels and Supply Chains: An Overview. *J. Mark. Channels* **2016**, *23*, 2–10. [CrossRef]

100. Woo, H.; Jin, B. Apparel firms' corporate social responsibility communications Cases of six firms from an institutional theory perspective. *Asia Pac. J. Mark. Logist.* **2016**, *28*, 37–55. [CrossRef]

101. Lock, I.; Schulz-Knappe, C. Credible corporate social responsibility (CSR) communication predicts legitimacy Evidence from an experimental study. *Corp. Commun.* **2019**, *24*, 2–20. [CrossRef]

102. de Abreu, M.C.S.; de Castro, F.; Soares, F.D.; da Silva, J.C.L. A comparative understanding of corporate social responsibility of textile firms in Brazil and China. *J. Clean. Prod.* **2012**, *20*, 119–126. [CrossRef]

103. Jung, S.J.; Jin, B. Sustainable Development of Slow Fashion Businesses: Customer Value Approach. *Sustainability* **2016**, *8*, 540. [CrossRef]

104. White, C.L.; Nielsen, A.E.; Valentini, C. CSR research in the apparel industry: A quantitative and qualitative review of existing literature. *Corp. Soc. Responsib. Environ. Manag.* **2017**, *24*, 382–394. [CrossRef]

105. Yadlapalli, A.; Rahman, S.; Gunasekaran, A. Socially responsible governance mechanisms for manufacturing firms in apparel supply chains. *Int. J. Prod. Econ.* **2018**, *196*, 135–149. [CrossRef]

106. Chen, T.; Larsson, A.; Mark-Herbert, C. Implementing a collective code of conduct-CSC9000T in Chinese textile industry. *J. Clean. Prod.* **2014**, *74*, 35–43. [CrossRef]

107. Wong, J.Y.; Dhanesh, G.S. Corporate social responsibility (CSR) for ethical corporate identity management Framing CSR as a tool for managing the CSR-luxury paradox online. *Corp. Commun.* **2017**, *22*, 420–439. [CrossRef]

108. Mann, M.; Byun, S.E.; Kim, H.; Hoggle, K. Assessment of Leading Apparel Specialty Retailers' CSR Practices as Communicated on Corporate Websites: Problems and Opportunities. *J. Bus. Ethics* **2014**, *122*, 599–622. [CrossRef]

109. Pangsapa, P.; Smith, M.J. Political economy of Southeast Asian borderlands: Migration, environment, and developing country firms. *J. Contemp. Asia* **2008**, *38*, 485–514. [CrossRef]

110. Lagoudis, I.N.; Shakri, A.R. A framework for measuring carbon emissions for inbound transportation and distribution networks. *Res. Transp. Bus. Manag.* **2015**, *17*, 53–64. [CrossRef]

111. Shen, L.X.; Govindan, K.; Shankar, M. Evaluation of Barriers of Corporate Social Responsibility Using an Analytical Hierarchy Process under a Fuzzy Environment A Textile Case. *Sustainability* **2015**, *7*, 3493–3514. [CrossRef]

112. Perry, P.; Wood, S.; Fernie, J. Corporate Social Responsibility in Garment Sourcing Networks: Factory Management Perspectives on Ethical Trade in Sri Lanka. *J. Bus. Ethics* **2015**, *130*, 737–752. [CrossRef]

113. Perry, P.; Towers, N. Conceptual framework development CSR implementation in fashion supply chains. *Int. J. Phys. Distrib. Logist. Manag.* **2013**, *43*, 478–500. [CrossRef]

114. Govindasamy, V.; Suresh, K. Corporate Social Responsibility in Practice: The Case of Textile, Knitting and Garment Industries in Malaysia. *Pertanika J. Soc. Sci. Humanit.* **2018**, *26*, 2643–2656.

115. Todeschini, B.V.; Cortimiglia, M.N.; Callegaro-de-Menezes, D.; Ghezzi, A. Innovative and sustainable business models in the fashion industry: Entrepreneurial drivers, opportunities, and challenges. *Bus. Horizons.* **2017**, *60*, 759–770. [CrossRef]

116. Pedersen, E.R.G.; Gwozdz, W.; Hvass, K.K. Exploring the Relationship Between Business Model Innovation, Corporate Sustainability, and Organisational Values within the Fashion Industry. *J. Bus. Ethics* **2018**, *149*, 267–284. [CrossRef]

117. Caniato, F.; Caridi, M.; Crippa, L.; Moretto, A. Environmental sustainability in fashion supply chains: An exploratory case based research. *Int. J. Prod. Econ.* **2012**, *135*, 659–670. [CrossRef]

118. Fu, B.L.; Shu, Z.; Liu, X.G. Blockchain Enhanced Emission Trading Framework in Fashion Apparel Manufacturing Industry. *Sustainability* **2018**, *10*, 1105. [CrossRef]

119. Pedersen, E.R.G.; Medelby, M.; Clemmensen, S.N. The Role of Corporate Sustainability in a Low-Cost Business Model-A Case Study in the Scandinavian Fashion Industry. *Bus. Strategy Environ.* **2015**, *24*, 344–359. [CrossRef]

120. de Lenne, O.; Vandenbosch, L. Media and sustainable apparel buying intention. *J. Fash. Mark. Manag.* **2017**, *21*, 483–498. [CrossRef]

121. Normann, U.; Ellegaard, C.; Moller, M.M. Supplier perceptions of distributive justice in sustainable apparel sourcing. *Int. J. Phys. Distrib. Logist. Manag.* **2017**, *47*, 368–386. [CrossRef]

122. Maldini, I.; Stappers, P.J.; Gimeno-Martinez, J.C.; Daanen, H.A.M. Assessing the impact of design strategies on clothing lifetimes, usage and volumes: The case of product personalization. *J. Clean. Prod.* **2019**, *210*, 1414–1424. [CrossRef]

123. Connell, K.Y.H.; Kozar, J.M. Sustainability knowledge and behaviors of apparel and textile undergraduates. *Int. J. Sustain. High. Educ.* **2012**, *13*, 394–407. [CrossRef]

124. Lee, S.H.N.; Kim, H.; Yang, K. Impacts of sustainable value and business stewardship on lifestyle practices in clothing consumption. *Fash. Text.* **2015**, *2*, s40691–s5015. [CrossRef]

125. Tama, D.; Cureklibatir Encan, B.; Ondogan, Z. University Students' Attitude Towards Clothes in Terms of environmental sustainability and slow fashion. *Tekst. Ve Konfeksiyon* **2017**, *27*, 191–197.

126. Baskaran, V.; Nachiappan, S.; Rahman, S. Indian textile suppliers' sustainability evaluation using the grey approach. *Int. J. Prod. Econ.* **2012**, *135*, 647–658. [CrossRef]

127. Arrigo, E. The flagship stores as sustainability communication channels for luxury fashion retailers. *J. Retail. Consum. Serv.* **2018**, *44*, 170–177. [CrossRef]

128. Kim, H.; Lee, S.H.; Yang, K. The heuristic-systemic model of sustainability stewardship: Facilitating sustainability values, beliefs and practices with corporate social responsibility drives and eco-labels/indices. *Int. J. Consum. Stud.* **2015**, *39*, 249–260. [CrossRef]

129. Moretto, A.; Macchion, L.; Lion, A.; Caniato, F.; Danese, P.; Vinelli, A. Designing a roadmap towards a sustainable supply chain: A focus on the fashion industry. *J. Clean. Prod.* **2018**, *193*, 169–184. [CrossRef]

130. Garcia-Torres, S.; Rey-Garcia, M.; Albareda-Vivo, L. Effective Disclosure in the Fast-Fashion Industry: From Sustainability Reporting to Action. *Sustainability* **2017**, *9*, 2256. [CrossRef]

131. Yang, Y.F.; Han, H.; Lee, P.K.C. An Exploratory Study of the Mechanism of Sustainable Value Creation in the Luxury Fashion Industry. *Sustainability* **2017**, *9*, 483. [CrossRef]

132. Na, Y.; Na, D.K. Investigating the sustainability of the Korean textile and fashion industry. *Int. J. Cloth. Sci. Technol.* **2015**, *27*, 23–33. [CrossRef]

133. Kemper, L.; Partzsch, L. Saving Water while Doing Business: Corporate Agenda-Setting and Water Sustainability. *Water* **2019**, *11*, 297. [CrossRef]

134. de Lagerie, P.B. Conflicts of Responsibility in the Globalized Textile Supply Chain. Lessons of a Tragedy. *J. Consum. Policy* **2016**, *39*, 397–416. [CrossRef]

135. Zhang, Y.; Liu, X.; Xiao, R.F.; Yuan, Z.W. Life cycle assessment of cotton T-shirts in China. *Int. J. Life Cycle Assess.* **2015**, *20*, 994–1004. [CrossRef]

136. Herva, M.; Franco, A.; Ferreiro, S.; Alvarez, A.; Roca, E. An approach for the application of the Ecological Footprint as environmental indicator in the textile sector. *J. Hazard. Mater.* **2008**, *156*, 478–487. [CrossRef]

137. McQueen, R.H.; Batcheller, J.C.; Moran, L.J.; Zhang, H.; Hooper, P.M. Reducing laundering frequency to prolong the life of denim jeans. *Int. J. Consum. Stud.* **2017**, *41*, 36–45. [CrossRef]

138. Koszewska, M. A typology of Polish consumers and their behaviours in the market for sustainable textiles and clothing. *Int. J. Consum. Stud.* **2013**, *37*, 507–521. [CrossRef]

139. Panigrahi, S.S.; Rao, N.S. A stakeholders' perspective on barriers to adopt sustainable practices in MSME supply chain: Issues and challenges in the textile sector. *Res. J. Text. Appar.* **2018**, *22*, 59–76. [CrossRef]

140. Song, S.Y.; Kim, Y.K. A Human-Centered Approach to Green Apparel Advertising: Decision Tree Predictive Modeling of Consumer Choice. *Sustainability* **2018**, *10*, 3688. [CrossRef]

141. Pather, A. Entrepreneurship and Regional Development: Case of Fashion Industry Growth in South Africa. *Entrep. Sustain. Issues* **2015**, *3*, 56–65. [CrossRef]

142. Adam, M. The Role of Human Resource Management (HRM) for the Implementation of Sustainable Product-Service Systems (PSS)-An Analysis of Fashion Retailers. *Sustainability* **2018**, *10*, 2518. [CrossRef]

143. Micheletti, M.; Stolle, D. Fashioning Social Justice through Political Consumerism, Capitalism, and the Internet. *Cult. Stud.* **2008**, *22*, 749–769. [CrossRef]

144. Svensson, G. The transparency of SCM ethics: Conceptual framework and empirical illustrations. *Supply Chain Manag. -Int. J.* **2009**, *14*, 259–269. [CrossRef]

145. Reilly, A.H.; Larya, N. External Communication About Sustainability: Corporate Social Responsibility Reports and Social Media Activity. *Environ. Commun. A J. Nat. Cult.* **2018**, *12*, 621–637. [CrossRef]

146. Athukorala, P.C.; Ekanayake, R. Repositioning in the global apparel value chain in the post-MFA era: Strategic issues and evidence from Sri Lanka. *Dev. Policy Rev.* **2018**, *36*, O247–O269. [CrossRef]

147. Klepp, I.G.; Laitala, K. Nisseluelandet-The Impact of Local Clothes for the Survival of a Textile Industry in Norway. *Fash. Pract. J. Des. Creat. Process Fash. Ind.* **2018**, *10*, 171–195. [CrossRef]

148. Lee, J.; Lee, Y. Effects of multi-brand company's CSR activities on purchase intention through a mediating role of corporate image and brand image. *J. Fash. Mark. Manag.* **2018**, *22*, 387–403. [CrossRef]

149. Yasmin, T. Burning death traps made in bangladesh: Who is to blame? *Labor Law J.* **2014**, *65*, 51–61.

150. Bartley, T.; Egels-Zanden, N. Beyond decoupling: Unions and the leveraging of corporate social responsibility in Indonesia. *Socio-Econ. Rev.* **2016**, *14*, 231–255. [CrossRef]

151. Bartley, T.; Egels-Zanden, N. Responsibility and neglect in global production networks: The uneven significance of codes of conduct in Indonesian factories. *Glob. Netw.* **2015**, *15*, S21–S44. [CrossRef]

152. Jammulamadaka, N. Bombay textile mills: Exploring CSR roots in colonial India. *J. Manag. Hist.* **2016**, *22*, 450–472. [CrossRef]

153. Crinis, V. Corporate Social Responsibility, Human Rights and Clothing Workers in Bangladesh and Malaysia. *Asian Stud. Rev.* **2019**, *43*, 295–312. [CrossRef]

154. Crinis, V. Sweat or No Sweat: Foreign Workers in the Garment Industry in Malaysia. *J. Contemp. Asia* **2010**, *40*, 589–611. [CrossRef]

155. Mezzadri, A. Indian Garment Clusters and CSR Norms: Incompatible Agendas at the Bottom of the Garment Commodity Chain. *Oxf. Dev. Stud.* **2014**, *42*, 217–258. [CrossRef]

156. Tran, A.N.; Jeppesen, S. SMEs in their Own Right: The Views of Managers and Workers in Vietnamese Textiles, Garment, and Footwear Companies. *J. Bus. Ethics* **2016**, *137*, 589–608. [CrossRef]

157. Knudsen, J.S. How Do Domestic Regulatory Traditions Shape CSR in Large International US and UK Firms? *Glob. Policy* **2017**, *8*, 29–41. [CrossRef]

158. Reimers, V.; Magnuson, B.; Chao, F. The academic conceptualization of ethical clothing. Could it account for the attitude behaviour gap? *J. Fash. Mark. Manag.* **2016**, *20*, 383–399. [CrossRef]

159. McNeill, L.; Moore, R. Sustainable fashion consumption and the fast fashion conundrum: Fashionable consumers and attitudes to sustainability in clothing choice. *Int. J. Consum. Stud.* **2015**, *39*, 212–222. [CrossRef]

160. International Organization for Standardization. Standards. Available online: https://www.iso.org/standards.html (accessed on 24 August 2020).

161. Pedersen, E.R.G.; Gwozdz, W. From Resistance to Opportunity-Seeking: Strategic Responses to Institutional Pressures for Corporate Social Responsibility in the Nordic Fashion Industry. *J. Bus. Ethics* **2014**, *119*, 245–264. [CrossRef]

162. Cooke, F.L.; He, Q.L. Corporate social responsibility and HRM in China: A study of textile and apparel enterprises. *Asia Pac. Bus. Rev.* **2010**, *16*, 355–376. [CrossRef]

163. Knudsen, J.S. Government Regulation of International Corporate Social Responsibility in the US and the UK: How Domestic Institutions Shape Mandatory and Supportive Initiatives. *Br. J. Ind. Relat.* **2018**, *56*, 164–188. [CrossRef]

164. Nassivera, F.; Troiano, S.; Marangon, F.; Sillani, S.; Nencheva, I.M. Willingness to pay for organic cotton Consumer responsiveness to a corporate social responsibility initiative. *Br. Food J.* **2017**, *119*, 1815–1825. [CrossRef]

165. Anner, M. CSR Participation Committees, Wildcat Strikes and the Sourcing Squeeze in Global Supply Chains. *Br. J. Ind. Relat.* **2018**, *56*, 75–98. [CrossRef]

166. Austgulen, M.H. Environmentally Sustainable Textile Consumption-What Characterizes the Political Textile Consumers? *J. Consum. Policy* **2016**, *39*, 441–466. [CrossRef]

167. Cho, E.; Gupta, S.; Kim, Y.K. Style consumption: Its drivers and role in sustainable apparel consumption. *Int. J. Consum. Stud.* **2015**, *39*, 661–669. [CrossRef]

168. Song, S.; Ko, E. Perceptions, attitudes, and behaviors toward sustainable fashion: Application of Q and Q-R methodologies. *Int. J. Consum. Stud.* **2017**, *41*, 264–273. [CrossRef]

169. Desore, A.; Narula, S.A. An overview on corporate response towards sustainability issues in textile industry. *Environ. Dev. Sustain.* **2018**, *20*, 1439–1459. [CrossRef]

170. Pedersen, E.R.G.; Andersen, K.R. Sustainability innovators and anchor draggers: A global expert study on sustainable fashion. *J. Fash. Mark. Manag.* **2015**, *19*, 315–327. [CrossRef]

171. Wu, G.C.; Ding, J.H.; Chen, P.S. The effects of GSCM drivers and institutional pressures on GSCM practices in Taiwan's textile and apparel industry. *Int. J. Prod. Econ.* **2012**, *135*, 618–636. [CrossRef]

172. Shubham; Charan, P.; Murty, L.S. Institutional pressure and the implementation of corporate environment practices: Examining the mediating role of absorptive capacity. *J. Knowl. Manag.* **2018**, *22*, 1591–1613. [CrossRef]

173. Li, B.; Wu, K.K. Environmental Management System Adoption and the Operational Performance of Firm in the Textile and Apparel Industry of China. *Sustainability* **2017**, *9*, 992. [CrossRef]

174. Borjeson, N.; Gilek, M.; Karlsson, M. Knowledge challenges for responsible supply chain management of chemicals in textiles as experienced by procuring organizations. *J. Clean. Prod.* **2015**, *107*, 130–136. [CrossRef]

175. Clarke-Sather, A.; Cobb, K. Onshoring fashion: Worker sustainability impacts of global and local apparel production. *J. Clean. Prod.* **2019**, *208*, 1206–1218. [CrossRef]

176. Hischier, R. Car vs. Packaging-A First, Simple (Environmental) Sustainability Assessment of Our Changing Shopping Behaviour. *Sustainability* **2018**, *10*, 3061. [CrossRef]

177. Lenzo, P.; Traverso, M.; Salomone, R.; Ioppolo, G. Social Life Cycle Assessment in the Textile Sector: An Italian Case Study. *Sustainability* **2017**, *9*, 2092. [CrossRef]

178. Resta, B.; Gaiardelli, P.; Pinto, R.; Dotti, S. Enhancing environmental management in the textile sector: An Organisational-Life Cycle Assessment approach. *J. Clean. Prod.* **2016**, *135*, 620–632. [CrossRef]

179. Roos, S.; Zamani, B.; Sandin, G.; Peters, G.M.; Svanstrom, M. A life cycle assessment (LCA)-based approach to guiding an industry sector towards sustainability: The case of the Swedish apparel sector. *J. Clean. Prod.* **2016**, *133*, 691–700. [CrossRef]

180. Karaosman, H.; Morales-Alonso, G.; Brun, A. From a Systematic Literature Review to a Classification Framework: Sustainability Integration in Fashion Operations. *Sustainability* **2017**, *9*, 30. [CrossRef]

181. Khurana, K.; Ricchetti, M. Two decades of sustainable supply chain management in the fashion business, an appraisal. *J. Fash. Mark. Manag.* **2016**, *20*, 89–104. [CrossRef]

182. Koksal, D.; Strahle, J.; Muller, M.; Freise, M. Social Sustainable Supply Chain Management in the Textile and Apparel Industry-A Literature Review. *Sustainability* **2017**, *9*, 100. [CrossRef]

183. Da Giau, A.; Macchion, L.; Caniato, F.; Caridi, M.; Danese, P.; Rinaldi, R.; Vinelli, A. Sustainability practices and web-based communication An analysis of the Italian fashion industry. *J. Fash. Mark. Manag.* **2016**, *20*, 72–88. [CrossRef]

184. Huq, F.A.; Stevenson, M.; Zorzini, M. Social sustainability in developing country suppliers An exploratory study in the ready made garments industry of Bangladesh. *Int. J. Oper. Prod. Manag.* **2014**, *34*, 610–638. [CrossRef]

185. Jung, S.J.; Jin, B.H. A theoretical investigation of slow fashion: Sustainable future of the apparel industry. *Int. J. Consum. Stud.* **2014**, *38*, 510–519. [CrossRef]

186. Macchion, L.; Da Giau, A.; Caniato, F.; Caridi, M.; Danese, P.; Rinaldi, R.; Vinelli, A. Strategic approaches to sustainability in fashion supply chain management. *Prod. Plan. Control* **2018**, *29*, 9–28. [CrossRef]

187. Briga-Sa, A.; Nascimento, D.; Teixeira, N.; Pinto, J.; Caldeira, F.; Varum, H.; Paiva, A. Textile waste as an alternative thermal insulation building material solution. *Constr. Build. Mater.* **2013**, *38*, 155–160. [CrossRef]

188. Koszewska, M. CSR Standards as a Significant Factor Differentiating Textile and Clothing Goods. *Fibres Text. East. Eur.* **2010**, *18*, 14–19.

189. Hwang, C.; Lee, Y.; Diddi, S.; Karpova, E. "Don't buy this jacket" Consumer reaction toward anti-consumption apparel advertisement. *J. Fash. Mark. Manag.* **2016**, *20*, 435–452. [CrossRef]

190. Liang, J.; Xu, Y. Second-hand clothing consumption: A generational cohort analysis of the Chinese market. *Int. J. Consum. Stud.* **2018**, *42*, 120–130. [CrossRef]

191. Dodds, R.; Pitts, R.E.; Smith, W.W. Willingness to pay for environmentally linked clothing at an event: Visibility, environmental certification, and level of environmental concern. *Tour. Recreat. Res.* **2016**, *41*, 283–290. [CrossRef]

192. Brennan, N.M.; Merkl-Davies, D.M. Rhetoric and argument in social and environmental reporting: The Dirty Laundry case. *Account. Audit. Account. J.* **2014**, *27*, 602–633. [CrossRef]

193. Kozlowski, A.; Searcy, C.; Bardecki, M. Corporate sustainability reporting in the apparel Industry An analysis of indicators disclosed. *Int. J. Product. Perform. Manag.* **2015**, *64*, 377–397. [CrossRef]

194. Stevenson, M.; Cole, R. Modern slavery in supply chains: A secondary data analysis of detection, remediation and disclosure. *Supply Chain Manag. Int. J.* **2018**, *23*, 81–99. [CrossRef]

195. Fang, T.; Gunterberg, C.; Larsson, E. Sourcing in an Increasingly Expensive China: Four Swedish Cases. *J. Bus. Ethics* **2010**, *97*, 119–138. [CrossRef]

196. Shen, B.; Choi, T.M.; Lo, C.K.Y. Enhancing Economic Sustainability by Markdown Money Supply Contracts in the Fashion Industry: China vs USA. *Sustainability* **2016**, *8*, 31. [CrossRef]

197. Choi, T.M. Local sourcing and fashion quick response system: The impacts of carbon footprint tax. *Transp. Res. Part E-Logist. Transp. Rev.* **2013**, *55*, 43–54. [CrossRef]

198. Salcito, K.; Wielga, C.; Singer, B.H. Corporate human rights commitments and the psychology of business acceptance of human rights duties: A multi-industry analysis. *Int. J. Hum. Rights* **2015**, *19*, 673–696. [CrossRef]

199. Diddi, S.; Niehm, L.S. Corporate Social Responsibility in the Retail Apparel Context: Exploring Consumers' Personal and Normative Influences on Patronage Intentions. *J. Mark. Channels* **2016**, *23*, 60–76. [CrossRef]

200. Anner, M. Monitoring Workers' Rights: The Limits of Voluntary Social Compliance Initiatives in Labor Repressive Regimes. *Global Policy* **2017**, *8*, 56–65. [CrossRef]

201. Lo, C.K.Y.; Yeung, A.C.L.; Cheng, T.C.E. The impact of environmental management systems on financial performance in fashion and textiles industries. *Int. J. Prod. Econ.* **2012**, *135*, 561–567. [CrossRef]

202. Benjamin, C.T.; Kit Fai, P. An Exploratory Study to Determine Archetypes in the Trinidad and Tobago Fashion Industry Environment. *West Indian J. Eng.* **2014**, *37*, 70–76.

203. Karell, E.; Niinimaki, K. Addressing the Dialogue between Design. Sorting and Recycling in a Circular Economy. *Des. J.* **2019**, *22*, 997–1013. [CrossRef]

204. Egels-Zanden, N.; Hyllman, P. Exploring the effects of union-NGO relationships on corporate responsibility: The case of the Swedish clean clothes campaign. *J. Bus. Ethics* **2006**, *64*, 303–316. [CrossRef]

205. Hong, H.; Kang, J.H. The impact of moral philosophy and moral intensity on purchase behavior toward sustainable textile and apparel products. *Fashion Text.* **2019**, *6*, 16. [CrossRef]

206. Albloushy, H.; Connell, K.Y.H. Purchasing environmentally sustainable apparel: The attitudes and intentions of female Kuwaiti consumers. *Int. J. Consum. Stud.* **2019**, *43*, 390–401. [CrossRef]

207. Lee, S.H.N.; Ha-Brookshire, J.; Chow, P.S. The moral responsibility of corporate sustainability as perceived by fashion retail employees: A USA-China cross-cultural comparison study. *Bus. Strategy Environ.* **2018**, *27*, 1462–1475. [CrossRef]

208. Mena, S.; Suddaby, R. Theorization as institutional work: The dynamics of roles and practices. *Hum. Relat.* **2016**, *69*, 1669–1708. [CrossRef]

209. Fornasiero, R.; Brondi, C.; Collatina, D. Proposing an integrated LCA-SCM model to evaluate the sustainability of customization strategies. *Int. J. Comput. Integr. Manuf.* **2017**, *30*, 768–781. [CrossRef]

210. Priyankara, H.P.R.; Luo, F.; Saeed, A.; Nubuor, S.A.; Jayasuriya, M.P.F. How Does Leader's Support for Environment Promote Organizational Citizenship Behaviour for Environment? A Multi-Theory Perspective. *Sustainability* **2018**, *10*, 271. [CrossRef]

211. Wijethilake, C.; Munir, R.; Appuhami, R. Strategic responses to institutional pressures for sustainability The role of management control systems. *Account. Audit. Account. J.* **2017**, *30*, 1677–1710. [CrossRef]

212. Leoni, G. Social responsibility in practice: An Italian case from the early 20th century. *J. Manag. Hist.* **2017**, *23*, 133–151. [CrossRef]

213. Chen, C.X.; Perry, P.; Yang, Y.X.; Yang, C. Decent Work in the Chinese Apparel Industry: Comparative Analysis of Blue-Collar and White-Collar Garment Workers. *Sustainability* **2017**, *9*, 1344. [CrossRef]

214. Bair, J.; Palpacuer, F. From Varieties of Capitalism to Varieties of Activism: The Anti sweatshop Movement in Comparative Perspective. *Soc. Probl.* **2012**, *59*, 522–543. [CrossRef]

215. Schmitt, J.; Renken, U. How to Earn Money by Doing Good!: Shared Value in the Apparel Industry. *J. Corp. Citizsh.* **2012**, 79–103. [CrossRef]

216. Burzynska, D.; Jablonska, M.; Dziuba, R. Opportunities and Conditions for the Development of Green Entrepreneurship in the Polish Textile Sector. *Fibres Text. East. Eur.* **2018**, *26*, 13–19. [CrossRef]

Employee's Corporate Social Responsibility Perception and Sustained Innovative Behavior: Based on the Psychological Identity of Employees

Yi-Bin Li [1], Gui-Qing Zhang [1], Tung-Ju Wu [2] and Chi-Lu Peng [3,*]

[1] School of Business Administration, Huaqiao University, Quanzhou 362021, China;
   liyibin@hqu.edu.cn (Y.-B.L.); 17014120001@stu.hqu.edu.cn (G.-Q.Z.)

[2] School of Management, Harbin Institute of Technology, Harbin 150001, China; tjwu@hit.edu.cn

[3] Business Intelligence School, National Kaohsiung University of Science and Technology, Kaohsiung 824303, Taiwan

* Correspondence: chilupeng@nkust.edu.tw

Abstract: Corporate social responsibility refers to the voluntary promises made by an enterprise to achieve sustainable development. When enterprises conduct prosocial activities, they must consider the feelings of their employees including employees' sense of identification and well-being. However, most existing corporate social responsibility studies have focused on the financial performance of enterprises; the effects of corporate social responsibility on employees have seldom been examined. Accordingly, this study conducted an empirical study examining the effects of employee perception of enterprise corporate social responsibility, employee well-being, and organizational identification on employee innovative behavior. A total of 431 valid questionnaires were retrieved. A structural equation modeling analysis revealed that a positive relationship exists between employee perception of enterprise execution of corporate social responsibility and employee innovative behavior. Furthermore, both employee well-being and organizational identification play mediating roles between the two variables. When conducting social responsibility activities, enterprises are suggested to inform their employees or even encourage their participation in their efforts to fulfill their social responsibility. Through interaction between internal and external stakeholders, substantial innovative behavior, beneficial for the subsequent development of enterprises, can be stimulated.

Keywords: corporate social responsibility perception; employee well-being; organizational identification; innovative behavior

1. Introduction

With the diversification and enrichment of communication technologies, network information, and knowledge dissemination media, available information has been made more transparent and the operation and management of many enterprises less mysterious. Information related to enterprise operations and management is, thus, open to public scrutiny [1,2]. When an unexpected event occurs, does an enterprise stand with society against the negative influences of the event? The reaction of enterprises in these critical moments influence public impressions of them. Scandals and philanthropic acts of corporations have an even more profound influence on their image and consumer trust [2,3]. Therefore, the emphasis of the public on the ethics and morals of enterprises has been sharpened, and the public is beginning to contemplate the roles played by enterprises. Enterprises depend on consumers to generate profits; however, the negative consequences of enterprise actions are frequently borne equally by these consumers, the environment, and the public [2–4]. Is such an outcome fair and reasonable? Current events concern the survival of many industries, and they are critical to the sustainable development of enterprises. Therefore, corporate social responsibility (CSR) is no longer merely a matter that society and the public follow with interest; it has become a manifestation of enterprises' own positioning, as well as their responsibilities toward every level of society [1,2,4,5]. Apart from profit generation, what other factors constitute critical factors in ensuring the sustainable development of enterprises? This is the question to be answered by enterprises in the 21st century. When proposing the future trends of enterprises, Drucker [6] mentioned that "the current century is an age of social charity" and "the new management fad should emphasize the incorporation of integrity and trust into practice." This indicates that the execution of social responsibility by enterprises has gradually become a crucial trend and critical factor in the development of enterprises.

CSR refers to voluntary promises made by an enterprise guided by sustainable development. Thus, other than their own financial and operational status, enterprises also need to consider the influence they have on society and the natural environment. Enterprises must also plan social activities that improve the quality of life of employees and their families, the local community, and society at large [7]. With the growing attention of industries and academia on CSR, scholars have urged the transformation of "CSR concepts that emphasize the fulfilling of duties and responsibilities" into "CSR strategic thinking that emphasizes proactiveness." Additionally, to gain an in-depth understanding of the influence of CSR on enterprises, the scope of examination should not be limited to financial indicators such as return on investment. The inclusion of nonfinancial indicators such as market share, brand positioning, corporate image, employee job satisfaction, and customer loyalty in the examination is necessary to gain an in-depth understanding of the influence of CSR on enterprises [8–10]. Enterprises should therefore take the initiative to plan and implement social responsibility measures targeting different stakeholders, such as employees.

Employees are the most important asset in a company [11–14]. With the entrenchment of economic globalization and the rapid development of science technologies, enterprises confront a highly competitive commercial environment. Many enterprises have realized that they must adjust and innovate constantly to cope with these changes, and organizational learning is a key means for employees to realize innovative behavior [11–14]. Enterprises gain a long-lasting competitive edge over their competitors only through rapid development and commercialization of new products, and this is possible only with persistent innovative behavior [14]. Additionally, enterprises are a type of organization that can be considered indispensable to the operation of society. Therefore, when carrying out economic activities, enterprises should also consider the influence of these activities on society and shoulder the corresponding social responsibility; accordingly, this is not only the demand of society on enterprises, but also a means for enterprises to lead by example. When employees are proud of the enterprise that they work for, they are more willing to contribute to the enterprise. Employees' autonomous innovative behavior can be increased by enhancing their sense of identification with and commitment toward the enterprise [13,15–17]. In recent years, the fulfillment of social responsibility by enterprises has been confirmed to enhance employees' sense of identification with the enterprise they work for [10,18,19]. However, whether the fulfillment of social responsibility by enterprises can lead to an increase in employee innovative behavior has yet to be confirmed. Therefore, the first motivation of the current study is to examine the relationship between CSR and employee innovative behavior.

Retaining talent and enhancing the senses of cohesiveness and identification with an enterprise have been long-standing problems in the realm of enterprise development. Retaining talent means the competitiveness of the enterprise is enhanced, leading in turn to the generation of better enterprise performance. Accordingly, many enterprises have started to pay attention to employee emotions and sense of well-being [20,21]. Additionally, most modern enterprises have adopted the goal of creating a happy enterprise. Creating a win–win situation by combining the cultivation of well-being with social responsibility fulfillment is a component that modern enterprises are working on [22]. For example, enterprises can invest resources into social charity activities or staff care and reexamine the core values of the enterprises. Subsequently, enterprises can generate employee perception of well-being and ultimately enhance job satisfaction [23]. Subtle measures, such as encouraging employees to participate in enterprise social responsibility activities and paying attention to employees' work-related feelings, can also enhance employees' sense of cohesiveness and sense of identification with the enterprise [24]. Some enterprises have even asserted they should treat employees in the same manner they treat customers; the same level of importance should be attached to both because both play a critical role in the performance of the enterprises [21,24]. Most studies have focused on the influence of employee well-being and sense of identification on enterprise performance. However, they have not specified which aspect of enterprise performance the two variables affect. This study believes that employee willingness to contribute to the enterprise or even engage in innovative behavior is likely to increase with their sense of well-being and organizational identification. Furthermore, the critical factor in the generation of innovative behavior in employees is their sense of well-being. Therefore, the second motivation of the study is to examine how enterprises can make employees feel the significance of fulfilling social responsibility, which in turn generates a sense of well-being among employees and ultimately increases their innovative behavior.

2. Literature Review

2.1. CSR and Employee Innovative Behavior

When defined broadly, CSR refers to enterprises' voluntary use of their resources to contribute to society and their shouldering of responsibilities toward shareholders and all relevant stakeholders; this is done through the adoption of legal and economic responsibilities as the underlying basis, and laws, ethics, and morals as the underlying standards [8,10]. Bettencourt [25] argued that enterprises should attempt to improve the quality of life of employees and their family members, the local community, and the public through sustainable economic development and make this a promise from the enterprises to these parties in enterprise operation. With the maximizing of benefits and the minimizing of harm as the goal, enterprises should carefully evaluate the impact of their activities and operations on the environment, society, and the economy. Wu and Chen [26] maintained that CSR contains voluntary activities related to cause marketing, charity, and employees, as well as other innovative activities. Cause marketing has the effect of strengthening enterprise brands, which would in turn lead to the attraction of more potential customers or the strengthening of employees' sense of honor; enterprises could generate profits from this, even though cause marking is regarded as a tool for relationship management [2,4,5]. CSR concepts have already been extended such that social responsibility is substantially incorporated into enterprise decision-making and project execution; this allows cooperation between enterprises and society, which in turns leads to mutually beneficial modes of collaboration [2–4].

Brunk [27] simplified the factors of CSR and divided them into five categories, namely customer responsibility, employee responsibility, environmental responsibility, economic responsibility, and community responsibility. Wu et al. [10] confirmed that fulfilling social responsibility can help enhance consumers' positive perception of enterprises, which would in turn lead to increased purchase intention among the consumers. Furthermore, most enterprises believe that the execution of social responsibility is an effort recognized by the public, and enterprises could use the shouldering of noneconomic factors of social responsibility to create a competitive edge for themselves; this includes creating a business reputation for themselves or enhancing proactive employee attitude and behavior [28]. If enterprises can shoulder their social responsibility, they might differentiate themselves from their competitors as well as establish a better image and reputation [9]. Zadek [29] argued that the CSR execution process is an organizational learning process. When an organization is fulfilling its social responsibility, it must coordinate relationships between different stakeholders. This would cause the organization to form a more open organizational culture, which would facilitate communication and interaction inside and outside the organization. Yadlapalli, Rahman, and Rogers [30] examined the relationship between suppliers' autonomous fulfilling of social responsibility and organizational learning from the perspective of a global supply chain and asserted that when organizations fulfill their

CSR, they possess people-oriented cultures, which exert a positive influence on organizational learning. Studies have also revealed that a close relationship exists between an enterprise's innovation capacity and its internal knowledge stock. Thus, without the support of relevant knowledge, enterprises face serious limitations in innovative behavior [4,28].

Additionally, to ensure development in the long run, enterprises set clear visions and strategic goals, and they may be more inclined to fulfill their social responsibility; this behavior would also facilitate knowledge sharing inside the enterprises [4,31]. The influence of CSR on enterprises is reflected in company culture, techniques, organizational structure, and member behavior; all these factors affect enterprises' operational performance and innovative behavior [32,33]. Majumdar and Marcus [34] stated that the autonomous fulfillment of CSR has a significant influence on the coordination and management style of organizations. Therefore, autonomous fulfillment of CSR can help enterprise managers develop better management skills. The management capacity of managers can be internalized through the enterprise's process of fulfilling social responsibility, which would lead to effective use of organizational resources and transformation of these resources into actual behavior that could enhance the operational performance of the enterprise [33]. Richter et al. [28] asserted that long-term investment behavior of enterprises guided by social responsibility could spark enterprises' motivation to engage in product innovation, development, and differentiation as well as entice employees to enact innovative behavior. In stakeholder theory, the execution of social responsibility can lead to the enhancement of enterprise reputation and improvement in relationships between the enterprise and various stakeholders, such as suppliers, customers, employees, or even government agencies. This would benefit the enterprise by increasing its internal and external social capital, facilitating the gathering of various operational resources (e.g., technical, capital, and talent) or even leading to the realization or enhancement of employee innovative behavior. Therefore, this study proposes H1 as follows: A significant and positive relationship exists between CSR and employee innovative behavior.

2.2. Mediating Roles of Employee Well-Being and Organizational Identification

Wu et al. [13] argued that well-being is a positive and proactive psychological state, and they regarded a sense of well-being as the intensity of life satisfaction, positive emotions, and negative emotions. Pignata et al. [24] agreed and proposed that work influences perception of life and well-being, and that one's sense of well-being is determined by one's level of satisfaction with work, life, and health. Existing research and measurements of sense of well-being have mostly used psychological feelings as their basis and developed concepts related to sense of well-being using the aspects of emotions and cognition. Lu [35] proposed one source of sense of well-being as being able to blend into groups in which an individual is accepted; through such blending and social activities, an individual can experience positive feelings such as identification, happiness, satisfaction, and sense of belonging. These feelings in turn lead to the generation of a sense of well-being. Sense of well-being is a sense of satisfaction that an individual can obtain under the condition of spiritual abundance, and morale is a critical factor [36]. This is because morale possesses the energy to make people engage in positive thinking, and positive thinking can transform negative emotions into positive ones, which can generate a sense of well-being through the enhancement of spiritual and life satisfaction. Therefore, positive thinking and kindly morale thinking are core sources of well-being.

Organizational identity refers to the feeling of having common goals or experiences with other members of an organization, being united, and being part of the organization. People with organizational identity also feel that members of the organization support each other and are loyal to one another. Organizational identity also refers to strong beliefs held by employees of an organization. Employees holding these beliefs accept the goals and values of the organization, are willing to contribute their efforts to the organization, and desire to become or remain part of the organization. From the perspective of organization management, Eisenberger et al. [17] asserted that organizational identity constitutes a type of benefit for enterprises because the sense of organizational identity would ensure that employees base their decision-making process on the interests of the organization. Even without the supervision of managers, employees who identify with the organization form a new set of self-values similar to those of the organization, based on their impressions and perceived values of the organization. Mael and Ashforth [37] defined organizational identity as follows: When organizational members regard themselves as part of an organization, they identify with the mission, values, and goals of the organization and consider the interests of the organization in their management decision-making. Briefly, organizational identification refers to individuals' generation of emotional connection to the organization that they belong to. The individual sees herself as part of the organization and is willing to identify with its culture, values, and goals. The individual would appreciate the fact that they are a member of the organization and contribute loyally to the organization [38]. Organizational identity reflects employee understanding of self-concepts, their role positioning within the organization, and the organization as a whole. Additionally, in organizational identity formation, employees seek to define their self-identity in the organization through self-selected standards. Therefore, employee identity is refracted through the organization. Therefore, organizational identity is not only the type of perception that employees have of the organization they work in; it is also, for employees, a type of emotional bonding [38,39]. Employee work intention is crucial to the effectiveness of an organization, and employee willingness to serve the organization can be enhanced by improving employee identification with the organization; work intention can be transformed into effective actual behavior when employees are willing to work with all their hearts and souls for the sake of the organization.

Dirks and Ferrin [20] argued that employee perception of the modus operandi of an enterprise influences the employees' perception of the enterprise's trustworthiness. Kim et al. [21] posited that enterprises' execution of social responsibility activities can enhance their external reputation, and employee perception of an enterprise's external reputation can enhance their sense of identification with it. When employees have actually participated in or formed connections with the CSR activities of their company, their perception of the fulfillment of CSR by the company are enhanced. These results indicate that the more an enterprise fulfills its social responsibility, the more likely an employee is to possess a favorable impression of the CSR activities of the enterprise. Employees would believe that the enterprise has a moral sense and a conscience, and they would therefore generate positive expectations toward the enterprise. Not only that, the feeling of sharing in the enterprise's prestige also enhances employees' loyalty [40] and commitment [38,39]. Additionally, the results of Loon, Otaye-Ebede, and Stewart [41] revealed that both organizational identification and employee well-being are positively correlated to employee performance. These results indirectly indicate that enterprise fulfillment of social responsibility would lead to the establishment of an explicit positive image, and that such effort would also exert a positive influence on employee sense of well-being and identification. Therefore, this study believes that enterprise fulfillment of social responsibility not only enhances employees' sense of identification with the enterprise, but also that such efforts could lead to the increase of positive emotions in employees and, in turn, enhance employees' sense of well-being and further promote their sense of identification with the enterprise. If employees then engage in their work with a positive and proactive mentality, the productivity, creativity, and commitment aspects of their performance are enhanced. Therefore, this study posits H2: Employee well-being plays a mediating role between CSR and employee innovative behavior; and H3: Organizational identification mediates the effect of CSR on employee innovative behavior.

3. Materials and Methods

3.1. Research Participants

To gain an understanding of employees' feelings regarding the fulfillment of CSR by the enterprises that they work in, the researchers designed a questionnaire based on the theories described. The participants of the study consisted of employees of the top 500 enterprises in Taiwan. Taiwan's top 500 enterprises are selected as research bases is that these enterprises have relatively complete

CSR systems, and their firm size and reputation are relatively strong. Therefore, it is meaningful to choose employees in these enterprises as research target. Moreover, we contacted human resources managers of top 500 enterprises to inquire as to whether they were willing to take part in our study, and 49 enterprises agreed. The researchers sampled in the electronics, financial, food and beverage, and general services industries. We distributed 10 questionnaires to each enterprise that was willing to participate in this research, and randomly conducted surveys of their employees. The questionnaire was divided into two parts. The first included content related to the measurement of four study variables, namely CSR, work well-being, organizational identification, and employee innovative behavior. The second part contained items examining the demographic information of the respondents, including their gender, age, educational attainment, job tenure, and type of industry they worked in. The researchers distributed a total of 490 questionnaires, and 431 valid questionnaires were retrieved. The average age of the study sample was 33 years, and majority of the respondents were women ($n = 296$; 68.7%). With regard to educational attainment, most had an academic qualification of bachelor's degree or beyond ($n = 392$; 91%). The average job tenure of the participants was 8.4 years, and majority worked in the general services industry ($n = 225$; 52.2%).

3.2. Measurement

Corporate social responsibility: For CSR, the researchers referred to the definition proposed by Bettencourt [25]. Bettencourt argued that enterprises should attempt to improve the quality of life of employees and their family members, the local community, and the public through sustainable economic development and make this a promise of the enterprise to these parties through enterprise operations. For this construct, the researchers adopted the Corporate Ethics Scale proposed by Brunk [27] as the measurement tool, with 21 items in five dimensions, namely customer responsibilities, employee responsibilities, environmental responsibilities, economic responsibilities, and community responsibilities. Using the second-order single-factor model for the CFA (Confirmatory Factor Analysis, CFA), the overall fit indices ($\chi2 = 244.39$, CFI (Comparative Fit Index) = 0.96, RMSEA (Root Mean Square Error of Approximation) = 0.05, NFI (Normed Fit Index) = 0.96, AGFI (Adjusted Goodness of Fit Index) = 0.91, and GFI (Goodness of Fit Index) = 0.95 appeared better than when the first-order five-factor model was used ($\chi2 = 1075.42$, CFI = 0.77, RMSEA = 0.09, NFI = 0.81, AGFI = 0.72, and GFI = 0.82). This section of the questionnaire had a Cronbach's α value of 0.93.

Employee well-being: For employee well-being, the researchers adopted the definition put forth by Wu et al. [13,14], who stated that well-being comprises satisfaction in one's work, life, and health; the higher an individual's satisfaction in these areas, the more intense the individual's sense of well-being. For this section of the questionnaire, the researchers used the Chinese Happiness Inventory developed by Lu [42]. This section of the questionnaire contained 10 items and had a Cronbach's α value of 0.91.

Organizational identification: Mael and Ashforth [37] suggested that organizational identification refers to an individual's generation of emotional connection to the organization that they belong to; the extent to which an individual sees herself as part of the organization and is willing to identify with the culture, values, and goals of the organization. If an individual appreciates that they are a member of the organization, they will contribute loyally to it. For this section of the questionnaire, the researchers used the Organization Identification Scale that Van Knippenberg and Sleebos [38] modified based on the original scale proposed by Mael and Ashforth [37]. This section contained six items and had a Cronbach's α value of 0.88.

Employee innovative behavior: Scott and Bruce [43] argued that employee innovative behavior refers to the worker behavior in which initiative is taken to provide new ideas, products, or processes to the enterprise to improve or enhance its performance [33]. For this section of the questionnaire, the researchers used the Organization Identification Scale proposed by Scott and Bruce [43]. The section contained six items and had a Cronbach's α value of 0.91. All the items were measured using a 7-point Likert scale. The measure details of this study are shown in Table 1.

Table 1. The instrumentals of this study.

Variable	Items	References
Corporate social responsibility	1. Can provide products and services that meet consumer needs. 2. Treat customers with ethics and integrity. 3. Think from the perspective of consumers. 4. Staff work efficiency is high. 5. Good service attitude. 6. I feel that employees love the company. 7. I feel the staff is full of energy. 8. I feel good working environment. 9. Reduce sales of over-packaged products. 10. Environmental protection production process. 11. Responsible for environmental protection. 12. Have environmental protection measures such as resource recycling. 13. Can promote industry development. 14. The marketing method is very attractive. 15. Often there is the development of innovative products. 16. Can enhance our country's economic activity. 17. Invest in public welfare activities. 18. Long-term donation of materials to impoverished areas. 19. Regular social education activities will be held to promote healthy eating concepts. 20. Sponsor activities related to arts and culture.	Brunk [27]
Employee well-being	1. I love my life. 2. I think life is very meaningful and purposeful. 3. My work always brings me a sense of success. 4. Everything that happened in life in the past was very pleasant. 5. I'm so happy. 6. I am satisfied with everything in life. 7. I feel I have infinite vitality. 8. The future is full of hope for me. 9. I am always happy and excited. 10. I can always understand the meaning of life.	Wu et al. [13,14] Lu [42]
Organizational commitment	1. When someone criticizes your company, it feels like a personal insult. 2. I am very interested in what others think about your company. 3. When I talk about this company, I usually say 'we' rather than 'they'. 4. This company's successes are my successes. 5. When someone praises this company, it feels like a personal compliment. 6. If a story in the media criticized the company, I would feel embarrassed.	Mael and Ashforth [37] Van Knippenberg and Sleebos [38]
Employee innovative behavior	1. Searches for new technologies, processes, techniques, and/or product ideas. 2. Generates creative ideas. 3. Promotes and champions ideas to others. 4. Investigates and secures funds needed to implement new ideas. 5. Develops adequate plans and schedules for the implementation of new ideas. 6. Is innovative.	Scott and Bruce [43]

4. Results

Common method variance is another important factor influencing the research model. The variance is tested using Harman's Single-Factor Test. An exploratory factor analysis through a principal components analysis has shown that the four factors selected explain 77.69% of the total variance; factor 1 explains 38.42% of the total variance, which is less than half of it. This proves that common method variance in this paper is well-controlled.

The Pearson's correlation coefficients for the study variables are presented in Table 2. All variables were significantly and positively correlated. Significant and positive relationships between CSR and all other variables were identified, and the directions of the relationships were consistent with the hypothesized directions. Additionally, all variables were significantly and positively correlated to employee innovative behavior; this result is consistent with results reported in relevant literature. To examine the mediating effects of other variables on employee well-being and organizational identification, the researchers employed the path analysis method of structural equation modeling (SEM).

Table 2. Results of correlation analyses.

	M	SD.	1	2	3	4
CSR	6.53	0.61	1			
Employee well-being	5.98	0.73	0.32 **	1		
Organizational identification	6.27	0.57	0.33 **	0.37 **	0.1	
Employee innovative behavior	6.34	0.48	0.28 **	0.39 **	0.37 **	0.1

$n = 431$; ** $p < 0.01$; CSR: Corporate social responsibility.

The final structure equation modeling (SEM) analysis revealed the following results: $\chi 2/DF = 1.58$, RMSEA = 0.05 (i.e., <0.08), GFI = 0.99, AGFI = 0.97, NFI = 0.97, and CFI = 0.98; all these values are larger than 0.95. PGFI = 0.6245, which is larger than 0.5. These values indicated that this model had good fit indices, which indicated that a good fit existed between the corrected model and the study sample. Furthermore, the construct reliability (CR) results yielded values greater than 0.7, showing that the underlying variables all have good internal consistency. The values of the average variance extracted (AVE) results are all greater than 0.5, which demonstrate that the average ability of the measurement indicators to explain the underlying variables is good. Therefore, it can be seen that the underlying variables have good construct reliability and validity. The path coefficients of the model reasonably and effectively reflect cause-and-effect relationships between the latent variables, and thus they can be used in examining the proposed hypotheses. Refer to Figure 1 for the operation results.

Figure 1. Path analysis. **$p < 0.01$; ***$p < 0.001$.

As Figure 1 reveals, the standardized path coefficient between employee CSR perception and employee innovative behavior is 0.38, and the relationship is significant at the $p < 0.01$ level; employee CSR perception exerts a significant and positive influence on employee innovative behavior. Therefore, H1 is assumed to be empirically supported. Furthermore, the standardized path coefficient between employee well-being and employee innovative behavior is 0.26; the relationship is significant at the $p < 0.01$ level. This result indicates that employee well-being exerts a significant and positive influence on employee innovative behavior. The standardized path coefficient between employee organizational identification and employee innovative behavior is 0.31, and the relationship is significant at the $p < 0.01$ level. This indicates that employee well-being exerts a significant and positive influence on the employee innovative behavior. The results also indicate that employee organizational identification exerts a significant and positive influence on employee innovative behavior.

Regarding the verification of H2 and H3, the researchers employed SEM to analyze the mediating effects of employee well-being and organizational identification. As described, CSR perception exerts a significant and positive influence on employee innovative behavior (the standardized path coefficient is 0.38 ***), and employee well-being also exerts a significant influence on employee innovative behavior (the standardized path coefficient is 0.26 **); this indicates that employee well-being exerts a significant partial mediating effect on the relationship between CSR perception and employee innovative behavior (the mediating effect is 0.29 **). Therefore, H2 is assumed to be empirically supported. Additionally, organizational identification also exerts a significant influence on employee innovative behavior (the standardized path coefficient is 0.31 **); this indicates that the employee's sense of identification with the organization exerts a significant partial mediating effect on the relationship between CSR perception and employee innovative behavior (the mediating effect is 0.25 **). Therefore, H3 is assumed to be empirically supported.

5. Discussion

This study examined whether employee perception of CSR affects their innovative behavior from the perspective of organizational learning and sharing. The roles of employee well-being and organizational identification as mediating variables were also examined. Empirical analysis of the data collected through questionnaires revealed that engagement in social responsibility by enterprises positively influence employee innovative behavior. Enterprises' executing social responsibility is beneficial for promoting employee creativity through the process of internal interaction, and it could also help enterprises facilitate their technical research and development and, ultimately, assist them in realizing their goals of fostering innovative behavior. Employee participation in CSR activities increases the employees' job satisfaction and improves their proactiveness in participating in the operation and management activities of enterprises. Ultimately, employee participation in CSR activities stimulates their ability to innovate and causes them to transform internal knowledge and apply this knowledge to other domains for the popularization, modification, and improvement of products and services. With regard to external stakeholders such as suppliers, consumers, and even government agencies, the fulfilling of social responsibility by the enterprise is beneficial for the establishment of external connections, which makes it easier for employees to obtain product- or service-related creative ideas from outside the enterprise, helping enhance the research and development of products and technologies.

Numerous studies have confirmed that when employees perceive that the enterprise they work in has fulfilled necessary CSR, they have a higher level of identification with and trust toward the enterprise. This leads to the generation of positive expectations and the enhancement of commitment to the enterprise. Our results indirectly indicate that the benefit of enterprise fulfillment of social responsibility is not limited to the establishment of explicit positive images—it also exerts a positive influence on employees' sense of well-being. If an enterprise can realize the integration of CSR and daily management, this integration may have a positive effect on job satisfaction. The results of the current study also indicate that enterprises' execution of social responsibility indirectly increase employee identification with the organization and also their sense of well-being. When enterprises engage in socially responsible activities, with conscience and responsibility fulfillment as the original intentions, they encourage their employees to participate in these efforts. As for employees, they discover the positive aspects of CSR activities in the process of participation; this leads to the generation of positive emotions and affection for enterprises and ultimately enhancement of employees' work well-being and identification with the organization. Under these ideal conditions, the influence of employee perception of enterprise execution of CSR on employee well-being and organizational identification are significant. Finally, the results suggest that when employees are able to perceive the original intention and motive of the enterprises conducting social responsibility activities, it is easier for them to identify with the organization as well as generate a sense of occupational well-being.

5.1. Theoretical Implications

There is a positive relationship between CSR and employees' good working behavior, especially in innovative behavior. It is recognized by consumers because the company abides by social responsibility, or employees increase their recognition of the company due to CSR, thus increasing employee performance and reducing management cost. The likelihood of employees contributing to the enterprise increases with their sense of work well-being and sense of identification with the enterprise they work in. These contributions are reflected not only in the financial performance of the enterprise, but also in their altered behavior or in the overall organizational climate. Thus, another finding of the study is that in fulfilling their social responsibility, enterprises can also indirectly enhance the sense of well-being and organizational identification of their employees, which in turns facilitates the generation of employee innovative behavior. This also indicates that both internal factors (associated with employees themselves) and external factors play an active role in facilitating the formation of innovative behavior in employees. The study has also confirmed that sense of work well-being and organizational identification are the critical intermediary mechanism in the transformation of employee innovative behavior. Thus, when an enterprise engages in practical activities not related to financial performance but related instead to society's interests, this would lead employees to believe that the enterprise is good. This would then cause them to generate a sense of well-being and pride associated with working with the enterprise. This would subsequently lead to an enhanced sense of identification with the enterprise and ultimately lead to the generation of employee innovative behavior that benefit the enterprise.

When examining the influence of CSR perception of eastern enterprise employees on sustained innovation performance, the researchers adopted an affective events theory as the study framework in an attempt to clarify the mediating effects of employee well-being and organizational identification. The researchers adopted the integrated theoretical perspective (as suggested by relevant literature [44]) in analyzing the relationship between employee CSR perception and innovative behavior; this perspective demonstrated unique theoretical value in clarifying the relationship between the two variables. Additionally, the current research also addressed the gap in theoretical understanding of the relationship between employee CSR perception and innovative performance in the eastern cultural context, a problem identified by one report [45]. In short, the findings of the current study provide a new theoretical basis for in-depth understanding of the relationship of CSR perception to innovation performance among enterprise workers in an eastern social context.

The study has further clarified the critical intermediary mechanism involved in the transformation of Taiwanese enterprise workers' sense of work well-being and organizational identification into innovative performance. Employees can possess the positive mentality that they have competency and value in contributing to the enterprise, and this can cause employees to generate innovative behavior beneficial for their organizations. This conclusion provides not only further theoretical support regarding the role played by self-concept in the formation process of individual innovative performance (in response to a research suggestion) [46], but also enriches and optimizes theoretical understanding of the origin and influence of employee organizational identification. At the same time, based on the perspective of group-based self-representation in indigenous psychology, the researchers also explained the predictive validity of inferences associated with Chinese transformations of the sense of well-being into behavior that benefits the group they are a member of [42]. The expansion from social psychology to organizational behavior injects new elements to the construction of employee innovation management theories that are suitable for the local context.

5.2. Practical Implications

The fulfilling of CSR has become a trend; the governments of many countries have made clear requests that enterprises disclose CSR-related information in their annual reports. Accordingly, an increasing number of enterprises are beginning to brief relevant stakeholders (e.g., employees, consumers, and even suppliers) on their policies, courses of action, and implementation results in three major dimensions, namely "economic," "environment", and "society", through the publication of CSR reports. The CSR perception, employee well-being, organizational identification, and employee innovative behavior evaluation indicators applied by this study could serve as tools for enterprises gauging the psychological status and behavior of their employees when conducting CSR activities. In fact, in terms of enterprise operations, CSR activities should not be regarded merely as "value-adding" projects for improving the financial performance of enterprises. When implementing CSR activities, enterprises should also pay attention to the needs of stakeholders and engage in communication and feedback with them. Among different stakeholders, one of the most essential is employees. This is because employee perception of their job and their level of identification with the enterprise are directly reflected in their work performance, which in turn influences the enterprise's operational performance or overall work climate. Therefore, enterprises should monitor employees' status to grasp and utilize the knowledge and abilities of employees effectively. Moreover, enterprises can enhance employee understanding of their CSR strategies and contributions through a variety of methods, such as the publication of CSR reports, the incorporation of relevant information into education and training materials for new employees, the publication of relevant information on the official website of the enterprise, and raising awareness through regular publication of electronic bulletins. In addition, employees' participation in the CSR implementation of the company will also increase their sense of identity with the organization. Because actually participating in corporate activities will deepen their understanding of the company, and then allow them to feel the pride of being a part of the company. Therefore, it is recommended that the human resources department of the enterprise use employee participation in corporate activities as a strategy to increase the employee's sense of identity and affective commitment.

Furthermore, enterprises should deepen employees' understanding of the connotations and effects of work well-being concepts (e.g., emotional well-being, perceived well-being, occupational well-being, and social well-being), regularly collect and evaluate information related to employees' sense of work well-being, and adopt the following measures to facilitate improvement of sense of work well-being among employees: First, to enhance employees' sense of emotional well-being, enterprises should attempt to create a warm and delightful work environment because this would facilitate the formation and maintenance of an active and optimistic attitude among employees. Enterprises should also provide employees with counseling options to help alleviate negative emotions that they experience at work; this helps reduce the influence of these negative emotions on employees' sense of well-being. Second, to cultivate the sense of perceived well-being in employees, enterprises can tailor-make job-relevant cognitive skill and concentration training sessions for employees. This would lead to improved employee cognitive performance at work. Third, to enhance the sense of occupational well-being in employees, enterprises should tailor-make individualized career life plans for employees to satisfy their career development needs. Additionally, to enhance employees' sense of job competence, enterprises could provide employees with education and training opportunities that strengthen their occupational competency. Enterprises must also provide positive feedback regarding the job performance of employees to facilitate the formation of the sense of occupational recognition. Fourth, to improve the sense of social well-being among employees, enterprises should create a united, harmonious, and sincere organizational climate in which enterprise members help each other out. Such a climate helps employees form friendly and close-knitted partnerships with the organization and members of the organization. If these four categories of measures can be implemented simultaneously, they would exert a significant combined effect on improving employees' sense of well-being, and this would set the foundation for increased innovative performance of employees.

5.3. Limitations

Employee experience of participating in CSR activities conducted by their companies is supposed to be a key variable in the current study. Based on common sense, employees who have the experience of participating in CSR activities should have a significantly higher level of CSR perception compared with those who do not possess such experience. Restated, when employees have actually participated in or formed connections with the CSR activities of companies, their perception of the fulfilling of CSR by their company would be enhanced, and this would in turn influence the psychological condition of employees. Therefore, the researchers propose that employee experience of participating in CSR activities be incorporated into future studies as one variable to be examined. Additionally, the stakeholders of enterprises include several main categories, including society, consumers, and employees. Therefore, enterprises should focus not only on their profit-generating capability (in financial aspects), but also on whether they have the ability to cope with external and internal changes, sustain errors and risks, and grow continuously in the future. Only through the implementation of CSR strategies and planning are enterprises able to generate competitiveness and move toward becoming sustainable organizations. Accordingly, future researchers can also adopt a diverse approach to the measurement of CSR; more valuable and constructive findings can perhaps be obtained if CSR issues were examined from the perspective of governments, consumers, and employees.

6. Conclusions

The conclusions of the study possess a certain degree of significance in advancing understanding of employee perception of social responsibility fulfillment by enterprises and the development of employee innovative behavior. (1) CSR can facilitate organizational learning. Therefore, enterprises should not regard the fulfilling of social responsibility as an undue burden. On the contrary, enterprises should incorporate social responsibility as a component of enterprise development strategy and make it an essential means for them to enhance organizational cohesiveness and enterprise competitiveness. (2) Employee well-being and organizational identification both play a mediating role between CSR and employee innovative behavior. This explains the extent to which employee well-being and organizational identification affect the relationship between social responsibility and employee innovative behavior. Therefore, when fulfilling their social responsibilities, enterprises should also consider the psychological feelings of their employees. Enterprises can convey their visions to employees and influence their sense of contributing to society through sharing, to enhance employees' sense of participation in enterprise CSR operations; these efforts would enhance the influence of CSR on employee innovative behavior. For managers who want to fulfill CSR and create a happy enterprise, this inside-out CSR implementation model is ideal. Internally, the implementation model can enhance employee well-being, cohesiveness, and creativity. Externally, this inside-out CSR implementation model can enhance the overall value of the enterprise, including through improving the corporate image and brand value and even bringing substantial profit for the enterprise through cause marketing.

Author Contributions: Conceptualization, Y.-B.L. and T.-J.W.; data curation, T.-J.W. and C.-L.P.; formal analysis, G.-Q.Z. and C.-L.P.; funding acquisition, Y.-B.L. and T.-J.W.; investigation, G.-Q.Z.; methodology, C.-L.P.; project administration, Y.-B.L.; software, G.-Q.Z. and C.-L.P.; supervision, Y.-B.L.; visualization, T.-J.W.; writing—original draft, Y.-B.L., G.-Q.Z., and C.-L.P.; writing—review & editing, T.-J.W. and C.-L.P. All authors have read and agreed to the published version of the manuscript.

Acknowledgments: The author is grateful to the valuable comments made by the reviewers. This research was supported by the China Postdoctoral Science Foundation (No. 2018M632573), and the National Natural Science Foundation of China (71702059).

References

1. Dangelico, R.M. Improving firm environmental performance and reputation: The role of employee green teams. *Bus. Strategy Environ.* **2015**, *24*, 735–749. [CrossRef]
2. Wei, A.P.; Peng, C.L.; Huang, H.C.; Yeh, S.P. Effects of corporate social responsibility on firm performance: Does customer satisfaction matter? *Sustainability* **2020**, *12*, 7545. [CrossRef]
3. Barrena-Martinez, J.; López-Fernández, M.; Romero-Fernandez, P. Drivers and barriers in socially responsible human resource management. *Sustainability* **2018**, *10*, 1532. [CrossRef]
4. Gangi, F.; Mustilli, M.; Varrone, N. The impact of corporate social responsibility (CSR) knowledge on corporate financial performance: Evidence from the European banking industry. *J. Knowl. Manag.* **2019**, *23*, 110–134. [CrossRef]
5. Wahba, H. Does the market value corporate environmental responsibility? An empirical examination. *Corp. Soc. Responsib. Environ. Manag.* **2008**, *15*, 89–99. [CrossRef]
6. Drucker, P.F. Managing oneself. *Harv. Bus. Rev.* **2005**, *83*, 100–109.
7. Shen, J.; Zhang, H. Socially responsible human resource management and employee support for external CSR: Roles of organizational CSR climate and perceived CSR directed toward employees. *J. Bus. Ethics* **2019**, *156*, 875–888. [CrossRef]
8. Campa, D.; Zijlmans, E.W.A. Corporate social responsibility recognition and support for the arts: Evidence from European financial institutions. *Eur. Manag. J.* **2019**, *37*, 818–827. [CrossRef]
9. Jose, A.; Lee, S.M. Environmental reporting of global corporations: A content analysis based on website disclosures. *J. Bus. Ethics* **2007**, *72*, 307–321. [CrossRef]
10. Wu, T.J.; Tsai, H.T.; Tai, Y.N. Would corporate social responsibility affect consumers' attitudes towards brand and purchase behavior? Buyer-seller guanxi as the moderator. *Rev. Cercet. Interv. Soc.* **2016**, *53*, 272–287.
11. Cho, Y.; Lee, C. Effect of coopetitive activity on innovation and management performances in the structural context. *Sci. Technol. Soc.* **2019**, *24*, 365–384. [CrossRef]
12. Lennerts, S.; Schulze, A.; Tomczak, T. The asymmetric effects of exploitation and exploration on radical and incremental innovation performance: An uneven affair. *Eur. Manag. J.* **2020**, *38*, 121–134. [CrossRef]
13. Wu, T.J.; Gao, J.Y.; Wang, L.Y.; Yuan, K.S. Exploring links between polychronicity and job performance from the person–environment fit perspective—The mediating role of well-being. *Int. J. Environ. Res. Public Health* **2020**, *17*, 3711. [CrossRef]
14. Wu, T.J.; Wang, L.Y.; Gao, J.Y.; Wei, A.P. Social Support and Well-Being of Chinese Special Education Teachers—An Emotional Labor Perspective. *Int. J. Environ. Res. Public Health* **2020**, *17*, 6884. [CrossRef] [PubMed]
15. Albort-Morant, G.; Ariza-Montes, A.; Leal-Rodríguez, A.; Giorgi, G. How does positive work-related stress affect the degree of innovation development? *Int. J. Environ. Res. Public Health* **2020**, *17*, 520. [CrossRef]
16. Dey, P.K.; Malesios, C.; De, D.; Chowdhury, S.; Abdelaziz, F.B. The impact of lean management practices and sustainably-oriented innovation on sustainability performance of small and medium-sized enterprises: Empirical evidence from the uk. *Br. J. Manag.* **2020**, *31*, 141–161. [CrossRef]
17. Eisenberger, R.; Fasolo, P.; Davis-LaMastro, V. Perceived organizational support and employee diligence, commitment, and innovation. *J. Appl. Psychol.* **1990**, *75*, 51. [CrossRef]
18. Brammer, S.; Millington, A.; Rayton, B. The contribution of corporate social responsibility to organizational commitment. *Int. J. Hum. Resour. Manag.* **2007**, *18*, 1701–1719. [CrossRef]
19. Kim, S.; Lee, H. The effect of CSR fit and CSR authenticity on the brand attitude. *Sustainability* **2020**, *12*, 275. [CrossRef]
20. Dirks, K.T.; Ferrin, D.L. Trust in leadership: Meta-analytic findings and implications for research and practice. *J. Appl. Psychol.* **2002**, *87*, 611. [CrossRef]
21. Kim, H.R.; Lee, M.; Lee, H.T.; Kim, N.M. Corporate social responsibility and employee–company identification. *J. Bus. Ethics* **2010**, *95*, 557–569. [CrossRef]

22. Wu, T.J.; Xu, T.; Li, L.Q.; Yuan, K.S. "Touching with heart, reasoning by truth"! The impact of brand cues on mini-film advertising effect. *Int. J. Advert.* **2020**, 1–29. [CrossRef]

23. Wu, T.J.; Yuan, K.S.; Yen, D.C.; Xu, T. Building up resources in the relationship between work–family conflict and burnout among firefighters: Moderators of guanxi and emotion regulation strategies. *Eur. J. Work Organ. Psychol.* **2019**, *28*, 430–441. [CrossRef]

24. Pignata, S.; Boyd, C.; Gillespie, N.; Provis, C.; Winefield, A.H. Awareness of stress-reduction interventions: The impact on employees' well-being and organizational attitudes. *Stress Health* **2016**, *32*, 231–243. [CrossRef] [PubMed]

25. Bettencourt, L.A. Change-oriented organizational citizenship behaviors: The direct and moderating influence of goal orientation. *J. Retail.* **2004**, *80*, 165–180. [CrossRef]

26. Wu, C.M.; Chen, T.J. Inspiring prosociality in hotel workplaces: Roles of authentic leadership, collective mindfulness, and collective thriving. *Tour. Manag. Perspect.* **2019**, *31*, 123–135. [CrossRef]

27. Brunk, K.H. Exploring origins of ethical company/brand perceptions—A consumer perspective of corporate ethics. *J. Bus. Res.* **2010**, *63*, 255–262. [CrossRef]

28. Richter, U.H.; Shirodkar, V.; Shete, N. Firm-level indicators of instrumental and political CSR processes—A multiple case study. *Eur. Manag. J.* **2020**, in press. [CrossRef]

29. Zadek, S. The path to corporate responsibility. In *Corporate Ethics and Corporate Governance*; Springer: Berlin/Heidelberg, Germany, 2007; pp. 159–172.

30. Yadlapalli, A.; Rahman, S.; Rogers, H. A dyadic perspective of socially responsible mechanisms for retailer-manufacturer relationship in an apparel industry. *Int. J. Phys. Distrib. Logist. Manag.* **2019**, *49*, 242–266. [CrossRef]

31. Obrenovic, B.; Jianguo, D.; Tsoy, D.; Obrenovic, S.; Khan, M.A.S.; Anwar, F. The enjoyment of knowledge sharing: Impact of altruism on tacit knowledge-sharing behavior. *Front. Psychol.* **2020**, *11*, 1496. [CrossRef]

32. Barney, J. Firm resources and sustained competitive advantage. *J. Manag.* **1991**, *17*, 99–120. [CrossRef]

33. Stoffers, J.; van der Heijden, B.; Schrijver, I. Towards a sustainable model of innovative work behaviors' enhancement: The mediating role of employability. *Sustainability* **2020**, *12*, 159. [CrossRef]

34. Majumdar, S.K.; Marcus, A.A. Rules versus discretion: The productivity consequences of flexible regulation. *Acad. Manag. J.* **2001**, *44*, 170–179.

35. Luo, L. Work motivation, job stress and employees' well-being. *J. Appl. Phycol. Manag. Stu.* **1999**, *8*, 61–72.

36. Liu, J.; Hui, C.; Lee, C.; Chen, Z.X. Why do i feel valued and why do I contribute? A relational approach to employee's organization-based self-esteem and job performance. *J. Manag. Stud.* **2013**, *50*, 1018–1040. [CrossRef]

37. Mael, F.; Ashforth, B.E. Alumni and their alma mater: A partial test of the reformulated model of organizational identification. *J. Organ. Behav.* **1992**, *13*, 103–123. [CrossRef]

38. Van Knippenberg, D.; Sleebos, E. Organizational identification versus organizational commitment: Self-definition, social exchange, and job attitudes. *J. Organ. Behav.* **2006**, *27*, 571–584. [CrossRef]

39. Epitropaki, O. A Multi-level investigation of psychological contract breach and organizational identification through the lens of perceived organizational membership: Testing a moderated–mediated model. *J. Organ. Behav.* **2013**, *34*, 65–86. [CrossRef]

40. Du, S.; Bhattacharya, C.B.; Sen, S. Maximizing business returns to corporate social responsibility (CSR): The role of CSR communication. *Int. J. Manag. Rev.* **2010**, *12*, 8–19. [CrossRef]

41. Loon, M.; Otaye-Ebede, L.; Stewart, J. The paradox of employee psychological well-being practices: An integrative literature review and new directions for research. *Int. J. Hum. Resour. Manag.* **2019**, *30*, 156–187. [CrossRef]

42. Lu, L.; Gilmour, R. Individual-oriented and socially oriented cultural conceptions of subjective well-being: Conceptual analysis and scale development. *Asian J. Soc. Psychol.* **2006**, *9*, 36–49. [CrossRef]

43. Scott, S.G.; Bruce, R.A. Determinants of innovative behavior: A path model of individual innovation in the workplace. *Acad. Manag. J.* **1994**, *37*, 580–607.

44. James, K.; Brodersen, M.; Eisenberg, J. Workplace affect and workplace creativity: A review and preliminary model. *Hum. Perform.* **2004**, *17*, 169–194. [CrossRef]

45. Lyubomirsky, S.; King, L.; Diener, E. The benefits of frequent positive affect: Does happiness lead to success? *Psychol. Bull.* **2005**, *131*, 803. [CrossRef] [PubMed]

46. Jaussi, K.S.; Randel, A.E.; Dionne, S.D. I am, I think I can, and I do: The role of personal identity, self-efficacy, and cross-application of experiences in creativity at work. *Creat. Res. J.* **2007**, *19*, 247–258. [CrossRef]

3

Corporate Social Responsibility at LUX* Resorts and Hotels: Satisfaction and Loyalty Implications for Employee and Customer Social Responsibility

Haywantee Ramkissoon [1,2,3,*] 🆔, **Felix Mavondo** [4] **and Vishnee Sowamber** [5]

[1] College of Business, Law & Social Sciences, Derby Business School, University of Derby, Derby DE22 1GB, UK
[2] School of Business & Economics, UiT, The Arctic University of Norway, 1621 Alta, Norway
[3] College of Business & Economics, Johannesburg Business School, University of Johannesburg, APB 17011 Johannesburg, South Africa
[4] Department of Marketing, Monash Business School, Clayton Campus, Monash University, Melbourne, VIC 3000, Australia; Felix.Mavondo@monash.edu
[5] Faculty Research Centre for Financial and Corporate Integrity, Coventry University, Coventry CV1 2TU, UK; sowamberv@uni.coventry.ac.uk
* Correspondence: H.Ramkissoon@derby.ac.uk

Abstract: Corporate Social Responsibility (CSR) remains a hot topic in management. Yet, little is known about how well managers, employees and consumers are responding to CSR initiatives to align with the 2030 Agenda for Sustainable Development. Underpinned by well-established theories, this study develops a single integrative model of managers', employees' and consumers' CSR. Data were collected from the LUX* group of resorts and hotels located on three Indian Ocean islands: Mauritius, Reunion and the Maldives. Structural equation modelling was employed. Findings reveal: (1) organizational CSR is positively related to employee social responsibility; (2) organizational CSR is negatively associated with customer social responsibility; (3) employee social responsibility is negatively related to customer social responsibility; (4) employee social responsibility is negatively related to customer delight; (5) customer social responsibility is positively related to customer satisfaction; and (6); customer social responsibility is positively related to customer delight. Strategic CSR initiatives with a multi-stakeholder engagement approach are discussed.

Keywords: corporate social responsibility; stakeholder engagement; employee; customer satisfaction; loyalty; post COVID-19 implications

1. Introduction

Research on environmental and social corporate social responsibility (CSR) have attracted significant attention. However, an integrated model with managers', employees' and consumers' approach to CSR initiatives to align with the 2030 Agenda for Sustainable Development is yet to be established. The United Nations Global Compact, a UN initiative, created in 2000, was introduced to engage multinational organizations and corporations to spot and evaluate their CSR activities. The initiative strives to advocate the inclusion, monitoring and reporting of the UN SDGs into their business operations [1]. With the 17 Sustainable Development Goals (SDGs) at the core of the Agenda, the objective is to collaborate to solve development challenges to balance economic, social and environmental sustainability contributing to identified priorities [2].

This needs to be done through diversity, inclusiveness, shared values and collaboration with key stakeholders including civil society and policy makers [3,4]. The United Nations proclaimed 2017 as the International Year of Tourism for Sustainable Development emphasizing the importance of this sector and its ability to contribute towards the achievement of some of the SDGs. The Travel and Tourism industry experienced growth in terms of GDP until the COVID-19 dramatic impact on global businesses [5]. Prior COVID-19, however, there was still growing concern regarding the contributions to SDGs. Examples include inequalities such as what is being done to ethically integrate marginalized people for them to benefit from tourism [6]. Revenue leakages and gaps have been observed [7]. Other examples include low remuneration for the number of hours worked [8], job insecurity [9], poor work–life balance [10] and emotional labor [11] resulting in low job satisfaction and high employee turnover in the tourism and hospitality sector [12]. Critics have described CSR as "hot air" or "corporate waffle" [13] fueling further research into its practices [14,15]. This required organizations to think of new strategies and business plans to operate successfully along with delivering benefits to the broader society.

Environmental reporting has been well established [16,17]. There is now growing focus on social impact of CSR and social reporting [18,19]. Literature evidences that despite the exigencies of the sector, employees who are taken care of by their employers tend to be more committed [20,21], which in turn increases customer satisfaction [22]. This shows that CSR plays a very important role in value creation [23]. CSR in tourism primarily focuses on advanced economies [24]. This demands more research in developing countries including small island developing states [25] to understand the phenomenon.

Considering the pivotal role of employee interaction with customers in service encounters [26], this study explores the nexus of relationships between the three groups to achieve marketplace goals for firms in the tourism industry. The present study is based on data collected at LUX* Resorts and Hotels, a 5-star Mauritian company with luxury resorts operating in several destinations in several countries. The study examines the relationship of organizational CSR initiatives and their impact on employees' CSR and its ultimate influence on customer social responsibility and finally on customer satisfaction and delight. CSR is used as an umbrella concept, which incorporates four major facets of company sustainability policies and activities, aimed for community stakeholders, employees, customers and government [27–29].

Our study's objectives and contributions are: (1) we develop and test a single integrative model exploring the pattern of interaction and influence between three dynamic forces: the organization, its employees and its customers, from a CSR perspective in tourism and hospitality, (2) we contribute to CSR studies using a multi stakeholder development approach across five-star resorts in small island developing states.

2. Literature Review

2.1. CSR in Tourism and Hospitality

The increasing awareness of environmental impacts of travel and tourism paved the way for adopting CSR principles that are congruent with social norms and expectations of good citizenship practices for firms in the tourism and hospitality industry [30]. This has generated the need for a clearly identified connection of firms' Corporate Social Responsibility (CSR) initiatives with its internal and external stakeholders. Managers recognize CSR and sustainability strategies are not just arbitrary altruistic acts but are "essential" business imperatives for their strategic market operations, innovations in customer interaction and even for the internal talent management [31]. Despite continual debate on precise policies of CSR in the industry, its practice has grown among both practitioners and researchers worldwide. Most of the firms in the travel, tourism and hospitality industries if not all, started practicing various CSR activities. Levy and Park (2011) identified 129 CSR activities adopted by ten prominent hotel chains i.e., those having the largest number of rooms in the world.

Firms operating in tourism and hospitality sectors are not homogeneous in terms of adoption of their CSR policies and practices. Moreover, with its characteristics of intangibility and variability in its services [32], tourism offers can make their brands "tangible" by ensuring brand-customer identification [33] based on good corporate citizenship [34]. For eco-tourism companies, more ethical and social components are integrated into their businesses [35–37].

CSR continues to attract importance in the travel, tourism, and hospitality industries in view of its adoption of sustainability strategies [38–40]. The focus has been on internal marketing issues, employee perspectives [41,42], business sustainability [43,44], influence on critical service process [45] and consumer preference, as well as business ethics and shared value [46] among others.

A PricewaterhouseCoopers' (PWC) survey of CEOs found that the latter intend to give more importance to CSR (PWC, 2011). More than 25% of Fortune 500 companies provide visibility on their environmental, social and sustainability commitments. The private sector is paying more and more attention to CSR and inclusiveness [47]. The service-profit chain model [48] illustrates that employee attitudes and behavior as well as customer satisfaction, delight [49] and loyalty in service industries are ultimately linked to firm profit. Organizational CSR establishes the enabling corporate culture for employee CSR practices. CSR promotions to the external marketplace establishes firms' citizenship image among customers [50] whereas internal marketing establishes the acceptability and participation of its employees to firms' CSR initiatives. The ultimate goal for the firm is to strengthen the corporate citizenship image.

2.2. Organisational CSR and Internal Stakeholders

A pool of research focused on the positive associations between organizational CSR and employee attitudes [51–54]. Several studies have also shown that consumers have positive evaluations for companies demonstrating CSR activities [55,56]. A number of studies have noted negative relationships between organizational CSR and consumers' CSR attitudes [57,58] when companies are more concerned with their firms' interests than with greater public interests. These inconsistencies demand for more research in the field [59,60].

CSR research has been underpinned by "theory of reasoned action", the "theory of planned behavior", "social identity theory" and "stakeholder engagement theory" in a number of studies exploring links between CSR, employee attitudes and related impacts on the organization [61]. The theory of reasoned action predicts an individual's behavioral intentions in engaging in a specific activity is associated with one's attitude and subjective norms. The theory of reasoned action [62] and theory of planned behavior [63] are extensions of the former and have been applied in various CSR studies [64,65]. Several CSR studies for example [66,67] have also drawn on social identity theory [68]).

Tourism has been increasingly contributing to significant global environmental change, notably climate change [69,70], biodiversity loss, land-use change, water use and invasive species [71,72]. International tourist numbers have been estimated to reach 1.8 billion by 2030 [73]. This means there will be even greater need for businesses to cater for this increase and if unmanaged, it will result in dire consequences for public and environmental health. Tourism has often been conceived as essentially pure marketing, as it is often based on packaging existing resources and assets of a destination, and subsequent promotion to new markets [74] without much consideration for the deleterious impacts it often brings along if not carefully managed [75].

The growth in tourist numbers until the COVID-19 health pandemic had forecasted an increase in negative environmental impacts if tourism operators were to continue to follow a "business as usual" path [76,77]. If there were to be no change, energy consumption was expected to increase by 154% greenhouse gas (GHG) emissions by 131%, water consumption by 152% and solid waste disposal by 251% [78]. The planet cannot sustain the current levels of consumption with its current carrying capacity. According to Met Office (2017), the year 2016 was officially reported as the warmest year on record. It was mentioned that the El Niño event was partly responsible but the main cause to global warming is human activities from increasing greenhouse gases in the atmosphere [79].

The global pandemic COV-SARS-2 has emphasized the climate change crisis; we need sustainable and urgent measures in place for the post pandemic economic structure. COVID-19 has had a tremendous halt on tourism and hospitality businesses [80], there will be an even greater need for responsible behaviors as business slowly starts getting back to normal [81]. Researchers argue that this could be a long-term process; hospitality businesses need to continue with a multi-stakeholder engagement approach [82] to generate collective benefits for the tourism and hospitality industry. There is further need for businesses to work more closely with governments as they have a more exponential influence on resources [83]. Firms are legislated to do so through good governance and ethical practice requirements. Fortunately, organizations do not engage in CSR initiatives solely because of compliance. The actions are triggered due to other factors such as demand for environmental and community friendly products and services and responsible management expectations by investors and other key stakeholders. This is likely to become more pronounced with consumers' collective efforts to become more pro-environmental [84] due to perceived threats of detrimental impacts of human activities on the environment and fear of a second wave of COVID-19 [85]. There are also other key benefits such as cost reduction and increased profitability [86].

The current global health crisis and climate change concerns clearly reinforce the need for businesses to align with sustainable development goals [87]. To promote behavioral change in a target audience in order to engender public good, social marketing of organizations utilizes marketing techniques linked to same [88–90]. The growing demand from tourists for ethical and sustainable practices is an important motivating factor for CSR in business practices [91,92]. Another key factor is that there is a great concern for the protection of local environment and culture [93] and environmental reporting to satisfy legal requirements [94].

Often in organizations, top management initiates the establishment and growth of a corporate culture that emphasizes CSR which gradually shapes employee attitude and performance around CSR initiatives [95]. As a social control system, the corporate culture can determine internal stakeholders' commitment and performance [96] through greater appreciation for socially appropriate norms [97] of business interaction. Moreover, when an employee perceives the strategic fit between his/her personal identity and firm's characteristics [98], they are likely to behave collaboratively to achieve the firm's CSR goal [99,100].

CSR initiatives of hospitality firms endorse greater trustworthiness for the intangible nature of service transaction, and this demands solid evidence to establish their accountability [101]. Firms, hence, create and retain the corporate culture of shared values among different levels of management to facilitate CSR activities to achieve their greater CSR goals effectively [102]. Companies often leverage their CSR strategies to attract and retain quality skilled employees and use this as a competitive advantage [103]. The key is for management to maintain a more holistic perspective, recognizing that employees identify with the firm, not only through efforts to save the natural environment, but also through those pertaining to community, employees, and customers [104]. As internal stakeholders, when employees have a clear vision of their organizations' CSR, they tend to accept and institutionalize these initiatives [105]. For service firm employees, every step of the service design and delivery are influenced by this corporate culture [106]. Drawing on social agency theory [91], employees' identity is influenced by their employers' social image, that is, the firm's accountability and responsible dealings with their stakeholders. Employees feel proud to contribute to the community. The employers' CSR programs often motivate employees to invest their time and effort for community benefits [107]. Employees' CSR performance is about the affective commitment and compliance one makes with the company's strategic initiative of CSR implementation. A service firm's CSR activities through their employees' performance, reflects the firm's characteristics to project their social citizenship [106].

Literature evidences a number of studies investigating CSR customer behavior [108–110]. The prevailing and rapidly changing COVID-19 and climate change contexts call for urgent actions to protect human and planetary health. The customer, as a member of the larger community holds the public view on corporate performances and CSR initiatives. Drawing on the social identity theory [111], we can argue that to build a distinct social identity and enhance their self-esteem, customers prefer and patronize service providers that are perceived as socially responsible. The resulting brand image from

CSR efforts plays an important role in attracting a segment of already socially aware customers [107]. The fit between a company and its CSR activities exerts an authentic effect on corporate image [112].

Customers' own sense of social responsibility and fit between company performance and customer expectation can bring success in business. Customers may perceive a firm's CSR initiatives as a promise to perform and deliver services in a socially acceptable way [113]. This may even generate a halo effect in other areas of firms' operations [114]. The rise in customer expectation due to firms' external CSR communication may have mixed effects on developing customer perception. Different CSR initiatives may favor customer satisfaction or other purchase decisions differently [115].

Some evidence in literature suggests that consumers found less trustworthiness in promotion-based CSR activities than the institutional implementation of CSR programs [116]. For a service firm, external communications make overt CSR promises [113] and corporate CSR culture in service delivery complements to fulfil customers' social responsibility expectations. A combination of corporate CSR initiatives, especially awareness campaigns and cause-related marketing activities can contribute to customer education; whereas, environmental and citizenship initiatives at the service point-of-sales affirm customers' social responsibility.

2.3. Employee CSR and Customer Engagement

The more engaged an employee is, the more efficient and hard-working he/she is [117] (Karatepe, 2013). This in turn has a positive impact on service quality for customers [118] (which impacts on customer satisfaction and loyalty [119,120]. Research shows that CSR is positively associated with organizational commitment [67,121]. CSR plays an important role in enhancing companies' reputation as an ethical business [122]. Organizations from different fields show different "responsibility profiles". Some sectors prioritise environmental protection, while some show more concern towards economic or social responsibilities [123]. It can also be observed that in developing countries, the political challenges play a role in shaping the practice of CSR [124]. This is evidenced by CSR awards promoted by tourism organizations for those located in emerging economies who are investing more efforts in social and economic sustainability. The CSR awards often demonstrate they have successfully implemented various initiatives in line with education, health and youth community development [125].

Managing risks and building reputation have been shown to be the key motivators for business CSR [126]. In parallel, CSR initiatives enhance the employees' organizational identification. This in turns increases employees' loyalty [112] and employees' trust and job satisfaction [105]. Some evidence [127] shows that employee engagement is positively related to their involvement in organizational Human Resource Management (HRM) e.g., in CSR-inspired initiatives such as environmental protection.

CSR may enhance leadership skills and motivation for employees who like to participate in CSR projects [128]. Studies show that engaging in CSR practices is very beneficial. It mitigates risks, establishes a legitimacy, builds good reputation, attracts employees and increases customer satisfaction [126,129]. There is a paucity of studies investigating the relationship between company induced employee CSR and its direct or indirect outcomes, in terms of generating greater customer satisfaction and delight. In contrast, there is growing evidence suggesting that general employee attitude and behavior at the critical interaction moment with customers, essentially influence customer perception of the organization, its offers and quality of services [130]. Employee CSR can be defined as the derivative of the compliance of company employees to the company CSR initiatives. In most cases, proper orientation makes employees comfortable with the firm's culture and proper internalization of corporate initiatives, leads to higher level of affective commitment and eventual decrease in turnover intention [42]. Although firms cannot expect an instant financial outcome, employees' CSR engagement and performance can accrue long-term economic benefits [131] from attractive workplace conditions [132], improved employee morale and commitment [133], and thus, a congenial environment for better customer relations.

For front-line employees, attaining customer desire demands an assessment of customers' perception about the company, even beyond the company's immediate offer [134]. CSR initiatives, offers, and events have become a relatively common conversation element for employees while communicating with customers that creates a window into the innermost values of the customers and thus, facilitates the social comparison between them [135] Relational identity [111] suggests that customers may identify company employees as members of the same social category or having similar fellow feelings toward the society when they come across company's corporate culture of employees' CSR performance at the service encounter. Employees who identify with customers consider themselves to belong to a common social group with customers [111]. Employee–customer identification goes beyond attitudes about customers or their perceived traits, reflecting their commonalities in terms of social orientation [134].

Corporate social responsibility has become a relatively common element in communicating with customers, with numerous ways in which an employee can develop beliefs about customers' CSR perceptions. Social responsibility activities can stimulate social comparison and social categorization, because such activities are often interpreted as a meaningful indication of a person's values [135]. Employees may interpret customer perceptions about the company's CSR to better understand their character.

At least three distinct research streams have been identified to establish the link between company CSR and customer satisfaction. Firstly, the stakeholder theory proposes that while caring about their own consumption experience, customers also care about firms' actions that have potential to enhance stakeholder value [136]. Secondly, company CSR performance record, if communicated effectively, creates a context for consumers' favorable evaluation of the firm [137] and increasing their level of support [138]) as they identify themselves with the company. It is likely that customer-company fit brings satisfaction for customers [139,140]. Third, customers' higher perceived value from firms' CSR activities, consequently, acts as an antecedent to higher satisfaction from transacting with a socially responsible company [136]. Such activities indicate greater customers' satisfaction.

Employee welfare is influenced by CSR; there is an increased commitment in CSR among international hotel chains [91,95]. Within the domain of CSR, a stream of research is gaining strength with more enlightened academic views on Personal Social Responsibility (PSR), realizing a firm's dependence on its employees' personal sense of responsibility [141]. In the services organization e.g., in the tourism and hospitality industry, where several boundary spanning roles determine the success of customer interaction [142], PSR may play an important part to portray strong citizenship messages though employees' personality disposition [143]. In the organizational CSR discourse, PSR puts the employees and their personal traits at the core [141]. Individuals acknowledge the societal and environmental consequences of one's own actions [144]. Surprisingly, the concept of employees PSR, its aspects and its sensitivity at the time of dealing with customers has received little attention in the hospitality or tourism literature [143] although employees' personality traits have long been acknowledged [145].

Based on their own life experiences and level of social justice awareness [143] employees often form their own perception to decide about the management's fairness with CSR programs that eventually trigger their behavioral responses in everyday life [105]. Research identifies values such as altruism and conscientiousness as employees' helping behavior [130], which can be the reflection of their personal sense of responsibility and good citizenship behavior. The presence of personal responsibility and social orientation makes it easier for employees to actively engage in CSR activities of their firms [143]. An employee's responsibility disposition is basically the sum of his/her cultural background, personal values and the company's ethical training [146]. Employees, performing as boundary spanners, come across company customers, interacting with them to generate service experiences. During such encounters, employees' representation of social responsibilities while presenting the company and its brand is not purely "corporate", a large part of it is explainable as attributed from individual characteristics [146].

Employees today are looking for jobs that are exciting, challenging and at the same time have a good fit with their own perception of fairness and justice [112]. Compliant employees' CSR performance is the reflection of their firms' CSR influencing their attitudes and behavior, which in turn influence consumers' evaluation of service quality, value, and satisfaction [147–149]. An investigation of how hospitality industry employees' CSR activities influence their attitudes at work, and their potential influence on customer satisfaction through quality customer interaction is warranted, to better evaluate customers' satisfaction from tourism experiences [100]. Notably, employees' CSR performances are also becoming more diagnostic of firms' real CSR initiatives. Heightened self-esteem encourages employees to contribute to their company by serving customer needs, as a key company success indicator [134], that results in greater customer satisfaction.

Most importantly, companies are to perform their service dependably, and reliably to their customers [142]. Customer judgment about the service performance can produce a pleasurable level of fulfilment, thus "satisfaction" from their intangible service consumption. As firms' CSR creates a positive impact on customer satisfaction [150], employees' CSR performance can enhance the quality of customer interaction at its functional level. However, when companies focus on firm serving motives leading to skepticism towards CSR, customer satisfaction is not achieved [59,60].

Although scholars and industry practitioners have sought to identify the relationship between firms' social responsibilities and customers' satisfaction, findings remain inconclusive. An extant review of the literature suggests that there may be a positive relationship between CSR initiatives and consumer outcomes [150].

Customer delight has been considered as a performance goal based on customer response [49] based on disconfirmation of their service experience from marketing organizations [120,151]. Customer delight has been conceptualized as an emotional response of customers from what is captured by measuring customer satisfaction and can be another distinct performance metric [152]. While customer satisfaction can be earned by delivering according to customer expectations [153], customer delight only can be achieved through exceptional services. Exceptional boundary spanners in direct contact with the customers are the face of the company to bring success in customer delight [154,155].

Although some, for example [156] argue that surprise is not essential to make customers delighted, most research in this stream mandates [151] surprise as a significant element to produce customer delight which creates a dilemma for all customers and loyal customers in specific. However, providing a delightful surprise has a definite impact on loyalty intention and generates positive word-of-mouth [157]. In a tourism and hospitality setting, where the customer encounter is characterized by infrequent and non-repetitive holiday experiences, greater opportunities are available to make the guest delighted relating to multiple aspects available in the destination [158]. The relationship between employees' CSR performance and its impact on the customer delight is yet to be further explored. However, as the significant correlation between positive affect (interest and joy—components measuring customer delight) and satisfaction has been observed [159], it can be argued that customer delight is the progression of customer satisfaction. So, similar forms of relationship between employee CSR and customer delight can be observed between employee CSR and customer satisfaction. The hospitality industry is characterized by high turnover rates and the increasing customer demand that can only be served by retaining exceptional, self -motivated employees at boundary spanning roles [155].Empowerment, involvement of employees in CSR initiatives and improving morale by taking part in a firm's CSR can act as a job motivator for employees. Motivated and committed employees usually show loyalty and great potential to deliver service [20] and customer delight. Another argument could come from increasing blame for businesses for worsening the social justice and natural environmental balance by the community and citizens. If customers realize businesses' CSR initiatives as coming across through company employees caring about the social responsibility issues, it may add to their "surprise" and increase the occurrence of a delighted situation.

The role of company employees, especially their personal social responsibility to generate customer delight is yet to be explored. Referring to our earlier discussion, as boundary spanners, employees' social responsibility orientation being supported by company CSR culture, is expected to generate customer satisfaction [134,150]. The surprise component in satisfaction can only be earned through extraordinary service experiences [157]. Creating an "extraordinary" service experience for the customer requires firms to rely on exceptional surface traits such as empathy, high degree of responsiveness to anticipate and meet customer needs and a strong drive to please them [154]. This requires working really hard, even pushing the boundary of the company service blueprint. Managers cannot expect their employees having such exceptional surface traits without ensuring their altruism and conscientiousness; those largely come from their socially responsible behavioral formation [130].

Customer satisfaction and delight mostly come from non-ordinary time, at an uncommon place, encouraging customers to express a release from their regular value system [49,143] while others are still firmly within their values. Although it is recommended to have a break and enjoy the delight [160] for boundary spanners it is a challenge to give the customers experience of delight moving beyond so-called subterranean values. In this particular situation, employees' personal integrity, sense of responsibility and humanity are much sought after traits for employers.

From the extant review of the literature we develop and propose our conceptual framework illustrated in Figure 1.

Figure 1. Conceptual Framework.

We propose the following hypotheses:

Hypothesis 1 (H1). *Organizational CSR is positively related to employee social responsibility.*

Hypothesis 2 (H2). *Organizational CSR is positively related to customer social responsibility.*

Hypothesis 3 (H3). *Employee social responsibility is positively related to customer social responsibility.*

Hypothesis 4 (H4). *Employee social responsibility is positively related to customer satisfaction.*

Hypothesis 5 (H5). *Employee social responsibility is positively related to customer delight.*

Hypothesis 6 (H6). *Customer social responsibility is positively related to customer satisfaction.*

Hypothesis 7 (H7). *Customer social responsibility is positively related to customer delight.*

3. Methodology

3.1. Study Context

Data were collected from, employees and customers across 3 LUX* resorts in 3 distinctive Indian Ocean islands of Mauritius, Reunion and the Maldives. LUX* is a Mauritian hotel group with luxury resorts also operating in China and other forthcoming ones in Europe and Asia-Pacific. The hotel industry in the Indian Ocean islands have developed rapidly over the past years, largely as a result of it being one of the industries initially opened to foreign investments. However, the islands are very fragile; CSR efforts are important to mitigate negative social and environmental impacts [161,162]. This will help with the industry's contribution to sustainable tourism for broader societal goals [28,163,164].

The LUX* group of resorts has received numerous awards including Corporate Reporting Award in Integrated Reporting by PWC (PricewaterhouseCoopers), various awards at the International Hotel Awards: "Best Large Hotel Mauritius", "Best Sustainable Hotel Mauritius" and "Best Sustainable Hotel Africa", through its CSR initiatives "Tread Lightly by LUX" and "Ray of Light by LUX*". LUX* is also the first hotel group listed on the Stock Exchange of Mauritius Sustainability Index and its resorts are certified Gold Travelife Sustainability. In addition to its resort development, LUX* operates a private islet "Ile des Deux Cocos" in Mauritius with renewable energy Solar system. The group's objective is to review its energy mix to include more renewable energy solutions.

3.2. Scale Measurements

Measurement scales on a 1–7 Likert scales were borrowed from well-established studies in literature [49,105,136] and adapted to the context of our study. Some examples of items borrowed from the literature are: LUX encourages employees to join civic organizations that support the community; LUX encourages partnerships with local businesses; LUX gives adequate contributions to charities; employees view themselves as partners of LUX; at LUX all employees commit to organizational goals. The questionnaire was reviewed by academics in hospitality and tourism for face validity. The questionnaire was further revised following their suggestions to ensure ease of communication [165].

3.3. Sample and Data Collection

Management and employees at the LUX resorts were sent the questionnaire and requested to participate in the study. The data collection was effected in 2016; the questionnaire was distributed through the Human Resource Departments. Completed questionnaires were deposited at central collection points. Respondents were assured of complete privacy. The greater the participation the more likely the greater representativeness of the sample. Studies show that CSR activities are better understood theoretically and tested empirically when they are organized by stakeholder types [121,166]. Firstly, questions were included in order to select front line employees, that is, those who are in direct contact with the guests during service delivery. Then employees who are in managerial positions were also requested to provide their perceptions. Thirdly, a sample of hotel customers was surveyed with a questionnaire that was distributed by the receptions. This was a shorter questionnaire to solicit larger response rate. Their responses were used as the dependent variables of interest to this study to minimize CMV. Structural Equation Modelling (SEM), a robust statistical technique [167,168], was employed to test the hypotheses. The measurement and the structural models were tested. The structural component of SEM tests the hypothesized relationships [169].

The sample for the analysis was 436. This was the smallest of the three categories of respondents i.e., managers and supervisors. There were more frontline employees, but only 436 were randomly picked for this data analysis. There were more customers (650) and a random sub-sample of 436 was picked. The three categories had to be equal to avoid missing values and the problems presented by analyzing unequal sample sizes in AMOS. The model had robust psychometric properties. Convergent and discriminant validity were established. The average variance extracted (AVE) were greater than 0.50 supporting convergent validity. The square root of AVE for each construct was greater than the correlations between latent constructs, thereby satisfying the discriminant validity criterion [170] (see Table 1).

Table 1. Correlation, square root of AVE and Reliability.

	1	2	3	4	5
1. Management CSR	**0.689**				
2. Employee CSR	0.043	**0.652**			
3. Customer Social Responsibility	−0.133 **	−0.156 **	**0.712**		
4. Customer Satisfaction	0.084	−0.194 **	0.840 **	**0.693**	
5. Customer Delight	0.028	−0.126 **	0.310 **	0.375 **	**0.723**
Internal Consistency	0.848	0.818	0.864	0.788	0.768
Cronbach alpha	0.828	0.812	0.864	0.803	0.667
Skewness	−1.069	−0.733	2.485	2.576	2.376
Kurtosis	1.015	−0.646	2.285	2.844	2.226

Note: * $p < 0.05$, ** $p < 0.01$, *** $p < 0.001$. Figures in bold on the diagonal are square roots of AVE.

We checked the robustness of the model following the approach by [171].

Robustness of model [171] uses the Chi-square difference between the SEM compared to the Measurement Model

$$\chi^2 = 621.779, df = 268; CMin/df = 2.320; GFI = 0.990, AGFI = 0.878; NFI = 0.869; TLI = 0.911; CFI = 0.920 \text{ (SEM Model)}$$

$$\chi^2 = 619.035, df = 265, CMin = 2.336; GFI = 0.900; AGFI = 0.877; NFI = 0.870; TLI = 0.910; CFI = 0.920 \text{ (Measurement Model)}$$

$\Delta\chi^2 = 2.744$; $\Delta df = 3$; Cmin/df= 0.915, $p > 0.90$ This suggests that the SEM is correctly specified, and the data fit the model very well. Thus, the discrepancy (i.e., Chi-square) is almost all accounted for by the measurement model. The path model fit statistics are robust suggesting no misspecification in the path model.

4. Results and Discussion

The sample consisted of mostly males for the managers (65%). In total, 55% were females among the employees. In total, 52% were females among the customers. The majority of managers (59.4%) and employees (55.6%) have been working at LUX for a period of three to five years. The demographic profile is attached in Supplementary Materials.

The structural model is shown in Figure 2. Our findings (see Table 2) show that organizational corporate social responsibility positively influences employee corporate social responsibility. Hypothesis 1 is confirmed (ß = 0.133; t = 2.345; $p < 0.05$). This finding is particularly illuminating in that it shows employees assimilate the organizational corporate responsibility to achieve organizational goals [99,100]. It also aligns with the social agency theory from [91] suggesting employees' identity is influenced by their employers' social image. Our findings further corroborate with [105] who suggest that when employees receive appropriate orientation, they tend to accept and institutionalize the organizational initiatives. This suggests that LUX* management has been able to communicate their corporate social responsibilities to the employees and the social responsibilities are well embedded in the organizational culture.

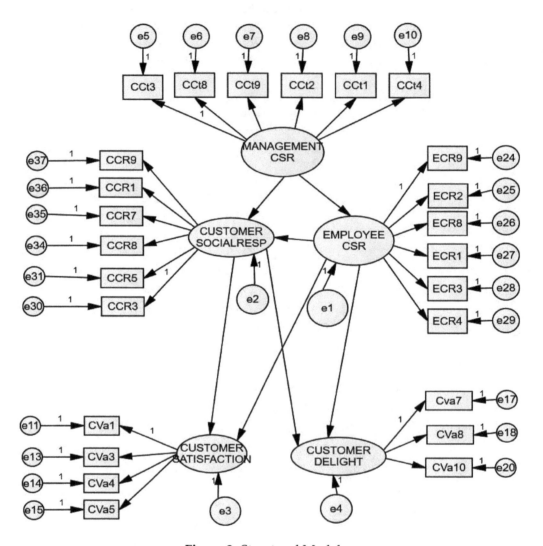

Figure 2. Structural Model.

Findings demonstrate that the relationship between organizational corporate social responsibility and customer social responsibility is negative and significant (ß = −0.144; t = −2.624; $p < 0.01$), thus, H2 is not supported. Previous studies [121,172] argue that CSR is positively associated with employee organizational commitment and plays an important role in enhancing companies' reputation as an ethical business. Organizational CSR, however, was found not to be a strong influencer of customer CSR [173,174]. Our findings suggest the need for LUX* to provide more subtle communication of its social responsibilities. Perhaps throwing in some incentives or redeemable points for future visits would be welcome. This finding raises interesting questions into the complex relations between tourists and the hotels they patronize. One gets the suspicion that tourists' sustainability concerns are one sided since the benefits are appropriated by the business without offering any tangible benefits to the visitors.

Table 2. Results.

Hypothesis	Standardized Regression (β)	t-Value	Supported/Not Supported
H1: Organizational CSR is positively related to Employee social responsibility	0.133	2.345 *	Supported
H2: Organizational CSR is positively related to Customer social responsibility	−0.144	−2.624 **	Not supported
H3: Employee Social responsibility is positively related to customer social responsibility	−0.182	−3.257 ***	Not supported
H4: Employee Social responsibility is positively related to customer satisfaction	−0.024	−0.727	Not supported
H5: Employee Social responsibility is positively related to customer delight	−0.0127	−2.134 *	Not supported
H6: Customer social responsibility is positively related to customer satisfaction	0.869	12.430 ***	Supported
H7: Customer social responsibility is positively related to customer delight	0.299	4.842 ***	Supported

Note: * $p < 0.05$, ** $p < 0.01$, *** $p < 0.001$.

The situation is complicated by the circumstances of staying at resorts. Visitors may see this as a few days of breaking from their routines and house chores, a time where they can essentially relax. They may perceive that they have paid the full price for goods and services and they are entitled to use them. This problem is compounded by the practice of resorts of not demonstrating how social responsibility can improve the environment or future visitation. In some way resorts need "to walk the talk" [175]. People become cynical if talk is not matched by behavior. Customers may view that their social responsibility is not rewarded by improved services or lower prices or some combination of the two and engaging in socially responsible behavior is not overtly recognized or incentivized by the resort.

Our findings also suggest that employees' social responsibility is negatively associated with customer social responsibility (ß = −0.182; t = −3.257; $p < 0.001$) thus, H3 is not supported. The suggestion is that visitors do not like to be pushed to take socially responsible actions during their vacation. This could have several interpretations. First, the nature of tourist visits is to seek relaxation and enjoy the holiday where someone else serves them [162] and not preach to them. Secondly, employees and customers are closely interacting and any apparent attitude suggesting the visitors are not behaving in a socially responsible manner may elicit a negative response from visitors. Third, perhaps it is a communication problem in that visitors may comply if the message is subtle or incentivized. Our findings and suggestions align with [173,176] arguments that CSR might be effective in driving positive attitudes and behavior in theory but are rarely matched at the consumption stage. This demands that a consistent approach to CSR be firstly adopted by management and employees and appropriate messages are delivered to customers [98,177] to trigger and promote the desired behaviors.

Hypothesis 4, proposing a positive relationship between employee social responsibility and customer satisfaction, was not supported (ß = −0.124; t = −0.727). This suggests that LUX* needs to pay attention to consumers' views on CSR initiatives, this aligns with [178]. Consumers are one of the main stakeholders for hospitality businesses [179] and yet their voices are often ignored. Companies need to strongly emphasize how their CSR initiatives are beneficial to the needy [25] thus helping to achieve broader societal goals. Dialogue between employees, customers, the government and the local community will ensure a participatory approach and information exchange to ensure continuous evaluation, monitoring and feedback on CSR benefits to the community.

Employees' level of corporate social responsibility does not influence customer delight (ß = −0.127; t = −2.134; $p < 0.05$) thus, H5 is not supported. There does not appear to be a quid pro quo for customers to behave in a socially responsible manner. Organizational CSR practices might not provide the desired convenience to customers and hence can negatively influence customer delight. This reflects the need for organizations to consult with and engage the consumers to make them aware of the benefits of their CSR strategies and practices. Our findings suggest that LUX* needs to invest further in providing messages conveying the clear focus of personal and social benefits to make customers opt for sustainability actions. People often act when they see the efficacy of their responsible actions [180]. Incentives can be provided for engaging in responsible behaviors, and rewards can enhance customer delight.

Hypothesis 6 was supported. Our findings show that customer social responsibility is significant and positively related to customer satisfaction ($ß = 0.869$; $t = 12.430$; $p < 0.001$). This is consistent with previous research (e.g., Luo and Bhattacharya, 2006), showing that customers' higher perceived value from firms' CSR activities acts as an antecedent to higher satisfaction from transacting with socially responsible companies. Scholars, for example [134,147,149] argue that CSR performance influences consumers' satisfaction and organizational CSR creates a positive impact on customer satisfaction [150]. On the other hand, employees' CSR can enhance the quality of customer interaction at its functional level. The subtle implication is that being socially responsible may lead to superior quality perceptions. This would suggest that where visitors voluntarily engage in socially responsible behavior, they would expect to receive superior service delivery. This would establish a win-win situation.

Hypothesis 7 was supported, the relationship between customer social responsibility and customer delight was significant and positive ($ß = 0.299$; $t = 4.842$; $p < 0.001$). Customers of LUX* are willing to be socially responsible to the extent that this maintains the convenience and enhances delight. There may be several explanations for this. First visitors wish to comply with generally acceptable behaviors for their benefit and for the benefit of other visitors. Visitors wish to maintain the reputation of the resort potentially to talk about it to friends and relatives. This corroborates with [112] who imply that the fit between a company and CSR activities exerts an authentic effect on corporate image. The fit between consumers' social responsibility expectations and firms' CSR activities may build potentially enduring customer relationships. Customers may also be willing to be socially responsible as they believe they are receiving value for money and have a positive evaluation of the resort enhancing customer delight [49].

5. Implications

5.1. Implications for Hotels and Resort Managers

An important process for hotels and resorts is to make CSR activities as visible as possible through signposting and advertising. Consumers need to able to readily access and verify the CSR information. For example, beach reclamation is a significant issue in many island states, it is important for hotels and resorts to establish a comprehensive understanding of CSR practices set to avoid negative effects of any change to the system. Consumers can make an informed decision based on their interpretations of the organizations' CSR performance and their willingness to pay a higher premium for CSR products [181]. It is recommended that CSR includes activities such as letting grass and flowers grow and using recycled water in gardening, to maintain biodiversity and protect environmental resources. Organizations need to visibly show employees' participation in these activities. Hotels and resorts could have a gardening site employee who encourage guests to actively engage in some fun, and creative low pro-environmental [84] gardening activities e.g., assisting staff in removal of weeds and raising beds for planting, watering plants at the hotel. Specific messages could also be set up across specific garden sites on the hotel premises to encourage participation. Effective communication can increase pro-environmental behavior compliance.

Organizations need to further explore local stakeholders to further support their CSR policies. Examples could include supporting the local community through sponsoring sports and education encouraging their employees and also those outside the organization to participate. Communicating about the projects through newsletters, displays and other channels will build awareness both locally and can also serve as an action for other organizations. Employees can be incentivized through recognition and bonuses for their continued commitment in encouraging and promoting CSR. Food waste is an important issue in hospitality organizations [182]. Restaurants in hotels and resorts generally tend to serve more food that customers will eat. Hotels and resorts can incentivize desirable behaviors such as free breakfast, lunch or dinner buffets for long-stay customers. We note that a lot of food in these feeding episodes is wasted, the actual financial cost of these incentives is small.

5.2. Implications for Academics

CSR has many similarities with sustainability, some discuss these terms as synonyms while others as two distinct concepts with the former focusing on social and the latter on environmental issues [183,184]. Synthesis and characterization of CSR still demands further work in the literature. Companies can be firm-oriented (serving interests of the organization) or public-serving [185]. CSR has been often a matter of perception rather than fact with fragmented discourses in the literature [181]. We argue that organizations can be financially, socially and environmentally sustainable. Our hope is to provoke further thinking and discussion among scholars and academics on how we can achieve financial, social and environmental goals synergistically. This may further allow for multi-stakeholder engagement for a common purpose, aligning with the UN Sustainable Development Goals [87]. Academic engagement with the hospitality sector is key and is now becoming increasingly important to cope with the immediate and plan for post-COVID-19 era [80].

5.3. Implications for Policy Makers

Our work is a considerable effort to highlight the need for a multi-stakeholder participatory approach for consistency and practicality. CSR can strengthen exchanges and communication and bring policy reforms. Government and private sector and local community participation are required in island tourism to reduce pollution of beaches and beach erosion, enhance biodiversity and promote social inclusivity to meet sustainable development goals. CSR can promote community support with further attention dedicated to the employee gender imbalance in the hospitality sector [179,186].

6. Conclusions and Suggestions for Future Research

An important remark is that our study was conducted in a pre-COVID-19 context. Since the start of the global health pandemic, there has been significant changes in tourist numbers due to travel restrictions imposed by many nations across the globe. SARS-COV-2 has had important implications for the travel and tourism businesses globally. As businesses start to re-open in some destinations, the need for sustainable business models and practices is being increasingly recognized. Our findings will be even more important in the post pandemic context to encourage businesses to further align employees' and customers' expectations to promote sustainable tourism development hence collectively contributing to the sustainable development goals.

Organizational corporate social responsibility managers can build on our study's findings to promote pro-sustainable cultures across management, employees and customers and hence contribute to achieving a better and more responsible society and contribute to planetary health. Our model has been tested in developing island states of the Indian Ocean. Future researchers are encouraged to replicate the study in other island destinations such as the Caribbean and the Pacific, this would have important implications for sustainable tourism development in small island developing states. The present study was conducted in a five-star group of hotels. Future researchers can test the model across different star-rating hotels to shed further light on the interactions of the relationships.

Author Contributions: Conceptualization, H.R. and F.M.; methodology, F.M., H.R. and V.S.; software, F.M., H.R. and V.S.; validation, F.M., H.R. and V.S.; formal analysis, H.R. and F.M. investigation, H.R., F.M. and V.S.; resources, H.R., F.M. and V.S.; data curation, H.R., F.M. and V.S.; writing—original draft preparation, H.R., F.M. and V.S.; writing—review and editing, H.R. and F.M.; visualization, H.R. and F.M.; supervision, H.R. and F.M. All authors have read and agreed to the published version of the manuscript.

References

1. UNWTO Annual Report 2016. Available online: https://www.e-unwto.org/doi/book/10.18111/9789284418725 (accessed on 1 May 2019).
2. United Nations Summit on Sustainable Development 2015, Informal Summary. Available online: https://sustainabledevelopment.un.org/content/documents/8521Informal%20Summary%20-%20UN%20Summit%20on%20Sustainable%20Development%202015.pdf (accessed on 1 May 2019).
3. Hristov, D.; Ramkissoon, H. Leadership in destination management organisations. *Ann. Tour. Res.* **2016**, *61*, 230–234. [CrossRef]
4. Scheyvens, R.; Biddulph, R. Inclusive tourism development. *Tour. Geogr.* **2018**, *20*, 589–609. [CrossRef]
5. He, H.; Harris, L. The Impact of Covid-19 Pandemic on Corporate Social Responsibility and Marketing Philosophy. *J. Bus Res.* **2020**, *116*, 176–182. [CrossRef] [PubMed]
6. Scheyvens, R.; Banks, G.; Hughes, E. The private sector and the SDGs: The need to move beyond 'business as usual'. *Sust. Dev.* **2016**, *24*, 371–382. [CrossRef]
7. Saarinen, J.; Rogerson, C.M. Tourism and the millennium development goals: Perspectives beyond 2015. *Tour Geog.* **2014**, *16*, 23–30. [CrossRef]
8. Ineson, E.M.; Benke, E.; László, J. Employee loyalty in Hungarian hotels. *Int. J. Hosp. Man.* **2013**, *32*, 31–39. [CrossRef]
9. Zhao, X.R.; Mattila, A.S. Examining the spillover effect of frontline employees' work–family conflict on their affective work attitudes and customer satisfaction. *Int. J. Hosp. Manag.* **2013**, *33*, 310–315. [CrossRef]
10. Deery, M.; Jago, L. A framework for work–life balance practices: Addressing the needs of the tourism industry. *Tour. Hosp. Res.* **2009**, *9*, 97–108. [CrossRef]
11. Lawson, K.M.; Davis, K.D.; Crouter, A.C.; O'Neill, J.W. Understanding work-family spillover in hotel managers. *Int. J. Hosp. Manag.* **2013**, *33*, 273–281. [CrossRef]
12. Lashley, C. Costing staff turnover in hospitality service organisations. *J. Serv Res.* **2001**, *1*, 3–24.
13. Mayer, A.E. Human Rights as a Dimension of CSR: The Blurred Lines Between Legal and Non-Legal Categories. *J. Bus. Ethic-* **2009**, *88*, 561–577. [CrossRef]
14. Sanjeev, G.M.; Birdie, A.K. The tourism and hospitality industry in India: Emerging issues for the next decade. *Worldw. Hosp. Tour. Themes* **2019**, *11*, 355–361. [CrossRef]
15. Sen, K.; Bhattacharya, A. Attracting and managing talent, how are the top three hotel companies in India doing it? *Worldw. Hosp. Tour. Themes* **2019**, *11*, 404–417. [CrossRef]
16. Coles, T.; Fenclova, E.; Dinan, C. Tourism and corporate social responsibility: A critical review and research agenda. *Tour. Manag. Perspect.* **2013**, *6*, 122–141. [CrossRef]
17. Font, X.; Lynes, J. Corporate social responsibility in tourism and hospitality. *J. Sustain. Tour.* **2018**, *26*, 1027–1042. [CrossRef]
18. Baniya, R.; Rajak, K. Attitude, Motivation and barriers for csr engagement among travel and tour operators in Nepal. *J. Tour. Hosp. Educ.* **2020**, *10*, 53–70. [CrossRef]
19. Jamali, D.; Lund-Thomsen, P.; Jeppesen, S. SMEs and CSR in developing countries. *Bus. Soc.* **2017**, *56*, 11–22. [CrossRef]
20. El-Kassar, A.N.; Messarra, L.C.; El-Khalil, R. CSR, organizational identification, normative commitment, and the moderating effect of the importance of CSR. *J. Dev. Areas* **2017**, *51*, 409–424. [CrossRef]
21. Way, S.A.; Sturman, M.C.; Raab, C. What matters more? *Cornell Hosp. Q.* **2010**, *51*, 379–397. [CrossRef]
22. Bakker, A.B.; Albrecht, S.L.; Leiter, M.P. Key questions regarding work engagement. *Eur. J. Work. Organ. Psychol.* **2011**, *20*, 4–28. [CrossRef]
23. Epstein, M.J.; Roy, M.J. Sustainability in action: Identifying and measuring the key performance drivers. *Long Range Plan.* **2001**, *34*, 585–604. [CrossRef]
24. Crouch, C. CSR and Changing Modes of governance: Towards corporate noblesse oblige? In *Corporate Social Responsibility and Regulatory Governance*; Utting, P., Marques, J.C., Eds.; Palgrave Macmillan: London, UK, 2010; pp. 26–49.
25. Sowamber, V.; Ramkissoon, H.; Mavondo, F. Impact of sustainability practices on hospitality consumers' behaviors and attitudes: The case of LUX* Resorts & Hotels. In *Routledge Handbook of Hospitality Marketing*; Routledge: Abingdon, UK, 2017; pp. 384–396.

26. Dewnarain, S.; Ramkissoon, H.; Mavondo, F. Social customer relationship management in the hospitality industry. *J. Hosp.* **2019**, *1*, 1–14.

27. Bhattacharya, C.B.; Sen, S.; Korschun, D. Using corporate social responsibility to win the war for talent. *MIT Sloan Manag. Rev.* **2008**, *49*, 37–44.

28. Ramkissoon, H.; Sowamber, V. Local support in tourism in Mauritius. In *Routledge Handbook of Tourism in Africa*; Novelli, M., Adu-Among, M.E., Ribeiro, A., Eds.; Routledge: London, UK, 2020.

29. Torelli, R.; Balluchi, F.; Furlotti, K. The materiality assessment and stakeholder engagement: A content analysis of sustainability reports. *Corp. Soc. Responsib. Environ. Manag.* **2020**, *27*, 470–484. [CrossRef]

30. Baird, T.; Hall, C.M.; Castka, P.; Ramkissoon, H. Migrant Workers' Rights, Social Justice and Sustainability in Australian and New Zealand Wineries: A Comparative Context. In *Social Sustainability in the Global Wine Industry*; Palgrave Pivot: Cham, Switzerland, 2020; pp. 107–118.

31. Levy, S.E.; Park, S.-Y. An analysis of CSR activities in the lodging industry. *J. Hosp. Tour. Manag.* **2011**, *18*, 147–154. [CrossRef]

32. He, H.; Li, Y. CSR and service brand: The mediating effect of brand identification and moderating effect of service quality. *J. Bus. Ethics* **2011**, *100*, 673–688. [CrossRef]

33. Marin, L.; Ruiz, S.; Rubio, A. The role of identity salience in the effects of corporate social responsibility on consumer behavior. *J. Bus. Ethics* **2009**, *84*, 65–78. [CrossRef]

34. Gardberg, N.A.; Fombrun, C.J. Corporate citizenship: Creating intangible assets across institutional environments. *Acad. Manag. Rev.* **2006**, *31*, 329–346. [CrossRef]

35. Bello, F.G.; Kamanga, G. Drivers and barriers of corporate social responsibility in the tourism industry: The case of Malawi. *Dev. South. Afr.* **2020**, *37*, 181–196. [CrossRef]

36. Thompson, B.S.; Friess, D.A. Stakeholder preferences for payments for ecosystem services (PES) versus other environmental management approaches for mangrove forests. *J. Environ. Manag.* **2019**, *233*, 636–648. [CrossRef]

37. Strasdas, W. Corporate Responsibility among international ecotourism and adventure travel operators. In *Corporate Sustainability and Responsibility in Tourism*; Lund-Durlacher, D., Dinica, V., Reiser, D., Fifka, M., Eds.; Springer: Cham, Switzerland, 2019; pp. 143–161.

38. Iazzi, A.; Pizzi, S.; Iaia, L.; Turco, M. Communicating the stakeholder engagement process: A cross-country analysis in the tourism sector. *Corp. Soc. Responsib. Environ. Manag.* **2020**, *27*, 1642–1652. [CrossRef]

39. Bickford, N.; Smith, L.; Bickford, S.; Bice, M.R. Evaluating the role of CSR and SLO in ecotourism: Collaboration for economic and environmental sustainability of arctic resources. *Resources* **2017**, *6*, 21. [CrossRef]

40. Sheldon, P.J.; Park, S.Y. An exploratory study of corporate social responsibility in the US travel industry. *J. Travel Res.* **2011**, *50*, 392–407. [CrossRef]

41. Supanti, D.; Butcher, K.; Fredline, L. Enhancing the employer-employee relationship through corporate social responsibility (CSR) engagement. *Int. J. Contemp. Hosp. Manag.* **2015**, *27*, 1479–1498. [CrossRef]

42. Wells, V.K.; Manika, D.; Gregory-Smith, D.; Taheri, B.; McCowlen, C. Heritage tourism, CSR and the role of employee environmental behaviour. *Tour. Manag.* **2015**, *48*, 399–413. [CrossRef]

43. Jones, P.; Hillier, D.; Comfort, D. Sustainability in the hospitality industry. *Int. J. Contemp. Hosp. Manag.* **2016**, *28*, 36–67. [CrossRef]

44. Modica, P.D.; Altinay, L.; Farmaki, A.; Gursoy, D.; Zenga, M. Consumer perceptions towards sustainable supply chain practices in the hospitality industry. *Curr. Issues Tour.* **2020**, *23*, 358–375. [CrossRef]

45. Chathoth, P.K.; Ungson, G.R.; Harrington, R.J.; Chan, E.S. Co-creation and higher order customer engagement in hospitality and tourism services. *Int. J. Contemp. Hosp. Manag.* **2016**, *28*, 222. [CrossRef]

46. Okumus, F.; Altinay, L.; Chathoth, P.; Koseoglu, M.A. *Strategic Management for Hospitality and Tourism*; Routledge: Abingdon, UK, 2019.

47. Camilleri, M.A. Advancing the sustainable tourism agenda through strategic CSR perspectives. *Tour. Plan. Dev.* **2014**, *11*, 42–56. [CrossRef]

48. Homburg, C.; Wieseke, J.; Hoyer, W.D. Social identity and the service-profit chain. *J. Mark.* **2009**, *73*, 38–54. [CrossRef]

49. Jiang, Y.; Ramkissoon, H.; Mavondo, F. Destination marketing and visitor experiences: The development of a conceptual framework. *J. Hosp. Mark. Manag.* **2016**, *25*, 653–675. [CrossRef]

50. Ramkissoon, H. Hospitality consumers' decision-making. In *Routledge Handbook of Hospitality Marketing*; Routledge: Abingdon, UK, 2018; pp. 271–283.

51. Barakat, S.R.; Isabella, G.; Boaventura, J.M.G.; Mazzon, J.A. The influence of corporate social responsibility on employee satisfaction. *Manag. Decis.* **2016**, *54*, 2325–2339. [CrossRef]

52. Bauman, C.W.; Skitka, L.J. Corporate social responsibility as a source of employee satisfaction. *Res. Organ. Behav.* **2012**, *32*, 63–86. [CrossRef]

53. Dögl, C.; Holtbrügge, D. Corporate environmental responsibility, employer reputation and employee commitment: An empirical study in developed and emerging economies. *Int. J. Hum. Resour. Manag.* **2014**, *25*, 1739–1762. [CrossRef]

54. Wong, I.A.; Gao, J.H. Exploring the direct and indirect effects of CSR on organizational commitment. *Int. J. Contemp. Hosp. Manag.* **2014**, *26*, 500–525. [CrossRef]

55. Du, S.; Bhattacharya, C.; Sen, S. Reaping relational rewards from corporate social responsibility: The role of competitive positioning. *Int. J. Res. Mark.* **2007**, *24*, 224–241. [CrossRef]

56. Wang, Y.; Xu, S.; Wang, Y. The consequences of employees' perceived corporate social responsibility: A meta-analysis. *Bus. Ethic- A Eur. Rev.* **2020**, *29*, 471–496. [CrossRef]

57. Wagner, T.; Lutz, R.J.; Weitz, B.A. Corporate Hypocrisy: Overcoming the Threat of Inconsistent Corporate Social Responsibility Perceptions. *J. Mark.* **2009**, *73*, 77–91. [CrossRef]

58. Walker, M.; Heere, B.; Parent, M.M.; Drane, D. Social responsibility and the olympic games: The Mediating role of consumer attributions. *J. Bus. Ethics* **2010**, *95*, 659–680. [CrossRef]

59. Peasley, M.C.; Woodroof, P.J.; Coleman, J.T. Processing contradictory CSR information: The influence of primacy and recency effects on the consumer-firm relationship. *J. Bus. Ethics* **2020**, 1–15. [CrossRef]

60. Rim, H.; Park, Y.E.; Song, D. Watch out when expectancy is violated: An experiment of inconsistent CSR message cueing. *J. Mark. Commun.* **2020**, *26*, 343–361. [CrossRef]

61. Hillenbrand, C.; Money, K.; Ghobadian, A. Unpacking the mechanism by which corporate responsibility impacts stakeholder relationships. *Br. J. Manag.* **2011**, *24*, 127–146. [CrossRef]

62. Fishbein, M. A theory of reasoned action: Some applications and implications. *Neb. Symp. Motiv.* **1979**, *27*, 65–116.

63. Ajzen, I. *Attitudes, Personality and Behaviour*; Open University Press: Milton Keynes, UK, 1988.

64. Alam, S.S.; Akter, S.; Ahmed, M.H.U. Explaining firms' behavioral intention towards environmental reporting in Bangladesh: An application of theory of planned behavior. *J. Int. Bus. Manag.* **2020**, *3*, 1–12. [CrossRef]

65. Darus, F.; Sawani, Y.; Zain, M.M.; Janggu, T. Impediments to CSR assurance in an emerging economy. *Manag. Audit. J.* **2014**, *29*, 253. [CrossRef]

66. Brammer, S.; Millington, A.; Rayton, B. The contribution of corporate social responsibility to organizational commitment. *Int. J. Hum. Resour. Manag.* **2007**, *18*, 1701–1719. [CrossRef]

67. Peterson, D.K. The relationship between perceptions of corporate citizenship and organizational commitment. *Bus. Soc.* **2004**, *43*, 296–319. [CrossRef]

68. Hogg, M.A. Social identity theory. In *Understanding Peace and Conflict through Social Identity Theory*; Springer: Cham, Switzerland, 2016; pp. 3–17.

69. Dube, K.; Nhamo, G. Vulnerability of nature-based tourism to climate variability and change: Case of Kariba resort town, Zimbabwe. *J. Outdoor Recreat. Tour.* **2020**, *29*, 100281. [CrossRef]

70. Scott, D.; Hall, C.M.; Gössling, S. A review of the IPCC Fifth assessment and implications for tourism sector climate resilience and decarbonization. *J. Sustain. Tour.* **2016**, *24*, 8–30. [CrossRef]

71. Rutty, M.; Gössling, S.; Scott, D.; Michael Hall, C. The global effects and impacts of tourism. In *The Routledge Handbook of Tourism and Sustainability*; Rutty, M., Gössling, S., Scott, D., Michael Hall, C., Eds.; Routledge: London, UK, 2015; pp. 36–62.

72. Scott, D.; Gössling, S.; Hall, C.M. International tourism and climate change. *Wiley Interdiscip. Rev. Clim. Chang.* **2012**, *3*, 213–232. [CrossRef]

73. UNWTO Annual Report. 2015. Available online: https://www.e-unwto.org/doi/pdf/10.18111/9789284418039 (accessed on 2 May 2019).

74. McCabe, S. *The Routledge Handbook of Tourism Marketing*; Routledge: London, UK, 2014.

75. Ramkissoon, H.; Smith LD, G.; Weiler, B. Testing the dimensionality of place attachment and its relationships with place satisfaction and pro-environmental behaviours: A structural equation modelling approach. *Tour. Manag.* **2013**, *36*, 552–566. [CrossRef]

76. Gössling, S.; Scott, D.; Hall, C.M. Pandemics, tourism and global change: A rapid assessment of COVID-19. *J. Sustain. Tour.* **2020**, *29*, 1–20. [CrossRef]

77. Scott, D.; Gössling, S.; Hall, C.M.; Peeters, P. Can tourism be part of the decarbonized global economy? The costs and risks of alternate carbon reduction policy pathways. *J. Sustain. Tour.* **2015**, *24*, 1–21. [CrossRef]

78. United Nations Environment Programme (UNEP) Report 2015. Available online: https://www.unenvironment.org/annualreport/2015/en/index.html (accessed on 14 May 2019).

79. MET Report 2017. Available online: https://www.metoffice.gov.uk/research/news/2018/annual-state-of-the-climate-report-for-2017-now-published (accessed on 5 May 2019).

80. Majeed, S.; Ramkissoon, H. Health, wellness and place attachment during and post health pandemics. *Front. Psychol.* **2020**, *11*, 3026.

81. Higgins-Desbiolles, F. Socialising tourism for social and ecological justice after COVID-19. *Tour. Geogr.* **2020**, *22*, 610–623. [CrossRef]

82. Nunkoo, R.; Ramkissoon, H. Stakeholders' views of enclave tourism: A grounded theory approach. *J. Hosp. Tour. Res.* **2016**, *40*, 557–558. [CrossRef]

83. Hristov, D.; Minocha, S.; Ramkissoon, H. Transformation of destination leadership networks. *Tour. Manag. Perspect.* **2018**, *28*, 239–250. [CrossRef]

84. Ramkissoon, H.; Mavondo, F.T. Pro-environmental behavior: Critical link between satisfaction and place attachment in Australia and Canada. *Tour. Anal.* **2017**, *22*, 59–73. [CrossRef]

85. Xu, S.; Li, Y. Beware of the second wave of COVID-19. *Lancet* **2020**, *395*, 1321–1322. [CrossRef]

86. Wymer, W.; Polonsky, M.J. The limitations and potentialities of green marketing. *J. Nonprofit Public Sect. Mark.* **2015**, *27*, 239–262. [CrossRef]

87. Ramkissoon, H. COVID-19 Place confinement, pro-social, pro-environmental behaviors, and residents' wellbeing: A new conceptual framework. *Front. Psychol.* **2020**, *11*, 2248. [CrossRef] [PubMed]

88. Kotler, P.; Lee, N. *Social Marketing: Influencing Behaviors for Good*; Sage Publications: Thousand Oaks, CA, USA, 2008.

89. Truong, V.D. Social marketing: A systematic review of research 1998–2012. *Soc. Mark. Q.* **2014**, *20*, 15–34. [CrossRef]

90. Truong, V.D.; Dang, N.V.; Hall, C.M.; Dong, X.D. The internationalisation of social marketing research. *J. Soc. Mark.* **2015**, *5*, 357–376. [CrossRef]

91. De Grosbois, D. Corporate social responsibility reporting by the global hotel industry: Commitment, initiatives and performance. *Int. J. Contemp. Hosp. Manag.* **2012**, *31*, 896–905. [CrossRef]

92. Dodds, R.; Joppe, M. *CSR in the Tourism Industry? The Status of and Potential for Certification, Codes of Conduct and Guidelines*; IFC: Washington, DC, USA, 2005.

93. Uduji, J.I.; Okolo-Obasi, E.N.; Asongu, S.A. Sustaining cultural tourism through higher female participation in Nigeria: The role of corporate social responsibility in oil host communities. *Int. J. Tour. Res.* **2020**, *22*, 120–143. [CrossRef]

94. Font, X.; Walmsley, A.; Cogotti, S.; McCombes, L.; Häusler, N. Corporate social responsibility: The disclosure–performance gap. *Tour. Manag.* **2012**, *33*, 1544–1553. [CrossRef]

95. Tsai, H.; Tsang, N.K.; Cheng, S.K. Hotel employees' perceptions on corporate social responsibility: The case of Hong Kong. *Int. J. Hosp. Manag.* **2012**, *31*, 1143–1154. [CrossRef]

96. Waddock, S.A.; Bodwell, C.; Graves, S.B. Responsibility: The new business imperative. *Acad. Manag. Perspect.* **2002**, *16*, 132–148. [CrossRef]

97. Andriof, J.; Waddock, S. Unfolding stakeholder engagement. In *Unfolding Stakeholder Thinking*; Routledge: Abingdon, UK, 2017; pp. 19–42.

98. Ramkissoon, H.; Mavondo, F.T. Managing customer relationships in hotel chains: A comparison between guest and manager perceptions. In *The Routledge Handbook of Hotel Chain Management*; Routledge: Abingdon, UK, 2016; pp. 295–304.

99. Chiang, C.F.; Jang, S.S. The antecedents and consequences of psychological empowerment: The case of Taiwan's hotel companies. *J. Hosp. Tour. Res.* **2008**, *32*, 40–61. [CrossRef]

100. Park, S.Y.; Levy, S. Corporate social responsibility: Perspectives of hotel frontline employees. *Int. J. Contemp. Hosp. Manag.* **2014**, *26*, 332–348. [CrossRef]

101. Choi, B.; La, S. The impact of corporate social responsibility (CSR) and customer trust on the restoration of loyalty after service failure and recovery. *J. Serv. Mark.* **2013**, *27*, 223–233. [CrossRef]

102. Carroll, A.B.; Laasch, O. From managerial responsibility to CSR and back to responsible management. In *The Research Handbook of Responsible Management*; Edward Elgar: Cheltenham, UK, 2020.

103. Kim, C.H.; Scullion, H. The effect of Corporate Social Responsibility (CSR) on employee motivation: A cross-national study. *Pozn. Univ. Econ. Rev.* **2013**, *13*, 5–30.

104. Schaefer, S.D.; Terlutter, R.; Diehl, S. Talking about CSR matters: Employees' perception of and reaction to their company's CSR communication in four different CSR domains. *Int. J. Advert.* **2020**, *39*, 191–212. [CrossRef]

105. Lee, E.M.; Park, S.Y.; Lee, H.J. Employee perception of CSR activities: Its antecedents and consequences. *J. Bus. Res.* **2013**, *66*, 1716–1724. [CrossRef]

106. Ramkissoon, H.; Mavondo, F.; Uysal, M. Social involvement and park citizenship as moderators for quality-of-life in a national park. *J. Sustain. Tour.* **2018**, *26*, 341–361. [CrossRef]

107. Tingchi Liu, M.; Anthony Wong, I.; Rongwei, C.; Tseng, T.H. Do perceived CSR initiatives enhance customer preference and loyalty in casinos? *Int. J. Contemp. Hosp. Manag.* **2014**, *26*, 1024–1045. [CrossRef]

108. Becker-Olsen, K.L.; Cudmore, B.A.; Hill, R.P. The impact of perceived corporate social responsibility on consumer behavior. *J. Bus. Res.* **2006**, *59*, 46–53. [CrossRef]

109. Carvalho, S.W.; Sen, S.; Mota, M.D.O.; De Lima, R.C. Consumer reactions to CSR: A Brazilian perspective. *J. Bus. Ethic-* **2010**, *91*, 291–310. [CrossRef]

110. Lee, S.; Park, S.-Y. Do socially responsible activities help hotels and casinos achieve their financial goals? *Int. J. Hosp. Manag.* **2009**, *28*, 105–112. [CrossRef]

111. Tajfel, H.; Turner, J.C. The social identity theory of intergroup behavior. In *Psychology of Intergroup Relations*; Worchel, S., Austin, W.G., Eds.; Nelson-Hall Publishers: Chicago, IL, USA, 1986; pp. 7–24.

112. Kim, H.R.; Lee, M.; Lee, H.T.; Kim, N.M. Corporate social responsibility and employee–company identification. *J. Bus. Ethics* **2010**, *95*, 557–569. [CrossRef]

113. Hess, D.; Ford, C.L. Corporate corruption and reform undertakings: A new approach to an old problem. *Cornell Int. Law J.* **2008**, *41*, 307.

114. Albus, H.; Ro, H. Corporate social responsibility: The effect of green practices in a service recovery. *J. Hosp. Tour. Res.* **2013**. [CrossRef]

115. Pérez, A.; Del Bosque, I.R. Measuring CSR image: Three studies to develop and to validate a reliable measurement tool. *J. Bus. Ethic-* **2013**, *118*, 265–286. [CrossRef]

116. Pirsch, J.; Gupta, S.; Grau, S.L. A framework for understanding corporate social responsibility programs as a continuum: An exploratory study. *J. Bus. Ethics* **2007**, *70*, 125–140. [CrossRef]

117. Karatepe, O.M. High-performance work practices and hotel employee performance: The mediation of work engagement. *Int. J. Hosp. Manag.* **2013**, *32*, 132–140. [CrossRef]

118. Salanova, M.; Agut, S.; Peiró, J.M. Linking organizational resources and work engagement to employee performance and customer loyalty: The mediation of service climate. *J. Appl. Psychol.* **2005**, *90*, 1217–1227. [CrossRef]

119. Deng, X.; Kang, J.-K.; Low, B.S. Corporate social responsibility and stakeholder value maximization: Evidence from mergers. *J. Financial Econ.* **2013**, *110*, 87–109. [CrossRef]

120. Oliver, C. Sustainable competitive advantage: Combining institutional and resource-based views. *Strateg. Manag. J.* **1997**, *8*, 697–713. [CrossRef]

121. Turker, D. Measuring corporate social responsibility: A scale development study. *J. Bus. Ethics* **2009**, *85*, 411–427. [CrossRef]

122. Epler Wood, M.; Leray, T. *Corporate Responsibility and the Tourism Sector in Cambodia*; Working Paper, No. 34658; World Bank Group: Washington, DC, USA, 2005; p. 1.

123. Ketola, T. Do you trust your boss?—A Jungian analysis of leadership reliability in CSR. *Electron. J. Bus. Ethics Organ. Stud.* **2006**, *11*, 6–14.

124. Idemudia, U. Corporate social responsibility and developing countries. *Prog. Dev. Stud.* **2011**, *11*, 1–18. [CrossRef]

125. Levy, S.E.; Hawkins, D.E. Peace through tourism: Commerce based principles and practices. *J. Bus. Ethic-* **2009**, *89*, 569–585. [CrossRef]

126. Kalisch, A. *Corporate Futures: Social Responsibility in the Tourism Industry; Consultation On Good Practice*; Tourism Concern: London, UK, 2002.

127. Lin, L.W. Corporate social responsibility in China: Window dressing or structural change. *Berkeley J. Int. Law* **2010**, *28*, 64. [CrossRef]

128. Cacioppe, R.; Forster, N.; Fox, M. A survey of managers' perceptions of corporate ethics and social responsibility and actions that may affect companies' success. *J. Bus. Ethic-* **2007**, *82*, 681–700. [CrossRef]

129. Ashley, C.; Haysom, G. From philanthropy to a different way of doing business: Strategies and challenges in integrating pro-poor approaches into tourism business. *Dev. South. Afr.* **2006**, *23*, 265–280. [CrossRef]

130. Barroso Castro, C.; Martín Armario, E.; Martín Ruiz, D. The influence of employee organizational citizenship behavior on customer loyalty. *Int. J. Serv. Ind. Manag.* **2004**, *15*, 27–53. [CrossRef]

131. Mackenzie, M.; Peters, M. Hospitality managers' perception of corporate social responsibility: An explorative study. *Asia Pac. J. Tour. Res.* **2014**, *19*, 257–272. [CrossRef]

132. Greening, D.W.; Turban, D.B. Corporate social performance as a competitive advantage in attracting a quality workforce. *Bus. Soc.* **2000**, *39*, 254–280. [CrossRef]

133. Rupp, D.E.; Ganapathi, J.; Aguilera, R.V.; Williams, C.A. Employee reactions to corporate social responsibility: An organizational justice framework. *J. Organ. Behav.* **2006**, *27*, 537–543. [CrossRef]

134. Korschun, D.; Bhattacharya, C.; Swain, S.D. Corporate social responsibility, customer orientation, and the job performance of frontline employees. *J. Mark.* **2014**, *78*, 20–37. [CrossRef]

135. Bartel, C.A. Social comparisons in boundary-spanning work: Effects of community outreach on members' organizational identity and identification. *Adm. Sci. Q.* **2001**, *46*, 379–413. [CrossRef]

136. Luo, X.; Bhattacharya, C.B. Corporate social responsibility, customer satisfaction, and market value. *J. Mark.* **2006**, *70*, 1–18. [CrossRef]

137. Sen, S.; Bhattacharya, C.B. Does doing good always lead to doing better? Consumer reactions to corporate social responsibility. *J. Mark. Res.* **2001**, *38*, 225–243. [CrossRef]

138. Lichtenstein, D.R.; Drumwright, M.E.; Braig, B.M. The effect of corporate social responsibility on customer donations to corporate-supported nonprofits. *J. Mark.* **2004**, *68*, 16–32. [CrossRef]

139. Bhattacharya, C.B.; Sen, S. Consumer-company identification: A framework for understanding consumers' relationships with companies. *J. Mark.* **2003**, *67*, 76–88. [CrossRef]

140. Dewnarain, S.; Ramkissoon, H.; Mavondo, F. Social customer relationship management: An integrated conceptual framework. *J. Hosp. Mark. Manag.* **2019**, *28*, 172–188. [CrossRef]

141. Makower, J. *Beyond the Bottom Line*; Simon: New York, NY, USA, 1994.

142. Wilson, A.; Zeithaml, V.; Bitner, M.J.; Gremler, D. *Services Marketing: Integrating Customer Focus across the Firm*; McGraw-Hill Education: London, UK, 2016.

143. McKercher, B.; Mackenzie, M.; Prideaux, B.; Pang, S. Is the hospitality and tourism curriculum effective in teaching personal social responsibility? *J. Hosp. Tour. Res.* **2012**. [CrossRef]

144. Soron, D. Sustainability, self-identity and the sociology of consumption. *Sustain. Dev.* **2010**, *18*, 172–181. [CrossRef]

145. Brown, T.J.; Mowen, J.C.; Donavan, D.T.; Licata, J.W. The Customer Orientation of Service Workers: Personality Trait Effects on Self-and Supervisor Performance Ratings. *J. Mark. Res.* **2002**, *39*, 110–119. [CrossRef]

146. Hemingway, C.A.; Maclagan, P.W. Managers' personal values as drivers of corporate social responsibility. *J. Bus. Ethics* **2004**, *50*, 33–44. [CrossRef]

147. Chi, C.G.; Gursoy, D. Employee satisfaction, customer satisfaction, and financial performance: An empirical examination. *Int. J. Contemp. Hosp. Manag.* **2009**, *28*, 245–253. [CrossRef]

148. Hartline, M.D.; Jones, K.C. Employee performance cues in a hotel service environment: Influence on perceived service quality, value, and word-of-mouth intentions. *J. Bus. Res.* **1996**, *35*, 207–215. [CrossRef]

149. Liao, H.; Chuang, A. A multilevel investigation of factors influencing employee service performance and customer outcomes. *Acad. Manag. J.* **2004**, *47*, 41–58.

150. Lee, S.; Heo, C.Y. Corporate social responsibility and customer satisfaction among US publicly traded hotels and restaurants. *Int. J. Hosp. Manag.* **2009**, *28*, 635–637. [CrossRef]

151. Finn, A. Customer delight: Distinct construct or zone of nonlinear response to customer satisfaction? *J. Serv. Res.* **2012**, *15*, 99–110. [CrossRef]

152. Oliver, R.; Rust, R.; Varki, S. Customer delight: Foundations, findings, and managerial insight. *J. Retail.* **1997**, *73*, 311–336. [CrossRef]

153. Ramkissoon, H.; Mavondo, F. Proenvironmental behavior: The link between place attachment and place satisfaction. *Tour. Anal.* **2014**, *19*, 673–688. [CrossRef]

154. Torres, E.N.; Kline, S. From customer satisfaction to customer delight. *Int. J. Contemp. Hosp. Manag.* **2013**, *25*, 642–659. [CrossRef]

155. Torres, E.N.; Milman, A.; Park, S. Delighted or outraged? Uncovering key drivers of exceedingly positive and negative theme park guest experiences. *J. Hosp. Tour. Insights* **2018**, *1*, 65–85. [CrossRef]

156. Kumar, A.; Olshavsky, R.W.; King, M.F. Exploring alternative antecedents of customer delight. *J. Consum. Satisf. Dissatisfaction Complain. Behav.* **2001**, *14*, 14.

157. Crotts, J.C.; Magnini, V.P. The customer delight construct. *Ann. Tour. Res.* **2011**, *38*, 719–722. [CrossRef]

158. Fuller, J.; Matzler, K.; Faullant, R. Asymmetric effects in customer satisfaction. *Ann. Tour. Res.* **2006**, *33*, 1159–1163. [CrossRef]

159. Oliver, R.L. Cognitive, affective, and attribute bases of the satisfaction response. *J. Consum. Res.* **1993**, *20*, 418–430. [CrossRef]

160. Urry, J. The consumption of tourism. *Sociology* **1990**, *24*, 23–35. [CrossRef]

161. Nunkoo, R.; Ramkissoon, H. Developing a community support model for tourism. *Ann. Tour. Res.* **2011**, *38*, 964–988. [CrossRef]

162. Ramkissoon, H.; Uysal, M.S. The effects of perceived authenticity, information search behaviour, motivation and destination imagery on cultural behavioural intentions of tourists. *Curr. Issues Tour.* **2011**, *14*, 537–562. [CrossRef]

163. Nunkoo, R.; Smith, S.L.; Ramkissoon, H. Residents' attitudes to tourism: A longitudinal study of 140 articles from 1984 to 2010. *J. Sustain. Tour.* **2013**, *21*, 5–25. [CrossRef]

164. Akhshik, A.; Rezapouraghdam, H.; Ramkissoon, H. Industrialization of Nature in the Time of Complexity Unawareness: The Case of Chitgar Lake, Iran. *J. Hosp. Tour. Res.* **2020**. [CrossRef]

165. Hair, J.F.; Black, W.C.; Babin, B.J.; Anderson, R.E. *Multivariate Data Analysis*; Prentice Hall: Upper Saddle River, NJ, USA, 2010.

166. Waddock, S. Parallel universes: Companies, academics, and the progress of corporate citizenship. *Bus. Soc. Rev.* **2004**, *109*, 5–42. [CrossRef]

167. Nunkoo, R.; Ramkissoon, H. Structural equation modelling and regression analysis in tourism research. *Curr. Issues Tour.* **2012**, *15*, 777–802. [CrossRef]

168. Ramkissoon, H.; Mavondo, F.T. The satisfaction–place attachment relationship: Potential mediators and moderators. *J. Bus. Res.* **2015**, *68*, 2593–2602. [CrossRef]

169. Nunkoo, R.; Ramkissoon, H.; Gursoy, D. Use of structural equation modeling in tourism research: Past, present, and future. *J. Travel Res.* **2013**, *52*, 759–771. [CrossRef]

170. Fornell, C.; Larcker, D.F. Evaluating structural equation models with unobservable variables and measurement error. *J. Mark. Res.* **1981**, *28*, 39–50. [CrossRef]

171. McDonald, R.P.; Ho, M.-H.R. Principles and practice in reporting structural equation analyses. *Psychol. Methods* **2002**, *7*, 64–82. [CrossRef] [PubMed]

172. Collier, J.; Esteban, R. Corporate social responsibility and employee commitment. *Bus. Ethic- A Eur. Rev.* **2007**, *16*, 19–33. [CrossRef]

173. Boccia, F.; Malgeri Manzo, R.; Covino, D. Consumer behavior and corporate social responsibility: An evaluation by a choice experiment. *Corp. Soc. Responsib. Environ. Manag.* **2019**, *26*, 97–105. [CrossRef]

174. Randle, M.; Kemperman, A.; Dolnicar, S. Making cause-related corporate social responsibility (CSR) count in holiday accommodation choice. *Tour. Manag.* **2019**, *75*, 66–77. [CrossRef]

175. Feldman, P.M.; Vasquez-Parraga, A.Z. Consumer social responses to CSR initiatives versus corporate abilities. *J. Consum. Mark.* **2013**, *30*, 100–111. [CrossRef]

176. Pomering, A.; Dolnicar, S. Assessing the prerequisite of successful CSR implementation: Are consumers aware of CSR initiatives? *J. Bus. Ethic-* **2009**, *85*, 285–301. [CrossRef]

177. Perks, K.J.; Farache, F.; Shukla, P.; Berry, A. Communicating responsibility-practicing irresponsibility in CSR advertisements. *J. Bus. Res.* **2013**, *66*, 1881–1888. [CrossRef]

178. Öberseder, M.; Schlegelmilch, B.B.; Murphy, P.E. CSR practices and consumer perceptions. *J. Bus. Res.* **2013**, *66*, 1839–1851. [CrossRef]

179. Nunkoo, R.; Ramkissoon, H. Gendered theory of planned behaviour and residents' support for tourism. *Curr. Issues Tour.* **2010**, *13*, 525–540. [CrossRef]

180. Ramkissoon, H.R.; Smith LD, G. The relationship between environmental worldviews, emotions and personal efficacy in climate change. *Int. J. Arts Sci.* **2014**, *7*, 93.

181. Pope, S.; Wæraas, A. CSR-washing is rare: A conceptual framework, literature review, and critique. *J. Bus. Ethics* **2016**, *137*, 173–193. [CrossRef]

182. Chen, H.S.; Jai, T.M. Waste less, enjoy more: Forming a messaging campaign and reducing food waste in restaurants. *J. Qual. Assur. Hosp. Tour.* **2018**, *19*, 495–520. [CrossRef]

183. Schwartz, M.S.; Carroll, A.B. Integrating and unifying competing and complementary frameworks: The search for a common core in the business and society field. *Bus. Soc.* **2008**, *47*, 148–186. [CrossRef]

184. Strand, R.; Freeman, R.E.; Hockerts, K. Corporate social responsibility and sustainability in Scandinavia: An overview. *J. Bus. Ethics* **2015**, *127*, 1–15. [CrossRef]

185. Austin, L.; Gaither, B.M. Perceived motivations for corporate social responsibility initiatives in socially stigmatized industries. *Public Relat. Rev.* **2017**, *43*, 840–849. [CrossRef]

186. Spence, L.J. The obfuscation of gender and feminism in CSR research and the academic community: An essay. In *Gender Equality and Responsible Business*; Routledge: Abingdon, UK, 2017; pp. 16–30.

4

A Study of the Relationship between Corporate Social Responsibility Report and the Stock Market

An-An Chiu [1], Ling-Na Chen [2,*] and Jiun-Chen Hu [2]

[1] Department of International Business, College of Business, Feng Chia University, Taichung 40724, Taiwan; aachiu@fcu.edu.tw

[2] Department of Accounting and Information Technology, College of Management, National Chung-Cheng University, Chiayi 621301, Taiwan; a12577364020@gmail.com

*   Correspondence: cln1010625@gmail.com

Abstract: This study mainly investigates the relationship between corporate social responsibility (CSR) reporting and the reaction in the stock market. Specifically, we utilize the data from Taiwanese stock market from 2012 to 2017 to examine whether the CSR report disclosed by the listed companies on the Taiwan Stock Exchange and the Taipei Exchange will cause abnormal returns on the short-, mid- or long-term horizon. The empirical results demonstrate that companies which disclose their CSR reports generate higher and more positive mid- to long-term abnormal returns than undisclosed companies. In addition to filling the gap of previous studies, this study also examines whether CSR reports mitigate the information asymmetry between management and stakeholders. Companies disclosing their CSR reports will boost the confidence of investors and lead to higher stock return valuations.

Keywords: corporate social responsibility report; CSR; ESG; abnormal return; event study

1. Introduction

Corporate social responsibility (CSR) was developed by Bowen in 1953. Amid the rapid development of the global economy and technologies, environmental protection is rising in awareness. Thus, CSR has become an important agenda for industries, governments, and academics. Crifo and Forget [1] suggest that CSR integrates social, environmental, ethical, human rights, and consumer issues into business operations and core strategies to maximize the benefits of shareholders and stakeholders. Shih et al. [2] posit that in addition to the pursuit of better profits and performance, companies should take responsibilities and obligations regarding society and the environment. In brief, CSR is a firm's efforts to create value for the society while it is seeking profits, which is achieved through adherence to moral standards and accountability to all stake holders. Owing to the separation of enterprise ownership and management rights, the owner hires managers to operate the company and managers should aim to pursue the company's values. However, the information asymmetry exists between shareholders and managers. Thus, the moral crisis may cause managers not to aim at pursuing the company's maximum value but pursing self-interest. Under this condition, managers will cause the company to lose their values. Given the information asymmetry, the disclosure of non-financial information enhances transparency, which can make investors accurately value firms. Kao et al. [3] found that socially responsible companies disclose their sustainability performance in CSR reports, which complements financial reports and keeps stakeholders informed of the strategy and allows information users to understand the firm value and the capability in business sustainability.

As the pursuit of carbon reduction and environmental protection has become a global consensus, the disclosure of environmental information is increasingly sophisticated, and consumers have started to pay attention to CSR issues. With the rise of citizenship and civic justice, environmental awareness and information transparency, stakeholders are increasingly concerned about social environmental pollution issues. Investment decisions will also be targeted at the environment, sustainability and governance (ESG) of the assessment [4]. CSR describes a company's socially responsible commitment, efforts and practices. On the other hand, ESG is a set of standards/criteria for investors and other stakeholders to evaluate a company's environmental, social and governance performance. The ESG concept proposed in the report of the United Nations Principles of Responsible Investment, which suggests that related-investors and stakeholders make their decisions should consider the key factor-ESG scores. In practice, management consulting firms and investors have widely used ESG scores as a major index to understand a firm's overall CSR performance. Besides the traditional financial information, CSR reports or ESG reports have become an irresistible global trend for enterprises to meet the needs of stakeholders and to disclose non-financial information [5]. Bowman and Haire [6] indicate that CSR initiatives enhance the social reputation, brand images, and competitiveness of companies, which leads to better performance and stronger financial results [7]. Socially conscious investors are willing to pay a premium for the shares of these companies [8]. This is why CSR achievements improve financial performances and bolster investors' confidence and willingness to invest. This in turn boosts the short-term and long-term performances of stock returns. In response to the global trends for CSR and its increasing importance, Taiwan has been promoting this idea to the public and to society since 2002. Companies can publish CSR reports voluntarily.

The Kaohsiung gas explosions and the Ting Hsin food scandals have dented the public's trust in Taiwan. To keep up with the global emphasis on CSR reports and to salvage citizens' confidence, the Financial Supervisory Commission (FSC) of Taiwan on 18 September 2014 announced the mandatory requirement for four groups of listed companies to compile CSR reports. The requirements for the first group of listed companies are particularly stringent in that CSR reports should be accompanied with opinions issued by auditors. This policy demonstrates the Taiwan government's ambition to address corporate social responsibilities for food and related industries and to embark on the era of mandatory CSR reporting. This disclosure requirement sets the tone for the development of CSR reports in Taiwan [9]. In contrast with overseas literature [8,10–14], there are few studies in Taiwan regarding the roles and influences of CSR reports in the local stock market. Will this mandatory requirement for CSR reporting rescue the confidence of consumers and the investing public? Is this just a compliance exercise that adheres to regulatory requirements, without any information substance? Given the variances in cultural and legal systems, the research findings may differ. It is also worth noting that the percentage of Taiwanese firms that produce CSR reports is lower than that in other countries. These are the research motivations of this paper and the focus on stock market reactions to CSR reporting and disclosure.

This paper is trying to test whether the stock returns of the companies affected by the FSC's mandatory requirement for CSR reporting change significantly. In advance, we continue to examine whether CSR reporting causes positive abnormal returns both in the mid- and in the long term. This paper adopts the event study method. The first step is to examine whether the FSC's mandatory requirement announced on 18 September 2014 for CSR reporting and disclosure affected the stock returns of the firms concerned. Next, the study identifies the significant and positive returns on the stock returns of the listed companies that published CSR reports from 2012 to 2017, with event dates defined as the CSR reporting dates. The purpose is to explore whether the stock market reacts differently in different periods (before and after the requirement from the FSC) or to CSR reports of different natures (compulsory vs. voluntary).

The empirical findings of this paper suggest that those firms required to disclose CSR reporting mandatorily have negative stock returns after the announcement date. This possibly leads to investors' negative attitudes, as they believe that expenses may incur for CSR activities after compiling the CSR reports, which may damage shareholders' equity. In general, the firms publishing CSR reports show the positive and abnormal returns on their stock performances. This suggests that investors are optimistic about companies publishing CSR reports. This study divides the sample by the publication time (before or after the mandatory requirement) or by nature (voluntary vs. compulsory). The results indicate that investors have greater confidence in the CSR reports published after the mandatory requirement or voluntary disclosure than before the mandatory requirement or compulsory disclosure. The stock market has reacted positively to the CSR publications after the announcement of the mandatory requirement by the FSC.

This paper makes the following contributions. First, few studies have been conducted in Taiwan on the relationship between CSR reports and the stock market. In practice, there are both positive and negative viewpoints on the influence of the mandatory CSR reporting on the stock market. This paper hopes to fill this research gap. Second, the empirical study provides a full picture of how investors react to the mandatory CSR reporting and disclosure. To analyze the impact of CSR report disclosures of the listed companies, this paper collects and divides CSR reports into mandatory and voluntary samples. Finally, firms can observe whether CSR reports mitigate the information asymmetry between management and stakeholders. This will boost the confidence of investors and lead to higher stock return valuations, which can then enhance the firms' willingness toward CSR reporting and disclosures.

The following sections of this paper are organized as follows. Section 2 conducts a literature review on CSR reporting and stock markets and develops research hypotheses accordingly. Section 3 explains the sample selection, data sources, variable definitions, and empirical modeling. Section 4 summarizes the empirical results and analysis. Section 5 presents conclusions and suggestions.

2. Literature Review and Hypothesis Development

2.1. Regulations and Studies on CSR Reporting

The World Business Council for Sustainability and Development (WBCSD) defines CSR as the continuing commitment of the business to behave ethically and contribute to economic development while improving the quality of life of the workforce and their families as well as of the local community and society at large. Gu [15] suggests that CSR requires companies to care about employees, the society, the environment, and the government while seeking profits and being held accountable to shareholders. The purpose is to create the value for all stakeholders and achieve the business sustainability for companies. CSR reports are the disclosure of CSR activities, as well as goals, achievements, commitment, and plans in sustainable operations and corporate social responsibilities. Therefore, CSR reports can be viewed as an effective non-financial communication tool, to give information users a clear picture of firm values and provide the capability of business sustainability [16].

The preparation of financial reports is governed by accounting principles such as the U.S. Generally Accepted Accounting Principles (U.S. GAAP) of International Financial Reporting Standards (IFRS). Similarly, there is a number of standards on CSR reporting such as the OECD Guidelines for Multinational Enterprises, ISO14000 Series, United Nations Global Compact, and Global Reporting Initiative (GRI). Most companies follow the GRI standards in the compilation of CSR reports [16]. GRI guidelines start with environmental issues and then expand to an equal emphasis on the economy, the environment, and society. Companies disclose their CSR involvement in a systematic manner.

The publication of non-financial CSR reports has become a global trend. To achieve business sustainability and enhance competitiveness, companies must establish CSR practices [17,18]. KPMG Global has been conducting a KPMG Survey of Corporate Responsibility Reporting once every two years since 1993. According to its 2017 global survey, 93% of the top 250 companies (G250) have been releasing CSR reports. The top 100 companies (N100) in 45 countries are following suit, with the percentage of CSR reporting up from 73% in 2015 to 75% in 2017. The percentage of the top 100 companies in Taiwan that publish CSR reports also witnessed significant growth, from 77% in 2015 to 88% in 2017.

Du et al. [19] suggest that socially responsible companies foster positive attitudes and behaviors among stakeholders and establish good corporate and brand images. Fombrun et al. [20] posit that the engagement of public welfare activities helps to enhance corporate and brand images and boost firm competitiveness. Chi and Hsieh [21] indicate that CSR reports provide relevant information that can reduce the cost of the capital and mitigate the information asymmetry. However, some scholars hold opposite views and argue that CSR damages shareholders' interest and props up funding costs [6]. Ullmann [22] points out that CSR increases corporate costs, affects product development, and hampers firm competitiveness. Friedman [23] mentions that CSR is not part of management's job. The implementation of CSR engagements may cause cash outflows and infringe the trust relationship between managers and shareholders.

The empirical research on CSR, finance, and accounting tends to focus on the connection between CSR and financial performances. Most studies support this positive relation. Orlitzky et al. [24] suggest that CSR performance and financial results are positively correlated, and they often affect each other. Tsoutsoura [25] contends that greater CSR involvement denotes higher return on equity, return on assets, and return on sales. Cornell and Shapiro [26] develop the social impact hypothesis, in which meeting the expectations of non-shareholder stakeholders such as employees and customers will enhance corporate reputations and better financial performances. Lev et al. [7] argue that socially responsible companies attract socially conscious consumers and are able to create good sales and financial results. Shen and Chang [27] prove that the listed companies in Taiwan honoring corporate social responsibilities perform better than those who do not when measured with financial metrics such as pre-tax earnings and net income margins. Dhaliwal et al. [28] suggest that CSR affects financial achievements and firm values via avenues relevant to the finance.

2.2. Studies on CSR Reports and Stock Markets

Hannon and Milkovich [29] indicate that stock returns of the companies witness positive and abnormal returns after two days post-announcement on the offering of the best work environment. Richardson and Welker [8] suggest that socially conscious investors are willing to pay a premium for the securities of socially responsible companies. Anderson and Smith [10] posit that companies with higher scores in social responsibility perform better on their stock returns. Kempf and Osthoff [11] contend that CSR investment portfolios exhibit positive, significant, and abnormal returns and even a net of transaction costs. This indicates that better CSR performance implies more trusts from the investors. Arya and Zhang [12] and Marna et al. [13] highlight the positive influence of CSR announcements and the disclosure on stock returns. Huang et al. [30] examine both awarded companies and companies reporting unlawful incidences in Taiwan in 2005–2010 to explore the effect of positive and negative CSR event announcements on abnormal stock returns. According to the empirical findings, positive CSR event announcements lead to positive abnormal stock returns, while negative CSR event announcements result in negative abnormal stock returns. Ahmed et al. [14] indicate that the CSR performance and stock returns have significant and positive effects.

2.3. Research Hypotheses

Chang [31] applies the event study method in examining the stock returns of the top 30 listed companies in Taiwan according to the CSR rankings by Common Wealth Magazine by assessing the short-term announcement effects and the long-term stock return performance based on the announcement of the ranking results. The empirical results suggest that these top 30 companies report significantly higher returns than the index. Huang et al. [30] also use the event study method to explore the impact of positive (negative) CSR events on stock returns. The empirical findings support that positive event announcements trigger positive abnormal stock returns, while negative event announcements generate negative abnormal stock returns. According to Worrell et al. [32] and Clinebell and Clinebell [33], the announcements of layouts and factory closures lead to negative abnormal stock returns. Richardson and Welker [8] suggest that more CSR disclosures may entail higher costs. Yu et al. [34] examine the market reaction to the announcement of material information regarding the mandatory requirements of CSR reporting in 2014 and 2015. The empirical results indicate negative and significant responses in stock returns. Investors anticipate greater costs than benefits for the new policy of compulsory compilation of CSR reports. Therefore, this paper examines the negative market reaction to the mandatory CSR reports news from the FSC on 18 September 2014 based on the short-term response of the stock market. Thus, this paper develops the following hypotheses.

Hypothesis 1 (H1). *The news of the mandatory CSR disclosure for specific firms have a negative effect on short-term stock returns.*

Furthermore, this study extends the market reaction period to mid- and long-term responses. Since the mandatory disclosure of CSR reports is only imposed on specific firms, the benefits of disclosing CSR activities would offset the costs of preparing the CSR report in a longer examination period. Then, this paper develops the hypothesis as follows.

Hypothesis 2 (H2). *The mandatory CSR disclosure reports for specific firms shows insignificant impacts on mid- to long-term stock returns.*

Schadewitz and Niskala [35] argue that CSR reports in compliance with GRI guidelines are the corporate communication tool. The research indicates that CSR reporting has a positive influence on stock returns, primarily because CSR disclosure mitigates the information asymmetry, and investors can use accurate information in the assessment of the true value of companies. Lin and Fu [18] find that the CSR disclosure of the listed electronics companies in Taiwan helps to convey a positive message to the investors and reduce the information asymmetry between management and shareholders. Cheng [17] indicates that companies publishing CSR reports enjoy higher stock returns and lower cost of capital. Liu [36] suggests that CSR reporting has positive effects on stock returns. CSR awards also bolster stock returns. Dhaliwal et al. [28] show that CSR reporting and good CSR performance can effectively lower the cost of capital and attract long-term institutional investors.

CSR reports are a showcase of the achievements in CSR. They enhance the transparency of the sustainability information, reinforce the corporate accountability, and serve as an important tool for communicating with stakeholders. Therefore, this paper infers that CSR reporting and disclosure of non-financial information in business sustainability, which emphasizes the corporate governance, the environmental protection, and social engagements, help to reduce the information asymmetry between companies and investors and result in positive mid- to long-term stock returns. Hence, this paper develops the following hypotheses.

Hypothesis 3 (H3). *CSR disclosure reports have positive effects on mid- to long-term stock returns.*

In response to food safety problems, the FSC in 2014 stipulated that companies should publish CSR reports. At the same time, both the Taiwan Stock Exchange and the Taipei Exchange required the listed companies to refer to the most recent guidelines from the GRI for the preparation of CSR reports. This will improve the robustness of the disclosure in CSR reports, reduce the information asymmetry, and create information content for investors. As pointed out by Grossman [37], even if companies conceal unfavorable information in the published CSR reports, investors are likely to make reasonable conjectures anyway. Zhang and Kuo [38] posit that certified CSR reports provide better information content and value, as well as reliable information for investment decisions. This paper believes that investors have better confidence in the CSR reports published under the mandatory requirement from the FSC and hence develops the following hypothesis.

Hypothesis 4 (H4). *Firms that disclose CSR reports show mid- to long-term positive stock returns after the mandatory requirement.*

The other focus of this paper is on the voluntary and compulsory nature of CSR reports. Lin et al. [39] found a positive and significant effect between the voluntary disclosure of environmental protection spending and the value of the companies. However, there is no significant relationship between mandatory disclosure and firm values. Marna et al. [13] indicate that CSR information is important to stakeholders. At the same time, voluntary disclosure of CSR information affects stock returns. Lee and Wu [40] argue that if information disclosure is regular and can be anticipated by the market, the market response to information disclosure will be smaller than expected. The mandatory disclosure of CSR reports is an event that can be anticipated by the market. Therefore, the investors will expect all the companies subject to this requirement to release CSR reports each year. Thus, this paper infers that voluntary disclosure of CSR reports leads to better mid- to long-term stock returns compared to mandatory disclosure of CSR reports. Hence, the following hypothesis is developed.

Hypothesis 5 (H5). *Firms that voluntarily disclose CSR reports have positive mid- to long-term stock returns.*

3. Research Method

3.1. Data Sources and Sample Selection

This paper examines companies listed on the Taiwan Stock Exchange and the Taipei Exchange that published CSR reports under the stipulation from the FSC and those companies that published CSR reports from 2012 to 2017. The list of companies under the mandatory stipulation can be found in the FSC "List of Listed Companies That Should File CSR Reports" and "Survey by the Taipei Exchange on Mandatory Requirement for Preparation of CSR Reports". The CSR reports and stock returns are collected from the corporate governance database of the Taiwan Economic Journal. In total, 1414 observations were sampled as of 31 May 2017.

3.2. Variable Definitions

3.2.1. Dependent Variables

(1)   Cumulative Abnormal Returns (CAR)

The event study method examines whether an event causes abnormal changes in the stock returns. This paper uses the market model to calculate the CAR, which is the most widely used one. The abnormal return is defined as the differences between the actual return and the expected return. We compute the CAR by summing the abnormal returns over different horizons. A statistical test is performed to see whether there exist significant abnormal returns within the event period in order to validate whether the event has affected the stock return performance.

(2)   Buy-and-Hold Abnormal Returns (BHAR)

This paper calculates buy-and-hold abnormal returns (BHAR) based on the method developed by Barber and Lyon [41]. The BHAR of these companies is compared with the BHAR of the industry peers of comparable size, but which do not publish CSR reports. The BHAR of the investment portfolio is estimated with the simple weighted average of the BHAR of individual securities (i.e., sampled companies). A statistical test is performed to that of CAR in order to validate whether the event has affected the stock return performance.

3.2.2. Independent Variables

(1)   Companies subject to mandatory requirements (Mand): a dummy variable equals to 1 if the firm is required by the FSC to disclose a CSR report, and 0 otherwise.

(2)   Companies that publish CSR reports (CSR): a dummy variable equals to 1 if the firm publishes CSR report, and 0 otherwise.

(3)   Companies that publish CSR reports after the disclosure requirement imposed by the FSC (AftPlcy): a dummy variable equals to 1 if the firm discloses CSR report after the mandatory requirement, and 0 otherwise.

(4)   Companies that voluntarily publish CSR reports (Volunt): a dummy variable equals to 1 if the firm voluntary discloses CSR report, and 0 otherwise.

3.2.3. Control Variables

(1)   Size: Conrad et al. [42] indicate that stock returns of large firms react faster to information than those of small firms. This paper measures firm size with the natural logarithm of the beginning of the period's assets.

(2)   Institutional holdings (Inst): Badrinath et al. [43] observe that the higher the institutional holdings are, the faster stock returns respond to information compared to securities with lower institutional shareholdings. Institutional shareholdings are measured by the total number of shares held by institutional investors divided by the total number of ordinary shares outstanding.

(3)   Trading volume (Volm): Lee and Wu [40] indicate that shares with higher trading volumes react faster to major announcements. This paper refers to Lee and Swaminathan [44] by measuring trading volumes with share turnover ratios. This is calculated by the monthly trading volume of ordinary shares during the previous period divided by the total number of ordinary shares outstanding at the end of the previous period.

(4)   Market-to-book (MTB): Hung and Lei [45] highlight an inverse relation between market-to-book values and stock returns. Market-to-book are calculated with market value divided by book values.

(5)   Listed on Taiwan Stock Exchange (TSE): Lin et al. [46] suggest that the investment risks associated with companies listed on the Taipei Exchange are greater than those listed on the Taiwan Stock Exchange. The dummy variable is 1 for a firm listed on the Taiwan Securities Exchange and 0 otherwise.

(6)   Industry (Ind): The stock returns of companies in different industries react to information with different levels of sensitivity. Therefore, this paper incorporates industries as a dummy variable to observe how stock returns in different sectors respond to CSR reporting announcements.

(7)   Year: This paper incorporates years as a dummy variable to control the effect of individual years on the announcement regarding CSR reporting.

3.3. Establishment of the Empirical Model

This paper establishes a regression Equation (1) to validate H1: There will be short-term and negative effect on the stock returns of the companies affected by the mandatory requirement for CSR reporting.

$$CAR_i = \beta_0 + \beta_1 \, Mand + \beta_2 \, Size + \beta_3 \, Inst + \beta_4 \, Volm + \beta_5 \, MTB + \beta_6 \, TSE + \varepsilon_i \qquad (1)$$

This paper establishes a regression Equation (2) to validate H2: There will be insignificant impacts on the mid- to long-term stock returns of mandatory CSR disclosure reports for specific firms.

$$CAR_i = \beta_0 + \beta_1 \, Mand + \beta_2 \, Size + \beta_3 \, Inst + \beta_4 \, Volm + \beta_5 \, MTB + \beta_6 \, TSE + \sum \beta_\alpha \, Ind + \sum \beta_\gamma \, Year + \varepsilon_i \qquad (2)$$

This paper establishes regression Equation (3) to validate H2: The effect of CSR disclosure reports shows mid- to long-term positive stock returns.

$$CAR_{it} = \beta_0 + \beta_1 \, CSR + \beta_2 \, Size + \beta_3 \, Inst + \beta_4 \, Volm + \beta_5 \, MTB + \beta_6 \, TSE + \sum \beta_\alpha \, Ind + \sum \beta_\gamma \, Year + \varepsilon_{it} \qquad (3)$$

This paper establishes regression Equation (4) to validate H3: Firms that disclose CSR reports show mid- to long-term positive stock returns after the mandatory requirement for CSR disclosure.

$$CAR_{it} = \beta_0 + \beta_1 \, AftPlcy + \beta_2 \, Size + \beta_3 \, Inst + \beta_4 \, Volm + \beta_5 \, MTB + \beta_6 \, TSE + \sum \beta_\alpha \, Ind + \varepsilon_{it} \quad (4)$$

This paper establishes regression Equation (5) to validate H4: Firms that voluntary disclose CSR reports show mid- to long-term positive stock returns.

$$CAR_{it} = \beta_0 + \beta_1 \, Volunt + \beta_2 \, Size + \beta_3 \, Inst + \beta_4 \, Volm + \beta_5 \, MTB + \beta_6 \, TSE + \sum \beta_\alpha \, Ind + \sum \beta_\gamma \, Year + \varepsilon_{it} \quad (5)$$

To enhance the robustness of the research results, this paper measures abnormal returns by using buy-and-hold abnormal returns (BHAR) developed by Barber and Lyon [41] in the validation of the influence of CSR reports on mid- to long-term stock returns.

4. Empirical Results and Analysis

4.1. Descriptive Statistics

Table 1 summarizes the descriptive statistics of respective variables. The number of observations is 1414 for H1 and H2; 1335 for H3; and 833 for H4 and H5. First, the short-term cumulative abnormal returns (CAR_News) of dependent variables are estimated with the market model, to measure the short-term cumulative abnormal returns of the companies before and after the FSC's mandatory requirement for CSR reporting. The mean is 0.001, and the median is −0.001, indicating that more than half of the companies posted negative and abnormal returns during the event period. Second, the mid- to long-term cumulative abnormal returns (CAR_90, CAR_180, CAR_270, CAR_360, BHAR_90, BHAR_180, BHAR_270, BHAR_360) of dependent variables report medians are between −0.020 to −0.038, also indicating that more than half of the companies posted negative and abnormal returns during the mid- to long-term period.

Table 1. Summary Statistics.

Variable	N	Mean	Median	SD	Max	Min
CAR_News	1414	0.001	−0.001	0.049	0.940	−0.782
Mand	1414	0.139	0.000	0.346	1.000	0.000
CAR_90	1335	−0.002	−0.020	0.145	0.985	−0.632
CAR_180	1335	−0.003	−0.022	0.201	1.342	−0.809
CAR_270	1335	0.004	−0.025	0.258	1.545	−0.854
CAR_360	1335	0.003	−0.037	0.323	2.791	−0.918
BHAR_90	1335	0.001	−0.021	0.152	1.277	−0.653
BHAR_180	1335	0.000	−0.032	0.220	1.953	−0.669
BHAR_270	1335	0.011	−0.038	0.306	2.790	−0.668
BHAR_360	1335	0.024	−0.054	0.458	5.972	−0.721
CSR	1335	0.624	1.000	0.485	1.000	0.000
AftPlcy	833	0.435	0.000	0.496	1.000	0.000
Volunt	833	0.516	1.000	0.500	1.000	0.000
Size	1335	16.855	16.598	1.824	22.795	11.408
Inst	1335	0.145	0.091	0.156	0.802	0.000
Volm	1335	0.080	0.038	0.126	1.237	0.000
MTB	1335	1.616	1.131	2.050	51.729	0.199
TSE	1335	0.784	1.000	0.412	1.000	0.000

Note: The definitions for variables used in this paper can be found in Appendix A.

With regard to independent variables, the mean of the number of companies which are subject to the mandatory requirement (Mand) is 0.139. The mean of the number of companies publishing CSR reports (CSR) is 0.624. The mean is close to 0.5, as a published CSR report matches non-publication of a CSR report. The mean of the CSR reports published after the mandatory requirement (AftPlcy) is

0.435. This refers to the CSR reports released after 18 September 2014. The research period is from 2012 to 2017. Following the stipulation from FSC, the number of companies preparing CSR reports has increased over the years. The mean of the number of voluntarily published CSR reports (Volunt) is 0.516. The segmentation of voluntary and compulsory publication of CSR reports indicates that more reports are published as required.

As far as control variables are concerned, the mean of institutional holdings (Inst) is 14.5%. The maximum value is 80.2%, and some companies have zero institutional holdings. The mean of market-to-book (MTB) values is 1.616. The maximum is 51 (i.e., market capitalization as 51 times the book value), and the minimum is only 0.2. The mean of the companies listed on the Taiwan Stock Exchange (TSE) is 0.784, indicating that 78.4% of the sampled companies are listed on the main board.

4.2. Empirical Model and Regression Analysis

This paper continues with a regression analysis. H1 examines whether the news on the mandatory CSR disclosure reports for specific firms shows short-term negative stock returns. As summarized by Model 1 of Table 2, there is a negative and significant effect between firms subject to the mandatory requirement (Mand) and short-term cumulative abnormal returns (CAR_News) (coefficient = −0.011, t-value = −3.44 ***). When we control industry and year variables, shown in Model 2 of Table 2, there is also a negative and significant effect between firms subject to the mandatory requirement (Mand) and short-term cumulative abnormal returns (CAR_News) (coefficient = −0.015, t-value = −3.32 ***). This suggests that compared with firms not subject to the mandatory requirement, firms covered by the mandatory requirement reported short-term, negative, and abnormal stock returns. This is consistent with the literature [30,32,33]; therefore, H1 is supported.

Table 2. The Impact of Mandatory Disclosure News on Stock Returns (For H1).

	Dependent Variable: CAR News	
Variables	**Model 1**	**Model 2**
Constant	−0.035	−0.034
	(−1.37)	(−1.26)
Mand	−0.011	−0.015
	(−3.44) ***	(−3.32) ***
Size	0.001	0.002
	(1.09)	(1.30)
Inst	−0.025	−0.028
	(−1.98) **	(−2.04) **
Volm	14.53	5.058
	(2.56) **	(0.84)
MTB	1.158	1.103
	(1.14)	(1.03)
TSE	0.011	0.012
	(3.24) ***	(3.38) ***
Ind/Year Dummies	-	Yes
N	1414	1414
R^2	0.023	0.005
F-value	5.62 ***	1.96 ***

Note: The dependent variable is the cumulative abnormal returns (CAR_News) over the window (−2, +2) where the mandatory disclosure of CSR news is $t = 0$. The t-statistics in parentheses are based on heteroskedasticity-robust standard errors. The superscripts *, ** and *** denote statistical significance at the 10%, 5% and 1% levels, respectively. The variable inflation factor (VIF) values of the main variables are between 1.21 to 2.83, which preclude severe multicollinearity concerns. Detailed descriptions of variables can be found in Appendix A.

H2 examines whether insignificant impacts on the mid- to long-term stock returns of mandatory CSR disclosure reports are for specific firms. As summarized in Panel A and B of Table 3, there is a negative but not significant effect between firms subject to the mandatory requirement

(Mand) and mid-term cumulative abnormal returns (CAR_90, CAR_180, BHAR_90, BHAR_180) (coefficient = −0.013, −0.007, −0.015, −0.004; t-value = −1.02, −0.38, −1.21, −0.20). There is a positive but not significant effect between companies subject to the mandatory requirement (Mand) and long-term cumulative abnormal returns (CAR_270, CAR_360, BHAR_270, BHAR_360) (coefficient = 0.015, 0.010, 0.015, 0.027; t-value = 0.64, 0.35, 0.53, 0.68). This suggests that there are insignificant impacts on the mid- to long-term stock returns of mandatory CSR disclosure reports. This is consistent with the literature [40]. Therefore, H2 is supported.

H3 explores whether CSR disclosure reports show mid- to long-term positive stock returns. As shown in Panel A and B of Table 4, the publication of CSR reports (CSR) and the mid-term cumulative abnormal returns (CAR_90, BHAR_90) show positive and significant effects (coefficient = 0.208, 0.022; t-value = 2.31 **, 2.33 **). The publication of CSR reports (CSR) and the long-term cumulative abnormal returns (CAR_180, CAR_270, CAR_360, BHAR_180, BH_270, BHAR_360) show positive but not significant effects (coefficient = 0.019, 0.015, 0.032, 0.018, 0.015, 0.045; t-value = 1.47, 0.95, 1.59, 1.28, 0.81, 1.62). In general, this is consistent with the literature [12,13,36]. Hence, H3 is supported.

H4 seeks to validate whether disclosed CSR reports show mid- to long-term positive stock returns after the mandatory requirement for CSR disclosure. As shown in Panel A and B of Table 5, the release of CSR reports as mandatorily required (AftPlcy) and the mid-term cumulative abnormal returns (BHAR_180) show positive and but not significant effects (coefficient = 0.015; t-value = 0.96). The release of CSR reports as mandatorily required (AftPlcy) and long-term cumulative abnormal returns (CAR_270, CAR_360, BHAR_270, BHAR_360) show positive and significant effects (coefficient = 0.048, 0.061, 0.058, 0.061; t-value = 2.84 ***, 3.03 ***, 2.82 ***, 3.03 ***). In general, this is consistent with the literature. Hence, H4 is supported.

H5 examines whether voluntary publication of CSR reports yields better mid- to long-term stock returns compared with the required publication of CSR reports. As shown in Panel A and B of Table 6, voluntary disclosure of CSR reports (Volunt) and mid-term cumulative abnormal returns (CAR_90, BHAR_90) show positive and significant effects (coefficient = 0.025, 0.025; t-value = 1.90 *, 1.85 *). The voluntary disclosure of CSR reports (Volunt) and the long-term cumulative abnormal returns (CAR_360) show positive but not significant effects (coefficient = 0.004; t-value = 0.16). In general, this is consistent with the literature [13,17,39]. Therefore, H5 is supported.

This paper uses the variable inflation factor (VIF) to test the collinearity among variables in the regression models. As shown in Table 2 to Table 6, the VIF values of the main variables are between 1.03 to 3.15, which preclude severe multicollinearity concerns.

Table 3. The Relationship between Mandatory CSR Disclosure and Mid- to Long-term Stock Returns (For H2).

Variables	Panel A: Dependent Variable: CAR				Panel B: Dependent Variable: BHAR			
	CAR_90	CAR_180	CAR_270	CAR_360	BHAR_90	BHAR_180	BHAR_270	BHAR_360
Constant	-0.024	-0.071	-0.028	0.232	-0.029	-0.073	-0.051	0.428
	(-0.42)	(-0.81)	(-0.24)	(1.16)	(-0.49)	(-0.76)	(-0.40)	(1.26)
Mand	-0.013	-0.007	0.015	0.010	-0.015	-0.004	0.015	0.027
	(-1.02)	(-0.38)	(0.64)	(0.35)	(-1.21)	(-0.20)	(0.53)	(0.68)
Size	0.004	0.004	0.001	-0.005	0.004	0.004	0.002	-0.008
	(1.19)	(0.88)	(0.09)	(-0.54)	(1.29)	(0.86)	(0.32)	(-0.62)
Inst	-0.039	-0.111	-0.112	-0.074	-0.038	-0.119	-0.126	-0.089
	(-1.31)	(-2.70) ***	(-2.25) **	(-1.21)	(-1.25)	(-2.79) ***	(-2.21) **	(-1.15)
Volm	-11.294	8.815	10.525	-60.831	-7.139	19.120	23.875	-43.446
	(-0.31)	(0.19)	(0.17)	(-0.85)	(-0.20)	(0.41)	(0.37)	(-0.59)
MTB	-3.734	-5.085	-7.487	-18.794	-4.483	-6.366	-12.186	-25.910
	(-1.27)	(-1.22)	(-1.34)	(-2.79) ***	(-1.52)	(-1.42)	(-2.01) **	(-3.43) ***
TSE	-0.041	-0.046	-0.035	-0.037	-0.039	-0.048	-0.040	-0.054
	(-3.45) ***	(-2.80) ***	(-1.64)	(-1.29)	(-3.17) ***	(-2.72) ***	(-1.67) *	(-1.32)
Ind/Year Dummies	Yes	Yes	Yes	Yes	Yes	Yes	Yes	Yes
N	1231	1231	1231	1231	1231	1231	1231	1231
R^2	0.052	0.048	0.075	0.072	0.055	0.045	0.073	0.076
F-value	2.01 ***	2.20 ***	3.31 ***	2.72 ***	2.11 ***	2.24 ***	3.21 ***	2.41 ***

Note: The dependent variable is the mid- to long-term cumulative abnormal returns (CAR, shown in Panel A) and the buy-hold abnormal returns (BHAR, shown in Panel B). The measures for the mid- and long-term abnormal returns are based on the CSR disclosure date $t = 0$ and cumulative over 90, 180, 270, and 360 days, respectively. The t-statistics in parentheses are based on heteroskedasticity-robust standard errors. The superscripts *, **, and *** denote statistical significance at the 10%, 5%, and 1% levels, respectively. The VIF values of the main variables are between 1.30 to 3.15, which preclude severe multicollinearity concerns. Detailed descriptions of variables can be found in Appendix A.

Table 4. The Relationship between CSR Disclosure and Mid- to Long-term Stock Returns (For H3).

Variables	Panel A: Dependent Variable: CAR				Panel B: Dependent Variable: BHAR			
	CAR_90	CAR_180	CAR_270	CAR_360	BHAR_90	BHAR_180	BHAR_270	BHAR_360
Constant	−0.023	−0.055	−0.048	0.131	−0.032	−0.082	−0.107	0.206
	(−0.41)	(−0.69)	(−0.45)	(0.88)	(−0.55)	(−0.92)	(−0.86)	(0.93)
CSR	0.208	0.019	0.015	0.032	0.022	0.018	0.015	0.045
	(2.31) **	(1.47)	(0.95)	(1.59)	(2.33) **	(1.28)	(0.81)	(1.62)
Size	0.003	0.002	0.001	−0.008	0.004	0.003	0.005	−0.011
	(1.03)	(0.39)	(0.17)	(−0.91)	(1.11)	(0.62)	(0.62)	(−0.81)
Inst	−0.055	−0.081	−0.064	−0.022	−0.062	−0.095	−0.087	−0.039
	(−1.67) *	(−1.74) *	(−1.06)	(−0.30)	(−1.74) *	(−1.89) *	(−1.21)	(−0.43)
Volm	−0.044	−0.102	−0.138	−0.288	−0.049	−0.127	−0.161	−0.341
	(−1.23)	(−2.03) **	(−2.10) **	(−3.41) ***	(−1.36)	(−2.43) **	(−2.54) **	(−3.37) ***
MTB	−0.007	−0.009	−0.011	−0.011	−0.006	−0.008	−0.010	−0.014
	(−2.15) **	(−2.04) **	(−2.76) ***	(−4.23) ***	(−2.32) **	(−2.15) **	(−3.63) ***	(−0.014) ***
TSE	−0.040	−0.051	−0.047	−0.047	−0.039	−0.056	−0.058	−0.070
	(−3.58) ***	(−3.32) ***	(−2.27) **	(−1.74) *	(−3.29) ***	(−3.31) ***	(−2.40) **	(−1.79) *
Ind/Year Dummies	Yes	Yes	Yes	Yes	Yes	Yes	Yes	Yes
N	1335	1335	1335	1335	1335	1335	1335	1335
R²	0.063	0.054	0.080	0.075	0.063	0.050	0.077	0.078
F-value	2.24 ***	2.60 ***	3.55 ***	3.22 ***	2.27 ***	2.66 ***	3.49 ***	2.82 ***

Note: The dependent variable is the mid- to long-term cumulative abnormal returns (CAR, shown in Panel A) and the buy-hold abnormal returns (BHAR, shown in Panel B). The measures for the mid- and long-term abnormal returns are based on the CSR disclosure date $t = 0$ and cumulative over 90, 180, 270, and 360 days, respectively. The t-statistics in parentheses are based on heteroskedasticity-robust standard errors. The superscripts *, **, and *** denote statistical significance at the 10%, 5%, and 1% levels, respectively. The VIF values of the main variables are between 1.14 to 2.53, which preclude severe multicollinearity concerns. Detailed descriptions of variables can be found in Appendix A.

Table 5. The Relationship between After Policy CSR Disclosure and Mid- to Long-term Stock Returns (For H4).

Variables	Panel A: Dependent Variable: CAR				Panel B: Dependent Variable: BHAR			
	CAR_90	CAR_180	CAR_270	CAR_360	BHAR_90	BHAR_180	BHAR_270	BHAR_360
Constant	0.024	−0.009	0.102	0.207	0.028	−0.036	0.068	0.207
	(0.39)	(−0.11)	(0.102)	(1.57)	(0.44)	(−0.37)	(0.49)	(1.57)
AftPlcy	−0.004	−0.014	0.048	0.061	−0.005	0.015	0.058	0.061
	(−0.39)	(1.01)	(2.84)***	(3.03)***	(−0.52)	(0.96)	(2.82)***	(3.03)***
Size	0.002	0.001	0.001	−0.002	0.002	0.003	0.003	−0.002
	(0.56)	(0.15)	(0.08)	(−0.21)	(0.51)	(0.49)	(0.40)	(−0.21)
Inst	−0.076	−0.101	−0.108	−0.110	−0.082	−0.127	−0.138	−0.110
	(−1.71)*	(−1.73)*	(−1.32)	(−1.15)	(−1.66)*	(−1.95)*	(−1.36)	(−1.15)
Volm	−0.049	−0.113	−0.236	−0.283	−0.062	−0.134	−0.263	−0.283
	(−1.14)	(−1.78)*	(−3.11)***	(−2.84)***	(−1.35)	(−2.05)**	(−3.47)***	(−2.84)***
MTB	−0.002	0.001	−0.006	−0.016	−0.003	0.001	−0.009	−0.016
	(−0.63)	(0.18)	(−1.00)	(−2.38)**	(−0.80)	(0.17)	(−1.38)	(−2.38)**
TSE	−0.037	−0.041	−0.045	−0.059	−0.033	−0.044	−0.053	−0.059
	(−2.62)***	(−2.07)**	(−1.77)*	(−1.91)*	(−2.21)**	(−2.05)**	(−1.79)*	(−1.91)*
Ind dummy	Yes	Yes	Yes	Yes	Yes	Yes	Yes	Yes
N	833	833	833	833	833	833	833	833
R^2	0.073	0.058	0.092	0.103	0.075	0.059	0.092	0.103
F-value	2.53***	2.98***	4.18***	7.14***	2.64***	2.84***	3.79***	7.14***

Note: The dependent variable is the mid- to long-term cumulative abnormal returns (CAR, shown in Panel A) and the buy-hold abnormal returns (BHAR, shown in Panel B). The measures for the mid- and long-term abnormal returns are based on the CSR disclosure date $t = 0$ and cumulative over 90, 180, 270, and 360 days, respectively. The t-statistics in parentheses are based on heteroskedasticity-robust standard errors. The superscripts *, **, and *** denote statistical significance at the 10%, 5%, and 1% levels, respectively. The VIF values of the main variables are between 1.03 to 2.73, which preclude severe multicollinearity concerns. Detailed descriptions of variables can be found in Appendix A.

Table 6. The Relationship between Voluntary CSR Disclosure and Mid- to Long-term Stock Returns (For H5).

Variables	Panel A: Dependent Variable: CAR				Panel B: Dependent Variable: BHAR			
	CAR_90	CAR_180	CAR_270	CAR_360	BHAR_90	BHAR_180	BHAR_270	BHAR_360
Constant	−0.028	−0.017	0.148	0.254	−0.027	−0.034	0.134	0.309
	(−0.49)	(−0.20)	(1.27)	(1.89)*	(−0.45)	(−0.39)	(1.02)	(1.72)*
Volunt	0.025	0.010	−0.001	0.004	0.025	0.006	−0.001	−0.006
	(1.90)*	(0.56)	(−0.05)	(0.16)	(1.85)*	(0.28)	(−0.24)	(−0.16)
Size	0.004	0.001	−0.001	−0.003	0.004	0.003	0.002	−0.002
	(1.21)	(0.27)	(−0.08)	(−0.33)	(1.16)	(0.56)	(0.20)	(−0.21)
Inst	−0.074	−0.098	−0.100	−0.100	−0.080	−0.124	−0.129	−0.168
	(−1.68)*	(−1.68)*	(−1.22)	(−1.04)	(−1.64)*	(−1.91)*	(−1.26)	(−1.27)
Volm	−0.055	−0.122	−0.256	−0.310	−0.067	−0.142	−0.285	−0.350
	(−1.26)	(−1.91)*	(−3.32)***	(−3.00)***	(−1.45)	(−2.16)**	(−3.67)***	(−3.35)***
MTB	−0.003	0.001	−0.006	−0.016	−0.003	0.001	−0.009	−0.207
	(−0.79)	(0.12)	(−1.08)	(−2.53)**	(−0.96)	(0.13)	(−1.46)	(−2.82)***
TSE	−0.038	−0.043	−0.048	−0.064	−0.035	−0.046	−0.056	−0.805
	(−2.71)***	(−2.14)**	(−1.89)*	(−2.04)**	(−2.29)**	(−2.10)**	(−1.91)*	(−1.71)*
Ind dummy	Yes	Yes	Yes	Yes	Yes	Yes	Yes	Yes
N	833	833	833	833	833	833	833	833
R^2	0.076	0.058	0.083	0.092	0.079	0.058	0.082	0.126
F-value	2.56***	2.86***	4.3***	5.23***	2.59***	2.76***	3.99***	4.37***

Note: The dependent variable is the long-term cumulative abnormal returns (CAR, shown in Panel A) and the buy-hold abnormal returns (BHAR, shown in Panel B). The measures for the mid- and long-term abnormal returns are based on the CSR disclosure date $t = 0$ and cumulative over 90, 180, 270, and 360 days, respectively. The t-statistics in parentheses are based on heteroskedasticity-robust standard errors. The superscripts *, **, and *** denote statistical significance at the 10%, 5%, and 1% levels, respectively. The VIF values of the main variables are between 1.19 to 2.94, which preclude severe multicollinearity concerns. Detailed descriptions of variables can be found in Appendix A.

5. Conclusions and Suggestions

In response to various problems with food safety and environmental protection over recent years, the FSC announced on 18 September 2014 that four groups of companies listed on the Taiwan Stock Exchange and on the Taipei Exchange are required to file CSR reports. This paper is trying to answer the following questions. First, this paper examines whether the stock returns of the companies affected by the mandatory requirement by the FSC for CSR reporting change significantly. This is followed by sampling the companies listed on the Taiwan Stock Exchange and on the Taipei Exchange that published CSR reports in 2012–2017. The results indicate negative stock returns on the announcement days. This paper notes that the higher the institutional holdings are, the stronger the negative response is. In other words, both the investors and professional investors viewed unfavorably the mandatory requirement by the FSC for CSR reporting. This may be due to the expectation that the preparation of CSR reports needs to be substantiated with CSR activities and will incur upfront expenses that have direct effects on the financials.

Second, this paper aims to validate whether CSR reporting causes positive abnormal returns both in the mid- and the long-term. In general, the results indicate that firms publishing CSR reports show positive abnormal stock returns. This suggests the optimism among investors with companies that do publish CSR reports. The next step is to divide the sample of CSR reports according to the time point of publication (before or after the mandatory requirement) or by nature (voluntary vs. compulsory). The results indicate that investors have greater confidence in the CSR reports published after the mandatory requirement or voluntary disclosure than before the mandatory requirement or compulsory disclosure. The stock market has reacted positively to the CSR publications after the announcement of the mandatory requirement by the FSC.

In sum, the stock market reacts with short-term negative returns to the FSC's mandatory requirement for CSR reporting. However, the mid- to long-term abnormal stock returns of firms who are mandatorily required or voluntarily release CSR reports are higher than those that do not publish CSR reports. The abnormal returns on the stock returns of companies that publish CSR reports after the announcement of the FSC's requirement (on 18 September 2014) are relatively higher.

The publication of CSR reports in Taiwan is not classified as material information or a major announcement. The investors can only access CSR reports from firm websites. The fulfillment of CSR has become a focal point of attention from investors. The Taiwan government has been advised to categorize CSR announcements as material information. The findings of this paper establish an understanding of the short-term, mid-term and long-term market reactions to the FSCs' mandatory requirement for CSR reporting and the CSR disclosure by listed companies. The research results can serve as a reference to academics. For companies, the preparation of CSR reports is about describing and articulating their CSR strategies and activities, in order to mitigate information asymmetry between managers and investors. The overall purpose is to bolster the confidence among investors, generate stock returns, and enhance a willingness for CSR reporting.

Author Contributions: Conceptualization, A.-A.C.; Data curation, A.-A.C. and J.-C.H.; Formal analysis, A.-A.C., L.-N.C. and J.-C.H.; Investigation, L.-N.C. and J.-C.H.; Methodology, A.-A.C., L.-N.C. and J.-C.H.; Project administration, L.-N.C.; Resources, J.-C.H.; Software, L.-N.C. and J.-C.H.; Supervision, A.-A.C.; Validation, A.-A.C. and L.-N.C.; Visualization, A.-A.C. and L.-N.C.; Writing—original draft, L.-N.C. and J.-C.H.; Writing—review & editing, A.-A.C. and L.-N.C. All authors have read and agreed to the published version of the manuscript.

Appendix A

Variables	Definition
CAR_News	The cumulative abnormal returns over the window $(-2, +2)$ where the mandatory disclosure of CSR report news is $t = 0$.
	The mid- to long-term cumulative abnormal returns, which are based on the CSR

CAR	disclosure date $t = 0$ and are cumulative over 90 (CAR_90), 180 (CAR_180), 270 (CAR_270), and 360 (CAR_360) days, respectively.
BHAR	The mid- to long-term cumulative buy-hold abnormal returns which are based on the CSR disclosure date $t = 0$ and cumulative over 90 (BHAR_90), 180 (BHAR_180), 270 (BHAR_270), and 360 (BHAR_360) days, respectively.
CSR	A dummy variable equals to 1 if the firm discloses CSR report, and 0 otherwise.
Mand	A dummy variable equals to 1 if the firm is required by the FSC to disclose a CSR report, and is 0 otherwise.
AftPlcy	A dummy variable equals to 1 if the firm discloses a CSR report after the mandatory requirement, and is 0 otherwise.
Volunt	A dummy variable equals to 1 if the firm voluntary discloses CSR report, and is 0 otherwise.
Size	Firm size is measured as the natural logarithm of total assets at the beginning of the year.
Inst	Institutional shareholdings are measured by the total number of shares held by institutional investors divided by the total number of ordinary shares outstanding.
Volm	Trading volume is measured by the monthly trading volume of ordinary shares divided by the total number of shares outstanding at the end of the previous period.
MTB	The market-to-book ratio is measured as market capitalization divided by book value.
TSE	A dummy variable equals to 1 if the firm is listed in the Taiwan Securities Exchange, and is 0 otherwise.
Ind	The industrial classification is based on the Taiwan Securities Exchange SIC code.
Year	Dummy variables to construct the sample year used in this study.

References

1. Crifo, P.; Forget, V.D. The economics of corporate social responsibility: A firm-level perspective survey. *J. Econ. Surv.* **2015**, *29*, 112–130. [CrossRef]
2. Shih, T.C.; Tsai, L.W.; Hsiang, H.P. A study on the determinants of the CSR implementation performance of Taiwan's listed companies: The perspectives of corporate governance and intellectual capital. *Rev. Account. Audit. Stud.* **2019**, *9*, 119–166.
3. Kao, L.P.; Huang, X.Y.; Pan, G.Y.; Chiang, Y. A study on the informativeness of corporate social responsibility report. *J. Tzu Chi Univ. Sci.* **2016**, *3*, 125–149.
4. Yang, X.Y. A Brief Discuss of Capital Market Sustainability Initiative and ESG Information Disclosure Drives. *Secur. Serv. Rev.* **2018**, *16*, 41–46.
5. Yoon, B.; Lee, J.H.; Byun, R. Does ESG performance enhance firm value? Evidence from Korea. *Sustainability.* **2018**, *10*, 3635. [CrossRef]
6. Bowman, E.H.; Haire, M. A strategic posture toward corporate social responsibility. *Calif. Manag. Rev.* **1975**, *18*, 49–58. [CrossRef]
7. Lev, B.; Petrovits, C.; Radhakrishnan, S. Is doing good good for you? How corporate charitable contributions enhance revenue growth. *Strateg. Manag. J.* **2010**, *31*, 182–200. [CrossRef]
8. Richardson, A.J.; Welker, M. Social disclosure, financial disclosure and the cost of equity capital. *Account. Organ. Soc.* **2001**, *26*, 597–616. [CrossRef]
9. Huang, C.C.; Shih, A.T.; Lin, C.S. Taiwan's listed company CSR report of the seven achilles heels. *Secur. Count.* **2014**, *174*, 53–57.
10. Anderson, J.; Smith, G. A great company can be a great investment. *Financ. Anal. J.* **2006**, *62*, 86–93. [CrossRef]
11. Kempf, A.; Osthoff, P. The effect of socially responsible investing on portfolio performance. *Eur. Financ. Manag.* **2007**, *13*, 908–922. [CrossRef]
12. Arya, B.; Zhang, G. Institutional reforms and investor reactions to CSR announcements: Evidence from an emerging economy. *J. Manag. Stud.* **2009**, *46*, 1089–1112. [CrossRef]

13. Marna, D.K.; Charl, D.V.; Chris, V.S. The influence of corporate social responsibility disclosure on share prices. *Pac. Account. Rev.* **2015**, *27*, 208–228.

14. Ahmed, S.U.; Abdullah, M.; Ahmed, S.P. Linkage between corporate social performance and stock return: An evidence from financial sector of Bangladesh. *J. Dev. Areas.* **2017**, *51*, 287–299. [CrossRef]

15. Gu, L.S. Deepen Taiwan's corporate governance and strengthen corporate social responsibility. *Secur. Serv.* **2019**, *669*, 5–9.

16. Lee, Y. Corporate social responsibility reporting new trends—The G4 era. *Account. Res. Mon.* **2014**, *339*, 22–30.

17. Cheng, H.Y. Corporate Governance and Corporate Responsibility Reports Disclosure. *Int. J. Account. Stud.* **2011**, *52*, 35–76.

18. Lin, W.L.; Fu, C.J. The disclosure of corporate social responsibility on the value—relevance of accounting information: An empirical analysis of the electronic industry in Taiwan. *Commer. Manag. Q.* **2011**, *12*, 209–229.

19. Du, S.; Bhattacharya, C.B.; Sen, S. Maximizing business returns to corporate social responsibility (CSR): The role of CSR communication. *Int. J. Manag. Rviews.* **2010**, *12*, 8–19. [CrossRef]

20. Fombrun, C.J.; Gardberg, N.A.; Barnett, M.L. Opportunity platforms and safety nets: Corporate citizenship and reputational risk. *Bus. Soc. Rev.* **2000**, *105*, 85–106. [CrossRef]

21. Chi, W.C.; Hsieh, S.H. To explore the accounting research of corporate social responsibility. *Money Watch. Credit Rat.* **2015**, *111*, 4–20.

22. Ullmann, A.A. Data in search of a theory: A critical examination of the relationships among social performance, social disclosure, and economic performance of U. S. firms. *Acad. Manag. Rev.* **1985**, *10*, 540–557.

23. Friedman, M. Capitalism and Freedom 2009. *Econ. Syst.* **2010**, *34*, 91–104.

24. Orlitzky, M.; Schmidt, F.L.; Rynes, S.L. Corporate social and financial performance: A meta-analysis. *Organ. Stud.* **2003**, *24*, 403–441. [CrossRef]

25. Tsoutsoura, M. *Corporate Social Responsibility and Financial Performance*; Working Paper 2004; Haas School of Business, University of California: Berkeley, CA, USA, 2004.

26. Cornell, B.; Shapiro, A.C. Corporate stakeholders and corporate finance. *Financ. Manag.* **1987**, *16*, 5–14. [CrossRef]

27. Shen, C.H.; Chang, Y. Ambition versus conscience, does corporate social responsibility pay off? The application of matching methods. *J. Bus. Ethics.* **2009**, *88*, 133–153. [CrossRef]

28. Dhaliwal, D.S.; Li, O.Z.; Tsang, A.; Yang, Y.G. Voluntary nonfinancial disclosure and the cost of equity capital: The initiation of corporate social responsibility reporting. *Account. Rev.* **2011**, *86*, 59–100. [CrossRef]

29. Hannon, J.M.; Milkovich, G.T. The effect of human resource reputation signals on share prices: An event study. *Hum. Resour. Manag.* **1996**, *35*, 405–424. [CrossRef]

30. Huang, C.Y.; Wang, K.Y.; Chang, F.C. The Relationship between CSR announcements and abnormal stock returns. *J. Contemp. Account.* **2013**, *14*, 175–204.

31. Chang, Y. Do companies with corporate social responsibility perform better in stock returns? *Fu Jen Manag. Rev.* **2011**, *18*, 79–118.

32. Worrell, D.L.; Davidson, W.N.; Sharma, V.M. Layoff announcements and stockholder wealth. *Acad. Manag. J.* **1991**, *34*, 662–678. [CrossRef]

33. Clinebell, S.K.; Clinebell, J.M. The effect of advance notice of plant closings on firm value. *J. Manag.* **1994**, *20*, 553–564. [CrossRef]

34. Yu, L.H.; Tseng, S.C.; Liu, C.C. Market reaction to the mandatory adoption of CSR report: Evidence from Taiwan. *Rev. Account. Audit. Stud.* **2017**, *7*, 1–22.

35. Schadewitz, H.; Niskala, M. Communication via responsibility reporting and its effect on firm value in Finland. *Corp. Soc. Responsib. Environ. Manag.* **2010**, *17*, 96–106. [CrossRef]

36. Liu, M.L. The Relationship between Stock Returns and Corporate Social Responsibility. Master's Thesis, National Chung Hsing University, Taichung, Taiwan, 2015.

37. Grossman, S.J. The informational role of warranties and private disclosure about product quality. *J. Law Econ.* **1981**, *24*, 461–483. [CrossRef]

38. Zhang, W.J.; Kuo, H.C. The relationship of corporate social responsibility reports' reason for issuance, assurance, and assurance type to stock price reaction. *J. Valuat.* **2019**, *13*, 17–58.

39.   Lin, H.F.; Cheng, Y.J.; Lin, P.H.; Chen, C.Y. The relationship between voluntary environment disclosure and firm value. *Tunghai Manag. Rev.* **2013**, *15*, 37–67.

40.   Lee, H.Y.; Wu, S.C. Analysis on information impact and transmission in Taiwan stock market. *Fu Jen Manag. Rev.* **2005**, *12*, 71–94.

41.   Barber, B.M.; Lyon, J.D. Detecting long-run abnormal stock returns: The empirical power and specification of test statistics. *J. Financ. Econ.* **1997**, *43*, 341–372. [CrossRef]

42.   Conrad, J.; Gultekin, M.N.; Kaul, G. Asymmetric predictability of conditional variances. *Rev. Financ. Stud.* **1991**, *4*, 597–622. [CrossRef]

43.   Badrinath, S.G.; Kale, J.R.; Noe, T.H. Of shepherds, sheep, and the cross-autocorrelations in equity returns. *Rev. Financ. Stud.* **1995**, *8*, 401–430. [CrossRef]

44.   Lee, C.M.; Swaminathan, B. Price momentum and trading volume. *J. Financ.* **2000**, *55*, 2017–2069. [CrossRef]

45.   Hung, J.H.; Lei, A. An empirical study on the relationship between stock return and firm size, stock price, price-to-earnings, and bok-to-market. *Manag. Rev.* **2002**, *21*, 25–48.

46.   Lin, C.H.; Liu, V.W.C.; Wu, C.S. The analysis of stock return and volatility in Taiwan otc stock market. *Asia Pac. Manag. Rev.* **2000**, *5*, 435–449.

5

Changes in the Influence of Social Responsibility Activities on Corporate Value over 10 Years in China

Feifei Zhang and Jin-young Jung *

College of Business Administration, Inha University, Incheon 22212, Korea; zhangfeifei2020@inha.edu
* Correspondence: jyjung@inha.ac.kr

Abstract: This study analyzes changes in how corporate social responsibility (CSR) affects corporate value in China. We use multiple regression analysis on a sample of A-share listed companies on the Shanghai and Shenzhen Stock Exchanges from 2009 to 2018. We divide the sample into 2009–2012 and 2013–2018 periods according to the development of CSR-related media and corporate policies. The dependent variable is corporate value, measured by Tobin's Q. The independent variable is the CSR score calculated and published by RKS, a widely recognized CSR evaluation agency in China. We use firm size, sales growth rate, return on equity, top 10 shareholders' equity, operating cash flow, and debt ratio as control variables. The panel-based regression models find no statistical correlation between CSR score and corporate value from 2009 to 2012 but find that the CSR score has a significantly positive influence on corporate value from 2013 to 2018. The impact of CSR activities on corporate value increases over the 10-year period. This decade saw the Chinese government shift its development strategy from a rapid growth model to a high-quality growth model and pursue sustainable development. This study is useful for Chinese companies considering adopting CSR activities to promote sustainable development.

Keywords: China; corporate social responsibility; corporate value; CSR; sustainability; Tobin's Q

1. Introduction

China's economy has been in a high-growth stage since the country's reform and opening-up began in 1978. During this stage, the primary objective was rapid growth in the economy. China's average growth rate has been 9.3% over this period. However, this economic growth has come at a heavy price. This price has come in two main forms: environmental destruction and a serious gap between the rich and poor. To solve these problems, the Chinese government has shifted its development strategy from a rapid growth model to a high-quality growth model and has pursued sustainable development.

Corporate social responsibility (CSR), as a prerequisite for achieving sustainable development and management, is getting more and more attention. CSR activities can make a major contribution to sustainable development [1] for several reasons. First, companies protect the environment when they engage in CSR activities, which forms the material basis for corporate sustainable development. Second, CSR activities enable companies to improve their management environment and sustainable management capacity by reducing friction between stakeholders. Third, a company can establish a good image by conducting CSR activities, which can accelerate its development.

The traditional corporate perception of CSR activities in China has tended to be passive. According to this view, CSR activities consume company resources and lower its economic power; it may improve corporate value in the long term, but it decreases it in the short term. In this perception, CSR activity is more about showing charity than doing it. However, in today's Internet age, the real CSR activity is the conduct of business itself. For example, Chinese delivery company MEITUAN reported on its CSR activities in 2018 by claiming that its drivers had delivered food to nearly 20 million elderly people who were unable to cook and made more than 14 million deliveries to white collar workers after 8 p.m. The report claims that this helped the company provide 19.6 million job opportunities and that 670,000 drivers out of 2.7 million job opportunities come from 781 poverty-stricken prefectures. Add to the Internet allows information to be transmitted anywhere in the world in seconds the public is able to obtain information on firms' CSR activities immediately. Sensitive investors can use this information to predict whether a company will do well and thus whether to invest. Therefore, more and more corporations have begun to attach importance to CSR activities and believe that conducting CSR activities can improve their corporate values and certainly help them to realize their long-term development.

This research is different from most of the previous studies that focused on the relationship between CSR and corporate value; we focused on the change of the relationship between them. This study is based on the sample of 111 listed Chinese companies for the period from 2009 to 2018. We find that the relationship between CSR and corporate value has changed from no relationship in 2009–2012 to a positive relationship in 2013–2018. The correlation between them has also become stronger.

This study contributes to the literature in several ways. First, most of the studies that have examined the relationship between CSR and corporate value have investigated whether the relationship is positive [2–34], negative [35–43], or there is no relationship [44–47] or have explored how CSR activities affect corporate value in the short or long term [48–52]. No study has examined how the relationship between CSR activities and corporate value changes in a rapidly changing economic environment. This study focuses on the changes in the impact of CSR activities on corporate value. Second, most of the research on the relationship between CSR activities and corporate value uses a maximum of three years of data [26,53,54], but this study's sample period spans 2009 to 2018, providing 10 years of data. This expanded sample size allows us to analyze recent trends in the impact of CSR activities on corporate value.

The rest of the paper is organized as follows. In the next section, we review the literature. Section 3 develops our research hypotheses. Section 4 explains the study's methodology. Section 5 presents the results. Finally, Section 6 concludes the paper.

2. Literature Review

2.1. The Development of CSR Theory

Corporate social responsibility requires companies to pursue profits and fulfil their legal responsibilities to shareholders and employees, as well as to consumers, society, and the environment. To do this, companies must go beyond the traditional ideology whereby profit is the only goal and emphasize human values in the production process and contribute to the welfare of the environment, consumers and society.

In Stage 1, the concept of CSR was established. British scholar Oliver Sheldon [55] first proposed the concept of CSR in 1923. He believed that CSR is more focused on ethics. In 1953, American scholar Howard Bowen [56] published *Social Responsibility of the Businessman* which examines the responsibilities businesspeople have to society. Bowen argues that businesses should consider social goals and values when setting policies and to guide their conduct. As this claim provides the first definition of CSR, Bowen is said to be the "father" of CSR.

In Stage 2, CSR theory was developed, and CSR activities gradually became popular in developed countries such as the United States and in Europe. In 1979, Archie Carroll [57] presented the theory of the "Pyramid of Corporate Social Responsibility." Carroll argued that CSR comprises a firm's economic, legal, ethical, and philanthropic expectations. The Pyramid of Corporate Social Responsibility has become the most widely used CSR theory. John Elkingtor proposed the "triple bottom line" theory in 1997. He believed that corporate social responsibility can be divided into economic responsibility, environmental responsibility, and social responsibility [58].

In Stage 3, CSR gained worldwide attention. In 2000, the American Commercial Social Responsibility Association announced that CSR is about respecting ethical values, legal requirements, people, local communities, and the environment when determining company policies. The Commission of the European Union (EU) announced in 2001 that CSR should always be voluntary and that a company's interest in society and the environment should be combined with its management and interactions with stakeholders. In 2010, 77 countries adopted the Guidance on Social Responsibility (ISO 26000); this provides a clear definition of social responsibility, describing it as a company's assumption of responsibility for the impact of its actions on society and the environment through transparency and moral conduct.

2.2. CSR in China

Since China's reform and opening in 1978, China has gone from being a planned economy to being a planned commodity economy, and finally a socialist economic system with Chinese characteristics. Corporate social responsibility emerged in China during the reform/opening-up period and has developed in unique ways over the past 40 years. This development can be divided into three stages.

Stage 1 occurred from 1978 to 2008. When China began its reform and opening-up, Deng Xiaoping's famous "black and white cat" theory (a good cat, whether white or black, catches mice) encouraged people to produce as much as possible, but it also created many social problems. The quantity of products greatly increased, but fake, low-quality goods became rampant due to product quality issues. Against this background, the legal system quickly addressed problems in areas such as consumer rights protection, workers' rights protection, and environmental protection. In this context, corporate management philosophies, corporate social values, and corporate and social relations became matters of increasing interest, which enhanced the profile of CSR among Chinese companies.

In 2003, the Hu Jintao-Wen Jiabao government established the scientific development perspective [22]. The first essence of the scientific development concept is economic development, the core is people-oriented, and the fundamental method is overall planning. In 2006, the government put forward the idea of building a harmonious society; such a society features democratic rule of law, fairness and justice, honesty and friendship, an energetic atmosphere, well-organized practices, and a harmonious coexistence between humans and nature. China's CSR has developed rapidly in accordance with the scientific development view and the "harmonious society" policy. Corporate social responsibility has appeared on China's national horizon, and Chinese leaders have endorsed CSR on several occasions.

The first year of CSR in China is said to be 2008, when a number of symbolic events occurred that promoted the development of Chinese CSR activities and ideology among the public [59]. In January 2008, the SASAC issued the Guidelines for Central Enterprises to Fulfill Social Responsibilities, which is considered a CSR milestone in China. In May 2008, the Shanghai Stock Exchange published the Notice on Strengthening the Social Responsibility Work of Listed Companies and the Guidelines on the Environmental Information Disclosure of Listed Companies. These all promoted the development of CSR in China. Moreover, several major events also helped promote CSR in 2008, such as the winter snowstorms, the Sichuan earthquake, and the Sanlu milk powder incident. First, starting on 3 January 2008, 20 provinces—including Shanghai, Jiangsu, and Henan—suffered from low temperatures, heavy snow, and ice to different degrees. In the face of the resulting disasters, various sectors of society participated in rescue efforts. Second, on 12 May 2008, a large earthquake occurred in Sichuan Province, leading to many geological disasters such as massive landslides, collapses, and debris flow. The damaged area totaled 100,000 km. Tens of thousands of people voluntarily went to the disaster area to assist in rescue missions, and many companies participated in relief efforts. Finally, on 11 September 2008, about 700 tons of baby formula made by Sanlu were found to contain melamine. About 290,000 infants in China developed urinary abnormalities due to milk powder containing melamine, more than 10,000 infants were treated in hospital, and six infants died. In a heartbreaking development, on 16 September, China's quality supervision agency announced the results of a test that extracted milk powder from more than 100 milk powder companies across the country: Melamine was detected in the milk powder of 22 companies, most of them famous in China. This case undermined public confidence in China's companies, and the public strongly condemned irresponsible corporate conduct.

Stage 2 occurred from 2009 to 2012. Due to the many cases of corporate irresponsibility that occurred in 2008, the Shanghai and Shenzhen securities exchanges required listed companies to disclose CSR information starting in December of that year. Thus, Chinese CSR underwent a period of rapid development from 2009 to 2012. During this period, all of Chinese society participated in CSR activities. Companies recognized the importance and necessity of social responsibility and carried out CSR activities accordingly. In 2009, the Chinese Academy of Social Sciences published China's Top 100 Social Responsibility Development Index (2009). As a result of this development, 290 companies released social responsibility reports in 2008, 371 did so in 2009, and 471 did so in 2010. The number of public companies releasing social responsibility reports is increasing significantly.

Stage 3 occurred from 2013 to 2018. During this stage, Chinese CSR was characterized by standardization, normalization, internationalization, and high-level attention. The Xi Jinping government, which began at the end of 2012, put increased CSR pressure on companies with the goal of eliminating poverty, narrowing the gap between rich and poor, solving environmental problems, eliminating corruption, and ensuring food safety as the top priorities. Xi Jinping argued in his book [60] that loving property is the only truly meaningful property and that companies that pursue CSR are the most competitive and vital. On 1 January 2015, the Environmental Protection Act was officially implemented. The act increases penalties for environmental pollution, and even forces companies that fail to protect the environment to stop production.

On 2 June 2015, the General Administration of Quality Supervision (AQSIQ) and the Standardization Administration of China jointly announced a series of social responsibility national standards. These include the Guidelines for Social Responsibility, the Guide to the Preparation of Social Responsibility Reports, and the Social Responsibility Performance Classification Guide. This series is China's first national standard document in the field of social responsibility. The presentation of this series helped raise the level of social responsibility in China. As the global division of labor continues to deepen and the supply chain continues to expand, the sense of social responsibility and supply chain partnerships in corporate management are important factors affecting firm competitiveness. Interest in corporate and social responsibility is increasing across all sectors of Chinese society, and Chinese governments at all levels have released guidance documents on social responsibility. About 40 social responsibility standards have been established by 20 commercial associations. Many universities have established professional CSR research standards. In addition, many media organizations have pursued activities such as holding social responsibility forums to promote the spread of the CSR ideology throughout society.

2.3. Research on Relationship between CSR and Corporate Value

The empirical research on the correlation between corporate value and social responsibility activities has offered three perspectives on the issue: They have found a positive correlation, negative correlation, and no correlation between corporate value and CSR.

A negative correlation between CSR and corporate value is found if a company's CSR activities are observed to degrade its value. Friedman [36] argued that the only responsibility of the corporation is to increase a company's profits by making full use of its resources in an environment of open and free competition. From the shareholders' perspective, the expenditures required to engage in social responsibility activities is seen as a waste of company resources, which causes agency problems. According to Aupperle et al. [37], CSR activities waste capital and other resources, and companies that engage in them cannot compete against those that do not. In the empirical study of Vance [35], CSR activities are found to have negative effects on corporate value.

On the other hand, Ullman [46] found no correlation between CSR activities and corporate value and argued that it is difficult to think of a reason why they would be correlated. Bauer et al. (2005) [47] showed that there is no significant difference in performance between CSR active companies and control group companies.

However, many studies have shown that CSR activities have a positive effect on corporate value and corporate financial performance. In this case, companies can increase their corporate value through CSR activities. According to the stakeholder approach proposed by Freeman [9] that CSR activities satisfy the interests of all of a firm's stakeholders can increase company profits in the long run. Frank (2018) [7] collected data of South African listed companies and found a positive and statistically significant relationship between social disclosure performance and firm value. Elif Akben-Seluck (2019) [3] used the listed company in Turkey as the sample shows that corporate social responsibility has a positive relationship with financial performance. Ju Hyoung Park (2018) [2] found that, on average, firms can increase their value through CSR activities in Korea.

Among the studies that examine the correlation between CSR and corporate value for Chinese companies, Li (2006) [38] investigated 521 companies listed on the Shanghai Stock Exchange in 2003 and found that CSR activities have a negative effect on corporate value in the current period but have a positive effect in the long run. Pan and Wang (2015) [44] studied the relationship between environmental protection investment and financial performance, finding no correlation in the short term (within one year) and a positive relationship in the long term (two years). Kong and Li (2010) [14] used stakeholder theory and found a positive relationship between social responsibility indicators and financial performance. In addition, Yang (2014) [15] shows that the companies listed on the Shanghai and Shenzhen Securities Exchange A markets display a positive correlation between CSR and financial performance through multiple regression analysis. Seo and Park (2015) [22] found that CSR had a positive effect on corporate value for companies listed on the Shanghai and Shenzhen Securities Exchange A markets from 2009 to 2013. Jin, Yang, Hong, and Choi [26] found that both Korean and Chinese companies show positive relationships between CSR activities and corporate value for both the next year ($t + 1$) and the next two years ($t + 2$).

3. Hypotheses

This study tests how the impact of CSR on corporate values changes in China between 2009 and 2018. We first divide the study period into two stages, 2009–2012 and 2013–2018, according to three dimensions: the development of government CSR-related policies, media issues, and corporate issues.

3.1. Government and Related Policy Dimension

The Xi Jinping government, in power since the end of 2012, has put forward the concept of building a moderately prosperous society in all respects and building a modern socialist country that is prosperous, strong, democratic, culturally advanced, and harmonious to realize the Chinese dream of the great rejuvenation of the Chinese nation. This is different from the scientific development concept proposed by the Hu Jintao government, in which development was the priority. Before 2013, the government's policy on corporate CSR activities was mainly to guide and advise. Since 2013, however, CSR activities have been applied to national strategies, and laws and regulations governing CSR activities have been increasing, while local governments have also issued guidance documents and implementation systems for CSR.

3.2. Media Dimension

Chinese mass media such as the *People's Daily Online* and *Xinhua* have promoted the spread of CSR in society by holding CSR forums, giving out CSR awards, and reporting on outstanding CSR practices. Meanwhile, the popularity of smartphones has produced the era of mobile Internet. As Figure 1 shows, the number of mobile netizens has been increasing since 2008, exceeding 500 million in 2013 and exceeding 800 million in 2018. The share of mobile netizens in the netizen population increased rapidly from 39.5% in 2008 to 80% in 2013, and then rose steadily to 98.6% by 2018. Figure 2 shows that the number of WeChat users has been rapidly increasing since it launched in January 2011. It has become the most widely used messenger platform in China. In this environment, new ways of spreading news, called "we-media," have emerged. The official WeChat account was developed in 2013 and is now the most-used we-media in China. Media platforms, companies, and individuals can all publish articles through WeChat's official accounts, and the Chinese have become used to watching news through WeChat. Such advances in technology have greatly promoted the spread of CSR among the Chinese public.

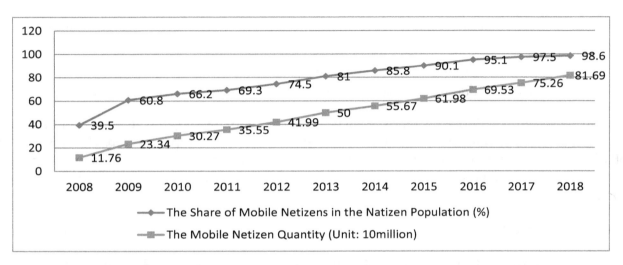

Figure 1. Mobile netizen quantity and share of mobile netizens in the netizen population.

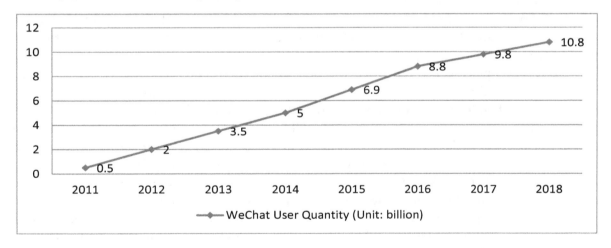

Figure 2. WeChat user quantity.

3.3. Corporate Dimension

As CSR has developed in China, companies have changed their attitudes toward it considerably and have recognized its importance to their performance. Whereas companies initially believed that CSR activities only increased their costs, companies are increasingly realizing that CSR is not only good for society but also plays an important role in their own development. An increasing number of companies are actively engaging in CSR activities, and many companies' CSR activities have penetrated through the firms' production management processes in an effort to promote sustainable development. As Figure 3 shows, the number of A-share companies reporting CSR via the Shanghai and Shenzhen Stock Exchanges increased between 2009 and 2018, exceeding 600 by 2013 and growing stably since then.

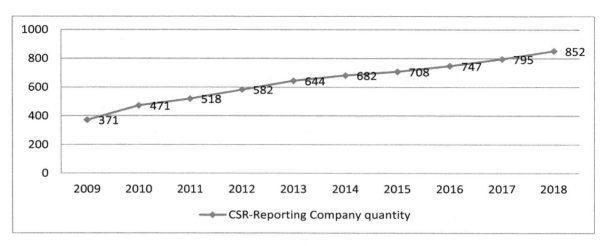

Figure 3. Corporate social responsibility (CSR)-reporting company quantity.

In the 2009–2012 period, the Chinese state was unclear about the proper CSR assessment standards, policies, and laws. The media were giving CSR little publicity, and companies were also unsure about CSR activities. In addition, prior studies suggest that CSR and corporate value have a mostly negative correlation or no correlations in this early period. Therefore, based on the above discussion, we propose the following:

Hypothesis 1. *From 2009 to 2012, CSR activities had a negative impact on corporate value for Chinese companies.*

The 18th National Congress of the Communist Party of China was held in November 2012, and a new government was elected. China entered a period of comprehensively deepening reforms. After 2013, the new government has emphasized CSR at the national strategy level, launched a number of policies related to CSR, and issued national CSR standards, while laws related to CSR have become stronger. The «Decision of the CPC Central Committee on several Major Issues concerning comprehensively deepening the Reform» adopted at the Third Plenary Session of the 18th CPC Central Committee held in 2013 for the first time promoted social responsibility work as a key task in the reform of state-owned enterprises. In 2014, the Fourth Plenary Session of the 18th CPC Central Committee adopted the «Decision of the CPC Central Committee on Several Major Issues concerning comprehensively advancing the rule of law», which clearly proposed to strengthen the legislation of corporate social responsibility as one of the tasks of strengthening legislation in key areas. In 2015 GB/T 36000-2015 «Guidelines for Social Responsibility», GB/T 36001-2015 «Guidelines for the compilation of social responsibility reports», GB/T 36002-2015 «Guidelines for the classification of social responsibility performance» three national standards were officially released. In addition, advances in science and technology enabled the media to quickly and accurately deliver CSR-related information to the public. The importance of CSR was disseminated to the public, whose interest in CSR increased. Companies also recognized the importance of CSR and actively participated in CSR activities. Moreover, the most recent studies show that CSR had a positive effect on corporate value. Therefore, we propose the following:

Hypothesis 2. *From 2013 to 2018, CSR activities had a positive impact on corporate value for Chinese companies.*

A 2018 case of vaccine manipulation led to widespread reflection in Chinese society. On 15 July 2018, an announcement from the State Drug Administration (SDA) reveals the inside story behind the manipulation of the Changchun Changsheng Biological Company. The 252,600 vaccines produced by the company had already been distributed to each province, 247,359 people had already been inoculated, 215,184 of them children. As soon as the manipulation took place, the WeChat Official Account reported on it, which aroused public anger. Premier Li Keqiang claimed that the vaccine case had crossed a moral line, that the nation deserved a clear explanation that the State Council would immediately send a group to thoroughly investigate the production and selling chain of the vaccine to uncover the truth as soon as possible, and that any wrongdoing would be severely punished regardless of who is involved. The case was later thoroughly investigated, and the company and its managers were severely punished. The company went bankrupt. However, in March 2009, Yanshen Company was similarly found to have manipulated vaccines. In this case, 180,000 vaccines had already been distributed to 21 provinces and had been used on humans. In this case, there was no recall or compensation, a fine of only 3 million yuan was imposed on the company and the general manager, and only five employees were found criminally guilty. Jiangsu Yanshen quickly makes a comeback. Just six months later, the firm received 1.6 million orders from the epidemic prevention department worth more than 100 million yuan. It was soon licensed to make swine flu vaccines. These two events are very similar, but the consequences for the two companies varied considerably depending on the timing of the events. Therefore, this study argues that social responsibility has a greater impact on corporate value over time. We thus propose the following:

Hypothesis 3. *The impact of CSR activities on corporate value in China was greater from 2013 to 2018 than it was from 2009 to 2012.*

4. Methodology

4.1. Data: Sample Selection and Sources

The sample used in this study comprises all Chinese companies listed on the Shanghai and Shenzhen Stock Exchanges' A markets between 2009 and 2018 that

1.   have financial information in China Stock Market & Accounting Research Database (CSMAR),
2.   have a settlement date of 31 December,
3.   have CSR activity scores in RKS (Rankins CSR Ratings),
4.   are non-financial companies.

The CSMAR economic and financial research database draws on the research and precision database specifically developed for the Chinese financial and economic fields, drawing on internationally renowned economic and financial database standards such as CRSP and Standard & Poor's Compustat from the University of Chicago. The data come from the Shanghai Stock Exchange, Shenzhen Stock Exchange, Shanghai Commodity Futures Exchange, Zhengzhou Commodity Futures Exchange, Dalian Commodity Futures Exchange, and other authoritative publishing agencies. These data are accurate, wide-ranging, complete in time, and abundant in indicators, and are therefore appropriate for the purposes of this study [26,61].

The CSR score provided by RKS is used as the company's CSR score in this study [22,26]. RKS was established in 2007 and is an authoritative third-party institution that evaluates Chinese corporate social responsibility. The study considers only companies with a settlement date of 31 December because different settlement dates may have different effects on firms' financial information depending on their economic environment. Moreover, financial companies have different financial statements, and the same indicators can have different meanings across firms. Thus, these firms are excluded from the sample.

As this study examines how the impact of CSR scores on corporate value changes during the sample period, the sample needs to be comparable over time. We select 111 companies according to the process shown in Table 1 below.

Table 1. Sample selection process.

	2009	2010	2011	2012	2013	2014	2015	2016	2017	2018
Listed companies with December settlement	1774	2215	2450	2578	2622	2737	2925	3219	3596	3690
Companies without CSR scores	1459	1743	1931	1995	1968	2055	2217	2471	2773	2833
Companies with CSR scores	315	472	519	583	654	682	708	748	823	857
Companies with insufficient financial information	189	346	393	457	528	556	582	622	697	731
Financial companies	15	15	15	15	15	15	15	15	15	15
Final sample	111	111	111	111	111	111	111	111	111	111

4.2. Model

We tested the changes in the impact of Chinese CSR activities on corporate value over 10 years by estimating Equations (1) and (2):

$$TQ09\text{-}12 = \beta 0 + \beta 1CSR09\text{-}12 + \beta 2SIZE09\text{-}12 + \beta 3SGR09\text{-}12 + \beta 4ROE09\text{-}12 + \beta 5OWN09\text{-}12 + \beta 6OCF09\text{-}12 + \beta 7LEV09\text{-}12 + \varepsilon 09\text{-}12 \tag{1}$$

where TQ09-12 = AVG (2009 TQ–2012 TQ), TQ = (market value of equity + book value of debt)/book value of total assets,

CSR09-12 = AVG (2009 CSR–2012 CSR), CSR = CSR total presented by RKS,
SIZE09-12 = AVG (2009 SIZE–2012 SIZE), SIZE = ln (Ending total assets),
SGR09-12 = AVG (2009 SGR–2012 SGR), SGR = (Current sales − Pre-sales)/Pre-sales,
ROE09-12 = AVG (2009 ROE–2012 ROE), ROE = Net income/Stockholder's equity,
OWN09-12 = AVG (2009 OWN–2012 OWN), OWN = Top 10 Shareholders' Equity Rate,
OCF09-12 = AVG (2009 OCF–2012 OCF), OCF = Operating cash flow/Beginning total assets,
LEV09-12 = AVG (2009 LEV–2012 LEV), LEV = Total debt/Total assets,
$\varepsilon 09\text{-}12$ = error term.

$$TQ13\text{-}18 = \beta 0 + \beta 1CSR13\text{-}18 + \beta 2SIZE13\text{-}18 + \beta 3SGR13\text{-}18 + \beta 4ROE13\text{-}18 + \beta 5OWN13\text{-}18 + \beta 6OCF13\text{-}18 + \beta 7LEV13\text{-}18 + \varepsilon 13\text{-}18 \tag{2}$$

where TQ13-18 = AVG (2013 TQ~2018 TQ), TQ = (market value of equity + book value of debt)/book value of total assets,

CSR13-18 = AVG (2013 CSR–2018 CSR), CSR = CSR total presented by RKS,
SIZE13-18 = AVG (2013 SIZE–2018 SIZE), SIZE= ln (Ending total assets),
SGR13-18 = AVG (2013 SGR–2018 SGR), SGR = (Current sales − Pre-sales)/Pre-sales,
ROE13-18 = AVG (2013 ROE–2018 ROE), ROE = Net income/Stockholder's equity,
OWN13-18 = AVG (2013 OWN–2018 OWN), OWN = Top 10 Shareholders' Equity Rate,
OCF13-18 = AVG (2013 OCF–2018 OCF), OCF = Operating cash flow/Beginning total assets,
LEV13-18 = AVG (2013 LEV–2018 LEV), LEV = Total debt/Total assets,
$\varepsilon 13\text{-}18$ = error term.

The values of the variables used in Equation (1) are the average values of each variable from 2009 to 2012, and the values of the variables used in Equation (2) are the average values of each variable from 2013 to 2018.

Tobin's Q is the dependent variable of this study. Commonly used proxy variables of corporate value include market value, market/book ratio, price-to-earnings ratio, Return on Assets, and Tobin's Q. As the latter is the most commonly used in the literature [22,23,26], we also adopt it for our analysis. Tobin's Q is the ratio between the market value of the company asset and the total replacement cost of the asset. The total cost of replacement here refers to the cost of repurchasing the retained tangible asset. The higher the value of Tobin's Q, the higher the value of the company on the market.

We use CSR as the independent variable. The CSR scores are calculated and published by RKS; the highest possible score is 100 points. The annual CSR scores for the sample are shown in Table 2.

As the table shows, the CSR scores' minimum, maximum, and average values all have upward trends over time.

Table 2. Sample's annual CSR scores.

	Minimum	Maximum	Mean	Std. Deviation
CSR2009	15.20	68.76	29.693	10.195
CSR2010	15.40	78.49	33.876	13.400
CSR2011	16.12	79.54	35.789	15.047
CSR2012	16.697	81.880	37.681	15.141
CSR2013	18.479	81.702	39.680	14.459
CSR2014	19.702	87.948	41.470	14.998
CSR2015	28.964	89.298	44.416	13.740
CSR2016	27.414	86.637	46.765	12.183
CSR2017	33.002	86.550	47.843	12.167
CSR2018	31.690	89.003	48.618	14.022

Company size (SIZE), sales growth rate (SGR), return on equity (ROE), top 10 shareholders' equity (OWN), operating cash flows (OCF), and the debt-to-equity ratio (LEV) are used as control variables. We consider that a larger company size implies higher firm value due to economies of scale [34]. Theoretically, the higher the value of SGR, OCF, and ROE, the higher the value of the company (i.e., they are positively related to the value of the company). If OWN is high, the probability of major shareholders having an information asymmetry problem is high, as the major shareholders are likely to seek their own profits rather than those of the company [33]. We thus conjecture that OWN has a negative relationship with company value. Moreover, the higher the LEV, the lower the company's ability to repay debt; thus, a negative relationship with company value is expected.

5. Results

5.1. Descriptive Statistics

Tables 3 and 4 below provide the descriptive statistics of the average values of the main variables for 2009–2012 and 2013–2018 used in the regression model. For 2009–2012, the company's TQ values are distributed between 0.794 and 6.576, with an average value of 1728. However, in 2013–2018, the company's TQ minimum values increase slightly to 0.811, but the maximum is 6271, and the average value decreases slightly to 1610. The CSR scores' minimum value, maximum value, and the average value for 2013–2018 are all higher than the values for 2009–2012. The standard deviation of the two periods is almost unchanged. While SIZE is higher from 2013 to 2018, SGR, ROE, OWN, OCF, and LEV are higher for 2009–2012.

Table 3. Descriptive statistics for 2009–2012.

Variable	Obs.	Minimum	Maximum	Mean	Std. Deviation	Variance
T Q 09-12	111	0.794	6.576	1.728	0.877	0.769
CSR 09-12	111	17.268	76.395	34.260	12.723	161.879
SIZE 09-12	111	20.313	26.851	23.133	1.454	2.113
SGR 09-12	111	−0.618	21.118	0.483	2.143	4.593
ROE 09-12	111	−0.092	0.267	0.105	0.071	0.005
OWN 09-12	111	10.148	75.123	40.846	15.420	237.782
OCF 09-12	111	−0.024	0.216	0.064	0.051	0.003
LEV 09-12	111	0.092	0.850	0.523	0.178	0.032

Table 4. Descriptive statistics for 2013–2018.

Variable	Obs.	Minimum	Maximum	Mean	Std. Deviation	Variance
TQ 13-18	111	0.811	6.271	1.610	0.859	0.738
CSR 13-18	111	30.560	85.910	44.799	12.766	162.974
SIZE 13-18	111	20.473	27.379	23.669	1.489	2.217
SGR 13-18	111	−0.703	4.550	0.270	0.576	0.332
ROE 13-18	111	−0.547	0.289	0.063	0.113	0.013
OWN 13-18	111	8.093	73.280	39.188	14.747	217.474
OCF 13-18	111	−0.041	0.233	0.058	0.050	0.003
LEV 13-18	111	0.097	0.869	0.518	0.186	0.035

5.2. Correlation Analysis

Table 5 shows the correlation between the average values of the main variables for 2009–2012. There is a significantly negative relationship between the CSR scores and corporate value (TQ), as expected. Carrying out CSR activities requires the company to spend large amounts of money and reduces its value in the short term. Looking at the correlation between corporate value (TQ) and other variables, company size (SIZE) surprisingly shows a negative relationship with corporate value (TQ). Return on equity (ROE) and operating cash flows (OCF) show positive relationships while debt-to-equity ratio (LEV) shows a negative relationship with corporate value (TQ), as predicted. Lastly, the sales growth rate (SGR) and the top 10 shareholders' equity (OWN) seem to have no statistical correlation with corporate value (TQ).

Table 5. Pearson correlation for 2009–2012.

	(1)	(2)	(3)	(4)	(5)	(6)	(7)	(8)	VIF
(1) TQ 09-12	1								-
(2) CSR 09-12	−0.228 **	1							1.77
(3) SIZE 09-12	−0.417 ***	0.611 ***	1						2.72
(4) SGR 09-12	0.025	−0.135	−0.105	1					1.09
(5) ROE 09-12	0.316 ***	0.150	0.292 ***	0.013	1				1.35
(6) OWN 09-12	−0.125	0.215 **	0.319 ***	−0.107	0.020	1			1.17
(7) OCF 09-12	0.303 ***	0.164 *	0.066	0.146	0.390 ***	0.131	1		1.53
(8) LEV 09-12	−0.521 ***	0.078	0.446 ***	−0.011	−0.087	0.029	−0.388 ***	1	1.77

Notes: ***, **, and * indicate significance at the 1%, 5%, and 10% levels, respectively.

None of the correlations among the variables shown in Table 5 exceeds 0.7, and the variance inflation factor (VIF) values are all less than 10; therefore, multicollinearity does not affect the results.

Table 6 shows the correlation between the mean values of the main variables for 2013–2018. Contrary to our prediction, a significantly negative relationship appears between the CSR score and corporate value (TQ) for 2013–2018, as it does for 2009–2012. Looking at the correlation between corporate value (TQ) and other variables, company size (SIZE) shows a negative relationship with corporate value (TQ), as it does for 2009–2012. In addition, return on equity (ROE) and debt-to-equity ratio (LEV) has the same relationship with corporate value (TQ) for 2009–2012. Just as we predicted, the top 10 shareholders' equity (OWN) shows a significantly negative relationship with corporate value (TQ). Lastly, the sales growth rate (SGR) and operating cash flow (OCF) are not statistically related to corporate value (TQ).

Table 6. Pearson correlation for 2013–2018.

	(1)	(2)	(3)	(4)	(5)	(6)	(7)	(8)	VIF
(1) TQ 13-18	1								-
(2) CSR 13-18	−0.162 *	1							1.87
(3) SIZE 13-18	−0.595 ***	0.632 ***	1						2.85
(4) SGR 13-18	0.094	−0.060	0.063	1					1.12
(5) ROE 13-18	0.182 *	0.194 **	0.142	0.064	1				1.41
(6) OWN 13-18	−0.159 *	0.246 ***	0.324 ***	−0.021	0.206 **	1			1.20
(7) OCF 13-18	0.148	0.169*	0.091	−0.199 **	0.403 ***	0.260 ***	1		1.39
(8) LEV 13-18	−0.594 ***	0.109	0.512 ***	−0.200 **	−0.292 ***	0.043	0.294 ***	1	2

Notes: ***, **, and * indicate significance at the 1%, 5%, and 10% levels, respectively.

Moreover, none of the correlations exceeds 0.7, and none of the VIF values exceeds 3; therefore, multicollinearity is not an issue.

However, this is just a simple correlation analysis. Testing the effect of CSR on corporate value requires a multiple regression analysis that controls for other variables affecting corporate value.

5.3. Multiple Regression Analysis

Table 7 shows the regression results for H1. The average value of the CSR score between 2009 and 2012 implies that CSR activities have a negative but insignificant relationship with corporate value. The correlation matrix (see Table 5) also shows the same. These results confirm our prediction that, from 2009 to 2012, corporate costs were high for CSR activities, and social responsibility was slow to convert into economic effects.

Table 7. Effect of CSR on corporate value for 2009–2012.

TQ 09-12	Coefficient	Standard Error	t-Value	p-Value	95% Confidence Interval		
Constant	7.279	1.335	5.451	0.000	4.631	9.928	***
CSR 09-12	−0.003	0.007	−0.495	0.622	−0.016	0.010	
SIZE 09-12	−0.228	0.072	−3.164	0.002	−0.370	−0.085	**
SGR 09-12	−0.012	0.031	−0.382	0.703	−0.073	0.050	
ROE 09-12	4.632	1.037	4.468	0.000	2.576	6.688	***
OWN 09-12	−0.000	0.004	−0.101	0.919	−0.009	0.008	
OCF 09-12	1.457	1.544	0.944	0.348	−1.605	4.519	
LEV 09-12	−1.390	0.474	−0.283	0.004	−2.330	−0.449	**
Adj_R Square		0.423			Sample size	111	
F-statistics		12.536 ***			Durbin–Watson	2.256	

Notes: *** and ** indicate significance at the 1%, 5%, and 10% levels, respectively.

Table 8 shows the regression results for H2. The average value of the CSR score for 2013–2018 implies that CSR activities have a positive and significant relationship with corporate value. This result is contrary to that for 2009–2012 because the Chinese government placed more emphasis on CSR activities after 2013, and investments were made to encourage companies to implement CSR activities and help the firms improve their corporate value through them.

Table 8. Effect of CSR on corporate value for 2013–2018.

TQ 13-18	Coefficient	Standard Error	t-Value	p-Value	95% Confidence Interval		
Constant	10.131	1.240	8.171	0.000	7.672	12.590	***
CSR 13-18	0.016	0.006	2.588	0.011	0.004	0.029	**
SIZE 13-18	−0.368	0.066	−5.533	0.000	−0.499	−0.236	***
SGR 13-18	0.012	0.108	0.108	0.914	−0.202	0.225	
ROE 13-18	1.097	0.615	1.785	0.077	−0.122	2.136	*
OWN 13-18	−0.003	0.004	−0.589	0.557	−0.011	0.006	
OCF 13-18	0.847	1.373	0.617	0.539	−1.876	3.569	
LEV 13-18	−1.095	0.445	−2.459	0.016	−1.978	−0.212	**
Adj_R Square		0.488			Sample size	111	
F-statistics		15.986 ***			Durbin–Watson	1.919	

Notes: ***, **, and * indicate significance at the 1%, 5% and 10% levels, respectively.

Finally, each regression formula for 2009–2012 and 2013–2018 is shown in the following:

TQ09-12 = 7.279 − 0.003CSR − 0.228SIZE − 0.012SGR + 4.632ROE − 0.000OWN + 1.457OCF − 1.390LEV

TQ13-18 = 10.131 + 0.016CSR − 0.368SIZE + 0.012SGR + 1.097ROE − 0.003OWN + 0.847OCF − 1.095LEV

Overall, the coefficient of CSR for 2009–2012 is −0.003, and that for 2013–2018 is 0.016. This implies that the impact of CSR activities on corporate value from 2013 to 2018 in China is greater than that from 2009 to 2012. These results support H3.

5.4. Robustness Test: Alternative Measure of Company Value

We ensure the robustness of our results using an alternative measure of corporate value, substituting Tobin's Q with MV (market value). The results using the alternative measure are reported for 2009–2012 and 2013–2018 separately in Tables 9 and 10. The coefficient of CSR for 2009–2012 remains insignificant ($p = 0.895$), and the coefficient of CSR for 2013–2018 also remains positively significant ($p = 0.002$). These results are consistent with those wherein corporate value is measured by Tobin's Q.

Table 9. Robustness checks: alternative measure of corporate value for 2009–2012.

MV 09-12	Coefficient	Standard Error	t-Value	p-Value	95% Confidence Interval		
Constant	3.734	0.510	7.318	0.000	2.722	4.746	***
CSR 09-12	0.000	0.003	0.132	0.895	−0.005	0.005	
SIZE 09-12	0.860	0.027	31.283	0.000	0.806	0.915	***
SGR 09-12	−0.001	0.012	−0.044	0.965	−0.024	0.023	
ROE 09-12	2.201	0.396	5.556	0.000	1.415	2.986	***
OWN 09-12	0.000	0.002	0.169	0.866	−0.003	0.004	
OCF 09-12	0.097	0.590	0.165	0.869	−1.073	1.267	
LEV 09-12	−0.614	0.181	−3.388	0.001	−0.973	−0.255	***
Adj_R Square		0.961			Sample size	111	
F-statistics		390.241 ***			Durbin–Watson	1.779	

Notes: *** indicate significance at the 1%, 5%, and 10% levels, respectively.

Table 10. Robustness checks: alternative measure of corporate value for 2013–2018.

TQ 13-18	Coefficient	Standard Error	t-Value	p-Value	95% Confidence Interval		
Constant	4.790	0.482	9.936	0.000	3.834	5.747	***
CSR 13-18	0.008	0.002	3.189	0.002	0.003	0.013	**
SIZE 13-18	0.808	0.026	31.263	0.000	0.756	0.859	***
SGR 13-18	0.001	0.042	0.012	0.990	−0.082	0.083	
ROE 13-18	0.690	0.239	2.885	0.005	0.215	1.164	**
OWN 13-18	−0.002	0.002	−0.991	0.324	−0.005	0.002	
OCF 13-18	0.376	0.534	0.704	0.483	−0.683	1.435	
LEV 13-18	−0.431	0.173	−2.488	0.014	−0.774	−0.087	**
Adj_R Square		0.964			Sample size	111	
F-statistics		423.322 ***			Durbin–Watson	1.611	

Notes: *** and ** indicate significance at the 1%, 5%, and 10% levels, respectively.

6. Conclusions

Nowadays, CSR is widely given importance in the international community. CSR is not only the demand of the enterprise's own development, but also the demand of national strategy and government governance of social issues. In the last decade in China, the views of governments, public and companies on CSR have all changed. This research is devoted to studying the changes in the relationship between CSR and corporate value using a sample of companies listed in the Chinese market from 2009 to 2018. The results are as follows. First, this study confirms that there is no statistical correlation between CSR activities and corporate value from 2009 to 2012. This implies that in this stage, the conduct of CSR activities had no influence on corporate value for companies. Second, we found that CSR activities had a positive effect on corporate value from 2013 to 2018. Third, our results show that the impact of CSR activities on corporate value has become much stronger over time. These results suggest that the conduct of CSR activities in China increased corporate value in the period from 2013 to 2018, supporting the results of most recent studies, and the influence is getting stronger and stronger.

CSR in Chinese traditional culture refers to righteousness. Confucius said that wealth and nobility are what people want, and if you do not get it by the way, you will not get anywhere [62]. We can know that righteousness was more important than profit in ancient times. Since the establishment of modern society, China has neglected corporate social responsibility in order to develop the economy, which has led to a series of problems. In order to solve these problems, all parties in China began to attach importance to corporate social responsibility. In the period of 2009–2012 CSR was developing rapidly, and its importance and necessity were being grasped in China. However, the investment costs of CSR activities were very high in this economic environment, and the government also had little input in encouraging companies to engage in social responsibility at this stage. In addition, it takes time for CSR activities to convert into economic benefits. This is likely why CSR is not correlated with corporate value at this stage. During the stage of 2013–2018, CSR activities in China were standardized and became more normative. In addition, the Chinese government emphasized CSR activities and implemented many policies to promote them during this period. Finally, CSR activities were converting into economic benefits more quickly because media reports on CSR activities were increasing, and the public could easily read them on the Internet. Therefore, CSR activities were having a positive effect on corporate value in the short term.

At present, most of the existing studies focus on the relationship between CSR and corporate value. Several studies on the impact of CSR activities on corporate value have shown both negative and positive correlations, as well as no correlation, with corporate value. Other studies have shown a negative relationship between CSR activities and corporate value in the current year and a positive relationship in the next year. Nevertheless, it makes it interesting to see the change of the relationship between them. Furthermore, unlike most of the previous studies which used a maximums of three years of data, we expanded the range to 10 years of data. Hence, we provide a new perspective on the relationship between CSR and corporate value.

Based on this study, corporations should realise that in the current environment, the conduct of CSR activities and the maximization of enterprise value are not two opposite things. Corporations' conduct of CSR activities will not reduce corporate value but increase corporate value. Especially in today's globalized world, the Chinese companies which want to go abroad can, through conduct of CSR activities, enhance their global competitiveness, and also have a reference of significance for these foreign companies which want to enter the Chinese market, or want to conduct transactions with Chinese companies to create company development strategy.

Our study has several limitations. First, the values of our variables are averages, making it impossible to determine the year in which the impact of CSR activities on corporate value changes. Second, we studied changes in the relationship between CSR activities and corporate values only in the current period; changes in the impact of CSR activities on corporate value in the next year and the next two years should also be studied. Third, restricting the sample to companies for which all necessary financial information is available from 2009 to 2018 may have led to sample selection bias. Future studies should seek to overcome these limitations and extend this line of research.

Author Contributions: Conceptualization, F.Z. and J.-y.J.; methodology, F.Z.; validation, F.Z. and J.-y.J.; formal analysis, F.Z.; investigation, J.-y.J.; resources, F.Z.; data curation, F.Z.; writing—original draft preparation, F.Z.; writing—review and editing, J.-y.J.; supervision, J.-y.J. and F.Z. All authors have read and agreed to the published version of the manuscript.

Acknowledgments: We appreciate support from Inha University.

References

1.   Zhang, D.Y.; Morse, S.; Ma, Q.Y. Corporate social responsibility and sustainable development in China: Current status and future perspectives. *Sustainability.* **2019**, *11*, 4392. [CrossRef]
2.   Park, J.H.; Park, H.Y.; Lee, H.Y. The effect of social ties between outside and inside directors on the association between corporate social responsibility and firm value. *Sustainability* **2018**, *10*, 3840. [CrossRef]
3.   Elif, A.S. Corporate social responsibility and financial performance: The moderating role of ownership concentration in Turkey. *Sustainability* **2019**, *11*, 3643.
4.   Liu, N.N.; Liu, C.Z.; Guo, Q.; Da, B.; Guan, L.N.; Chen, H.Y. Corporate social responsibility and financial performance: A quantile regression approach. *Sustainability* **2019**, *11*, 3717. [CrossRef]

5.   Sial, M.S.; Zheng, C.M.; Khuong, N.V.; Khan, T.; Usman, M. Does firm performance influence corporate social responsibility reporting of Chinese listed companies? *Sustainability* **2018**, *10*, 2217. [CrossRef]

6.   Yang, M.H.; Bento, P.; Akbar, A. Does CSR influence firm performance indicators? Evidence from Chinese pharmaceutical enterprises. *Sustainability* **2019**, *11*, 5656. [CrossRef]

7.   Sampong, F.; Song, N.; Boahene, K.O.; Wadie, K.A. Disclosure of CSR performance and firm value: New evidence from south Africa on the basis of the GRI Guidelines for sustainability disclosure. *Sustainability* **2018**, *10*, 4518. [CrossRef]

8.   Li, K.; Khalili, N.R.; Cheng, W.Q. Corporate social responsibility practices in China: Trends, context, and impact on company performance. *Sustainability* **2019**, *11*, 354. [CrossRef]

9.   Freeman, R.; Liedtka, J. Corporate social responsibility: A critical approach. *Bus. Horizons* **1991**, *34*, 92–98. [CrossRef]

10. Cornell, B.; Shapiro, A.C. Corporate Stakeholders and Corporate Finance. *Financial Manag.* **1987**, *16*. [CrossRef]

11. Zeng, T. Corporate social responsibility, tax aggressiveness, and firm value. *Account. Perspect.* **2016**, *15*, 455–462. [CrossRef]

12. Li, S. The evolution of corporate social responsibility theory and literature review. *North. Econ.* **2007**, *11*, 46–49. (In Chinese)

13. Zhu, Y.Q. An empirical study of corporate social responsibility and corporate value. *Res. Financ. Econ. Issues* **2010**, *2*, 102–106. (In Chinese)

14. Kong, Y.S.; Li, J. Research on the correlation between corporate social responsibility and financial performance: Taking Shanghai A-share manufacturing industry as an example. *Financ. Account. Mon.* **2010**, *5*, 14–17. (In Chinese)

15. Yang, H.X. Research on the correlation between corporate social and financial performance based on multiple regression model. *Fri. Account.* **2014**, *5*, 105–108. (In Chinese)

16. Yu, X.H.; Wu, W.J. Corporate governance, corporate social responsibility and corporate value. *Res. Cont. Econ. Res.* **2014**, *5*, 74–78. (In Chinese)

17. Yun, F. *Research on the Correlation between Social Responsibility and Corporate Value of My Country's Electric Power Listed Companies*; North China Electric Power University: Beijing, China, 2016.

18. Ji, C.L.; Yang, P. Research on the correlation between the corporate social responsibility and corporate value of E-commerce platform companies-Based on the Empirical Analysis of Alibaba, JD and Jumei Youpin. *Econ. Manag.* **2016**, *30*, 89–96. (In Chinese)

19. Sun, M.; Zhang, Y. Corporate governance, corporate social responsibility and corporate value. *Friends Account.* **2012**, *10*, 100–103. (In Chinese)

20. Wang, Y.L. *Research on the Correlation between Corporate Social Responsibility and Financial Performance from the Perspective of Ownership Structure*; Qingdao University: Qingdao, China, 2015. (In Chinese)

21. Jiang, H.C. *Corporate Social Responsibility, Ownership Structure and Corporate Value*; Yangzhou University: Yangzhou, China, 2019. (In Chinese)

22. Seo, W.; Park, M.Y. Corporate social responsibility and firm value in China. *Financ. Account. Inf. J.* **2015**, *15*, 103–125. (In Korean)

23. Dai, M.; Kang, H.J. The effect of corporate social responsibility on firm value to Chinese companies. *J. Korea Cont. Assoc.* **2013**, *12*, 422–427. (In Korean) [CrossRef]

24. Shin, M.S.; Kim, S.U.; Kim, B.S. The impact of corporate social responsibility spending on corporate value. *Financ. Eng. Res.* **2011**, *10*, 99–125. (In Korean)

25. Jeon, I.; Seol, Y.M.; Kim, C.K. The relationship between corporate social responsibility and corporate value. *Manag. Res.* **2012**, *27*, 361–387. (In Korean)

26. Jin, L.; Yang, D.H.; Hong, Y.D.; Choi, J.H. International comparison of the relationship between corporate social responsibility and firm value: Korea and China. *Korean Account.* **2016**, *25*, 67–112. (In Korean)

27. David, P.; Kline, S.; Dai, Y. Corporate Social Responsibility Practices, Corporate Identity, and Purchase Intention: A Dual-Process Model. *J. Public Relations Res.* **2005**, *17*, 291–313. [CrossRef]

28. Waddock, S.A.; Graves, S.B. The corporate social performance-financial performance link. *Strateg. Manag. J.* **1997**, *18*, 303–319. [CrossRef]

29. Deng, D.M. Analysis of the relationship between corporate social responsibility and corporate performance. *Sci. Tech. Entr. Mon.* **2005**, *18*, 116–117. (In Chinese)

30. Li, S.C.; Zhang, C.W.; Li, F. Research on the relationship between social responsibility and financial performance of electric power companies-based on panel data of 51 companies from 2011 to 2013. *Friends Account.* **2015**, *24*, 60–64. (In Chinese)

31. Zhang, W.B. *An Empirical Study on the Relationship between Corporate Social Responsibility and Financial Performanc*; Soochow University: Suzhou, China, 2010. (In Chinese)

32. Yin, K.G.; Liu, X.Q. Research on the relationship between corporate social responsibility and financial performance based on endogeneity-empirical evidence from Chinese listed companies. *China Soft Sci.* **2014**, *29*, 98–107. (In Chinese)

33. Ko, S.C.; Park, R.S. Determinants of corporate social responsibility and corporate value. *Tax. Account. J.* **2011**, *12*, 105–134. (In Korean)

34. Kim, C.S. Corporate social responsibility and corporate value. *Korea Sec. Sch. J.* **2009**, *38*, 507–545. (In Korean)

35. Vance, S.C. Are socially responsible corporations good investment risk? *Manag. Rev.* **1975**, *64*, 18–24.

36. Friedman, M. The social responsibility of business is to increase its profits. *N. Y. Tim. Mag.* **1970**, *13*, 32–33.

37. Aupperle, K.E.; Carroll, A.B.; Hatfield, J.D. An empirical examination of the relationship between corporate social responsibility and profitability. *Acad. Manag. J.* **1985**, *28*, 446–463.

38. Li, Z. Research on the correlation between corporate social responsibility and corporate value: Empirical evidence from listed companies on the Shanghai Stock Exchange. *Chin. Ind. Econ.* **2016**, *2*, 77–83. (In Chinese)

39. Makni, R.; Francoeur, C.; Bellavance, F. Causality between corporate social performance and financial performance: From Canadian firms. *J. Bus. Ethics* **2009**, *3*, 409–422. [CrossRef]

40. Yang, W.S.; Yang, S.L. An empirical study on the relationship between corporate social responsibility and financial performance in the Chinese context-Based on the comparative analysis of large, medium and small listed companies. *China Manag. Sci.* **2016**, *24*, 143–150. (In Chinese)

41. Brammer, S.; Brooks, C.; Pavelin, S. Corporate social performance and stock returns: UK evidence from disaggregate measures. *Financ. Manag.* **2006**, *35*, 97–116. [CrossRef]

42. Shane, P.B.; Spicer, B.H. Market response to environmental information produced outside the firm. *Account. Rev.* **1983**, *58*, 521–538.

43. Wright, P.; Ferris, S.P. Agency conflict and corporate strategy: The effect of divestment on corporate value. *Strateg. Manag. J.* **1997**, *18*, 77–83. [CrossRef]

44. Pan, F.; Wang, L. Research on the relationship between corporate environmental investment and economic performance. *New Account.* **2015**, *4*, 6–11. (In Chinese)

45. Chen, K.; Li, S.T. The impact of corporate social responsibility on financial performance: A key element perspective. *Stat. Res.* **2010**, *27*, 105–111. (In Chinese)

46. Ullman, A. Data in search of a theory: A critical examination of the relationship among social performance, social disclosure, and economic performance. *Acad. Manag. Rev.* **1985**, *10*, 540–577.

47. Bauer, R.; Koedijk, K.; Otten, R. International evidence on ethical mutual fund performance and investment style. *J. Bank. Financ.* **2005**, *29*, 1751–1767. [CrossRef]

48. Wen, S.B.; Fang, Y. An empirical study on the relationship between corporate social responsibility and financial performance-Panel data analysis from the perspective of stakeholders. *Chin. Ind. Econ.* **2008**, *10*, 150–160. (In Chinese)

49. Tu, H.; Zheng, H. Corporate social responsibility, ownership and company value. *Nankai J.* **2018**, *6*, 147–156. (In Chinese)

50. Derwall, J.; Guenster, N.; Bauer, R.; Koedijk, K. The eco-efficiency premium puzzle. *Financ. Anal. J.* **2005**, *61*, 51–63. [CrossRef]

51. Liu, L.J.; Chen, X.M. Research on the impact of corporate responsibility on financial performance. *Stat. Dec.* **2010**, *14*, 149–151. (In Chinese)

52. Zhang, Z.G.; Jin, X.C.; Li, G.Q. An empirical study on the intertemporal impact of corporate social responsibility and financial performance. *Account. Res.* **2013**, *8*, 32–39. (In Chinese)

53. Wang, N. *The Study on the Relationship between Social Responsibility Fulfillment and Firm Value in Private Enterprises—A Case Study of Chengzhang Group*; Xi'an University: Xi'an, China, 2018. (In Chinese)

54. Wu, Y. *Property Rights, Corporate Social Responsibility and Enterprise Value—Taking Agricultural Listed Companies as an Example*; Wuhan Polytechnic University: Wuhan, China, 2018. (In Chinese)

55. Sheldon, O. *The Philosophy of Management*; Sir Isaac Pitman and Sons Ltd.: London, UK, 1924.

56. Schnepp, G.J.; Bowen, H.R. Social Responsibilities of the Businessman. *Am. Cathol. Sociol. Rev.* **1954**, *15*, 42. [CrossRef]

57. Carroll, A. A three-dimensional conceptual model of corporate social performance. *Acad. Manag. Rev.* **1979**, *4*, 497–505. [CrossRef]

58. Yin, Q. On the impact of CSR on the sustainable development of enterprises based on John Elkingtor's "Triple Bottom Line' theory. *Oriental Enterprise Culture.* **2012**, *7*, 203–204. (In Chinese)

59. Li, H.Y.; He, B.; Chen, H.; Wu, J.Q. My country's CSR large sample empirical research: Theory, method and data processing. *Financ. Account. Mon.* **2019**, *15*, 122–132. (In Chinese)

60. Xi, J.P. Zhi jiang xin yu. *Zhejiang Dly.* **2007**, *251*. Available online: https://books.google.com.hk/books/about/%E4%B9%8B%E6%B1%9F%E6%96%B0%E8%AF%AD.html?id=4jrgDwAAQBAJ&printsec=frontcover&source=kp_read_button&redir_esc=y#v=onepage&q&f=false (accessed on 2 November 2020). (In Chinese).

61. Zhou, X.M. *Corporate Social Responsibility and Stake Holder Value Maximization -Based on the Perspective of Mergers and Acquistions*; Jilin University: Jilin, China, 2018. (In Chinese)

62. Ogasawara, K. Analects of Confucius. *Jpn. J. Radiol. Technol.* **2011**, *67*, 67. (In Chinese) [CrossRef]

6

The Impact of Corporate Social Responsibility Disclosure on the Future Earnings Response Coefficient (ASEAN Banking Analysis)

Istianingsih [1,*][ID]**, Terri Trireksani** [2] **and Daniel T. H. Manurung** [3][ID]

[1]   Economics and Business Faculty, Universitas Bhayangkara Jakarta Raya, Kota Jakarta Selatan, Daerah Khusus Ibukota Jakarta 12550, Indonesia

[2]   Murdoch Business School, Murdoch University, Murdoch 6150, Australia; t.trireksani@murdoch.edu.au

[3]   STIE Widya Gama Lumajang, Jawa Timur 67352, Indonesia; dtmanurung@gmail.com

*   Correspondence: istianingsih@dsn.ubharajaya.ac.id

Abstract: Corporate social responsibility in the banking industry has an impact on the environment and society. Research was conducted on the impacts of environmental social responsibility disclosure on future income response coefficients of The Association of South East Asian Nations (ASEAN) Banking to determine the level of concern ASEAN banks have in disclosing corporate responsibility, and to understand the levels of future revenue response coefficients. The variable in this research was measured by corporate social responsibility disclosure, while the variable of the Future Earnings Response Coefficient (FERC) was based on the value of banking stocks. Other variables—size, growth, earning persistence, and earnings volatility—were the control variables. The sampling method used was a purposive sampling approach; a research sample of 280 banks in 5 ASEAN countries was determined with this provision: banking report data were taken from the stock exchanges of each country and sustainability reports, using the Global Reporting Initiative (GRI) standard version 4 (G4) from 2014 to 2018. The researchers used conducted multiple regression analysis to examine the variables. The analysis tools used included panel data, so that data processing was carried out using review software. The results of the study show that corporate social responsibility disclosure has a positive and significant effect on the future earnings response coefficient, whereas other variables (i.e., company size, growth, and earnings persistence), do not have a relationship with the disclosure of corporate responsibility or FERC. Only the volatility of earnings has an influence on disclosure of corporate social responsibility and FERC.

Keywords: corporate social responsibility; earnings response coefficient; stock prices

JEL Classification: G32; G34

1. Introduction

Financial information cannot reflect all changes that occur in business operations [1]. A financial report is considered a "fail" when describing coverage areas of intangible asset values, bringing out the increase of information asymmetry between company and user. It creates inefficiency in the process of resource allocation in the stock market (Refs [1–3] Accounting failures show that the intangible resources owned by a company emphasize claims that traditional financial reports have lost their relevance as decision-making instruments [4].

Ref [1] argue that financial reports that mostly value the tangible assets of a company have seen a decrease of value–relevance, especially in an industry sector that is dominated by knowledge-intensive and innovative organizations. This should encourage companies to raise awareness to external parties about the different (non-financial) conditions. For example, corporate social responsibility (CSR) is still a worthy topic to be examined because it can lead to conflict between two different parties. The potential conflicts can happen to two types of shareholders that are affiliated with the company (insider), and other shareholders, such as institutions or small individual investors, who are not affiliated with the [5].

Ref [5] They found a relationship between insiders and CSR ratings. The insider has a personal advantage when the company has a high CSR rating. The CSR conflict can be seen from two different perspectives. On the one hand, we find that greater levels of CSR spending can maximize a company's value [5,6]. On the other hand, CSR activity is considered an expense for the company, so that it can decrease shareholder value.

Corporate social responsibility is needed to maintain the harmony of relationships between companies and the environment. The World Bank defines CSR as a business commitment to contribute to sustainable economic development, through collaboration with employees and their representatives, their families, local communities, and the general public, to improve the quality of life, in ways that are beneficial for both business and development. Ref [7] stated that the disclosure of information in annual reports, conducted by companies, can reduce information asymmetry and agency problems. The research conducted by [8] showed that one of the reasons that management performs social reporting is for strategic reasons. From an economic perspective, the company will disclose information if it can increase the value of the company. This indicates that companies implementing CSR expect positive response from market participants.

Corporate social responsibility was previously seen as a new concept for Asian business culture; however, many scholars have found that this may not be the case—that a notion appropriate to CSR behavior exists within Asian philosophy [9].The evolution of CSR in ASEAN originated from the establishment of industrialization in 1990, which affected the Asian Economic era. In this period, the CSR program focused on human rights, politics, gender equality, employment conditions, and environmental concerns, due to the increasing use of natural resources [10–12].

The ASEAN Stock Exchange requires disclosure of financial and non-financial information that can be used to predict future conditions of a company [9]. The ASEAN stock exchange may play an increasingly important role in shaping the development of financial reporting in ASEAN. A high level of harmony exists within the disclosure requirements of the five ASEAN countries. Nevertheless, there are important national differences in volume and disclosure levels, as well as sources of authority [9].

By disclosing their CSR activities, it is expected that companies will obtain a good reputation in order to attract investors, so that future earnings of the company can be predicted. The existence of voluntary disclosure in a company's annual report allows investors to obtain additional information to accurately assess future earnings of the company [13]. A lack of information disclosure limits the ability of capital and labor markets to monitor and discipline managers [14]. The higher disclosure can also reduce the cost of equity capital by reducing non-diversifiable risk [15]. Ref [13] examined the relationship between the extent of voluntary disclosure and stock price informatization to predict future earnings. The results of the research show that the future earnings response coefficient (FERC) for a high disclosure company is significantly larger than FERC in a low disclosure company.

Ref [16] explored how the company environmental reputation (CER) affects the relationship between a company's current annual earnings and future annual earnings. They found that companies with higher CER scores show higher levels of stock price anticipation against earnings than companies with lower CER scores. Therefore, environmental problems will most likely influence an investor's ability to forecast future earnings and, hence, their decision to buy corporate securities [16].

In contrast to [16], this study aims to examine the effect of CSR disclosure in a company's annual report on prediction of future earnings, as measured by FERC. Samples in this research include banking companies in five selected ASEAN countries: Indonesia, Malaysia, Philippines, Singapore, and Thailand. Banking companies are selected as samples in this study because, according to the

Association of Chartered Certified Accountants (ACCA) report 2010, the percentage of banks in ASEAN that make the CSR report is still very small, although it increases every year. There is increasing recognition that banks should provide disclosure on social, environmental, and economic (CSR) aspects of their operations, as CSR can enhance bank reputation and investor confidence [17].

The concept of CSR generally states that a company's responsibility is not only to its owners or shareholders, but also to stakeholders who are affected by company operations. Companies that carry out CSR activities will pay attention to the impact of their operations on social and environmental conditions, and strive for positive impacts. So, with the concept of CSR, it is hoped that environmental damage that occurs in the world, such as deforestation, air and water pollution, and climate change, can be reduced. The future earnings response coefficient (FERC) is the relationship between this year's return and next year's earnings, which shows stock price informativeness [18].

The future earnings response coefficient (FERC) is often used as a measure to predict future earnings. FERC reflects more than just persistence. If income smoothing makes earnings more informative, then returns should reflect more information on future earnings, and FERC should be higher for firms, with greater smoothing. If income smoothing merely garbles information, then returns should reflect less future earnings information, and the FERC should be lower for firms with greater smoothing. A more negative correlation indicates more income smoothing. The understanding (that has been explained) is based on several studies related to research on corporate responsibility, and is something that must be done by companies, especially banks.

Ref [19] reported that CSR is desirable because it adds a unique dimension to the attributes of income and is useful for company valuation. In particular, their FERC-based testing results show that companies with higher-CSR smoothness reflect more information about future earnings than companies with lower-CSR smoothness. FERC measurements in [19] referred to the model developed by [20], and also used in [21]. The method approach used in corporate social responsibility is Global Reporting Initiative version 4 (GRI G4), while for the future earnings response coefficient (FERC) uses future stock prices. The control variables in this study are firm size, growth, earnings persistence, and volatility. Profit is a moderating variable. Thus, the study was conducted to determine the impact of disclosure of corporate responsibility on the efficiency of future income responses (ASEAN Banking Analysis).

2. Literature Review and Hypotheses

The agency problem occurs due to information asymmetry between principals and agents. In reducing information discrepancy, a company discloses their annual reports, including a corporate social responsibility disclosure. One strategy to maintain a harmonious relationship with company stakeholders is to implement CSR—With expectations that the company can realize the desires of stakeholders. A harmonious relationship between the company and its stakeholders will help the company achieve sustainability.

Differences in the quality of information between companies occur because of the special characteristics in each company. Due to information discrepancies (information asymmetry) between companies, the manager may try to give a signal about the information to investors. Signaling theory states that there are two ways to give a signal: direct and indirect. Direct signals can be given through, for example, voluntary disclosure of the company's financial statements [22,23].

Investor predictions on future earnings of a company can be tested, for example, with the stock price informativeness model, where the current stock return would reflect the earnings of the next period. This study uses the stock price informativeness model, where the profit prediction rate can be expected from the coefficient of regression result between the current stock return and next period earnings, by adding some control variables, such as those done by [23,24].

In general, study results on the relationship between the levels of information disclosure by companies, with company market performances, are still very diverse. The contents and timing of other expressions (besides financial statement information) may affect the usefulness of financial statements, as disclosed by [25]. Disclosure of information in annual reports conducted by companies is expected to reduce information asymmetry and agency problems [7].

Ref [22] examined the relationship between the extent of voluntary disclosure and stock price informativeness. The [22] studies have hypothesized that the more disclosures, the higher the informativeness of the price, as measured by FERC, ceteris paribus. The results of the research conducted by [22] show that FERC for high disclosure companies is significantly greater than FERC for low disclosure companies.

Research conducted by [26] used a wide range of voluntary disclosures in the annual report as a proxy for the uncertainty on future prospects of the company. CSR reflects the company's efforts to improve the company's image (to be seen as a responsible company). This raises the notion that CSR disclosure has a positive effect on firm value. The existence of voluntary disclosure in the company's annual report allows investors to obtain additional information to accurately assess future earnings of the company in the future, so that uncertainty about future prospects of the company will be reduced. CSR brings many benefits to the banking sector; thus, enhances a bank's reputation and financial performance [27].

FERC is the relationship between this year's return and next year's earnings, which shows stock price informativeness [20]. The future earnings response coefficient (FERC) is often used as a measure to predict future earnings. The [20] model is an approach developed by [20] to examine the amount of information on future earnings that is reflected in changes in current earnings. This approach is used to estimate the direct relationship between future earnings and current earnings and past earnings. To see the ability of the stock market to predict future earnings, the proxy used is the future earnings response coefficient (FERC). This coefficient is obtained by regressing this year's stock return with the annual earnings from the company, plus the control variable. According to [20], investors would have better ability to predict earnings, which would then be reflected in stock prices, which can lead to anticipation of better future profits (and, as a result, produce higher FERC). The approach by [20], hereinafter CKSS, provided evidence that income smoothing increases past and present earnings informativeness, concerning future earnings and cash flow. We do this by investigating the relationship between this year's stock returns and future earnings for firms with different leveling rates. We call this association the future earnings response coefficient (FERC).

Ref [28] support a positive relationship between firm size and ERC. The positive relationship between firm size and earnings response coefficient is good (regarding economic profit). In addition, the more information available about a company's activities, the easier it is for the market to interpret the information in financial statements. Companies that have large total assets indicate that the company has reached the maturity stage, where, at this stage the company has good prospects for a relatively long period of time, is predicted to be relatively stable, and more able to generate profits than small companies. Meanwhile, research [29] states that income has a significant positive effect on ERC, but a significant negative effect on FERC. Meanwhile, leverage has no significant effect on ERC, but has a significant negative effect on FERC. In addition, dividends and firm size have no effect on ERC and FERC.

According to [30,31], theoretically, large companies will not only bound to pressure, but also have more operating activities, and have a greater influence on society, and may have more shareholders, who will always pay attention to social programs made by the company, so that the disclosure of corporate social information will be even wider. This resulted in larger companies being required to disclose their social responsibilities. Ref [32] state that there is a relationship between company size and CSR, where, the bigger the company, the greater the demands to implement CSR, so it can be said that there is a positive correlation between size and social performance.

Anticipating future access to capital markets, firms with higher growth prospects might disclose forward-looking information to reduce information asymmetry [33]. If a company's future earnings are unstable, then they are more difficult to predict and, thus, the amount of future earnings information confiscated in the current share price is low. In addition, firm stock prices may provide more information on future earnings when there is more personal information-seeking activity by institutional analysts and investors [21]. According to [34], the dividend payout ratio and growth in assets have no significant effect on stock price volatility, while earnings volatility has a significant negative effect on stock price volatility. Ref [35] regarding the factors that affect the volatility of share prices in non-financial public companies, stated that the dividend payout ratio and growth asset variables significantly affect stock price volatility. It may be argued that the use of single-segment firms as controls for macroeconomic changes during our sample period, is inadequate, since firms that expand the number of segments will, most likely, use growth options, market valuation of growth, and future options. Ref. [24], also looked at the impact of SFAS No. 131 Business Segment Data on the Market's Ability to Anticipate Future Earning. Their study was conducted in reference to the stock market boom of the late 1990s which resulted in increased income of the companies sample study. They concluded that the Market's Ability to Anticipate Future Income is not due to changes in standards but in response to broad economic events.

Ref [36] concluded that companies experiencing a growth phase have a cash flow relevance value that is higher than the net income relevance value. Ref [37], found that the ability of financial information, such as income and cash flow, to predict the benefits of investment is useful for predicting changes in earnings and cash. The ratio of profit and gross profit to sales is quite significant in predicting changes in profit in the following year. However, it is not significant in predicting cash flow. The variables that are significant in predicting changes of income and cash flow include sales and administration costs and gross profit.

Ref [38] use the earnings return correlation as a proxy for information asymmetry in the context of an adverse selection model. A low earnings return correlation indicates that earnings information provides little information about a firm's value, so that information asymmetry remains high. Therefore, with the aim of reducing information asymmetry, the expression will be more in companies that have a lower earnings return correlation, or, in other words, the earnings return correlation is negatively related to the extent of the expression. Ref [22] tested the relationship between the extent of voluntary expression and informativeness of stock prices. This study found that the ERC future for high disclosers was significantly greater than the ERC future for low disclosers. They did not specifically test for the broad association of voluntary expression with current ERCs, or if the effect of informativeness on current ERCs may be positive or negative. Ref [22,39] tested the relationship between the extent of voluntary expression and informativeness of stock prices. This study found that the ERC future for high disclosers was significantly greater than the ERC future for low disclosers. They did not specifically test for the broad association of voluntary expression with current ERCs, or if the effect of informativeness on current ERCs may be positive or negative. According to the authors, the broad influence of expressions on current ERC may be positive, because, usually, companies that disclose a lot of information are companies that have good news. Research conducted by [26] states that the voluntary level of corporate disclosure published in annual reports has a negative effect on FERC, while the results of the significance test for model 2 (not presented) indicates that, of the five ERC determinants tested, namely earnings persistence, systematic risk, leverage, growth, and company size, only earnings persistence variables were found to have a positive effect on ERC.

Concerning environmental protection and management [40–42] reveals that CSR disclosure in annual reports is one way for companies to build, maintain, and legitimize corporate contributions from an economic and political perspective. CSR is a mechanism for an organization to voluntarily integrate environmental and social concerns into its operations and interactions with stakeholders, which goes beyond the organization's responsibility in the legal field [43,44]. CSR can be interpreted as an industrial commitment to be responsible for the impact of operations in the social, economic, and environmental dimensions, and to maintain that these impacts contribute to the benefits of society and the environment [45]. Companies are increasingly aware that a company's survival also depends on the company's relationship with the community and its environment. Corporate social responsibility occurs between a company and all stakeholders, including customers, employees, communities, owners or investors, government, suppliers, and even competitors [46]. The banking industry also mentions the social responsibility aspect in its annual reports, although, in a relatively simple form, it should be based on economic, environmental, labor, human rights, community/social, and product performance indicators. The reason banking companies in Indonesia conduct social reporting is because of a change in the paradigm of accountability, from management to share owners and stakeholders.

Investor considerations will affect the market response to company profits (FERC) because investors not only use earnings information in making investment decisions, but the information contained in the CSR report [41]. This means that the information contained in CSR will reduce, or negatively affect, the level of use of earnings information by investors [42]. According to [39], research on voluntary disclosure shows that a higher level of disclosure is associated with better market performance (as measured by stock returns) and the correlation of earnings and company stock returns are used as a proxy for information asymmetry. The low correlation of earnings and stock returns indicate that earnings information provides little information about a firm's value, indicating that there is still high information asymmetry. This disclosure aims to reduce information asymmetry, especially for companies that have a low correlation of earnings/returns, so that there is a negative relationship between the correlation of earnings/returns (FERC) and the level of disclosure.

Hypothesis 1. *Corporate social responsibility disclosure has a positive effect on the company's future earnings prediction level as measured by FERC.*

3. Research Methods

3.1. Population and Sample

The populations in this study are banking companies in five ASEAN countries (Indonesia, Singapore, Malaysia, Thailand, and Philippines). Purposive sampling was conducted for unqualified population members, not selected as the study sample.

Sampling was based on the following criteria:

(1)   Banking and financial companies listed in the Stock Exchange in the five ASEAN countries: Indonesia, Malaysia, Philippines, Singapore, and Thailand.
(2)   Companies using the Global Reporting Initiative (GRI) version 4 (G4) standard in disclosure of corporate social responsibility.
(3)   The companies had complete data in accordance with the needs of the study sample.

3.2. Definition and Operation of Variables

3.2.1. Future Earnings Response Coefficient (FERC)

This study follows the model used by Ettredge et al. (2005) and Istianingsih (2011). The model that estimates FERC in this research is as follows:

$$R_t = a_0 + b_0 E_{t-1} + b_1 E_t + b_2 E_{t+1} + b_3 R_{t+1}$$

where E_{t-1} and E_t respectively represent earnings for year $t - 1$ and t, and E_{t+1} represents profit t year +1. R_{t+1} is the annual stock return in year $t + 1$. The coefficient (b_0) is predicted to be negative, the coefficient of ERC (b_1) is predicted to be positive, the coefficient of future returns (b_3) is predicted to be negative because it associates to the unexpected component of E_{t+1}.

The FERC is measured following the measurements used by Ettredge et al. (2005) and Istianingsih (2011). The basic FERC model used in this study is as follows:

$$R_t = a_0 + b_0 E_{t-1} + b_1 E_t + b_2 E_{t+1} + b_3 R_{t+1}$$

where:

R_t: daily stock return year t, calculated 12 months that ends on March 31.

E_t: retained earnings year t, divided by equity at the end of March.

E_{t-1}: retained earnings year $t - 1$, divided by equity at the end of March.

E_{t+1}: retained earnings year $t + 1$, divided by equity at the end of March.

R_{t+1}: daily stock return year $t + 1$, calculated 12 months that ends on March 31.

The value of FERC is coefficient b_2.

3.2.2. CSR Disclosure Index (CSRI)

In this study, an independent variable is the disclosure of corporate social responsibility (CSR). CSR disclosure is measured by using CSR index. Disclosures are measured using the GRI Standard, covering economic, environmental, and social indicators. CSRI is calculated by using dichotomy on each research instrument for each item of CSR where disclosure is given as a value of 1, and if it is not disclosed, it is given a value of 0. Next, the score of each item are totaled to get an overall score for each company. For the calculation formula of CSRI, it is as follows:

$$CSRI_J = \frac{\Sigma X_{ij}}{n_J}$$

The approach to calculate CSRI uses a content analysis approach, where each CSR item in a research instrument is assigned a value of 1 if it is disclosed, and a value of 0 if it is not disclosed. Next, the value of each item is totaledto earn the overall value for each company.

$CSRI_j$: corporate social responsibility disclosure index.

n_j: Total item in GRI 4.0 (161 item).

X_{ij}: content analysis: 1 = if item i disclosed; 0 = if item i not disclosed.

Therefore, $0 \leq CSRI_j \leq 1$.

3.2.3. Company Size (SIZE)

The variable size is calculated by using the logarithmic proxy of the market capitalization of the company. Company size is used to control the possibility of influence of the company size and information environment on FERC, as used in [21,23,24].

3.2.4. Company Growth (SG)

The growth variable in this study is used to see the effect on the relationship between the current return to the future earnings of the company, as used in [14,21,24,47]. The growth variable is measured from the sales growth rate, which is the growth rate of net sales.

$$SG_t = \frac{SALES_t - SALES_{t-1}}{SALES_{t-1}}$$

3.2.5. Earning Persistence (PERSIS)

Earnings persistence is used to control the effect of earnings persistence on FERC, as used in [14,21,24,47]. The earnings persistence is measured by a dummy variable with a value of 1 for a company that has a negative next year profit and 0 for the other. According to [14], if the company's earnings is to turn negative in the following year, then it will be more difficult to predict than companies that have positive future earnings that are more normal and persistence.

3.2.6. Earnings Volatility (VOLA)

The earnings volatility is used to control the effect of earnings volatility on FERC, as used in [14,21,24,47]. Companies with high earnings volatility will be more difficult to predict. This variable is measured by the standard deviation of earnings before interest and tax from year $t - 1$ to year $t + 1$.

3.3. Research Design

The model used to test the factors affecting FERC in this study is a model that has been used in [14,24]. This study follows [14] in the use of realized earnings for year $t + 1$ in lieu of expectation of year end income t. The realization of $t - 1$ year earnings is used as the forecast of the previous year's earnings. To reduce errors due to the use of realized profits, this study uses the yield $t + 1$ year stock, as conducted in [14,24].

The model used to test the factors affecting FERC in this study is as follows:

$$
\begin{aligned}
R_t = a_0 &+ b_0 E_{t-1} + b_1 E_t + b_2 E_{t+1} + b_3 R_{t+1} + b_4 CSDI + b_5 SIZE + b_6 GROW \\
&+ b_7 PERSIS + b_8 VOLA + b_9 CSDI + b_9 CSDI * E_{t-1} + b_{10} CSDI * E_t \\
&+ b_{11} CSDI * E_{t+1} + b_{12} CSDI * R_{t+1} + b_{13} SIZE * E_{t-1} \\
&+ b_{14} SIZE * E_t + b_{15} SIZE * E_{t+1} + b_{16} SIZE * R_{t+1} \\
&+ b_{17} GROW * R_{t-1} + b_{18} GROW * E_t + b_{19} GROW * E_{t+1} \\
&+ b_{20} GROW * R_{t+1} + b_{21} PERSIS * E_{t-1} + b_{22} PERSIS * E_t \\
&+ b_{23} PERSIS * E_{t+1} + b_{24} PERSIS * R_{t+1} + b_{25} VOLA * E_{t-1} \\
&+ b_{26} VOLA * E_t + b_{27} VOLA * E_{t+1} + b_{28} VOLA * R_{t+1} + \varepsilon
\end{aligned}
$$

where:

R_t:	Daily stock return year t, calculated using 12 months ended on March 31.
E_t:	Retained earnings year t, divided by market equity at the end of March.
E_{t-1}:	Retained earnings year $t{-}1$, divided by market equity at the end of March.
E_{t+1}:	Retained earnings year $t + 1$, divided by market equity at the end of March.
R_{t+1}:	daily stock return year $t + 1$, calculated using 12 months ended on March 31
CSRI:	Corporate social responsibility disclosure index (measuring the type of CSR disclosed by the company in its annual report), is a content analysis with a value of 1 if the item is disclosed, and value 0 if the item is not disclosed.
SIZE:	Size of company calculated by logarithm market capitalization.
GROWTH:	Sales growth company i in year t, measured by sales growth rate which is the growth rate of net sales.
PERSISTENT:	Earnings persistence is a dummy variable with value 1 for company that has negative annual profit, and 0 for the other.
VOLATILITY:	Earnings volatility, measured by the standard deviation of earnings before interest and tax from year $t - 1$ to year $t + 1$.

It is expected that the regression coefficient of interaction variables CSRI and E2010 will be greater than 0 to support the existing hypothesis. The effect of control variable on FERC can be seen from the regression coefficient of interaction variables SIZE, GROW, PERSIS, and VOLA with E_{t+1}.

4. Results and Discussion

4.1. Descriptive Statistic

Populations in this research are banks in five ASEAN countries (Indonesia, Malaysia, Philippines, Singapore, and Thailand). Sampling was done by the purposive sampling method. Unqualified population members were not selected as the sample. After the selection of data for each company selected to sample, there were 56 companies selected, with a final sample of 280 companies obtained from 2014 to 2018. This sample consists of 56 banks from five countries, namely Indonesia (as many as 37 banks), Malaysia (seven banks), Thailand (seven banks), Singapore (two banks), and the Philippines (three banks). Data from 37 banks were taken from annual reports and financial reports, as well as their share prices for 5 years, from 2014 to 2018. In particular, profit data were taken from 2013 to 2019 as this study required profit data for the past year and future profits (1 year ahead). For data used to calculate stock returns—data from 2014 to 2019 were used because return data are needed until the next year.

Refer to Table 1 the results show that the average CSRI is 0.15 (15%), with a maximum is 0.3956 (39%) and a minimum is 0.0110 (1%). It can be concluded that the average disclosure of banking companies in ASEAN that follow the ASEAN CG Scorecard assessment is still very low. This is possible because CSR is still a voluntary disclosure and has not been required by financial accounting standards. As a result, companies simply voluntarily disclose the social information. This voluntary disclosure is not required by the standards, but is recommended, and will add value to the companies. The number of companies that disclose social responsibility information in their annual reports is growing [7].

Table 1. Descriptive Statistics.

Variable	N	Minimum	Maximum	Mean	Std. Deviation
R_t	280	−0.5431	7.87	0.20	0.87
R_{t+1}	280	−0.8056	123.68	0.32	1.44
CSRI	280	0.0110	0.40	0.15	0.10
Persistence	280	0.0000	1.00	0.97	0.16
Growth	280	−0.1740	5.16	0.25	0.54
Size	280	46.819	8.94	6.83	1.05
Leverage	280	0.0324	8.86	1.40	0.93
Volatility	280	0.0024	0.93	0.18	0.18
E_{t-1}	280	−81,740	24,253,845	1,342,804	4,154,244
E_t	280	−54,550	25,410,788	1,327,796	4,419,705
E_{t+1}	280	−6,483,084	26,227,991	1,253,784	4,392,954
CSRI × E_{t-1}	280	−18,863	7,263,220	326,843	1,172,528
CSRI × E_t	280	−12,588	7,438,205	329,034	1,247,190
CSRI × E_{t+1}	280	−1,211,125	6,973,318	310,019	1,186,516
Persistence × E_{t-1}	280	−54,550	24,253,845	1,342,468	4,154,333
Persistence × E_t	280	0	25,410,788	1,329,092	4,419,305
Persistence × E_{t+1}	280	−6,483,084	26,227,991	1,258,156	4,391,431
Growth × E_{t-1}	280	−66,604	7,026,602	291,192	1,031,955
Growth × E_t	280	−61,303	6,388,087	285,186	1,037,430
Growth × E_{t+1}	280	−436,420	7,403,463	296,998	1,128,610
Size × E_{t-1}	280	−570,097	216,919,242	11,281,113	35,679,239
Size × E_t	280	−380,460	227,266,600	11,189,949	38,091,541
Size × E_{t+1}	280	−53,561,380	234,575,423	10,653,507	38,441,481
Leverage × E_{t-1}	280	−96,578	30,757,781	1,559,749	4,893,271
Leverage × E_t	280	−64,452	32,224,971	1,523,727	5,236,725
Leverage × E_{t+1}	280	−7,742,784	33,261,316	1,508,695	5,499,659
Volatility × E_{t-1}	280	−43,632	2,231,165	119,233	328,590
Volatility × E_t	280	−29,118	1,888,115	92,770	253,115
Volatility × E_{t+1}	280	−4,614,122	1,307,709	39,097	490,124
Valid N (list-wise)	280				

Based on the CSRI graph for the average score of CSRI as per country, it shows that the highest CSRI value is the Philippines and the lowest is Malaysia.

Table 2 summarizes the results of correlation testing between variables in the FERC model. This table is used to see the correlation between variables in the research model used to test the effect of corporate social responsibility disclosure on FERC. From Table 3, it can be seen that the correlation between CSRI and E_{t+1} is positive but not significant. This is not in accordance with the initial prediction that the higher the CSRI, the stronger the relationship between current return and future earnings or the higher the FERC.

Table 2. Correlation Test.

	R_t	E_{t-1}	E_t	E_{t+1}	R_{t+1}	CSRI	GROW	PERSIS	SIZE	VOLA
R_t	1									
E_{t-1}	−0.039	1								
E_t	−0.067 *	0.472 **	1							
E_{t+1}	−0.040	0.381 **	0.514 **	1						
R_{t+1}	−0.013	−0.077 **	0.003	0.006	1					
CSRI	−0.059 *	0.043	0.063 *	0.046	−0.034	1				
GROW	0.046	0.040	0.209 **	0.126 **	−0.053 *	0.044	1			
PERSIS	0.000	0.249 **	0.326 **	0.550 **	−0.023	0.129 **	0.141 **	1		
SIZE	−0.069 **	0.086 **	0.065 *	0.019	−0.180 **	0.257 **	0.123 **	0.205 **	1	
VOLA	0.006	−0.070 **	−0.098 **	0.029	0.051	−0.152 **	−0.056 *	−0.293 **	−0.283 **	1

* = significant at 1%; ** = significant at 5%. R_t: Daily stock return year t, calculated using 12 months ended on March 31. E_t: Retained earnings year t, divided by market equity at the end of March. E_{t-1}: Retained earnings year $t - 1$, divided by market equity at the end of March. E_{t+1}: Retained earnings year $t + 1$, divided by market equity at the end of March. R_{t+1}: daily stock return year $t + 1$, calculated using 12 months ended on March 31. CSRI: Corporate social responsibility disclosure index (measuring the type of CSR disclosed by the company in its annual report), is a content analysis with a value of 1 if the item is disclosed, and value 0 if the item is not disclosed. SIZE: Size of company calculated by logarithm market capitalization. GROW: Sales growth company i in year t, measured by sales growth rate which is the growth rate of net sales. PERSIS: Earnings persistence is a dummy variable with value 1 for company that has negative annual profit, and 0 for the other. VOLA: Earnings volatility, measured by the standard deviation of earnings before interest and tax from year $t - 1$ to year $t + 1$.

Table 3. Summary of Test Results.

Variable	Coefficient	Std. Error	t-Statistic	Prob.
C	(0.524999)	0.155451	(3.377256)	0.0011
R_{t+1}	0.281152	0.056739	4.955225	0.0000
CSRI	(0.478390)	0.245706	(1.946999)	0.0549
GROW	(0.047333)	0.048188	(0.982243)	0.3288
SIZE	0.098013	0.028369	3.454979	0.0009
LEVERAGE	0.068324	0.019128	3.571938	0.0006
VOLATILITY	0.144405	0.109238	1.321929	0.1898
E_{t-1}	(5.43×10^{-6})	8.84×10^{6}	(0.614756)	0.5404
E_t	1.31×10^{5}	1.26×10^{-5}	1.038909	0.3018
E_{t+1}	(2.76×10^{-6})	3.58×10^{-6}	(0.772226)	0.4421
CSRI $\times E_t$	(1.57×10^{-6})	1.19×10^{-6}	−1.324824	0.1888
CSRI $\times E_{t-1}$	1.94×10^{-7}	1.14×10^{-6}	0.169433	0.8659
CSRI $\times E_{t+1}$	**1.60×10^{-6}**	**6.14×10^{-7}**	**2.612443**	**0.0106**
PERSISTENT $\times E_{t-1}$	(1.17×10^{-5})	8.71×10^{-6}	(1.342755)	0.1830
PERSISTENT $\times E_t$	2.01×10^{-6}	1.26×10^{-5}	0.159798	0.8734
PERSISTENT $\times E_{t+1}$	2.66×10^{-6}	3.09×10^{-6}	0.861875	0.3912
GROWTH $\times E_{t-1}$	2.14×10^{-6}	4.00×10^{7}	5.348892	0.0000
GROWTH $\times E_t$	(1.99×10^{-6})	3.08×10^{7}	(6.456691)	0.0000
GROWTH $\times E_{t+1}$	(7.03×10^{-7})	3.60×10^{7}	(1.950104)	0.0545
SIZE $\times E_{t-1}$	2.05×10^{6}	1.79×10^{7}	11.47542	0.0000
SIZE $\times E_t$	(1.74×10^{-6})	3.11×10^{7}	(5.594689)	0.0000
SIZE $\times E_{t+1}$	8.20×10^{9}	2.46×10^{7}	0.033306	0.9735
LEVERAGE $\times E_{t-1}$	(2.31×10^{-8})	2.20×10^{7}	(0.105032)	0.9166
LEVERAGE $\times E_t$	1.80×10^{7}	3.77×10^{7}	0.477367	0.6343
LEVERAGE $\times E_{t+1}$	(5.39×10^{-7})	4.61×10^{7}	(1.167694)	0.2462
VOLATILITY $\times E_{t-1}$	(7.36×10^{-7})	2.51×10^{7}	(2.937680)	0.0043
VOLATILITY $\times E_t$	(7.96×10^{-7})	4.64×10^{7}	(1.716082)	0.0898
VOLATILITY $\times E_{t+1}$	**4.92×10^{6}**	**2.18×10^{7}**	**2.261116**	**0.0263**

		Weighted Statistics	
R-squared	0.982338	Mean dependent variable	0.571032
Adjusted R-squared	0.976661	S.D. dependent variable	2.630946
S.E. of regression	0.372378	Sum squared residual	11.64788
F-statistic	173.0398	Durbin–Watson stat	1.932477
Prob (F-statistic)	0.000000		

Table 3. *Cont.*

Variable	Coefficient	Std. Error	t-Statistic	Prob.
	Unweighted Statistics			
R-squared	0.838360	Mean dependent variable		0.203361
Sum squared residual	13.64601	Durbin–Watson stat		1.600378

Numbers marked in bold are the main focus to prove the hypothesis. E_{t+1}: Retained earnings year $t + 1$, divided by market equity at the end of March. R_{t+1}: daily stock return year $t + 1$, calculated using 12 months ended on March 31. *CSRI*: Corporate social responsibility disclosure index (measuring the type of CSR disclosed by the company in its annual report), is a content analysis with a value of 1 if the item is disclosed, and value 0 if the item is not disclosed. *SIZE*: Size of company calculated by logarithm market capitalization. *GROW*: Sales growth company i in year t, measured by sales growth rate which is the growth rate of net sales. *PERSIS*: Earnings persistence is a dummy variable with value 1 for company that has negative annual profit, and 0 for the other. *VOLA*: Earnings volatility, measured by the standard deviation of earnings before interest and tax from year $t - 1$ to year $t + 1$.

4.2. Results

Table 3 shows the results of multiple linear regression analysis on the examined variables.

Table 3 shows that the value of Adjusted R-squared is 0.976661. It means that 97.66% of the variability of independent variable data are used in the study, while the remaining 2.44% is explained by other independent variables outside the model or residual.

Table 3 shows that corporate social responsibility disclosure positively affects the prediction level of future earnings of the company as measured with FERC ($t = 2.612$; $p = 0.0106$). It can be interpreted that the higher the value of CSR disclosure, the higher the prediction value of future earnings of the company as measured by FERC. The results of this research are in line with the results of [26,28,40].

Corporate social responsibility disclosure and earnings do not affect the stock returns. This is very interesting because when the CSR and earnings are viewed individually, they do not affect the stock return, but when the two variables interact, they have a significant effect ($t = 2.612$; $p = 0.0106$). Thus, the interaction between CSR and earnings is informative for future stock prices. In other words, investors cannot only see from one side, either from profit or CSR, but they must see from both sides in order to predict future earnings.

Corporate social responsibility to the public will provide additional information for investors to predict future earnings. This can reduce information asymmetry that occurs between the agent (as the manager of the company) and the principal (as the owner of the company). When information asymmetry is reduced, the investor, as the owner of the company, or the principal, will be more loyal, which is marked by the fluctuation of stock return. Ref [22] examined the relationship between the extent of voluntary disclosure and stock price informativeness. The results of the research show that future earnings response coefficient (FERC) for a high disclosure company is significantly larger than FERC in a low disclosure company.

Ref [8] show that one reason management performs social reporting is for strategic reasons. From an economic perspective, the company will disclose information if it will increase the value of the company. This indicates that companies implementing CSR expect positive response from market participants. This is also supported by [26], who stated that CSR reflects a company's efforts to improve the company's image (to be seen as a responsible company); thus, raising the notion that CSR disclosure has a positive effect on a firm's value.

This study also applies earnings persistence, growth, size, leverage, and earnings volatility as control variables, whether those variables can control the influence of corporate social responsibility disclosure affects the level of prediction of future earnings of the company, as measured by FERC. Table 2 shows that all control variables have no effect on FERC, except earnings volatility. Earnings volatility has value ($t = 2.26116$; $p = 0.0263$). This means that earnings volatility can control the effect of corporate social responsibility disclosure variable to FERC.

Testing of each research variable states that the corporate responsibility disclosure variable has a coefficient value of 2.612, meaning that there is a positive and significant relationship to the future earnings response coefficient (FERC). The results of the study agree with research conducted by [22], namely, the relationship between the extent of voluntary disclosure and stock price informativeness. This study found that the ERC future for high disclosers was significantly greater than the ERC future for low disclosers. They did not specifically examine the relationship between broad voluntary expressions and current ERCs, or if the effect of informativeness on current ERCs may be positive or negative. According to [28], income smoothing firms with higher corporate social responsibility (CSR) experience a higher contemporaneous earnings–return relationship, greater Tobin's Q, and stronger current return–future earnings relationships. The **Q** ratio, also known as Tobin's Q, equals the market value of a company divided by its assets' replacement cost. The results show that CSR is desirable as it adds a unique "quality dimension" to earnings attributes and is useful for firm valuation. The results of different research conducted by [26] show that the voluntary level of corporate disclosure published in annual reports has a negative effect on FERC, while the results of the significance test for model 2 (not presented) indicate that, of the five ERC determinants tested, namely earnings persistence, risk, systematic, leverage, growth, and firm size, only earnings persistence variables were found to have a positive effect on ERC.

As for the control variables in research related to corporate social responsibility, such as company size, growth, earnings persistence, and earnings volatility, it is intended to control the variable corporate social responsibility disclosure, but, as the results of the study agree, only the earnings volatility variable has an influence on the disclosure of corporate social responsibility and FERC. With research conducted, dividend policy has an influence on stock prices because the decision contains important information regarding the distribution of operating income and company performance. This information provides a reaction for each investor, thereby affecting the volatility of stock prices in the market. The fluctuation of profit can make it difficult for companies to get external funds, because the company is unstable. The higher the profit volatility level, the greater the capital gain that will be obtained by investors when the profit reaches its maximum level, so that investors tend to keep the shares they own (hold) for the future. Because not many sales that occurred, the level of stock price volatility tends to be low [34].

Likewise, the company size variable has no relationship to corporate responsibility disclosure, and the FERC research results are not in line with the research [29] which states that the income of a company has a significant positive effect on ERC, but has a significant negative effect on FERC. Meanwhile, leverage has no significant effect on ERC, but has a significant negative effect on FERC. In addition, dividends and firm size have no effect on ERC and FERC. The growth variable is stated to have no relationship with the disclosure of corporate responsibility and FERC, the results of this study do not agree with the research by [8], which concluded that companies experiencing a growth phase have a cash flow relevance value that is higher than the value of net income relevance. [16] found that the ability of financial information, such as income and cash flow, to predict the benefits of investment is useful for predicting changes in earnings and cash. The ratio of profit and gross profit to sales is quite significant in predicting changes in profit for the following year. However, it is not significant in predicting cash flow. Changes in income and cash flow are significantly affected by earnings persistence. However, earnings persistence has no impact on CSR disclosure and FERC. This is in line with [48] who define earnings persistence as a revision of expected future accounting earnings based on profit from current year earnings. The earnings component as a result of the application of the accrual accounting concept for impairment, write-off, or allowance for losses has limited relevance when applied to the evaluation of a firm [49].

5. Conclusions

Based on the results of the analysis and testing of data on the effect of corporate social responsibility disclosure, on the level of predictions of a company's future earnings (as measured by FERC), the following conclusions are obtained:

Disclosure of corporate social responsibility has a positive effect on the level of predictions of future earnings of a company, as measured by FERC, while company size, growth, earnings persistence, and earnings volatility are control variables. The results of the study state that a significant level of the future earnings response coefficient (FERC) is able to predict the disclosure of corporate social responsibility. Where it states that the higher the level of profit in banks, the banks will carry out corporate social responsibility activities. As for the control variables in research related to corporate social responsibility, such as company size, growth, earnings persistence, and earnings volatility, it is intended to control those related to the disclosure of corporate social responsibility, but only the earnings volatility variable has an influence on corporate social responsibility disclosure and FERC, while the size variable company, growth, and earnings persistence have no relationship with corporate responsibility disclosure and FERC. This states that the size of the company, both large and small, does not have an impact on the disclosure of corporate responsibility and FERC, for the growth variable, it only states that there is information related to future income, where the predictions of stock prices are uncertain, so that it will have an impact on the disclosure of corporate responsibility. Moreover, the variable earnings persistence can only predict and maintain future profits so that it will have an impact on the disclosure of corporate social responsibility.

5.1. Theoretical Contribution

The results of previous research that tested the relationship between the information contained in CSR disclosures and the acquisition of stock returns that reflect a company's future earnings are still very limited. This research is expected to be able to provide an overview of the relationship between the current return received by investors and a company's future earnings, as measured by FERC. The closer the relationship between the current return received by investors and the company's future earnings, after the existence of CSR disclosure information, shows that this information is useful for making investment decisions. In other words, CSR information can be used to predict a company's future earnings.

5.2. Practical Contribution

Management needs to pay attention to CSR disclosure to attract investors. With evidence that investors can use information on CSR disclosure as a material to assess a company's ability, company management needs to pay more attention to CSR disclosure as a signal of the company's future capabilities. Other than that, investors also need to consider the company's CSR. The better the company's CSR, the higher the chances of getting a return on investment in the future.

Limitations that we must address include the following:

a.   There is an imbalance in the number of research samples from each country. This occurs because the number of banks registered in the Securities Exchange of each country sampled was different.

b.   Literature on results of previous studies are still very rare.

c.   This study does not accommodate the time difference between samples taken from 2014 to 2018. This is done, considering the number of samples is very small, so we treat all samples in a cross-sectional (not time-series) manner. This research does not consider the possibility of influence from time-to-time, from year-to-year. The use of data for 5 years in this study was only carried out with the aim of increasing the number of observations, in order to be estimated by the weighted least square method, and not to see any difference in influence between times. Future studies need to consider the possibility of influence over time, from year-to-year. Testing needs to be done that can represent the influence of time differences that can provide richer analysis results.

d.   This study only tests the linear relationship between the variables used. There is the possibility of a non-linear relationship between the variables in this study. Future studies can test if there are non-linear relationships between variables in research on CSR Disclosure and FERC.

Author Contributions: I. and T.T. conceived the paper; I. and D.T.H.M. analysed the data; I., T.T. and D.T.H.M. wrote and finalised the manuscript. All authors have read and agreed to the published version of the manuscript.

References

1. Lev, B.; Zarowin, P. The Boundaries of Financial Reporting and How to Extend Them. *J. Account. Res.* **1999**, *37*, 353–385. [CrossRef]
2. Barth, M.E.; Beaver, W.H.; Landsman, W.R. The relevance of the value relevance literature for financial accounting standard setting: Another view. *J. Acc. Econ.* **2001**. [CrossRef]
3. Istianingsih. The Effect of Corporate Social Responsibility and Good Corporate Governance on Pharmaceutical Company Tax Avoidance in Indonesia. *Syst. Rev. Pharm.* **2020**, *11*. [CrossRef]
4. Oliveira, L.; Rodrigues, L.L.; Craig, R. Intangible assets and value relevance: Evidence from the Portuguese stock exchange. *Br. Account. Rev.* **2010**. [CrossRef]
5. Barnea, A.; Rubin, A. Corporate Social Responsibility as a Conflict between Shareholders. *J. Bus. Ethics* **2010**. [CrossRef]
6. Brown, J.; Fraser, M. Approaches and perspectives in social and environmental accounting: An overview of the conceptual landscape. *Bus. Strategy Environ.* **2006**. [CrossRef]
7. Healy, P.M.; Palepu, K.G. Information asymmetry, corporate disclosure, and the capital markets: A review of the empirical disclosure literature. *J. Account. Econ.* **2001**. [CrossRef]
8. Basalamah, A.S.; Jermias, J. Social and Environmental Reporting and Auditing in Indonesia: Maintaining Organizational Legitimacy? *Gadjah Mada Int. J. Bus.* **2005**. [CrossRef]
9. Huerta, M.C.; Ken, O. Communication of Corporate Social Responsibility in Latin American and ASEAN Countries: A Comparative content Analysis of Corporate websites of Leading Companies. *Int. J. Res. Manag.* **2012**, *1*, 130–145.
10. Febrilyantri, C.; Istianingsih. The Influence of Intellectual Capital and Good Corporate Governance on Earnings Response Coefficient (Case Study on Banks listed on IDX 2013–2015). *Int. J. Sci. Res. (IJSR)* **2018**. [CrossRef]
11. Mukti, A.H.; Istianingsih. The Impact of Ownership Structure on Intellectual Capital Disclosure. *Int. Bus. Manag.* **2018**, *12*, 337–345. [CrossRef]
12. Tanudjaja, B.B. Perkembangan Corporate Social Responsibility Di Indonesia. *Nirmana* **2016**, *8*. [CrossRef]
13. Kisno, K.; Istianingsih, I. Detection earnings management by deferred tax expense and firm characteristic. *J. Ris. Akunt. Terpadu* **2016**, *9*. [CrossRef]
14. Istianingsih, I. Efisiensi Modal Intelektual Dan Dampaknya Terhadap Kinerja Perusahaan. *Akuntabilitas* **2014**, *7*. [CrossRef]
15. Botosan, C.A.; Plumlee, M.A. Disclosure Level and Expected Cost of Equity Capital: An Examination of Analysts' Rankings of Corporate Disclosure and Alternative Methods of Estimating Expected Cost of Equity Capital. *SSRN Electron. J.* **2005**. [CrossRef]
16. Hussainey, K.; Salama, A. The importance of corporate environmental reputation to investors. *J. Appl. Account. Res.* **2010**. [CrossRef]
17. Shen, C.H.; Wu, M.W.; Chen, T.H.; Fang, H. To engage or not to engage in corporate social responsibility: Empirical evidence from global banking sector. *Econ. Model.* **2016**. [CrossRef]
18. Gul, F.A.; Srinidhi, B.; Ng, A.C. Does board gender diversity improve the informativeness of stock prices? *J. Account. Econ.* **2011**. [CrossRef]
19. Gao, L.; Zhang, J.H. Firms' earnings smoothing, corporate social responsibility, and valuation. *J. Corp. Financ.* **2015**. [CrossRef]
20. Collins, D.W.; Kothari, S.P.; Shanken, J.; Sloan, R.G. Lack of timeliness and noise as explanations for the low contemporaneuos return-earnings association. *J. Account. Econ.* **1994**. [CrossRef]
21. Tucker, J.W.; Zarowin, P.A. Does income smoothing improve earnings informativeness? *In Account. Rev.* **2006**. [CrossRef]
22. Gelb, D.S.; Zarowin, P. Corporate disclosure policy and the informativeness of stock prices. *Rev. Account. Stud.* **2002**. [CrossRef]

23. Istianingsih. Impact of firm characteristics on CSR disclosure: Evidence from Indonesia stock exchange. *Int. J. Appl. Bus. Econ. Res.* **2015**, *6*, 4265–4281.

24. Ettredge, M.L.; Kwon, S.Y.; Smith, D.B.; Zarowin, P.A. The impact of SFAS No. 131 business segment data on the market's ability to anticipate future earnings. *Account. Rev.* **2005**. [CrossRef]

25. Foster, W.K.; Pryor, A.K. The strategic management of innovation. *J. Bus. Strategy* **1986**. [CrossRef]

26. Widiastuti, H. Pengaruh Luas Ungkapan Sukarela dalam Laporan Tahunan terhadap Earnings Response Coefficient (ERC). *J. Akunt. Dan Investasi* **2004**, *5*, 187–207.

27. Ali, W.; Frynas, J.G.; Mahmood, Z. Determinants of Corporate Social Responsibility (CSR) Disclosure in Developed and Developing Countries: A Literature Review. *Corp. Soc. Responsib. Environ. Manag.* **2017**. [CrossRef]

28. Cho, J.Y.; Jung, K. Earnings Response Coefficients: A Synthesis of Theory and Empirical Evidence. *J. Account. Lit.* **1991**, *10*, 85–116.

29. Firmansyah, A.; Herawaty, V. Pengaruh income smoothing, kebijakan deviden, leverage dan ukuran perusahaan terhadap earnings response coefficient dan future earnings response coefficient. *J. Inf. Perpajak. Akunt. Dan Keuang. Publik* **2019**. [CrossRef]

30. Cowen, S.S.; Ferreri, L.B.; Parker, L.D. The impact of corporate characteristics on social responsibility disclosure: A typology and frequency-based analysis. *Account. Organ. Soc.* **1987**. [CrossRef]

31. Tulhasanah, D.; Nikmah, N. Pengaruh Corporate Social Responsibility Disclosure (Csrd) Terhadap Rasio Profitabilitas Dan Earning Response Coefficient (ERC). *J. Akunt.* **2019**. [CrossRef]

32. Filemon, C.N.; Krisnawati, A. Pengaruh corporate social responsibility disclosure terhadap return on assets pada perusahaan telekomunikasi yang terdaftar di bursa efek indonesia. *J. Manaj. Indones.* **2017**. [CrossRef]

33. Frankel, R.; Mayew, W.J.; Sun, Y. Do pennies matter? Investor relations consequences of small negative earnings surprises. *Rev. Account. Stud.* **2010**. [CrossRef]

34. Rowena, J.; Hendra, H. Earnings Volatility, Kebijakan Dividen, dan Pertumbuhan Asset Berpengaruh Terhadap Volatilitas Harga Saham Pada Perusahaan Manufaktur Di BEI Periode 2013–2015. *J. Adm. Kant.* **2017**, *5*, 2237–6694.

35. Nurfadilah, D.; Sudarmawan, S. Factors That Influence Stock Market Volatility: A Case Study From Malaysia. *Int. J. Bus. Stud.* **2017**, *1*. [CrossRef]

36. Jecheche, P. Dividend policy and stock price volatility: A case of the Zimbabwe stock exchange. *J. Comprehnsive Res. Account. Financ.* **2012**, *10*, 1–13.

37. Koijen, R.S.J.; Van Nieuwerburgh, S. Predictability of returns and cash flows. *Annu. Rev. Financ. Econ.* **2011**. [CrossRef]

38. Guo, Z. Evaluation of Financial Ability of Port Listed Companies Based on Entropy Weight TOPSIS Model. *J. Coast. Res.* **2020**. [CrossRef]

39. Lang, M.; Lundholm, R. Cross-Sectional Determinants of Analyst Ratings of Corporate Disclosures. *J. Account. Res.* **1993**. [CrossRef]

40. Sayekti, Y.; Wondabio, L.S. Pengaruh CSR Disclosure Terhadap Earning Response Coefficient: Suatu Studi Empiris Pada Perusahaan yang Terdaftar Di Bursa Efek Jakarta. In *Simposium Nasional Akuntansi X.*; Ikatan Akuntan Indonesia, Universitas Hasanudin: Makasar, Indonesia, 2007.

41. Guthrie, J.; Parker, L.D. Corporate Social Disclosure: A Rebuttal of Legitimacy Theory. *Account. Bus. Res.* **1989**, *19*, 343–352. [CrossRef]

42. Awuy, V.P.; Sayekti, Y.; Indah, P. Pengaruh Pengungkapan Corporate Social Responsibility (CSR) terhadap Earnings Response Coefficient (ERC). *J. Akunt. Dan Keuang.* **2016**. [CrossRef]

43. Wijayanti, I.; Mawardi, R.; Halim, A.B. The Effect of Corporate Social Responsibility Disclosure, Leverage, Firm Size, and Profitability Toward Earnings Response Coefficient. *Int. J. Innov. Creat. Chang.* **2020**, *13*, 1202–1216.

44. Silalahi, S.P. Pengaruh Corporate Social Responsibility (CSR) Disclosure, Beta dan Price to Book Value (PBV) Terhadap Earnings Response Coefficient (ERC). *J. Ekon.* **2014**, *22*, 1–14.

45. Syam, M.H.; Aqimuddin, E.A.; Nurcahyono, A.; Setiawan, E. Corporate Social Responsibility in ASEAN: Case Study ASEAN CSR Network. *Adv. Soc. Sci. Educ. Humanit. Res.* **2020**, *409*. [CrossRef]

46. Matten, D.; Moon, J. Reflections on the 2018 decade award: The meaning and dynamics of corporate social responsibility. *Acad. Manag. Rev.* **2020**. [CrossRef]

47.   Orpurt, S.F.; Zang, Y. Do direct cash flow disclosures help predict future operating cash flows and earnings? *Account. Rev.* **2009**. [CrossRef]

48.   Penman, S.H.; Zhang, X.J. Accounting conservatism, the quality of earnings, and stock returns. *Account. Rev.* **2002**. [CrossRef]

49.   Hayn, C. The information content of losses. *J. Account. Econ.* **1995**. [CrossRef]

7

Corporate Social Responsibility (CSR) in the Travel Supply Chain

Eneko Ibarnia [1],*[ID], Lluís Garay [2][ID] and Antonio Guevara [3][ID]

[1] Tourism Department, Deusto University, Universities Avenue, 24, 48007 Bilbao, Spain
[2] Economics and Management Department, Open University of Catalonia (UOC),
    Avinguda Tibidabo, 39, 08035 Barcelona, Spain; lgaray@uoc.edu
[3] Faculty of Tourism, Málaga University, León Tolstoy St., Campus de Teatinos, 29071 Malaga, Spain;
    guevara@uma.es74
*   Correspondence: enekoibarnia@uma.es

Abstract: Traditional travel agencies and tour operators are recognized as relevant stakeholders in the tourism distribution chain, even though their role as transforming agents in the achievement of more sustainable tourism is beginning to be accepted. This study aims at reviewing the main topics and the most recent approaches from the academic literature in its analysis of corporate social responsibility (CSR) practices developed by these intermediaries. The work has been structured around six recurring themes in most of the studies carried out: the new intermediaries that operate on the Internet; the role of travel agencies and tour operators in tourism sustainability; the influence of the size of the company; CSR as a disruptive innovation in this sector; the potential of the sustainable tourism supply chain; and the motivations and attitudes of the managers of these businesses when they engage with responsibility. This last topic is developed in greater detail since it is closely linked to the previous ones and dictates, in most cases, the meaning and function of the sustainable performance. The conclusions show how tourism intermediaries have only just begun to develop CSR policies, and those that are committed to their implementation mostly opt for actions aimed at the environment.

Keywords: corporate social responsibility; sustainability; travel supply chain; tourism intermediaries; SME; large corporations; motivations

1. Introduction

As far as sustainability is concerned, it seems to be the consensus to appreciate it as a balance between economic, socio-cultural and environmental returns and impacts [1]. Concerning the enterprise level, one of the most prolific trends in the analysis of sustainability links it with corporate social responsibility (CSR), understanding sustainability as the ultimate objective of indefinitely maintaining the viability of our economies, the societies in which they are immersed and the environment on which they depend, while CSR refers to business activities, particularly their contribution to achieving this economic, social and environmental sustainability [2]. Although the direct and close relationship of the tourism sector with its physical, economic and social environment is increasingly evident, the research production in the field of tourism and management on CSR is still scarce compared to other sectors [3], even if a soaring interest in it is noticeable [4,5]. It is important to bear in mind that tourism is not a homogeneous productive sector but rather a multisector made up of a great diversity of companies from various sectors—hotels, transport, travel agencies, tour operators, restaurants, activities providers, etc.—with very heterogeneous characteristics, which makes its study and holistic analysis difficult from a traditional microeconomic perspective, usually applied to other economic sectors based on the goods they produce. To solve this obstacle, various authors advocate the separate study of these sectors, adapting the research to each of them and with different perspectives [6,7].

This paper aims to explore what has been studied related with CSR about one of the less investigated stakeholders in tourism: intermediaries, and among them, particularly the traditional intermediaries, tour operators and travel agencies. Intermediary tourism companies play a decisive role in promoting and supplying products and assisting in the exchange of information [8], where some of them can shape travel volume and movements, combine and stimulate the thoughts and practices of tourism actors and influence destinations and communities [9,10]. The Eurobarometer statistical analyses establish that 20% of the total travel bookings made by Europeans are contracted in an offline travel agency and that about 15% of the reserved trips were circuits planned by tour operators. These figures are not only stabilized but even moved upwards in recent years [11]. Besides, the figures are higher if we consider their economic weight, since most of the reservations made through offline intermediaries involve a greater outlay by the consumer in such a way that it is estimated that 30% of tourism income flows through these intermediaries. In addition, it is also known that in certain countries, such as those in southern Europe or in developing countries, these percentages tend to amount to about 10 percentage points or even more [12]. Consequently, the decision of those intermediaries to become progressively more involved in the use of CSR seems relevant, on the one hand, due to greater consumer awareness and receptivity towards ecologically and socially compatible behaviors [13] and, on the other hand, on account of their central role in the distribution chain. These compelling reasons warrant why it has begun to be considered important that these stakeholders are responsible and focused on the three pillars of sustainable tourism and CSR: the environment, socio-cultural aspects and the economy [14–17].

Additionally, during the last decades, the evolution of information and communication technology (ICT) based on the Internet has questioned the structure of the existing tourism distribution channel and the role played by some of its stakeholders, mainly the traditional firms, leading to new processes, such as reintermediation, disintermediation or hypermediation [18,19]. In this context, intermediary companies have made great efforts in innovating their processes and products, in achieving revenue growth and in maintaining or improving their profit margins. However, innovations are often costly and time consuming, requiring considerable investment. In any case, it is understood that the innovation process in tourism intermediation must continue to advance in the use of new tools and, above all, in collaboration between all members of the value chain [20].

For many researchers, CSR must be understood as an innovative key factor for competitiveness and development in all the tourism industry, including its intermediaries [21,22], especially in crisis situations. In contexts of economic and social crisis, business organizations are considered as one of the clues in their overcoming, in particular, given the evolution in society's expectations regarding the role of companies as citizens with obligations [23]. The current COVID-19 crisis has severely impacted the tourism industry but also seems to offer an opportunity of innovation [12]. Therefore, it is not surprising that some authors argue that this pandemic depression may offer an opportunity to rethink and reset tourism towards a better path for the future [24,25]—specifically, for the intermediaries to develop, more than ever, their ability to take advantage of their capacity to add value through their provision of security, guarantee, advice, personalization, proximity and access to proven information, all of them upward values among tourism consumers in the post-COVID era. Reliably, a reconfiguration of the sector is intuited, whether it would be more desirable that it is done by equipping these stakeholders with sustainable strategies and tools than by encouraging CSR. Given its central situation in the tourism market, an analysis turns out to be pertinent as to why and how these enterprises are acquiring their responsibility in the actual crisis.

Based on this context, the following research questions are based on knowing the existing literature and its current status on these issues:

RQ1: What are the main research topics in the study of this subject and on which aspects do they focus their studies?

RQ2: Are these stakeholders taken into account by researchers in the ultimate goal of achieving more sustainable tourism?

2. Corporate Social Responsibility in the Tourism Industry

Tourism is, perhaps, the industry that shows the most significant growth rates, in relation to the contribution to the GDP and employment of people of many countries. It involves both benefits and tensions and conflicts [26], which is why it is key to mitigate the negative repercussions that occur in it, not only for the good of the environment and the society but also for the survival of the industry itself [27]. In this sense, although the relationship between tourism and sustainability has been extensively outlined [28], the same has not happened with the approaches of the tourism industry to the challenges of this sustainability. Nevertheless, there is a general agreement that the answer in this analysis of the tourism companies must be given by CSR [29].

Due to the comparatively recent pursuit of this field, there are still no clear standards on how to implement CSR in firms related to tourism activity [29,30]. Studies continually present inconclusive or contradictory findings regarding the financial impact [31], often with meaningless CSR reports [32] and causing consumer cynicism about proposals perceived as a facelift [33]. The problem derives from the same definition of what CSR is or should be in the tourism sector, indistinctly applying the numerous definitions of the term existing in the generalist literature, as well as its models and indicators, which denotes a lack of critical conceptualization for the sector, especially because its own peculiarities are not taken into account [30].

Overall, the hotel sector monopolizes most of the analyses carried out to date, followed far behind by aviation [34]. Therefore, the rest of the tourism sectors are relegated to sporadic studies, although with an increasing presence in the literature [5,17]. Likewise, the research on CSR in tourism is focused, for the most part, on certain aspects, such as environmental measures or the communication of undertaken actions [35], and not on a comprehensive application of the concept in the sector [36]. From a review of the state of the art, it can be deduced that the actions carried out in CSR are mainly focused on the environmental dimension [31,37–39], with little disclosure of these policies [40], where those aspects that reduce costs and have repercussions in economic profitability, such as saving water or energy efficiency, are predominant [41].

Given the predominance of environmental issues, a large part of the published studies has been focused on the impacts produced by the tourism industry and on the creation and development of sustainability indicators for their management and control. In this line, several studies assess the use of energy in the sector and advances in the commitment to the use of renewables, as well as the reduction in waste generation and water consumption [42]. To a lesser extent, although increasing in recent years, researchers' agendas have been incorporating topics such as technology for sustainability [38], stakeholders participation [5], gender equality [43], business ethics [44,45], tourism in favor of poverty alleviation [46], certifications of sustainability [47], marketing [48], consumer perceptions [49,50] or the perspectives and intentions of employees [51]. Meanwhile, there is a growing academic interest in topics such as the role of the industry in promoting the sustainable consumption of tourism, opportunities in the face of changing social habits, sustainable industry–tourist communication or the motivations and sustainable behaviors of entrepreneurs [42].

3. Corporate Social Responsibility in the Travel Supply Chain

3.1. Research Methods and Process

This paper consists of a systematic literature review (SLR) about CSR research among tourist intermediaries, especially tour operators and travel agencies. Organized, transparent and replicable procedures were employed in this SLR, as recommended in the literature [52], and were carried out in three stages: planning the review; conducting the review; and reporting and dissemination [53]. Table 1 presents a summary of the main activities conducted in each stage. In the first stage, an exploratory literature overview of the main related constructs was conducted, such as corporate social responsibility, sustainability, tourism intermediaries, travel agencies, tour operators and travel supply chain. This was conducted in a non-structured way to build an initial perception of the research field, based on snowball logic (accessing references of references) and trial-and-error (testing combinations of keywords for filters in paper databases). An important result of this stage is the preliminary version of the research question. Another result is the definition of criteria for the filters used for the paper sample. This definition is crucial for the research since it determines the quality of the results.

Table 1. Stages of research.

Stage 1 Planning the Review	Stage 2 Conducting the Review	Stage 3 Reporting and Dissemination
- Exploratory literature search on CSR and tourism intermediaries - Proposal for preliminary research question - Definition of criteria for paper sample selection	- Selection of studies: Initial paper sample based on criteria defined in previous stage - Data analysis: (1) Title and abstract: Elimination of papers non-related to the research, resulting in a refined sample with 145 papers (2) Full paper, with focus on introduction, research method and conclusions (3) Focused readings: Deeper content analysis about CSR approaches and its relationship with the travel intermediaries	- Initial draft of introduction section after about 20% of readings in the second round - Simultaneous data analysis and reporting elaboration with mutual benefits for both processes as deeper understanding of the sample was developed - Proposal of a conceptual framework

Source: Adapted from Tranfield et al., 2003, with inclusion of activities conducted in the present research.

The second stage represents the review itself [53], which was initiated with the data collection. For this step, a collection of articles on CSR and travel supply chain was obtained by querying the Institute for Scientific Information (ISI) Web of Knowledge (Web of Science) and Scopus databases, seeking research publications in the period between the years 2000 and 2020. These databases were chosen given their comprehensiveness of papers, including titles from Emerald, Elsevier, Springer, Willey, Taylor and Francis and JStor, among others. The following filters were used: (1) in the title: Corporate Social Responsibility or CSR or sustainability; (2) in the title or keyword or abstract: travel agenc* OR tour operator* OR travel supply chain* OR tourism supply chain* OR travel distribution* OR tourism distribution OR travel intermediat* OR tourism intermediat*. The symbol (*) has the function to include any variation on the terms searched. The first reading of the papers was restricted to title and abstract, with the objective of excluding papers without adherence to the present research and without the available full paper. The final sample consists of 145 papers.

Data analysis was initiated with the second round of readings, which included the full text, with a focus on introduction, research method and conclusion sections. In this step of data analysis, a brief description of the content related to CSR and its relationship with the travel intermediaries was made, and the main studied topics were extracted. When references used by the papers of the sample contributed to the discussion of results, they were also included to support the data analysis. The third stage of the research, the dissemination [53], was conducted simultaneously with the data analysis.

3.2. Results: Main Academical Discussions

After an exhaustive reading of the existing literature, six topics were considered the most studied or relevant: (a) the role of tourism intermediaries towards sustainability; (b) the firms' size factor; (c) online intermediaries' commitment; (d) the use of the CSR as an innovative strategy; (e) the sustainable tourism supply chain; (f) and the behavior and motivations of the managers facing CSR. In order to confirm the relevancy of these topics, a content study was carried out with the qualitative analysis software Nvivo, which analyzed the 500 most-mentioned words in all the articles, manually excluding the connecting words (prepositions, etc.) (see Figure 1). The results of this test offer clear coincidences with the assessments obtained from the reading of the articles, where words such as product, sustainability, operators, impact or consumer(s) (topic a), large, small, local or brand (topic b), online, media, global or Internet (topic c), innovation, future, quality, change, process (topic d), value, supply, community, suppliers (topic e) and behavior (topic f) confirm the relevance of the issues.

Figure 1. Cloud of concepts with the most-mentioned words in the articles.

As noted, CSR studies in tourism have focused mostly on hotels and mainly on environmental elements rather than on intermediaries [14], despite the fact that these companies are key players in the tourism industry. Notwithstanding the tough competition due to the eruption of ICT and the Internet, the evolution of the tourism industry has consolidated travel intermediaries in recent decades [54]. Nowadays, not only do the traditional offline intermediaries and the online intermediaries live together in the tourism distribution channel, but each one takes advantage of their comparative assets and their market niches [55]. The review of the research in the field of CSR among these stakeholders, whatever the distribution channel is, reflects an imbalance between online and offline intermediaries' studies, where traditional actors almost comprise all the weight of the literature, revealing a gap in the knowledge of how the commitment of online intermediaries with CSR is. Nonetheless, an incipient interest is emerging in the academy, trying to analyze this emptiness (see Table 2).

One of the main investigation lines followed by the research involves the role and possibilities that the intermediaries have (or should have) confronted the challenges of CSR, including the dealt barriers and the accomplished actions, as well as accepting and acknowledging their central role in sustainability [9,10]. Generally, the major outbound tourism market structures are configured with a few large tour operators and travel agency groups, who control a high percentage of these markets, and a large group of small and medium enterprises (SMEs), who try to survive them through product and quality differentiation [56,57]. Many studies have focused on the different approaches that companies perform in their approach to CSR, depending on their size. With that in mind, aligned with what happens in other well-studied sectors, the differentiating factors for large companies were based on the nature of their structure and objectives, and for SMEs, on their underlying motivations [58].

Table 2. Main discussions about CSR and tourism intermediaries.

Discussion	Author(s)
The role of tour operators and travel agencies in sustainability	Khairat and Maher [9]; Sigala [10]; Lund-Durlacher [13]; Schwartz et al. [54]; Zapata et al. [59]; Richards and Font [60]; Tigu et al. [61]; Budeanu [62]; Goodwin [63]; Font et al. [64]; Villarino and Font [65]; Dolnicar, and Laesser [66]; McKercher et al. [67]; Chen and Peng [68]; Alonso et al. [69]; Xin and Chan [70]; Jenkins [71]; Chubchuwong [72]
The firms' size factor	Sigala, [10]; Anderson et al. [47]; Udayasankar [58]; Zapata el al. [59]; Garay et al. [73]; Van Wijk and Persoon [74]; Norbit et al. [75]; Garay et al. [76]; Tapper [77]; Carey et al. [78]; Kilipiris and Zardava [79]; Budeanu [80]; Clarke [81]; Salvado [82];Russo and Tencati [83]; Sardianou et al. [84]
Online intermediaries' commitment	Coles et al. [17]; Salvado [82]; Panda and Modak [85]; He et al. [86]; Chunjou and Pang [87]; Lozano [88]; Dube and Nhamo [89]
CSR as an innovative strategy	Camisón and Monfort-Mir [21]; Mei et al. [22] Richards and Font [60]; Chubchuwong [72]; Alonso et al. [90]; Ioncică et al. [91]; Ko et al. [92]; Kraesgenberg et al. [93]; Balaguer [94]; Thomas et al. [95]; Almunawar et al. [96]; Mourshed et al. [97]; Alegre and Sard [98]; Chapuis [99]; Huët [100]; Baniya et al. [101]
The sustainable tourism supply chain	Sigala [10]; Peña et al. [27]; Zapata et al. [59]; Richards and Font [60]; Salvado [82]; Panda and Modak [85]; Xu and Gursoy [102]; Mwesiumo and Halpern [103]; Tsaur et al. [104]; Baddeley and Font [105]; Allen et al. [106]; Brockhaus et al. [107]; Font et al. [108]; Kwon and Suh [109]; Piboonrungroj and Disney [110]
Management behavior and motivations	Lin et al. [14]; Alonso et al. [69]; Garay et al. [73]; Sardianou et al. [84]; Tsaur et al. [104]; Cheng et al. [111]; Okech [112]; Font et al. [113]; Goffi et al. [114]; Atanase and Schileru [115]; Wong and Lee [116]; Erdogan [117]; Mossaz and Coghlan [118]

In addition, as indicated above, those traditional intermediaries that operated in the 1990s have taken advantage of the Internet and ICTs in recent decades to survive, where their main concern has been how to adopt and assimilate these innovations to obtain and maintain a competitive advantage [119,120]. Similarly, the adoption of CSR has been studied from its link with the innovation and these companies' proven capacity for embracing it. Thus, intermediary managers can take advantage in change scenarios to use their CSR initiatives in an innovative way [90]. This can be induced through the design of strategies and the formulation of new forms of work, which, in other sectors, have led many companies to redefine their business models [121]. Undoubtedly, one of the most prolific fields of research between CSR and intermediaries has been to gain a clearer understanding of the specific sustainable requirements, opportunities and constraints at each point in the tourism supply chain in order to identify common success criteria, barriers and opportunities to sell more responsible tourism [102]. Furthermore, travel intermediaries have the ability to influence travelers' choices, other supply chain member strategies and destination development plans, so it has seemed to be useful in the understanding of their contribution to the sustainable tourism supply chain through CSR [59]. Finally, a last and very prolific line of research has identified a series of managers' motivations that may lead them to adopt CSR, all of them in accordance with the motivations set out for the industry in general and the tourism sector in particular [14,73,111]. Typically, these motives include responding to stakeholder pressure, gaining a competitive advantage, adhering to government regulations, avoiding fines and other regulatory actions and improving their image. In addition, managers may also have internal ethical values to guide business decisions. This may involve a responsible conscience that prompts owners and managers to do "the right thing" [47].

3.3. The Role of Travel Agencies and Tour Operators toward Sustainability

The literature indicates that in recent years, there has been a nascent trend among tourism intermediaries to be increasingly involved in the implementation of CSR measures, precisely due to the growing awareness and sensitivity of consumers towards ecological and social behavior. These tourism actors face extraordinary challenges when implementing CSR in their businesses as they not only have to evaluate CSR measures within their own company but also throughout the value chain [13]. The development of CSR in this subsector of the tourism industry has particularly responded to issues related to the promotion of sustainable tourism practices, with very few initiatives for full integration of responsible policies in organizations. Although interest in responsible tourism is high and currently a recurring debated topic, it is not very widespread among intermediaries, and coherence in CSR policies, programs and practices is still sought [61], so much so that the factors that shape the adoption of sustainability practices by intermediaries show how sustainability strategies, practices and standards seem to be conceived primarily as a means of risk management (to prevent a negative public image), as a competitive advantage (brand equity and reputation) and as a strategy to manage regulation [54] rather than as a means to provide better customer services, cost savings or business opportunities [62]. Research suggests that the incorporation of intermediary companies in a process of setting the CSR agenda is primarily a response to customer concerns, non-governmental organizations (NGO) activities or due to negative publicity from their activities [59].

There seems to be an agreement that among intermediaries, a relevant part of their conception of what is responsible is directly related to the need to source and sell more sustainable products. Yet, despite growing product offerings, supported by apparently strong business cases, sustainable tourism still accounts for only a remarkably small proportion of the total tourism supply [63], with a sense of lost opportunities and low involvement faced with a demand for distinctive and sustainable experiences without translation into additional sales [60]. In this sense, it is known that tourism companies that integrate sustainable practices tend to find it difficult to effectively communicate their commitment to sustainability and the derived benefits for the client [64,65]. Nevertheless, there is little evidence to support these companies in communicating their sustainable actions in a more persuasive way, although some studies have provided evidence in this direction [122,123].

Hence, travel intermediaries must also play the role of information intermediaries, or professional infomediaries [66], particularly when exclusive and specialized experiences are involved. Consequently, they can have significant power to shape the relationship between tourism products and services and tourists themselves, preferentially selling and targeting some of them in particular. Despite this, little research has been conducted on their role as potential responsible tourism actors, although there are studies that demonstrate a resistance of the subsector to understand and integrate the concept of sustainable tourism [67]. More specifically, little is known about their role in developing ethical considerations in sustainable tourism supply chains that ultimately shape the development of this sector [68], although studies have outlined the relevant fields of action for the development of a correct CSR policy within these companies: the internal management, the product development, the supply chain, the customer relations and the cooperation with the destinations [9].

3.4. The Firm's Size Factor

When the literature related to sustainability has made reference to a subsector as relevant as this, it has focused especially on large international tour operators, generally ignoring travel agencies [76], which are not only basic in the sectoral structure of most international destinations but are also leading major transformations in the sector, both in disintermediation and reintermediation processes [19,124]. This uneven analysis can be extrapolated to each stakeholder separately; thus, tour operators have been mainly studied by large corporations, while travel agencies have a priority focus on SMEs [59,73]. Early studies highlighted the disparity of business approaches in this regard, depending on small, medium and large companies [77]. In CSR performance, although worse than in other tourism subsectors, large firms were more advanced than medium and small ones, while medium-sized companies, in turn, performed better than small companies [74]. In contrast, previous pioneering research already showed that small-scale specialized intermediaries were more interested in protecting the environment and tended to be more active, encouraging policymakers at destinations to develop viable long-term strategies [78].

The latest studies have delved into the different performances between SMEs and large companies when CSR is concerned. In fact, among large corporations, given how their priorities are established, the main practices towards CSR are internal policies that are oriented with codes of conduct and certification systems that serve as marketing tools [59]. On the contrary, those who stand out for their CSR practices and policies are the smaller organizations [76,79,125], which emphasizes that having small operations can be a success factor for the development of sustainable tourism [126], implicitly excluding the possibility that large organizations can adopt it. While examples of responsible small-scale practices flourish, the lack of empirical evidence in mass tourism suggests that charitable actions, the adoption of codes of conduct and environmental measures are applicable improvements for large-scale operations [127], expanding its conceptual dissociation from sustainable tourism. The limited adoption of sustainable product development procedures by large companies indicates the possible existence of deeper organizational barriers, causing only a few large intermediaries to have formal sustainable product development procedures, sometimes justified by their managers' unfamiliarity with the concept of CSR or the erroneous idea that it is not a profitable product for them if not for smaller companies [62].

As Budeanu indicated [80], large companies and their own retail subsidiaries were the first to adopt a more proactive attitude and who have begun to develop responsible policies and plans in recent years. However, the viability of their structural adjustment has proven to be very low since most of these groups are not innovative enough in this field to consider it in all its breadth and to be able to face the presumed expenses and investments that it would entail [81]. The other two models of tourism intermediaries linked to large networks, franchisees and associates, have little place in tourism research, much less in specific topics, such as CSR, with few exceptions in which these two models are analyzed as a brand of the large companies with which they are related, without taking into account their own characteristics and specificities [82].

As in the rest of the tourism sector, in the specific case of SME intermediary companies, they do not usually have complex management structures and are generally managed by their owners, oriented towards solving the day-to-day business, establishing informal and close relationships with their interest groups and living in a reality dependent on the dynamics of the sector, determined, on many occasions, by the actions of larger companies [83]. These largely independent small-scale companies position their value propositions [128] through their presence on the Internet to reinforce their differential factors, including sustainability, making ICT a basic element of tourism marketing [129]. The perception within these travel agencies in this matter is coincident and they think that their possibility of sustainable actions is limited within the sector as a whole. They adduce how the size of the company can be a determining factor but warn that they can become decisive in this area, particularly with regard to its environmental aspect. Consequently, they have to improve their knowledge and information in this regard, at the same time that a more active role from agency/tour operator associations and the management groups to which they belong is indispensable.

Small- and medium-sized tour operators can respond to their own challenges through CSR, although their proposals are often reduced to suit their own capabilities [75]. This happens because typically, most are too focused on short-term goals to maximize profits, with a penchant for being tactical in their strategy, with their primary focus on customers who are their direct source of immediate information and short-term income, secondarily considering other objectives, such as competitive advantage, branding, etc. Consequently, economic subsistence is the first and foremost goal among tourism intermediaries, regardless of size [130]. Along these lines, there is an academic discussion which sustains that the size of the tourism intermediary company does not seem to be related to the desire to develop responsible practices, since the vast majority of the managers report receptivity towards more sustainable models. This development would seem to be related to price, where companies for which this is the most important factor would be less willing to bet on CSR, while those that attach greater importance to responsible practices, even taking price into account, show a higher interest and knowledge of CSR, which makes them more inclined to implement it [47].

3.5. Online Intermediaries' Commitment

Given their prominent role in the present society, online intermediaries are increasingly expected to act according to current social and cultural values, which raises questions as to what kind of responsibilities they should bear and which ethical principles should guide their actions [131]. There is a largely specialized literature that has studied the implications of online distribution in the tourism supply chain, mainly attending to cost, price and service level [132,133], on the effects on traditional intermediaries [57,134–136] and on the trust and quality achieved by the companies operating in this channel [137,138]. In contrast, few studies have analyzed the development of CSR in online tourism intermediaries [17,82,85], but findings show that the acceptance of the new channel by consumers and the cost advantage it brings to these intermediaries, together with the profit sharing rate and the distributor's CSR behavior, jointly influence the choice of the sales channel and prices, showing that CSR behavior of online intermediaries could benefit the tourism supply chain and a greater acceptance of this channel among tourists [86].

The few research studies that have been published on online intermediaries and their responsibilities have followed the general trend of the sector of an environmental approach, prioritizing the websites of these intermediaries as relevant in attracting consumers to low-carbon trips. In other words, the web would not only provide travel information resources for tourists but would also motivate them to participate in more responsible travel [87]. These authors indicate that environmentally responsible travel promotions can hardly be found, concluding that online wholesale and retail travel agencies have not been generically implementing actions related to CSR. In addition, these few research studies have basically focused on the case of large tour operators [88], paying marginal attention to the case of retailers.

However, one of the most notable aspects in tourism intermediation regarding online marketing, as researchers have pointed out, is the transition of traditional companies to the online world, combining both sales channels, a clear example of the resilience of this subsector. Most of them have been digitized by using e-marketing to reach customers instead of printing brochures, which come with a considerable amount of greenhouse gas emissions. In this sense, almost all intermediaries use various online platforms to communicate with customers, ranging from Facebook, Twitter and YouTube to blogs, websites and other web-based applications, instead of traditional marketing methods, thereby increasing their market share [89].

3.6. CSR as an Innovative Strategy

There is unanimity among academics that innovations represent a key factor for competitiveness and development in all areas of activity, including the tourism industry and its intermediaries [21,22].

On the contrary, there is no such consensus regarding the contents and typology of innovations in the tourism intermediation sector since, traditionally, these have been associated with the need to identify and solve technical problems. Another important and controversial problem from the point of view of innovation research in the activity of intermediation agencies is related to the link between innovation and the size of the company [91], an aspect that would influence the sale of sustainable tourism products and its impact on the efficiency of the activity of intermediaries and their responsibility, according to the latter authors. Many researchers affirm that innovation is associated with an entrepreneurial spirit characteristic, mainly of new companies of small dimensions, which is why it is suggested that the innovative activities of SMEs are the most important determinant of their success [92]. On the other hand, large companies maintain the advantages that their size gives them to support the commercial development of new ideas by having the necessary financial resources to carry out experiments and prototypes or pilot operations.

Although CSR is not the panacea or the only measure to ensure the success of a business, even in crisis outlooks, the literature shows that many of the actions that are proposed to overcome the challenges are derived from the innovative conception of CSR and are directly related to factors that are integrated into the responsibility of the companies [93]. Above all, they have a lot to do with investment and innovation strategies that allow the integration of analysis criteria based on the sustainability of companies, with strict accountability measures, and on regulated business transparency frameworks, with the analysis of social and environmental impacts integrated in the risk management, and, finally, with the adoption of responsible structures for corporate governance and independent and external supervision [94]. As a result, the access to knowledge and innovation increases their capacity for internationalization, reduces their costs, increases their competitiveness and encourages the creation of work and support networks [95].

Moreover, unlike a few decades ago, tourists demand innovation in services and products, a requirement that must be adequately answered by intermediaries, which requires sustainable innovation, both in the development of processes and in products, to achieve sustainability in business [96]. To meet this demand and promote sustainability, the exchange of information is considered necessary in order to reduce inefficiency and waste of resources [97]. However, sustainability is not just about innovation and technology adoption but also about taking customer behavior into account when offering more sustainable products or services. Nevertheless, studies coincide in highlighting that the adoption of responsible practices and innovations by tourism intermediaries seems to go relatively unnoticed by their customers

It is a fact that many tourism intermediaries operate with small profit margins, and the resulting pressure from suppliers to lower prices may limit their ability to invest in quality improvements and innovations or other strategies that do not have a relatively immediate return [98]. However, there is a vanguard of companies that understand the concept of CSR innovation as applicable to their business initiatives, creating a de facto specific market niche, which consider social awareness work and offer services aimed at changing social practices of the trip [99], appealing to both individual and collective responsibility. For these, the responsible tourism middleman must be exemplary, with everything and everyone. Its responsible policies list evidence of its good behavior with the environment (use of recycled paper, free software, etc.), with its employees (reconciliation of work and family life, fair wages, etc.), with travelers, with the rest of the companies in the sector and with the destination and its population. Its credibility is based on the manifestation of a close commitment to responsible tourism [100].

3.7. The Sustainable Tourism Supply Chain

The study of the sustainable supply chain in tourism has focused mainly on understanding the adoption of sustainability governance mechanisms [59,80,139] and on resource efficiency and cost savings [10,105]. Other lines of research have also exposed the exercise of power and unequal control over providers by tour operators [140,141]. In this sense, some authors point out several fields in which a more detailed analysis of CSR in the tourism supply chain would be beneficial, such as the role of different actors in the sustainable supply chain [60,103,142], or, to obtain a clearer understanding of the specific sustainability requirements, opportunities and limitations at each point of the tourism supply chain [102,143]. However, a very important factor not sufficiently recognized in the tourism literature is the complex set of corporate and contractual international agreements that characterize tourism intermediators, a factor that adds difficulties in achieving a sustainable supply chain since it is difficult to verify the commitment to CSR of each and every one of the companies with which it collaborates [59]. The problems and difficulties in persuading external contractors and small tourism providers to jointly commit to CSR are also emphasized. Given the large number of SMEs, as well as their importance for the socioeconomic viability of many destinations, studies that investigate how to overcome these troubles and support these SMEs in their commitment to sustainability are noted to be essential [10].

Similar conclusions are reached by other researchers who highlight how tourism intermediaries have limited potential to achieve sustainable management of the supply chain, caused by a lack of understanding of sustainability by their managers, a lack of values at the company level with respect to sustainability, budget constraints, supply chain conflicts, a lack of personnel trained in sustainability and a lack of planning [102]. On the contrary, it seems undeniable that the relationship between the two traditional travel agency models, tour operators and travel agencies, is aimed at mutual collaboration and associationism, where the ideal would be a useful relationship in which both companies could create added value, share information and increase market opportunities [104]. These authors suggest that interpersonal behavior in their relationships, the offer of support and the mutual search for customer satisfaction motivate managers to increase the quality of the relationship between travel wholesalers and retailers, where the duration of the relationship and importance of the product would affect this relational behavior.

Therefore, a supportive organizational culture is a prerequisite for the success of companies that want to increase the volume of sustainable products that they source and sell. Sustainability is only sold when it contributes to an organization's ability to meet its service quality requirements, especially in relation to the suitability of products for its target markets and the strengthening of professional and trustworthy relationships. Business-to-business marketing requires suppliers to understand the relative importance of sustainability to each of their providers and, in response, develop appropriate arguments to explain the importance of sustainability within the organizational needs of their buyers [60]. In this sense, the literature underscores the lessons to be learned from tourism supply chain research on how tour operators and local suppliers can collaborate effectively to foster sustainable tourism. Based on the literature review in this regard [54,102,105–110], these lessons can be grouped into six areas: (a) collaborative visions that include well-coordinated communication (including shared values), exchange and joint planning of information, "socialization" (for example, meetings, conferences or visits to the destination) and establishment of cross-functional teams to maximize opportunities for information transfer and collaboration related to sustainability; (b) training and advice, including awareness-raising interventions, targeted training, well-designed sustainability manuals and support for internal auditing, certification, monitoring and reporting; (c) contractual and procurement incentives, including preferred partner status, fair purchase and contractual conditions; (d) financial support, including soft loans; (e) rewards and incentives; (f) and promotional opportunities.

3.8. Management Behavior and Motivations

In their role as intermediaries for tourism consumption, the perceptions, opinions, beliefs, attitudes and work practices of these stakeholders make important contributions, negative and positive, to the sustainable development of tourism. Despite this, studies on tourism intermediaries and managers are fairly recent and limited in quantity and quality, especially in the non-Western world. In this subsector, the degree of behavior based on opinions and attitudes in daily business practices is barely known since the structural environment of economic and political decision-making is marked by personal and organizational objectives, power relations and dominance. There are numerous variables, internal and external, that intervene in the form of an adequate and improved CSR performance when translating their responsible attitudes and principles into concrete operational changes [117].

In the same way as other sectors, motivations and responsible behaviors tend to differ notably between large companies' and SMEs' intermediaries, and even the behavior of managers of small- and medium-sized companies with regard to CSR is far from being homogeneous [73]. In large corporations. there are usually coercive and regulatory pressures from the top down, so the managers of the delegations and sales offices have little room to maneuver and implement their own CSR initiatives, although there may be lines of business that are not passive recipients of these pressures and small responsible practices can be carried out outside the institutional guidelines [59].

In SMEs, on the other hand, the difficulties have been considered more than the advantages when it comes to introducing CSR, although the literature is modifying this vision. As a rule, the lack of resources [144] or information about market requirements and the opportunities for change related to these practices [145] are recurrent in most discussions. Researchers also point out the existence of differences between large tourism companies and SMEs, which are sometimes key for the development of CSR policies, especially in economic, financial and information resources [146]. These academic contributions also tend to refer to the strengths of SMEs, such as the advantage of reacting more quickly and flexibly to certain aspects (including those related to CSR) and the closer relationship with their stakeholders [71]. In addition, in this business model, decision-making in this regard results, in many cases, in an extension of the owner's personality [147], and in the case of entrepreneurs, this can be decisive to stimulate a responsible culture and to ensure that it is related to values other than profit maximization as the sole criterion [126]. These considerations justify the fact that in the context of small- and medium-sized intermediate firms, a wide degree of divergence is observed in the introduction of responsibility practices, depending on the different company profiles [76].

Finally, several of these studies have identified a series of managers' motivations that may lead them to adopt CSR, all of them in accordance with the motivations set out for the industry in general and the tourism sector in particular [14,73,111]. These typically include responding to stakeholder pressure, gaining a competitive advantage, adhering to government regulations, avoiding fines and other regulatory actions and improving their image. Moreover, managers may also have internal ethical values to guide business decisions. This may involve a responsible conscience that prompts owners and managers to do "the right thing" [49].

3.8.1. The Business Case

A first type or category of intermediary is described with a markedly opportunistic profile and is aimed at gaining market share with sustainability. These companies, normally large groups and also some medium-sized ones, have a high technological capacity and introduce sustainability as a market strategy and "image washing", so their mission, in relation to sustainability, responds more to the achievement of finalist objectives than to a certain vision of the world [76]. When addressing the motivations underlying their adoption of CSR, improving the company's image is considered the most important factor [54], followed by public relations, both motivations related to marketing programs. In fact, the construction of a positive public image is the most important motivator that drives large intermediary companies to adopt more responsible strategies, even more than responding to the demand of customers, which ranks second [9]. Therefore, a greater commitment to CSR for instrumental reasons can be expected from larger and more structured corporations than from SMEs [114].

The implementation of CSR programs for the managers of these firms is supported by an expected direct, positive and significant impact on the financial results of the company [148]. Any practice that improves the performance and business competitiveness of these businesses (image, customer satisfaction, employee satisfaction, etc.) has a positive impact on the company's results [149–153]. This relationship of CSR with results and competitiveness is relevant and motivating for these managers and has proven proactivity in sectors, especially those affected by crises and in which there is a continuous movement, such as in tourism intermediation [154]. The presumed competitive advantage, tax advantages, fashion, mandatory compliance from the parent company or external pressure (media, NGO, public, government, etc.) are, consequently, additional motivations highlighted by the existing literature [61].

3.8.2. The Stakeholders' Rationale

The second profile is the tourism intermediary who tries to consider and reconcile the interests of the consumer and the variables that condition their purchasing decision processes, the supplier and its profitability strategies and the destination territory with the local population and its sustainable development from an environmental, social and economic point of view [155]. This type of manager is open to sustainability as an element of improving its competitiveness through business differentiation in relation to competitors. It is a profile that can respond to any type of intermediary but, above all, affects conventional medium-sized agencies which have a business structure that facilitates the introduction of sustainability practices as a competitive factor [76]. Studies in this area have understood that the commitment of tour operators and travel agencies to sustainability gives them a competitive advantage through added value [156]. Certainly, their proposals are based on a responsible policy, understanding that environmental, socio-cultural, economic and quality aspects must be covered in the definition of where they want to go, how and why [157], with the main purpose of achieving strategic competitiveness and success in the formulation and implementation of value creation from this strategy [158].

In this group of businesses concerned with justifying themselves to their stakeholders, among the methods to increase their competitiveness are seeking the trust of the customers and the improvement of their image in the market, and it is in these businesses where more normative use of the implementation of quality requirement standards and the attainment of quality management system certifications is carried out [113]. Likewise, more and more travel intermediaries give a relevant role to suppliers and, in fact, it is more common for retailers to require certificates or documents proving good practices. It seems to be related to recognizing exemplary corporate behaviors around this issue and being able to identify CSR policies related to those developed in the organization itself.

3.8.3. Lifestyle and Personal Values

Lastly, there is a third intermediary profile that fits with the conscientious small entrepreneur, with less symbolic sustainable initiatives and that is more convincing than that of large corporations [15]. They are highly specialized SMEs with a commitment that supports relationships beyond the competitive reinforcement of the company based on win–win acquaintances with destinations, society and the clients themselves [76]. In these businesses, managers' altruist attitudes, further than the appreciation of the benefits for the company, motivate CSR practices, along with their decisions used to be shown and informed due to their understanding of subjective norms, their personal perceptions and their own abilities to be successful [14]. Despite this, the understanding of which role ethics plays in tourism has been largely neglected regarding the function of intermediaries within the tourism supply chain [118]. The results show that smaller intermediaries are more committed to sustainability, which demonstrates that many socio-economic initiatives and certain environmental practices do not necessarily require massive investments (those that only large companies can afford) but rather derive from a different business philosophy, where the personal sense of obligation, the values and the formal engagement of the manager are crucial to adopt CSR policies and measures [114].

A strong belief in values and in the possibility of a change is usually what has led to the creation of these companies, where there is a high degree of commitment acquired by the intermediary and it is consistent with their own ethical principles. In fact, these entrepreneurs often reverse the sense of purpose and the means: sustainability becomes the final objective, while the trip is reduced to the condition to achieve it (tourism is used as a tool to meet sustainable development). The intermediary minimizes the commercial component and puts their vocation, values and principles ahead [99]. Similar studies have been based on the assumption that relational networks play an important role in the value chain of the altruistic behavior of tourism brokerage managers, which is key to the development of the company and its partners. If the interaction between businesses is strengthened, factors such as emotion, trust, reliability and reputation become indispensable. In this way, the altruistic behavior of managers plays an important role in creating commercial value [111].

These innovative projects, apart from being of interest to the market, above all, personally satisfy the entrepreneur. The motivation to incorporate sustainability in these business models, represented by small- and medium-sized specialized intermediaries, is especially associated with a personal factor, motivation linked to a vital business project rather than to the search for new markets or economic results in the short term. However, organizations that are committed to sustainability rely on the vital and innovative nature of their project to obtain benefits, to improve their competitiveness and to access new markets, in such a way that the business case also appears, albeit implicitly [76].

4. Discussion and Conclusions

Despite the relevance of tour operators and travel agencies in the distribution of tourism products, their role within the supply chain has been scarcely studied, and even less with regard to their performance towards more sustainable practices. In this sense, the development of CSR in these companies seems to be the best way to achieve more responsible goals. After an exhaustive review of the literature, this work has collected the most recent lines of research on tourism intermediaries and CSR, among which the evolution or emergence of current issues, such as online intermediaries, the tourism sustainable supply chain or the underlying managers' motivations in their commitment to sustainability, could be noteworthy. Likewise, throughout this review, various gaps have appeared, for the most part, due to the barely existing literary production which are likely to be studied in future research. In this sense, researchers could delve into the approaches to CSR of very widespread intermediary business models in tourism, such as the franchise and the company associated with a large corporation, the practices in sustainability of OTAs and other new online intermediaries, or the role that each actor in the tourism value chain must assume in order to achieve more responsible tourism.

Most of the research highlights how tourism intermediaries have only just begun to develop CSR policies in their companies, and those that are committed to their implementation mostly opt for actions aimed at the environment, generally because they are the simplest and the most noticeable. However, it seems clear that given its relevant position in the distribution channel, its commitment can be improved highly, beyond the creation and promotion of sustainable tourism products. That is why researchers have pointed out the relevance of the supply chain and the necessary collaboration between all its stakeholders, a very incipient measure in the subsector, where very competitive commercial policies are still being carried out, inherited from market structures that are already distant in time. In connection with this aspect, the studies highlight the innovative nature of CSR as a crucial factor in the survival of these intermediaries, not only in relation to possible internal control and process management measures but also in a clear commitment to the co-creation of value throughout the supply chain. Today more than ever, the use of new technologies and sustainable innovations seems to be the necessary bet for this intermediation sector to be able to overcome the crisis to which the COVID-19 pandemic has led it.

Furthermore, and as in other tourism subsectors, the view on the CSR of the owners and managers of travel intermediary organizations is far from being homogeneous, detecting factors that explain the different views and behaviors. In the first place, it should be noted that corporate factors related to business management processes or the search for markets are also present when explaining the positioning of these companies in their approaches to CSR, but there are other types of factors, such as altruism and lifestyle, which explain more accurately the differences in motivations and behaviors. In this case, altruism has not so much to do with the maturity of the companies in their approach to sustainability as with a personal factor applied to a specific intermediation business model. Altruism as an explanatory factor is related to a specific intermediary profile (SME and specialized) but also to the owner profile and, what is quite convincing, with the use of information technologies and social networks.

Author Contributions: Conceptualization, E.I. and L.G.; methodology, E.I. and L.G.; investigation, E.I.; writing—original draft preparation, E.I.; writing—review and editing, L.G. and A.G.; supervision, L.G. and A.G. All authors have read and agreed to the published version of the manuscript.

References

1. Alhaddi, H. Triple bottom line and sustainability: A literature review. *Bus. Manag. Stud.* **2015**, *1*, 6–10. [CrossRef]

2. Jenkins, H. A critique of conventional CSR theory: An SME perspective. *J. Gen. Manag.* **2004**, *29*, 37–57. [CrossRef]

3. Martos, M. Responsabilidad social corporativa y turismo. ¿Realidad o postureo? *Tur. Soc.* **2018**, *XXII*, 25–44. [CrossRef]

4. Bohdanowicz, P.; Zientara, P. Corporate social responsibility in hospitality: Issues and implications. A case study of Scandic. *Scand. J. Hosp. Tour.* **2008**, *8*, 271–293. [CrossRef]

5. Font, X.; Lynes, J. Corporate social responsibility in tourism and hospitality. *J. Sustain. Tour.* **2018**, *26*, 1027–1042. [CrossRef]

6. Sheldon, P.J.; Park, S.Y. An exploratory study of corporate social responsibility in the U.S. travel industry. *J. Travel Res.* **2011**, *50*, 392–407. [CrossRef]

7. Nicolau, J.L. Corporate social responsibility. Worth-Creating activities. *Ann. Tour. Res.* **2008**, *35*, 990–1006. [CrossRef]

8. Buhalis, D.; Law, R. Progress in information technology and tourism management: 20 years on and 10 years after the Internet. The state of eTourism research. *Tour. Manag.* **2008**, *29*, 609–623. [CrossRef]

9. Khairat, G.; Maher, A. Integrating sustainability into tour operator business: An innovative approach in sustainable tourism. *Tourismos* **2012**, *7*, 213–233.

10. Sigala, M. A supply chain management approach for investigating the role of tour operators on sustainable tourism: The case of TUI. *J. Clean. Prod.* **2008**, *16*, 1589–1599. [CrossRef]

11. European Commission. *Preferences of Europeans Towards Tourism. Eurobarometer No 432*; Directorate-General for Communication: Brussels, Belgium, 2016.

12. Rivera, J.; Pastor, R. ¿Hacia un turismo más sostenible tras el COVID-19? Percepción de las agencias de viajes españolas. *Gran Tour Rev. Investig. Tur.* **2020**, *21*, 206–229.

13. Lund-Durlacher, D. Corporate social responsibility and tourism. In *Education for Sustainability in Tourism—A Handbook of Processes, Resources, and Strategies*; Moscardo, P., Benckendorff, G., Eds.; Springer: Berlin/Heidelberg, Germany, 2015; pp. 59–72.

14. Lin, L.P.L.; Yu, C.Y.; Chang, F.C. Determinants of CSER practices for reducing greenhouse gas emissions: From the perspectives of administrative managers in tour operators. *Tour. Manag.* **2018**, *64*, 1–12. [CrossRef]

15. Tixier, M. Will sustainable management be a clear differentiator for tour operators? *Int. J. Tour. Hosp. Res.* **2009**, *20*, 461–466. [CrossRef]

16. Wells, V.K.; Manika, D.; Gregory-Smith, D.; Taheri, B.; McCowlen, C. Heritage tourism, CSR and the role of employee environmental behaviour. *Tour. Manag.* **2015**, *48*, 399–413. [CrossRef]

17. Coles, T.; Fenclova, E.; Dinan, C. Tourism and corporate social responsibility: A critical review and research agenda. *Tour. Manag. Perspect.* **2013**, *6*, 122–141. [CrossRef]

18. Runfola, A.; Rosati, M.; Guercini, S. New Business Models in Online Hotel Distribution: Emerging Private Sales versus Leading IDS. *Serv. Bus.* **2013**, *7*, 183–205. [CrossRef]

19. Standing, C.; Tang-Taye, J.P.; Boyer, M. The Impact of the Internet in Travel and Tourism: A Research Review 2001. *J. Travel Tour. Mark.* **2014**, *31*, 82–113. [CrossRef]

20. Pastor, R.; Rivera, J. Airbnb and tourism intermediation. Competition or coopetition? The perception of travel agents in Spain. *Empres. Humanismo* **2020**, *XXIII*, 107–132. [CrossRef]

21. Camisón, C.; Monfort-Mir, V.M. Measuring innovation in tourism from schumpeterian and the dynamic—Capabilities perspectives. *Tour. Manag.* **2012**, *33*, 776–789. [CrossRef]
22. Mei, X.Y.; Arcodia, C.; Ruhanen, L. Towards tourism innovation: A critical review of public policies at the national level. *Tour. Manag. Perspect.* **2012**, *4*, 92–105. [CrossRef]
23. Derevianko, O. Reputation stability vs anti-crisis sustainability: Under what circumstances will innovations, media activities and CSR be in higher demand? *Oeconomia Copernic.* **2019**, *10*, 511–536. [CrossRef]
24. Higgins-Desbiolles, F. Socialising tourism for social and ecological justice after COVID. *Tour. Geogr.* **2020**, 1–14. [CrossRef]
25. Gössling, S.; Scott, D.; Hall, C.M. Pandemics, tourism and global change: A rapid assessment of COVID. *J. Sustain. Tour.* **2020**, 48–52. [CrossRef]
26. Garay, L. El sector empresarial turístico como agente de desarrollo económico. In *Cooperación en Turismo. Nuevos Desafíos, Nuevos Debates*; Universitat Oberta de Catalunya—Laboratori del Nou Turisme; Universitat de Barcelona: Barcelona, Spain, 2013; pp. 307–328.
27. Peña, D.D.; Guevara, A.; Fraiz, J.A. La investigación de la responsabilidad social empresarial en el sector hotelero. Análisis y revisión de la literatura científica. *Tur. Soc.* **2016**, *18*, 137–158.
28. Buckley, R. Sustainable tourism: Research and reality. *Ann. Tour. Res.* **2012**, *39*, 528–546. [CrossRef]
29. Font, X.; Walmsley, A.; Cogotti, S.; Mccombes, L.; Häusler, N. Corporate social responsibility: The disclosure-performance gap. *Tour. Manag.* **2012**, *33*, 1544–1553. [CrossRef]
30. Farrington, T.; Curran, R.; Gori, K.; O'Gorman, K.D.; Queenan, C.J. Corporate social responsibility: Reviewed, rated, revised. *Int. J. Contemp. Hosp. Manag.* **2017**, *29*, 30–47. [CrossRef]
31. Inoue, Y.; Lee, S. Effects of different dimensions of corporate social responsibility on corporate financial performance in tourism-related industries. *Tour. Manag.* **2011**, *32*, 790–804. [CrossRef]
32. De Grosbois, D. Corporate social responsibility reporting by the global hotel industry: Commitment, initiatives and performance. *Int. J. Hosp. Manag.* **2012**, *31*, 896–905. [CrossRef]
33. Pope, S.; Wæraas, A. CSR-washing is rare: A conceptual framework, literature review, and critique. *J. Bus. Ethics* **2015**, *137*, 173–193. [CrossRef]
34. Kang, K.H.; Lee, S.; Huh, C. Impacts of positive and negative corporate social responsibility activities on company performance in the hospitality industry. *Int. J. Hosp. Manag.* **2010**, *29*, 72–82. [CrossRef]
35. Flores, D.; Barroso, M.O.; Castro, N.J. Reflexiones teóricas sobre el análisis de la responsabilidad social en el sector turístico. *Rev. Estud. Empres. Segunda Epoca* **2016**, *2*, 5–16. [CrossRef]
36. Fernández, M.T.; Cuadrado, R. La responsabilidad social empresarial en el sector hotelero: Revisión de la literatura científica. *Cuad. Tur.* **2011**, *28*, 47–57.
37. Ayuso, S. Adoption of voluntary environmental tools for sustainable tourism: Analysing the experience of Spanish hotels. *Corp. Soc. Responsib. Environ. Manag.* **2006**, *13*, 207–220. [CrossRef]
38. Budeanu, A.; Miller, G.; Moscardo, G.; Ooi, C.S. Sustainable tourism, progress, challenges and opportunities: An introduction. *J. Clean. Prod.* **2016**, *111*, 285–294. [CrossRef]
39. Horng, J.S.; Hsu, H.; Tsai, C.Y. An assessment model of corporate social responsibility practice in the tourism industry. *J. Sustain. Tour.* **2018**, *26*, 1085–1104. [CrossRef]
40. Rodríguez, J.M.; Alonso, M.M.; Celemín, M.S. Responsabilidad social corporativa en las cadenas hoteleras españolas: Un estudio de casos. *Rev. Responsab. Soc. Empres* **2013**, *13*, 15–50.
41. Font, X.; Guix, M.; Bonilla-Priego, M.J. Corporate social responsibility in cruising: Using materiality análisis to create shared value. *Tour. Manag.* **2016**, *53*, 175–186. [CrossRef]
42. Bramwell, B.; Higham, J.; Lane, B.; Miller, G. Twenty-five years of sustainable tourism and the journal of sustainable tourism: Looking back and moving forward. *J. Sustain. Tour.* **2017**, *25*, 1–9. [CrossRef]
43. Álvarez, A.; Rego, G.; Leira, J.; Gomis, A.; Caramés, R.; Andrade, M.J. La responsabilidad social corporativa como oportunidad para las empresas turísticas. *Rotur* **2009**, *2*, 11–43. [CrossRef]
44. Garzón, M.A.; Pérez, L.A. Consideraciones para el código de ética empresarial de las empresas afiliadas a la AMAV-México. *Orinoquia* **2016**, *20*, 87–101. [CrossRef]
45. Yaman, H.R.; Gurel, E. Ethical ideologies of tourism marketers. *Ann. Tour. Res.* **2006**, *33*, 470–489. [CrossRef]
46. Schilcher, D. Growth versus equity: The continuum of pro-poor tourism and neoliberal governance. *Curr. Issues Tour.* **2007**, *10*, 166–193. [CrossRef]

47. Anderson, L.; Mastrangelo, C.; Chase, L.; Kestenbaum, D.; Kolodinsky, J. Eco-labeling motorcoach operators in the North American travel tour industry: Analyzing the role of tour operators. *J. Sustain. Tour.* **2013**, *21*, 750–764. [CrossRef]

48. Borden, D.S.; Coles, T.; Shaw, G. Social marketing, sustainable tourism, and small/medium size tourism enterprises: Challenges and opportunities for changing guest behaviour. *J. Sustain. Tour.* **2017**, *25*, 903–920. [CrossRef]

49. Gao, J.; Huang, Z.; Zhang, C. Tourists' perceptions of responsibility: An application of norm-activation theory. *J. Sustain. Tour.* **2017**, *25*, 276–291. [CrossRef]

50. Liu, M.T.; Wong, I.A.; Rongwei, C.; Tseng, T.H. Do perceived CSR initiatives enhance customer preference and loyalty in casinos? *Int. J. Contemp. Hosp. Manag.* **2014**, *26*, 1024–1045.

51. Park, S.Y.; Levy, S.E. Corporate social responsibility: Perspectives of hotel frontline employees. *Int. J. Contemp. Hosp. Manag.* **2014**, *26*, 332–348. [CrossRef]

52. Littell, J.H.; Corcoran, J.; Pillai, V. *Systematic Reviews and Meta-Analysis*; Oxford University Press: New York, NY, USA, 2008.

53. Tranfield, D.; Denyer, D.; Smart, P. Towards a methodology for developing evidence-informed management knowledge by means of systematic review. *Br. J. Manag.* **2003**, *14*, 207–222. [CrossRef]

54. Schwartz, K.; Tapper, R.; Font, X. A sustainable supply chain management framework for tour operators. *J. Sustain. Tour.* **2008**, *16*, 298–314. [CrossRef]

55. Lacalle, L. Agencias de viajes en España. Una industria convulsa. *Pap. Tur.* **2013**, *54*, 122–138.

56. Flores, D.; Salazar, L.; Santana, M.Á. ¿Desaparecerán los tour operadores? El papel de los intermediarios en la distribución turística: Análisis del caso de Tenerife. *PASOS Rev. Tur. Patrim. Cult.* **2011**, *9*, 341–351.

57. Pastor, R. *Las Agencias de Viajes Tradicionales en España Frente al Reto de la Nueva Intermediación. Nuevas Formas de Relación con Clientes y Proveedores*; Universidad Rey Juan Carlos: Madrid, Spain, 2019.

58. Udayasankar, K. Corporate social responsibility and firm size. *J. Bus. Ethics* **2008**, *83*, 167–175. [CrossRef]

59. Zapata, M.J.; Hall, C.M.; Backlund, S. Can MNCs promote more inclusive tourism? Apollo tour operator's sustainability work. *Tour. Geogr.* **2018**, *20*, 630–652. [CrossRef]

60. Richards, P.; Font, X. Sustainability in the tour operator–ground agent supply chain. *J. Sustain. Tour.* **2019**, *27*, 277–291. [CrossRef]

61. Ţigu, G.; Popescu, D.; Hornoiu, R.I. Corporate social responsibility—An European approach through the tourism SME's perspectives. *Amfiteatru Econ. J.* **2016**, *18*, 742–756.

62. Budeanu, A. Exploring organizational antecedents for sustainable product development for international tour operating businesses. *CLCS Work. Pap. Ser.* **2012**, *9*, 1–24.

63. Goodwin, H. *Responsible Tourism: Using Tourism for Sustainable Development*, 2nd ed.; Goodfellow: Oxford, UK, 2016.

64. Font, X.; Elgammal, I.; Lamond, I. Greenhushing: The deliberate under communicating of sustainability practices by tourism businesses. *J. Sustain. Tour.* **2017**, *25*, 1007–1023. [CrossRef]

65. Villarino, J.; Font, X. Sustainability marketing myopia: The lack of persuasiveness in sustainability communication. *J. Vacat. Mark.* **2015**, *21*, 326–335. [CrossRef]

66. Dolnicar, S.; Laesser, C. Travel agency marketing strategy: Insights from Switzerland. *J. Travel Res.* **2007**, *46*, 133–146. [CrossRef]

67. McKercher, B.; Mak, B.; Wong, S. Does climate change matter to the travel trade? *J. Sustain. Tour.* **2014**, *22*, 685–704. [CrossRef]

68. Chen, A.; Peng, N. Recommending green hotels to travel agencies' customers. *Ann. Tour. Res.* **2014**, *48*, 284–289. [CrossRef]

69. Alonso, M.M.; Bagur, L.; Llach, J. The adoption of quality management practices and their impact on business performance in small service companies: The case of Spanish travel agencies. *Serv. Bus.* **2015**, *9*, 57–75.

70. Xin, T.K.; Chan, J.K.L. Tour operator perspectives on responsible tourism indicators of Kinabalu National Park, Sabah. *Procedia Soc. Behav. Sci.* **2014**, *144*, 25–34. [CrossRef]

71. Jenkins, H. A 'business opportunity' model of corporate social responsibility for small- and medium-sized enterprises. *Bus. Ethics A Eur. Rev.* **2009**, *18*, 21–36. [CrossRef]

72. Chubchuwong, M. The impact of CSR satisfaction on destination loyalty: A study of MICE travelers in Thailand. *Asia Pac. J. Tour. Res.* **2019**, *24*, 168–179. [CrossRef]

73. Garay, L.; Gomis, J.M.; González, F. Management, altruism, and customer focus as drivers of corporate social responsibility in tourism intermediation. *Tour. Anal.* **2017**, *22*, 255–260. [CrossRef]

74. Van Wijk, J.; Persoon, W. A long-haul destination: Sustainability reporting among tour operators. *Eur. Manag. J.* **2006**, *24*, 381–395.

75. Norbit, N.; Nawawi, A.; Salin, P.; Azlin, A.S. Corporate social responsibility practices among the smes in Malaysia—A preliminary analysis. *Manag. Account. Rev.* **2017**, *16*, 17–40. [CrossRef]

76. Garay, L.; Gomis, J.M.; González, F. El valor de la sostenibilidad como factor de diferenciación en los procesos de intermediación turística: Un análisis para el caso de las pymes catalanas. *Cuad. Tur.* **2018**, *41*, 219–248. [CrossRef]

77. Tapper, R. Tourism and socio-economic development: UK tour operators' business approaches in the context of the new international agenda. *Int. J. Tour. Res.* **2001**, *3*, 351–366. [CrossRef]

78. Carey, S.; Gountas, Y.; Gilbert, D. Tour operators and destination sustainability. *Tour. Manag.* **1997**, *18*, 425–431. [CrossRef]

79. Kilipiris, F.; Zardava, S. Developing sustainable tourism in a changing environment: Issues for the tourism enterprises (travel agencies and hospitality enterprises). *Procedia Soc. Behav. Sci.* **2012**, *44*, 44–52. [CrossRef]

80. Budeanu, A. Environmental supply chain management in tourism: The case of large tour operators. *J. Clean. Prod.* **2009**, *17*, 1385–1392.

81. Clarke, J. A synthesis of activity towards the implementation of sustainable tourism: Ecotourism in a different context. *Int. J. Sustain. Dev.* **2002**, *5*, 232–250. [CrossRef]

82. Salvado, J. Travel experience ecosystem model. Building travel agencies' business resilience in Portugal. *Eur. J. Tour. Hosp. Recreat.* **2011**, *2*, 95–116.

83. Russo, A.; Tencati, A. Formal vs. informal CSR strategies: Evidence from Italian micro, small, medium- sized, and large firms. *J. Bus. Ethics* **2009**, *85*, 339–353. [CrossRef]

84. Sardianou, E.; Kostakis, I.; Mitoula, R.; Gkaragkani, V.; Lalioti, E.; Theodoropoulou, E. Understanding the entrepreneurs' behavioural intentions towards sustainable tourism: A case study from Greece. *Environ. Dev. Sustain.* **2016**, *18*, 857–879. [CrossRef]

85. Panda, S.; Modak, N.M. Exploring the effects of social responsibility on coordination and profit division in a supply chain. *J. Clean. Prod.* **2016**, *139*, 25–40. [CrossRef]

86. He, P.; He, Y.; Xu, H.; Zhou, L. Online selling mode choice and pricing in an O2O tourism supply chain considering corporate social responsibility. *Electron. Commer. Res. Appl.* **2019**, *38*, 100894. [CrossRef]

87. Chunjou, M.; Pang, S.F.H. An exploratory study of corporate social responsibility of travel agency websites and consumers' low carbon travel intention. In Proceedings of the 2013 7th International Conference on Complex, Intelligent, and Software Intensive Systems, CISIS 2013, Taichung, Taiwan, 3–5 July 2013; IEEE: Piscataway, NJ, USA, 2013; pp. 661–666.

88. Lozano, J.; Arbulú, I.; Rey-Maquieira, J. The greening role of tour operators. *Environ. Manag.* **2016**, *57*, 49–61. [CrossRef] [PubMed]

89. Dube, K.; Nhamo, G. Greenhouse gas emissions and sustainability in Victoria Falls: Focus on hotels, tour operators and related attractions. *Afr. Geogr. Rev.* **2020**, 1–16. [CrossRef]

90. Alonso, M.M.; Bagur, L.; Llach, J.; Perramon, J. Sustainability in small tourist businesses: The link between initiatives and performance. *Curr. Issues Tour.* **2018**, *21*, 1–20. [CrossRef]

91. Ioncică, M.; Petrescu, E.C.; Ioncică, D.E. Innovations in selling tourism products and their impact on the efficiency of the activity of travel agencies and sustainability. *Int. J. Econ. Pract. Theor.* **2015**, *5*, 495–502.

92. Ko, W.W.J.; Liu, G.; Ngugi, I.K.; Chapleo, C. External supply chain flexibility and product innovation performance: A study of small- and medium-sized UK-based manufacturers. *Eur. J. Mark.* **2018**, *52*, 1981–2004. [CrossRef]

93. Kraesgenberg, A.L.; Beldad, A.D.; Hegner, S.M. The impact of corporate social responsibility (CSR) program type, crisis response strategy, and crisis type on postcrisis consumer trust and purchase intention. In *Creating Marketing Magic and Innovative Future Marketing Trends*; Springer: Cham, Switzerland, 2017; pp. 673–677.

94. Balaguer, M.R. Propuestas de la responsabilidad social corporativa en un contexto de crisis financiera internacional. *Prism. Soc.* **2013**, *10*, 157–190.

95. Thomas, R.; Shaw, G.; Page, S.J. Understanding small firms in tourism: A perspective on research trends and challenges. *Tour. Manag.* **2011**, *32*, 963–976. [CrossRef]

96. Almunawar, M.N.; Anshari, M.; Susanto, H. Crafting strategies for sustainability: How travel agents should react in facing a disintermediation. *Oper. Res.* **2013**, *13*, 317–342. [CrossRef]

97. Mourshed, M.M.; Matipa, W.M.; Keane, M.; Kelliher, D. Towards interoperability: ICT in academic curricula for sustainable construction. In Proceedings of the CIB W107 1st International Conference: Creating a Sustainable Construction Industry in Developing Countries, CIB Publications, Ottawa, ON, Canada, 1 March 2000; pp. 11–13. [CrossRef]

98. Alegre, J.; Sard, M. When demand drops and prices rise. Tourist packages in the balearic islands during the economic crisis. *Tour. Manag.* **2015**, *46*, 375–385. [CrossRef]

99. Chapuis, L. *Análisis Argumentativo del Discurso de las Agencias de Viaje Expertas en Turismo Sostenible*; Universidad de Sevilla: Sevilla, Spain, 2013; pp. 87–107.

100. Huët, R. Quand les chefs d'entreprise célèbrent leurs engagements ethiques. Étude de la symbolique des cérémonies publiques de signature des chartes. *Commun. Inf. Médias Théories Prat.* **2011**, *28*. [CrossRef]

101. Baniya, R.; Thapa, B.; Kim, M.S. Corporate social responsibility among travel and tour operators in Nepal. *Sustainability* **2019**, *11*, 2771. [CrossRef]

102. Xu, X.; Gursoy, D. Motivators and inhibitors of implementing sustainable hospitality supply chain management. In *Collaboration in Tourism Businesses and Destinations: A Handbook*; Emerald: London, UK, 2015; pp. 299–320.

103. Mwesiumo, D.; Halpern, N. Acquiescence and conflict in exchanges between inbound tour operators and their overseas outbound partners: A case study on Tanzania. *Tour. Manag.* **2018**, *69*, 345–355. [CrossRef]

104. Tsaur, S.H.; Yung, C.Y.; Lin, J.H. The relational behavior between wholesaler and retailer travel agencies: Evidence from Taiwan. *J. Hosp. Tour. Res.* **2006**, *30*, 333–353. [CrossRef]

105. Baddeley, J.; Font, X. Sustainability, health and safety, or quality? Tour operator supply chain management under scrutiny. *Tour. Recreat. Res.* **2011**, *44*, 1–23.

106. Allen, M.W.; Walker, K.L.; Brady, R. Sustainability discourse within a supply chain relationship: Mapping convergence and divergence. *J. Bus. Commun.* **2012**, *49*, 210–236. [CrossRef]

107. Brockhaus, S.; Kersten, W.; Knemeyer, A.M. Where do we go from here? Progressing sustainability implementation efforts across supply chains. *J. Bus. Logist.* **2013**, *34*, 167–182. [CrossRef]

108. Font, X.; Tapper, R.; Schwartz, K.; Kornilaki, M. Sustainable supply chain management in tourism. *Bus. Strateg. Environ.* **2008**, *17*, 260–271. [CrossRef]

109. Kwon, I.W.G.; Suh, T. Trust, commitment and relationships in supply chain management: A path analysis. *Supply Chain Manag. Int. J.* **2005**, *10*, 26–33. [CrossRef]

110. Piboonrungroj, P.; Disney, S.M. Supply chain collaboration in tourism: A transaction cost economics analysis. *Int. J. Supply Chain Manag.* **2015**, *4*, 25–31.

111. Cheng, M.L.; Liu, T.H.; Lin, C.C. Case study of altruistic behavior and relational network with business value on local travel agencies. *J. Res. Bus. Econ. Manag.* **2017**, *8*, 1455–1464.

112. Okech, R.N. The role of tour operators in sustainable ecotourism: Lessons from Kenya. *Tour. Today* **2004**, *4*, 78–88.

113. Font, X.; Garay, L.; Jones, S. Sustainability motivations and practices in small tourism enterprises in european protected areas. *J. Clean. Prod.* **2016**, *137*, 1439–1448. [CrossRef]

114. Goffi, G.; Masiero, L.; Pencarelli, T. Rethinking sustainability in the tour-operating industry: Worldwide survey of current attitudes and behaviors. *J. Clean. Prod.* **2018**, *183*, 172–182. [CrossRef]

115. Atanase, A.; Schileru, I. Quality and vision in the Romanian tourism agencies. *Amfiteatru Econ.* **2014**, *16*, 1075–1088.

116. Wong, J.Y.; Lee, W.H. Leadership through service: An exploratory study of the leadership styles of tour leaders. *Tour. Manag.* **2012**, *33*, 1112–1121. [CrossRef]

117. Erdogan, N. Environmental views and practices in tourism industry: A study on travel agency managers. *J. Bus. Res.* **2012**, *4*, 52–65.

118. Mossaz, A.; Coghlan, A. The role of travel agents' ethical concerns when brokering information in the marketing and sale of sustainable tourism. *J. Sustain. Tour.* **2017**, *261*. [CrossRef]

119. Theodosiou, M.; Katsikea, E. Antecedents and performance of electronic business adoption in the hotel industry. *Eur. J. Mark.* **2012**, *46*, 258–283. [CrossRef]

120. Buhalis, D.; Jun, S.H. E-tourism. *CTR Contemp. Tour. Rev.* **2011**, *1*, 2–38.

121. Asongu, J. Innovation as an argument for corporate social responsibility. *J. Bus. Public Policy* **2007**, *1*, 1–21.

122. Gössling, S.; Buckley, R. Carbon labels in tourism: Persuasive communication? *J. Clean. Prod.* **2016**, *111*, 358–369. [CrossRef]

123. Wehrli, R.; Priskin, J.; Demarmels, S.; Schaffner, D.; Schwarz, J.; Truniger, F.; Stettler, J. How to communicate sustainable tourism products to customers: Results from a choice experiment. *Curr. Issues Tour.* **2017**, *20*, 1375–1394. [CrossRef]

124. Law, R.; Leung, R.; Lo, A.; Leung, D.; Fong, L.H.N. Distribution channel in hospitality and tourism. Revisiting disintermediation from the perspectives of hotels and travel agencies. *Int. J. Contemp. Hosp. Manag.* **2015**, *27*, 431–452. [CrossRef]

125. Garay, L.; Font, X. Corporate social responsibility in tourism small and medium enterprises evidence from Europe and Latin America. *Tour. Manag. Perspect.* **2013**, *7*, 38–46.

126. Komppula, R. Developing the quality of a tourist experience product in the case of nature based activity services. *Scand. J. Hosp. Tour.* **2006**, *6*, 136–149. [CrossRef]

127. Luck, M. The "New Environmental Paradigm": Is the scale of Dunlap and Van Liere applicable in a tourism context? *Tour. Geogr.* **2002**, *5*, 228–240. [CrossRef]

128. Aguiar, T.; Moreno, S.; Picazo, P. How could traditional travel agencies improve their competitiveness and survive? A qualitative study in Spain. *Tour. Manag. Perspect.* **2016**, *20*, 98–108.

129. Berné, C.; García-González, M.; García-Uceda, E.; Múgica, M. Modelización de los cambios en el sistema de distribución del sector turístico debidos a la incorporación de las tecnologías. *Cuad. Econ. Dir. Empres.* **2012**, *15*, 117–129. [CrossRef]

130. Crane, A.; Matten, D. *Business Ethics: Managing Corporate Citizenship and Sustainability in the Age of Globalization*, 3rd ed.; Oxford University Press: New York, NY, USA, 2016.

131. Frosio, G.F. Why keep a dog and bark yourself? From intermediary liability to responsibility. *Int. J. Law Inf. Technol.* **2018**, *26*, 1–33. [CrossRef]

132. Inversini, A.; Masiero, L. Selling rooms online: The use of social media and online travel agents. *Int. J. Contemp. Hosp. Manag.* **2014**, *26*, 272–292. [CrossRef]

133. Wang, C.; Leng, M.; Liang, L. Choosing an online retail channel for a manufacturer: Direct sales or consignment? *Int. J. Prod. Econ.* **2018**, *195*, 338–358. [CrossRef]

134. Del Chiappa, G.; Zara, A. Offline versus online intermediation: A study of booking behavior of tourists travelling to Sardinia. In *Information and Communication Technologies in Tourism, ENTER Proceedings of the International Conference in Lugano, Switzerland*; Springer: Cham, Switzerland, 2015; pp. 709–721.

135. Kaewkitipong, L. Disintermediation in the tourism industry: An investigation of Thai tourism SMEs. *Int. J. Electron. Bus.* **2011**, *9*, 516–535. [CrossRef]

136. Rodríguez, A.; Pastor, R.; Fernández-Villarán, M.A. Evolución de la intermediación turística en España tras la aparición de las TIC en el sector. *Rev. Empres. Humanismo* **2017**, *XX*, 87–106. [CrossRef]

137. Agag, G.M.; El-Masry, A.A. Why do consumers trust online travel websites? Drivers and outcomes of consumer trust toward online travel websites. *J. Travel Res.* **2017**, *56*, 347–369. [CrossRef]

138. Min, S.R.; Lee, S.M. A study on the behavior of the user according to the distribution development of online travel agency. *J. Distrib. Sci.* **2020**, *18*, 25–35.

139. Van der Duim, R.; van Marwijk, R. The implementation of an environmental management system for Dutch tour operators: An actor-network perspective. *J. Sustain. Tour.* **2006**, *14*, 449–472. [CrossRef]

140. Bastakis, C.; Buhalis, D.; Butler, R.W. The perception of small and medium sized tourism accommodation providers on the impacts of the tour operators' power in Eastern Mediterranean. *Tour. Manag.* **2004**, *25*, 151–170. [CrossRef]

141. Medina, R.D.; Medina, D.; García, J.M. Understanding European tour operators' control on accommodation companies: An empirical evidence. *Tour. Manag.* **2003**, *24*, 135–147. [CrossRef]

142. Cho, M.; Bonn, M.A.; Giunipero, L.; Jaggi, J.S. Contingent effects of close relationships with suppliers upon independent restaurant product development: A social capital perspective. *Int. J. Hosp. Manag.* **2017**, *67*, 154–162. [CrossRef]

143. Xu, X.; Gursoy, D. Influence of sustainable hospitality supply chain management on customers' attitudes and behaviors. *Int. J. Hosp. Manag.* **2015**, *49*, 105–116. [CrossRef]

144. Worthington, I.; Ram, M.; Jones, T. 'Giving something back': A study of corporate social responsibility in UK South Asian small enterprises. *Bus. Ethics A Eur. Rev.* **2006**, *15*, 95–108. [CrossRef]

145. Condon, L. Sustainability and small to medium sized enterprises—How to engage them. *Aust. J. Environ. Educ.* **2004**, *20*, 57–67. [CrossRef]

146. Harness, D.; Ranaweera, C.; Karjaluoto, H.; Jayawardhena, C. The role of negative and positive forms of power in supporting CSR alignment and commitment between large firms and SMEs. *Ind. Mark. Manag.* **2018**, *75*, 17–30. [CrossRef]

147. Perrini, F. SMEs and CSR theory: Evidence and implications from an Italian perspective. *J. Bus. Ethics* **2006**, *67*, 305–316. [CrossRef]

148. Bagur, L.; Perramon, J.; Amat, O. Impact of quality and environmental investment on business competitiveness and profitability in small service business: The case of travel agencies. *Total Qual. Manag. Bus. Excell.* **2015**, *26*, 840–853. [CrossRef]

149. Alonso, M.M.; Rodríguez, J.M.; Rubio, L. Reasons for implementing certified quality systems and impact on performance: An analysis of the hotel industry. *Serv. Ind. J.* **2012**, *32*, 919–936. [CrossRef]

150. Bagur, L.; Llach, J.; Alonso, M.M. Is the adoption of environmental practices a strategic decision for small service companies? An empirical approach. *Manag. Decis.* **2013**, *51*, 41–62. [CrossRef]

151. Llach, J.; Perramon, J.; Alonso, M.M.; Bagur, L. Joint impact of quality and environmental practices on firm performance in small service businesses: An empirical study of restaurants. *J. Clean. Prod.* **2013**, *44*, 96–104. [CrossRef]

152. Bernal, J.A.; Briones, A.J.; de Nieves, C. Impacts of the CSR strategies of technology companies on performance and competitiveness. *Tour. Manag. Stud.* **2017**, *13*, 73–81. [CrossRef]

153. Pozo, H.; Tachizawa, T. Marketing and social responsibility: An exploratory study of local tourism. *Tour. Mang. Stud.* **2018**, *14*, 39–49. [CrossRef]

154. Dervitsiotis, K.N. An innovation-based approach for coping with increasing complexity in the global economy. *Total Qual. Manag. Bus. Excell.* **2012**, *23*, 997–1011. [CrossRef]

155. Waligo, V.M.; Clarke, J.; Hawkins, R. Implementing sustainable tourism: A multi-stakeholder involvement management framework. *Tour. Manag.* **2013**, *36*, 342–353. [CrossRef]

156. Goodwin, H.; Francis, J. Ethical and responsible tourism: Consumer trends in the UK. *J. Vacat. Mark.* **2003**, *9*, 271–284. [CrossRef]

157. Castro, L.D.; Ramírez, L.P.; Rodríguez, L.V.; Sierra, L.C.; Torres, S.C.; Torres, L.M. Servi Travel Ltda. A management proposal to improve its competitiveness and sustainability in the tourism sector. *Tur. Soc.* **2016**, *19*, 193–212.

158. Hitt, A.; Duane, R.; Hoskisson, R. *Administración Estratégica: Competitividad y Globalización. Conceptos y Casos*; Cengage Learning EMEA: Bogotá, Colombia, 2008.

8

Effects of Corporate Social Responsibility on Firm Performance: Does Customer Satisfaction Matter?

An-Pin Wei [1], Chi-Lu Peng [2,]*[ID], Hao-Chen Huang [3] and Shang-Pao Yeh [4]

[1] International School of Business and Finance, Sun Yat-sen University, Zhuhai 519082, China; weianp@mail.sysu.edu.cn

[2] Business Intelligence School, National Kaohsiung University of Science and Technology, Kaohsiung 82445, Taiwan

[3] Department of Public Finance and Taxation, National Kaohsiung University of Science and Technology, Kaohsiung 82445, Taiwan; haochen@nkust.edu.tw

[4] Department of Hospitality and M.I.C.E. Marketing Management, National Kaohsiung University of Hospitality and Tourism, Kaohsiung 812301, Taiwan; shangpao@mail.nkuht.edu.tw

* Correspondence: chilupeng@nkust.edu.tw

Abstract: Academic research has shed light on the empirical relationships among a firm's corporate social responsibility (CSR), corporate social irresponsibility (CSiR) and firm performance and on the firm's customer satisfaction–firm performance relationship in different markets. However, little notice has been taken of whether the coexistence of corporate social responsibility, corporate social irresponsibility and customer satisfaction has an interactive effect on firm performance. This study aims to examine the effects of their interaction on firm performance from an investment perspective. Using unbalanced panel regression to test a sample of publicly traded firms from the United States, this study finds that, in general, firms with higher customer satisfaction earn positive changes in abnormal stock returns. For firms that engage in CSR, CSR positively affects corporate performance, whereas firms' social irresponsibility activities reduce firms' financial performance. All else equal, a positive interactive effect of CSiR and customer satisfaction on stock return was observed. The results reveal that high customer satisfaction can alleviate the negative effect of corporate social irresponsibility on firms' financial performance. Our findings will help management executives and investors to understand that the negative effect of a firm's unforeseen events on firm performance can be weakened by increasing customer satisfaction.

Keywords: corporate social responsibility; corporate social irresponsibility; American Customer Satisfaction Index; stock returns

1. Introduction

Prior studies have examined the influences of corporate social responsibility (hereafter, CSR) on important outcomes in the financial markets. Recent studies have examined various elements of this relationship. For example, Chen, Dong and Lin [1], Nguyen, Kecskés and Mansi [2] and Oikonomou, Yin and Zhan [3] investigate the relevance of CSR to investors' investment decisions; Jin, Cheng and Zeng [4] investigate the stock market's impact on firms' corporate socially irresponsible (hereafter, CSiR) events. While previous research explicitly indicates CSR and customer satisfaction as intangible assets that work in achieving a firm's sustainable competitive advantage and higher performance. However, research regarding the impact of CSR, CSiR, customer satisfaction and their interaction on firm performance for a firm is relatively few. From an investment perspective, this paper investigates the relationship between CSR, CSiR, customer satisfaction and their interaction and stock returns.

In 2015, 92% of the world's 250 largest companies released a CSR report to illustrate the importance that they attached to CSR activities. According to a recent special report in the Harvard Business Review [5], Fortune Global 500 companies annually spend approximately US$20 billion on socially responsible investment (SRI). SRI is becoming increasingly popular because of the increase in funds invested according to socially responsible criteria, constituting more than US$11.6 trillion in assets under management in the Unites States in 2018. (https://www.ussif.org/files/2018%20_Trends_OnePager_ Overview(2).pdf) A recent survey indicated that a large majority of chief executive officers (CEOs) believe that CSR improves firm competitiveness and is crucial for a firm's future success [6]. CSR is a high-profile notion that has strategic importance to numerous companies. During the last two decades, the concept of CSR performance has become a mainstream preoccupation in the corporate world as well as the academic domain. The widespread practice of emphasizing CSR goals and multiple theoretical perspectives supporting a firm's strategic emphases imply that empirical evidence on the CSR–performance relationship should consistently support a positive relationship [7–9]. However, a qualitative review of the literature reveals that evidence of the CSR–performance relationship is relatively inconsistent [10–12]. One reason for the conflicting findings on the CSR–performance relationship is the aggregation of CSR and corporate social irresponsibility (CSiR) into an overall measure by the majority of studies [13,14]. Another potential question to address before we proceed is this: do investors follow firms' CSR or CSiR announcements?

CSR initiatives are a firm's activities which aim to improve the wellbeing of stakeholders or society at large [15]. By contrast, CSiR refers to a firm's actions that negatively affect the welfare of stakeholders or society at large [16]. Strike, Gao and Bansal [17] and Lee, Oh and Kim [18] indicate that a firm is likely to simultaneously engage in CSR and CSiR. For instance, Walmart has implemented fair labor practices in its foreign subsidiaries and suppliers; however, the Bangladeshi factories that produced goods for Walmart were found to have mistreated their workers [19]. Lenz et al. [13] decompose a firm's CSR activities into CSR and CSiR activities and determine that a positive CSR–performance relationship is significantly attenuated by the existence of CSiR. Kim et al. [14] demonstrate that CSR enhances firm value when a firm's competitive action level is high, whereas CSiR improves firm performance when the competitive action level is low. However, studies have extensively used Tobin's Q, a financial-market-based measure used as a proxy for firm performance, to examine the link between CSR activities and firm performance (for reviews of the literature, see [8,20]). Scholars have emphasized the theoretical relevance of Tobin's Q as a financial determinant of investment behavior [21]; however, the performance of investments such as asset expected returns is essential to the financial wellbeing of investors and thus affects their trading decisions [22]. From an investment perspective, these results raise the intriguing question of whether CSR relates to a firm's stock returns as it does to a firm's Tobin's Q.

From the market force perspective, Brønn and Vrioni [23] indicate that strong CSR implies a powerful cause-related marketing tool that can enhance customer perceptions such as loyalty; strong CSR builds and shape a company's reputation, thereby increasing profitability, and therefore, a firm's CSR activities can be viewed as a form of reputation building or maintain [24], and CSR strategies can be used to create a sustainable competitive advantage [25]. The stakeholder theory literature also confirms the evidence of CEOs beliefs that CSR strategies can reinforce intangible assets such as reputation, contributing to a firm's competitiveness and economic performance [14,20]. However, CSR addresses social objectives and stakeholders other than shareholders [26], implying that firms' intangible assets are developed through voluntary corporate actions instead of efforts regarding products or services. Researchers and managers have begun to examine which factors affect firms' intangible assets, such as company reputation, and thus influence firm value. A rising strand of research shows that intangible values of firms in the form of customer satisfaction bring about significant benefit to stakeholders [27–29]. In particular, customer value is on the mission statements of many large corporations (e.g., Amazon, TOYOTA and CISICO) and has become a sought-after source of competitive advantage. According to a resource-based view of the firm [25], CSR strategies can be used to create sustainable competitive advantage. We posed the following question: if customer satisfaction is associated with firm value, can higher customer satisfaction facilitate (alleviate) the positive (negative) relationship between CSR (CSiR) and firm performance?

As mentioned above, there is a rich body of literature that examines the linkage between customer satisfaction and financial performance [29,30] or analyzes the influence of firms' CSR and CSiR activities on firms' value [13,14]. However, Luo and Bhattacharya [7] conducted the first study investigating the potential relationship between CSR, customer satisfaction and firm performance. Because of data availability, they do not examine the potential negative effect of CSiR on firm performance. The relationship between CSR and firm performance is discovered to be amplified in firms with higher product quality. They conclude that a proper mix of internal corporate abilities such as customer satisfaction and external CSR initiatives are more likely to generate and sustain firm value. Surroca, Tribó and Waddock [31] suggest that internal corporate capabilities such as customer satisfaction can moderate the relationships between CSR and market value. Based on a resource-based view of the firm, the present study relies on the insight of Luo and Bhattacharya [7] that the impact of CSR on firm performance depends on the level of customer satisfaction. We expect that customer satisfaction may negatively affect the relationship between CSiR and firm stock return. Accordingly, the second goal of this study is to investigate whether CSR (CSiR) and customer satisfaction synergistically affect firms' stock returns. Following the criteria of Kim et al. [14], this study decomposes CSR initiatives into CSR and CSiR to investigate whether CSR, CSiR, customer satisfaction and the interactive effects between CSR (CSiR) and customer satisfaction influence stock returns.

The rest of this paper is organized as follows. Section 2 presents the literature review and develops our research hypotheses from an investment perspective to reconcile our evidence. Section 3 details the empirical models in this study. Section 4 describes the data. This is followed by a discussion of the empirical results and managerial implications. Finally, the conclusions are presented.

2. Theoretical Framework

2.1. CSR and Firm Performance

Although the definition of CSR is not always clear [12], the literature suggests that it is a general measure of how a firm serves other stakeholders, communities and the environment. Recent studies show that, through CSR activities, firms can not only generate favorable stakeholder attitude and better improve support behaviors but also earn reputation, strengthen stakeholder–company relationships, enhance stakeholders' advocacy behaviors [32], gain traction in the evolving investor and consumer market, as well as, eventually, enhance firm value [5]. These facts align well with the notion that CSR enhances firm value. Skroupa [33] reports that approximately 70% of high-net-worth millennials invest more money in companies with a higher level of CSR. Meier and Cassar [34] demonstrate that the CSR activities of the world's 250 largest companies, according to the companies themselves, increased from 64% in 2005 to 92% in 2015. Brière, Peillex and Ureche-Rangau [35] mention that the market scale of CSR mutual funds constituted more than US$8 trillion in assets under management in the United States in 2016.

Accordingly, many studies have examined whether CSR positively affects firm value represented, for example, by Tobin's Q. From the market force perspective, recent studies have indicated that engaging in CSR initiatives can help firms to earn reputation and obtain support from diverse stakeholders, eventually increasing the firm's financial performance [14] and reducing risks [36]. Lins et al. [36] show that, during the 2008–2009 financial crisis, firms with higher CSR experienced higher profitability, growth and sales per employee relative to firms with lower CSR. From the perspective of resource-based theory, McWilliams and Siegel [25] indicate that CSR strategies can be used to build a firm's sustainable competitive advantage. Meanwhile, sustainable competitive advantages positively influence cross-sectional stock returns [37]. Although there appears to be more support for the view that CSR activities are positively related to Tobin's Q and other accounting ratios [9], some studies have reported a weak or neutral relationship between CSR and firm performance. Kim et al. [14] observe that CSR significantly positively affects firm performance, whereas the relationship between CSiR and firm performance is insignificantly positive. Lenz et al. [13] confirm a positive relationship between CSR and firm performance and determine that the positive effect of CSR on firm performance is significantly attenuated by the existence of CSiR. Accordingly, the results appear to be inconclusive owing to the failure to decompose CSR into socially responsible and socially irresponsible activities.

Investors' trading behavior may significantly affect asset prices. Brzeszczyński and McIntosh [10] and Statman, Fisher and Anginer [38] report that investors are willing to sacrifice their investment returns if social benefits can be achieved through their investments. Bollen [39] determines that investors have a multi-attribute utility function: they combine their investments' social responsibility and return characteristics during their investment decision making. However, much less notice has been taken of the increasing attention of investors to sustainable investment [10] and its impact on individual stock returns. From an investment perspective, this study expects that investors should pay attention to CSR and thereby positively affect their investment returns. Therefore, we propose the following hypothesis:

Hypothesis 1. *An increase in CSR leads to a positive change in stock price.*

2.2. CSiR and Firm Performance

CSiR, the antithesis of CSR, refers to firm actions that adversely affect the wellbeing of stakeholders or society at large. The literature documents that CSiR undermines a firm's corporate reputation and brand image [32] as well as affecting the firm's relationship with various stakeholders, ultimately harming firm performance and increasing firm risk [40]. According to Massa [41] and Bollen [39], investors are concerned about the moral and social wellbeing connotations of corporate activity and are likely to profit from SRI. However, the performance differential between SRI and benchmark market returns is found to be insignificant or significantly negative [10,35,42]. The reason for the conflicting evidence of the positive boom in SRI and underperforming investment is that CSR and CSiR, conceptually distinct constructs, should be considered separately and simultaneously rather than being combined.

Recent articles have indicated that firms engage in CSR and CSiR concurrently [14,16,17] and have indicated that CSiR regularly occurs in the majority of firms that engage in CSR [43]. For instance, positive stakeholder news is released around CEO stock option granting dates [44]. In 2000, Exxon Mobil offered strong retirement benefits programs for its employees; simultaneously, the company faced major controversies related to workforce health and safety issues [40]. Socially irresponsible firms may be involved in more negative messages and negative stories than others when their faults become public [45]. Thus, stakeholders may interpret firms' CSiR activities as insincere, and these are likely to induce higher physiological activation than others [18], which reduces stakeholders trust, affects firm reputation and attenuates or inverses the positive CSR impact on firm value. Studies have indicated that a firm's CSR is ineffective in offsetting the negative effects of CSiR on firm performance [16]. Jayachandran, Kalaignanam and Eilert [46] indicate that the negative impact of CSiR is stronger than CSR's positive effect on firm performance. We decompose CSR into socially responsible and socially irresponsible activities to investigate the coexisting influences of CSR and CSiR on individual firms' stock return and hypothesize the following:

Hypothesis 2. *An increase in CSiR leads to a negative change in stock returns.*

2.3. Effects of CSR, CSiR and Customer Satisfaction on Stock Return

According to stakeholder theory, CSR is viewed as an intangible asset that significantly positively affects customer-related outcomes such as loyalty, stakeholder attitudes and advocacy behaviors, leading to future cash flows and market share gains [7,13,17]. Studies on customer satisfaction have indicated that the beneficial effects of CSR on customers' and investors' behaviors result in increased firm value. Empirical evidence has been obtained showing that firms with higher customer satisfaction can earn higher loyalty, reduce the costs of attracting new customers and have higher reputation in the marketplace, thereby leading to higher stock market returns [30,47].

CSR and customer satisfaction are potentially crucial sources of intangible capital that positively influences firm value. Huberman and Regev [48] indicate that prices react to new information only when investors pay attention to it. Whether investors follow firms' CSR and strong customer satisfaction information announcements to help make investment decisions is unclear. Recent studies have documented that awareness of a company's CSR initiatives among its stakeholders is typically low [26], but investors follow American Consumer Satisfaction Index (ACSI) announcements, and such announcements encourage their trading, thereby generating significantly positive stock returns [41,42]. Moreover, engaging in CSR and increasing customer satisfaction could be regarded as strategies to create a sustainable competitive advantage that is positively related to future stock returns [37]. Thus, this study expects that firms embark on both CSR and attempt to satisfy customers to reap the benefits of the synergistic interaction between CSR and strong customer satisfaction to ensure a high stock return, in addition to using the independent effects of CSR and ACSI. Correspondingly, this study proposes the following hypothesis:

Hypothesis 3. *After controlling for the independent effects of change in CSR and the strong customer satisfaction indicator, the interaction of positive change in CSR and strong customer satisfaction is positively related to a firm's stock return.*

As mentioned, firms can be simultaneously socially responsible and socially irresponsible. CSiR weakens CSR's positive effects on firm value. In view of resource-based theory, CSiR may weaken the sustainable competitive advantage of a firm and has a negative effect on a firm's stock returns. One question is then whether investors pay attention to a firm's CSiR initiatives when people are unaware of the firm's CSR activities. Tench et al. [45] reveal that the media always report negative stories concerning a firm's CSiR. The mass media's coverage of a firm's CSiR initiatives undermines the firm's value and thereby negatively affects investors' trading behavior and firm performance. CSiR may be the intentional or unintentional actions of a firm [43]; a firm may thus simultaneously satisfy customers and have CSiR. Peng et al. [47] report that firms with high ACSI generate significantly positive abnormal returns when markets are pessimistic. They conjecture that the intangible value of high customer satisfaction can insulate a firm's returns from economic downturns. Therefore, this study proposes the following hypothesis:

Hypothesis 4. *After controlling for the independent effects of change in CSiR and the customer satisfaction indicator, the interaction of positive changes in CSiR and strong customer satisfaction is positively related to a firm's stock return.*

3. Methods

3.1. Data and Variable Construction

In order to examine the effects of CSR, CSiR, customer satisfaction and their interaction on firm's financial performance separately, this study acquires data on CSR, CSiR and customer satisfaction from various databases: the Kinder, Lydenburg, Domini (KLD) Research and Analytics data set and ACSI database. Firstly, this study obtains CSR and CSiR ratings from the KLD database, which contains the most comprehensive and detailed data on firm-level CSR scores used in the literature [1,2,49] and has been widely used by academics and practitioners as a source of information on corporate social responsibility [1–3,26,49–51]. The KLD contains data on various CSR strengths and concerns (weaknesses) for seven socially irresponsibility ratings—community, corporate governance, diversity, employee relations, environment, human rights and product—for a large set of US companies since 1991.

The database uses sources both internal to the firm (e.g., annual reports) and external (e.g., articles in the business press) to conduct annual assessments of the social performance of the 3000 largest US publicly traded firms by market capitalization. Based on company filings, government data, nongovernmental organization data and more than 14,000 global media sources, the KLD covers several strengths and concerns across the seven social dimensions mentioned. It provides differentiation of strength and concern binary-item measures based on whether a firm meets certain strength and concern criteria, enabling disentanglement of CSR and CSiR rather than capturing them simultaneously using an overall approach [1,13,52]. The KLD's strength and concern criteria are assigned values of 0 or 1, and the number of measures for most dimensions has evolved over time as KLD has refined the database. The raw CSR and CSiR scores are the sum of seven-dimension scores based on the number of measures for strengths and concerns, respectively. However, the simple summation approach has a disadvantage, because the number of strength and concern measures varies considerably between years due to slight changes of the KLD measures. Therefore, the raw CSR and CSiR scores may not be helpful in evaluating a firm's actual CSR activities over the years [49]. Accordingly, directly comparing raw CSR or CSiR scores within a category over years is inappropriate [26,49].

To overcome this concern and obtain consistent comparisons in unbalanced panel data structure, this study follows Lenz et al. [13] and Cao et al. [49], dividing the number of strengths (concerns) with a KLD rating for each firm-year within each CSR category by the maximum possible number of strengths (concerns) within the domain in the respective year. We scale the strengths and concerns for each firm-year to obtain two indicators that range from 0 to 1. The resulting scores of CSR and CSiR are scaled for each firm-year within each domain to a range of zero to one. We then sum these scaled numbers of strengths (concerns) across the seven domains, resulting in a measure anchored by 0 and 7. According to the definition, for each firm i, we can obtain two adjusted CSR and CSiR measures, denoted by $CSR_{i,t}$ and $CSiR_{i,t}$. Higher CSR scores indicate that the firm engages in more CSR activities in time t. By contrast, higher CSiR scores indicate that the firm is more involved in CSiR in time t.

Following prior studies in marketing and finance, this study collected the customer satisfaction data from the American Customer Satisfaction Index (ACSI), which is computed annually and has been employed in a large number of studies [7,27,28,30,47,53–57]. Since 1994, the ACSI has been developed and maintained by the National Quality Research Center at the University of Michigan. By interviewing consumers regarding their comprehensive level of satisfaction, the ACSI measures customer satisfaction as a score on a 0 to 100 scale that is experienced by the broader and larger sample of customers instead of experts, which can reduce sampling error and delimit biases from regional differences in satisfaction tendencies [58]. (For a detail description of the ACSI database, see e.g., Aksoy et al. [30], Peng et al. [47], and Fornell, Morgeson and Hult [59]. All the ACSI data are available at https://www.theacsi.org/) Moreover, the firms in the ACSI list account for the majority of market share in their industry sectors, which are broadly representative of the US economy serving US households [30,47]. Although reporting at an annual level on the ACSI website, these ACSI scores are collected in four quarterly instalments, and a subset of firms' ACSI scores is released in each specific release quarter. Annual satisfaction scores for each firm were collected on a quarterly basis for different industries and it is assumed that the ACSI scores for firms maintained until new ACSI scores were released in next year. By using the firms' names as shown on the ACSI website, we merge data from KLD and ACSI databases to span the publicly traded firms in the universe of firms in our sample that received ACSI scores in each year.

Firms which do better than their competition in terms of satisfying customers generate superior performance [59]. Customer satisfaction has been recognized as a key driver of firm profitability and market value [7] but shown not to move stock prices around the public release date. This seems to suggest that it is necessary to consider both level and changes in ACSI scores because the stock market do not seem to respond immediately to changes in the score [30]. According to the method of prior studies [30,47], this study classifies each firm into one of four categories according to whether the firm's ACSI is higher or lower than the national average-adjusted mean ACSI and whether it was non-decreasing or decreasing. The firms with high and non-decreasing ACSI are termed the strong portfolio in Aksoy et al. [30]. In this study, we classify firms belonging to the strong portfolio as strong ACSI firms by defining the dummy variable $ACSI_{i,t}$ that equals 1 if firm i is classified as a strong ACSI firm in time t. This study assesses whether a firm has both a changing CSR (CSiR) and strong customer satisfaction score and whether the synergistic interaction of change in CSR (CSiR) and strong customer satisfaction results in higher stock return. The raw data used to calculate control variables such as stock returns, firm size, cash asset ratio, leverage, firm profitability, turnover, liquidity and firm risk are collected from the Center for Research in Security Prices (CRSP) and Compustat. After cross-referencing these databases and accounting for lags and changes in CSR (CSiR), ACSI and financial information variables, this study obtains cross-sectional and time-series combined unbalanced panel data consisting of 285 publicly traded firms with approximately 4328 observations from 1995 to 2013 as the final sample.

3.2. Empirical Models

Following Cai, Jo and Pan [60], this study develops a model to predict an individual firm's stock return as a function of the variables described in the previous section. Working with changes also enables us to avoid problems of spurious regression and control for firm-specific information that is not modeled [61]. The model used to test the proposed hypotheses is as follows:

$$
\begin{aligned}
\Delta Performance_{i,t+1} &= \alpha_0 + \beta_1 \Delta CSR_{i,t} + \beta_2 \Delta CSiR_{i,t} + \beta_3 ACSI_{i,t} \\
&+ \beta_4 \Delta CSR_{i,t} \times ACSI_{i,t} + \beta_5 \Delta CSiR_{i,t} \times ACSI_{i,t} \\
&+ \Gamma_{Control} \times \Delta Control_{i,t} + \Sigma_k \delta_k Industry_{i,t}^k + \Sigma_m \eta_m Month_{i,t}^m + \varepsilon_{i,t}
\end{aligned}
\tag{1}
$$

where $\Delta Performance_{i,t+1}$ denotes the change in annual cumulative abnormal return of stock i in time t + 1, measured by the risk-adjusted returns of the capital asset pricing model (CAPM), the Fama and French three-factor model [62] or the Carhart four-factor model [63], respectively. To obtain the annual risk-adjusted returns of each company i in month t, this study follows Peng et al. [47] and Carhart [51], running regressions on the CAPM as well as the Fama and French three-factor or Carhart four-factor models, with a rolling window over the preceding 36 monthly returns, to obtain the time-varying factor loadings over time using the following equation:

$$
R_{i,t} - R_{f,t} = \alpha_{i,T} + \beta_{i,T}^{rmrf} RMRF_t + \beta_{i,T}^{smb} SMB_t + \beta_{i,T}^{hml} HML_t + \beta_{i,T}^{mom} MOM_t + \varepsilon_{i,t}
\tag{2}
$$

where $R_{i,t}$ denotes the return on firm i in period t, and $R_{f,t}$ denotes the risk-free rate in period t. $RMRF_t$, SMB_t, HML_t and MOM_t denote the index investing, size investing, value investing and momentum investing strategy returns, respectively. The intercepts (alpha) from these regressions can be interpreted as risk-adjusted returns of an individual firm related to Carhart's model. (The monthly factor-loadings data used in this study are obtained from the Kenneth R. French Data Library: http://mba.tuck.dartmouth.edu/pages/faculty/ken.french/data_library.html.) Following Peng et al. [47], we retrieve the value of alpha by estimating the expected return in excess over the realized risk premium. We use the realized factor loading of firm i during specific time periods by subtracting the firm's monthly returns from the product of each factor realization and its estimated loadings to obtain a series of individual firm i's monthly abnormal returns at time t ($AR_{i,t}$) as follows:

$$
\begin{aligned}
AR_{i,t} &= (R_{i,t} - R_{f,t}) \\
&- \left(\hat{\alpha}_{i,T} + \hat{\beta}_{i,T}^{RMRF} RMRF_t + \hat{\beta}_{i,T}^{SMB} SMB_t + \hat{\beta}_{i,T}^{HML} HML_t + \hat{\beta}_{i,T}^{MOM} MOM_t \right)
\end{aligned}
\tag{3}
$$

This study examines the relationship between change in CSR, change in CSiR and their interactive effect on strong ACSI firms and stock return on a yearly basis. Annual cumulative abnormal returns are computed as follows:

$$
Performance_{i,t} = \left[\prod_{k=1}^{12} (1 + AR_{i,t+k}) \right] - 1
\tag{4}
$$

In each case, changes in adjusted CSR and CSiR measures are denoted as $\Delta CSR_{i,t}$ and $\Delta CSiR_{i,t}$. Following past studies [36,64], this study accounts for observable heterogeneity with many control variables found to influence firm performance, including change in $\Delta LnSize_{i,t}$ (the logarithm of total assets) [13,52], change in $\Delta Leverage_{i,t}$ (total debt to common equity ratio; D/E ratio) [20,52], change in $\Delta Profit_{i,t}$ [36] (operating income divided by total assets), change in $\Delta Liquidity_{i,t}$ (current ratio, as calculated by dividing book value of current assets by debt in current liabilities) [13,14], changes in $\Delta Turnover_{i,t}$ (dividing the total number of shares traded over month t by the number of shares outstanding for the period) [65], change in $\Delta Idiosy_{i,t}$ (the standard deviation of the residuals from the fitted market models, estimated by the rolling regression with period $t - 1$ and including the past 36 months of returns) [30] and the lagged dependent variable ($\Delta Performance_{i,t}$) [66] to control for the potential lagged effect of stock performance changes. Moreover, we include the industry dummies (based on all four-digit Standard Industrial Classification (SIC) code industries) and monthly time dummies to account for unobserved heterogeneity across industries and time, respectively. $Industry_k$ and $Month_m$ are the dummies for industry and time fixed effects and $\varepsilon_{i,t} \sim N(0, \sigma^2)$. This study used the lagged independent variables as instrumental variables to reduce potential endogeneity concerns. Moreover, we follow Petersen [67] to test the significance of the estimated coefficients in the regression by using t-statistics based on standard errors corrected for firm and time clustering.

4. Empirical Results

4.1. Summary Statistics

Panel A and Panel B of Table 1 summarize the descriptive statistics of raw scores of our main independent variables, CSR and CSiR, during our sampling period. Consistent with Lenz et al. [13], the mean CSR and CSiR scores are all positive, indicating that CSiR actions regularly occur in firms also engaging in CSR. Table 1 demonstrates that, on average, firms' CSiR scores are significantly higher than their CSR scores—approximately 0.30 higher (t = 10.02) during 2001 and 2009. Firms' CSR scores are higher than their CSiR scores by approximately 0.45 between 2010 and 2013, indicating that the firms engaged in more socially responsible actions and fewer and fewer socially irresponsible initiatives after 2009 (see Figure 1).

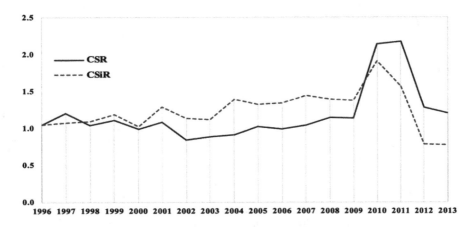

Figure 1. Mean CSR and CSiR scores for our sample firms over period 1996–2013.

As mentioned above, this study obtains firms' customer satisfaction data from the ACSI website. The average (median) of ACSI is 75.546 (76) and the maximum and minimum values are 90 and 54, respectively. The standard deviation of ACSI is 5.882, indicating that the level of customer satisfaction with the firms in our sample varied considerably. A dummy is assigned for a strong ACSI firm if the firm has a high and increasing ACSI in time $t - 1$. The summary statistics of the dependent variable and our control variables—changes in firm size, leverage, profit, liquidity, turnover and idiosyncratic risk—are reported in Table 2.

Table 1. Summary statistics of main independent variables: CSR and CSiR.

				Panel A Scores of CSR				
Times	Mean	S.D.	Max.	Q. 75th	Median	Q. 25th	Min.	# of Firms
1996	1.052	0.765	4.050	1.450	0.975	0.500	0.000	51
1997	1.200	0.868	4.000	1.750	1.000	0.688	0.000	52
1998	1.042	0.878	4.250	1.500	0.750	0.500	0.000	46
1999	1.108	0.975	4.250	1.583	0.667	0.333	0.000	44
2000	0.992	0.926	4.250	1.333	0.750	0.333	0.000	43
2001	1.057	0.820	3.750	1.583	0.917	0.417	0.000	45
2002	0.834	0.655	3.500	1.250	0.750	0.333	0.000	57
2003	0.857	0.661	3.000	1.333	0.833	0.333	0.000	63
2004	0.910	0.722	3.417	1.333	0.833	0.333	0.000	66
2005	1.024	0.776	3.767	1.367	0.833	0.667	0.000	64
2006	0.985	0.810	4.183	1.250	0.733	0.500	0.000	65
2007	1.038	0.797	4.136	1.488	0.829	0.536	0.000	64
2008	1.143	0.841	4.279	1.569	0.893	0.643	0.000	76
2009	1.137	0.870	4.429	1.619	0.929	0.571	0.000	83
2010	2.139	1.199	4.981	2.876	2.305	1.186	0.000	85
2011	2.177	1.235	4.981	2.981	2.305	1.186	0.000	87
2012	1.281	0.973	4.067	1.767	1.167	0.500	0.000	85
2013	1.204	0.778	3.350	1.667	1.067	0.667	0.000	83

				Panel B Scores of CSiR				
Times	Mean	S.D.	Max.	Q. 75th	Median	Q. 25th	Min.	# of Firms
1996	1.050	0.841	3.000	1.500	1.000	0.500	0.000	51
1997	1.077	0.782	3.500	1.500	1.000	0.500	0.000	52
1998	1.095	0.870	3.333	1.792	0.833	0.500	0.000	46
1999	1.223	0.912	3.667	1.833	1.000	0.500	0.000	44
2000	1.018	0.788	2.833	1.750	0.750	0.500	0.000	43
2001	1.270	0.964	4.250	1.833	1.000	0.500	0.000	45
2002	1.119	0.773	3.583	1.521	0.833	0.500	0.000	57
2003	1.079	0.758	3.083	1.500	1.000	0.500	0.000	63
2004	1.388	0.914	4.667	1.833	1.333	0.833	0.000	66
2005	1.318	0.814	3.917	1.500	1.167	0.667	0.000	64
2006	1.338	0.837	4.500	1.833	1.250	0.750	0.000	65
2007	1.440	0.869	4.500	2.000	1.333	0.750	0.000	64
2008	1.389	0.861	4.500	2.000	1.250	0.750	0.000	76
2009	1.370	0.857	4.500	2.000	1.250	0.750	0.000	83
2010	1.908	1.102	5.467	2.767	1.950	1.083	0.000	85
2011	1.565	0.846	5.600	2.050	1.500	0.950	0.200	87
2012	0.780	0.784	4.233	1.000	0.650	0.200	0.000	85
2013	0.782	0.720	4.267	1.100	0.600	0.200	0.000	83

Notes: Summary statistics of corporate responsibility scores (scaled scores, i.e., the initial scores divided by the max scores at time t).

Table 2. Descriptive statistics for dependent variable and independent variables.

	Mean	S.D.	Max.	Q. 75th	Median	Q. 25th	Min.	# of Obs.
ΔPerformance	0.001	0.038	0.306	0.018	0.000	−0.018	−0.415	4328
ΔCSR	0.037	0.640	3.252	0.167	0.000	−0.143	−3.081	4328
ΔCSiR	−0.006	0.585	2.433	0.250	0.000	−0.250	−2.583	4328
ACSI	0.400	0.490	1.000	1.000	0.000	0.000	0.000	4328
ΔLnSize	0.059	0.152	1.131	0.098	0.041	−0.007	−0.856	4328
ΔLeverage	−0.046	54.870	1530.6	0.197	−0.012	−0.212	−1477.9	4328
ΔProfit	0.000	0.022	0.375	0.004	0.000	−0.003	−0.300	4328
ΔLiquidity	−0.001	0.301	2.990	0.123	0.000	−0.119	−3.367	4328
ΔTurnover	0.012	0.254	2.121	0.091	0.011	−0.068	−3.110	4328
ΔIdiosy	0.074	0.042	0.341	0.088	0.062	0.046	0.022	4328

Table 3 presents the Pearson (lower triangular matrix) and Spearman (upper triangular matrix) correlation coefficients and the variance inflation factors (VIFs) of all the independent variables in our empirical models. Although the pairwise correlations among the independent variables are not particularly high, $\Delta CSR_{i,t}$ ($\Delta CSiR_{i,t}$) is correlated with the interactive term of $\Delta CSR_{i,t}$ ($\Delta CSiR_{i,t}$) with $ACSI_{i,t}$, with a correlation coefficient of 0.65 (0.62). The highest correlation coefficient between independent variables is lower than 0.7, indicating that the regression model should not exhibit the multicollinearity problem [68]. Furthermore, this study tests for potential multicollinearity by checking the VIFs in our models. Table 3 reports the VIFs of independent variables and reveals no severe multicollinearity concern, with the VIFs ranging from 1.01 to 2.37. Given that all VIFs are below the threshold of 10 and the average full collinearity of the VIF of 1.47 satisfies the 3.3 limit of Kock [69], we conclude that multicollinearity does not pose a threat to the results.

Table 3. Correlation matrix and VIFs.

	(1)	(2)	(3)	(4)	(5)	(6)	(7)	(8)	(9)	(10)	(11)	(12)
(1) ΔPerformance	1.00	0.00	−0.03	0.04	0.01	0.00	−0.08	−0.04	0.05	0.02	−0.00	0.04
(2) ΔCSR	0.02	1.00	0.39	−0.02	0.62	0.22	0.02	−0.06	0.03	0.01	0.01	0.06
(3) ΔCSiR	−0.03	0.49	1.00	−0.03	0.21	0.61	0.02	−0.05	0.01	0.05	0.03	0.03
(4) ACSI	0.03	−0.01	−0.04	1.00	0.06	−0.02	0.05	−0.02	0.00	−0.03	−0.02	−0.03
(5) ΔCSR × ACSI	0.01	0.65	0.29	0.03	1.00	0.32	0.00	−0.05	0.03	−0.01	0.01	0.04
(6) ΔCSiR × ACSI	0.01	0.31	0.62	−0.04	0.47	1.00	0.02	−0.04	0.01	0.05	0.03	0.04
(7) ΔLnSize	−0.10	−0.00	0.03	0.04	0.00	0.02	1.00	0.07	−0.12	0.01	−0.05	−0.06
(8) ΔLeverage	0.02	0.01	−0.02	−0.02	−0.01	0.00	0.03	1.00	−0.18	−0.20	0.10	−0.04
(9) ΔProfit	0.03	0.02	0.01	0.00	0.04	0.03	−0.03	0.02	1.00	0.05	−0.10	0.06
(10) ΔLiquidity	0.05	0.00	0.05	−0.03	0.01	0.04	−0.02	−0.01	0.05	1.00	−0.06	0.03
(11) ΔTurnover	−0.02	0.00	0.02	−0.03	0.02	0.02	−0.03	0.00	−0.11	−0.06	1.00	−0.01
(12) ΔIdiosy	0.08	0.03	0.01	−0.04	0.03	0.05	−0.07	−0.02	0.09	0.01	−0.06	1.00
VIFs	1.47	2.37	2.21	1.01	2.30	2.13	1.01	1.00	1.02	1.01	1.02	1.02

Notes: The upper and lower triangular matrixes are the Spearman and Pearson correlation coefficients, respectively. The mean VIF is presented in the first column of the row entitled variance inflation factors (VIFs).

4.2. Empirical Results

Table 4 details the independent variables, control variables and variables of interest: CSR, CSiR, ACSI and their interactions. Hypotheses 1 and 2 state that CSR and CSiR have contrasting relationships with stock return performance. After controlling factors found to influence firm performance, Model 1 indicates the separate direct effects of CSR and CSiR on firm performance. An increase in a firm's CSR score is associated with an increase in the firm's risk-adjusted returns, indicating that investors investing in firms that engage in more CSR initiatives receive higher stock returns. Thus, Hypothesis 1 is supported. By contrast, an increase in firms' CSiR is negatively related to performance, suggesting that firms' CSiR actions directly damage investors' stock returns. Thus, Hypothesis 2 is supported. The separate positive and negative effects of CSR and CSiR scores on firm stock return are found. CSiR is discovered to more strongly affect stock return than CSR. This evidence echoes previous findings, such as those of Jayachandran et al. [46], who report that CSiR's negative effect on firm performance exceeds CSR's positive effect. As indicated in Model 2 of Table 4, the coefficient of a strong ACSI dummy is positive and significant, supporting earlier findings that firms with a strong ACSI generate higher investment returns than those with lower ACSI [47].

Hypothesis 3 states that the interaction between $\Delta CSR_{i,t}$ and $ACSI_{i,t}$ affects the positive relationship between CSR and firms' stock returns. Hypothesis 4 states that a strong ACSI effect negatively moderates the relationship between CSiR and firms' stock return. We rely on Model 4 to test our hypothesis because this model is a fully specified model and provides an accurate picture of the impact of each variable. Model 4 of Table 4 reports the results concerning the direction of the effects of $\Delta CSR_{i,t}$, $\Delta CSiR_{i,t}$ and $ACSI_{i,t}$. Consistent with the results obtained from Model 3, we find a significant positive direct effect of CSR and a significant negative effect of CSiR. We discover that the interaction between $\Delta CSR_{i,t}$ and $ACSI_{i,t}$ is insignificantly negative, whereas the coefficient of the interaction between $\Delta CSiR_{i,t}$ and

$ACSI_{i,t}$ is significantly positive and higher than that of the direct effect of CSiR on firm stock return. This result implies that firms that maintain higher customer satisfaction have the capacity to mitigate the negative effect of CSiR on firm performance. The results confirm past studies which state that firms with a strong ACSI generate positive abnormal returns.

Model 4 illustrates the interaction effects of $\Delta CSR_{i,t}$ ($\Delta CSiR_{i,t}$) and $ACSI_{i,t}$ on the relationship between $\Delta CSR_{i,t}$ ($\Delta CSiR_{i,t}$) and firm performance. The coefficient of the interaction variable, $\Delta CSR_{i,t} \times ACSI_{i,t}$, is negatively but insignificantly associated with a firm's stock returns. By contrast, the coefficient of the interaction between $\Delta CSiR_{i,t}$ and $ACSI_{i,t}$ is positive and significant. There is no evidence that firms engaging in CSR generate positive market value from their higher customer satisfaction. However, our evidence supports the notion that CSiR's negative effect on stock return is significantly weakened for firms with strong customer satisfaction. Therefore, the results obtained from Model 4 support Hypothesis 4 and refute the alternative Hypothesis 3. Regarding control variables, $\Delta LnSize_{i,t}$ is significantly negatively related to a firm's stock return, Furthermore, the relationships of $\Delta Leverage_{i,t}$, $\Delta Liquidity_{i,t}$ and $\Delta Idiosy_{i,t}$ with firm stock return are significantly positive.

Table 4. Effects of change in CSR (change in CSiR) and strong ACSI on stock return.

	Model 1		Model 2		Model 3		Model 4	
	Coef.	t-Stat	Coef.	T-Stat	Coef.	t-Stat	Coef.	t-Stat
Intercept	−0.0013	−0.1220	−0.0007	−0.0682	−0.0026	−0.2856	−0.0009	−0.0873
$\Delta CSR_{i,t}$	0.0021 *	1.9379			0.0021 *	1.9317	0.0033 **	2.1416
$\Delta CSiR_{i,t}$	−0.0027 **	−2.0765			−0.0026 **	−1.9922	−0.0048 ***	−2.7895
$ACSI_{i,t}$			0.0035 ***	2.3718	0.0034 **	2.3043	0.0036 ***	2.4265
$\Delta CSR_{i,t} \times ACSI_{i,t}$							−0.0028	−1.3963
$\Delta CSiR_{i,t} \times ACSI_{i,t}$							0.0055 ***	2.3353
$\Delta LnSize_{i,t}$	−0.0237 ***	−4.2898	−0.0247 ***	−4.5122	−0.0243 ***	−4.4216	−0.0244 ***	−4.4312
$\Delta Leverage_{i,t}$	0.0001 ***	2.9735	0.0001 ***	3.1265	0.0001 ***	3.0957	0.0001 ***	3.0283
$\Delta Profit_{i,t}$	0.0119	0.3065	0.0121	0.3100	0.0115	0.2946	0.0110	0.2823
$\Delta Liquidity_{i,t}$	0.0060 **	2.2098	0.0059 ***	2.1749	0.0061 ***	2.2546	0.0061 **	2.2601
$\Delta Turnover_{i,t}$	0.0005	0.1325	0.0005	0.1501	0.0007	0.1834	0.0007	0.1896
$\Delta Idiosy_{i,t}$	0.0839 ***	2.4031	0.0852 ***	2.4356	0.0844 ***	2.4151	0.0826 ***	2.3683
$Month_m$	YES		YES		YES		YES	
$Industry_k$	YES		YES		YES		YES	
Adj. R^2	0.0320		0.0324		0.0335		0.0343	
F-stat	4.0391		4.1525		4.1206		4.0736	
# of Obs.	4328		4328		4328		4328	

Notes: The dependent variables are estimated by Carhart four-factor model. The main independent variables are change in CSR (CSiR) from time $t − 1$ to t and change in firm characteristics from time $t − 1$ to t. Following Petersen [53], the t-statistics are estimated corrections of standard errors for heteroscedasticity and autocorrelation. ***, ** and * indicate significance at the 1%, 5% and 10% levels, respectively. Regarding the F-test, all explanatory variables together have an effect at the 10% significance level at least.

We also examine the CAPM and Fama and French risk-adjusted returns of our empirical models. The impact of the interaction between $\Delta CSiR_{i,t}$ and $ACSI_{i,t}$ is found to be positive and significant on both the CAPM and Fama and French risk-adjusted returns (Table 5). We rely on the fully specified models in Table 5 to test our arguments. For controlling for the potential persistence of firm performance over time, in Table 6, this study follows Brennan et al. [66] and examines whether there are lagged effects from the dependent variable ($\Delta Performance_{i,t}$) to stock performance changes ($\Delta Performance_{i,t+1}$). After considering the lagged return effect, Table 6 shows that the coefficient of the interaction variable, $\Delta CSR_{i,t} \times ACSI_{i,t}$, is negatively but insignificant associated with a firm's stock returns. Meanwhile, the coefficient of the interaction between $\Delta CSiR_{i,t}$ and $ACSI_{i,t}$ is positive and significant. Regarding control variables, $\Delta LnSize_{i,t}$ and $\Delta Performance_{i,t}$ are significantly negatively related to a firm's stock return changes. Furthermore, the relationships of $\Delta Leverage_{i,t}$, $\Delta Liquidity_{i,t}$ and $\Delta Idiosy_{i,t}$ with firm stock return are significantly positive. Our evidence indicates that the interaction between $\Delta CSR_{i,t}$ and $ACSI_{i,t}$ has an insignificantly negative effect, whereas that between $\Delta CSiR_{i,t}$ and $ACSI_{i,t}$ has a significant positive effect. This study explains the significantly positive interaction term of $\Delta CSiR_{i,t} \times ACSI_{i,t}$ on firm performance that (1) the stock market appears to underreact to CSiR when a firm's ACSI is high and that (2) a firm's strong ACSI can mitigate CSiR's negative effect on firm performance. The results are presented in Tables 4–6.

Table 5. Impacts of CSR, CSiR and ACSI on changes in cumulative stock return.

	CAPM		Three-Factor	
	Coef.	t-Stat	Coef.	t-Stat
Intercept	−0.0013	−0.3222	−0.0011	−0.1002
$\Delta CSR_{i,t}$	0.0028 *	1.9253	0.0033 **	2.1426
$\Delta CSiR_{i,t}$	−0.0054 ***	−3.4479	−0.0048 ***	−2.7936
$ACSI_{i,t}$	0.0034 **	2.3726	0.0034 ***	2.3782
$\Delta CSR_{i,t} \times ACSI_{i,t}$	−0.0027	−1.4582	−0.0027	−1.3742
$\Delta CSiR_{i,t} \times ACSI_{i,t}$	0.0039 *	1.7570	0.0053 **	2.2826
$\Delta LnSize_{i,t}$	−0.0277 ***	−4.7021	−0.0239 ***	−4.5213
$\Delta Leverage_{i,t}$	0.0001 ***	2.5678	0.0001 ***	2.9930
$\Delta Profit_{i,t}$	0.0351	0.8431	0.0115	0.2977
$\Delta Liquidity_{i,t}$	0.0034	1.3929	0.0059	2.3803
$\Delta Turnover_{i,t}$	−0.0006	−0.1329	0.0006	0.1741
$\Delta Idiosy_{i,t}$	0.0523	1.3735	0.0820	2.3659
$Month_m$	YES		YES	
$Industry_k$	YES		YES	
Adj. R^2	0.0360		0.0348	
F-statstic	4.2277		4.1237	
# of Obs.	4328		4328	

Notes: The dependent variables are estimated by the CAPM and Fama and French three-factor model, respectively. The main independent variables are change in CSR (CSiR) from time t − 1 to t and change in firm characteristics from time t − 1 to t. Following Petersen [53], the t-statistics are estimated corrections of standard errors for heteroscedasticity and autocorrelation. ***, ** and * indicate significance at the 1%, 5% and 10% levels, respectively.

Table 6. Impacts of CSR, CSiR and ACSI on changes in cumulative stock return, including lagged dependent variable ($\Delta Performance_{i,t}$).

	CAPM		Three-Factor		Four-Factor	
	Coef.	t-Stat	Coef.	t-Stat	Coef.	t-Stat
Intercept	0.0009	0.2242	0.0025	0.2448	−0.0032	−0.2324
$\Delta CSR_{i,t}$	0.0030 **	2.0919	0.0038 **	2.4314	0.0029 **	1.9743
$\Delta CSiR_{i,t}$	−0.0054 ***	−3.3903	−0.0048 ***	−2.8093	−0.0040 **	−2.3180
$ACSI_{i,t}$	0.0041 **	2.7746	0.0042 ***	2.8422	0.0031 **	2.1544
$\Delta CSR_{i,t} \times ACSI_{i,t}$	−0.0029	−1.5419	−0.0032	−1.6178	−0.0029	−1.4927
$\Delta CSiR_{i,t} \times ACSI_{i,t}$	0.0036	1.5856	0.0052 **	2.2170	0.0041 *	1.7665
$\Delta LnSize_{i,t}$	−0.0286 ***	−4.7815	−0.0242 ***	−4.4714	−0.0189 ***	−3.6680
$\Delta Leverage_{i,t}$	0.0000 ***	2.3996	0.0000 ***	2.9204	0.0000 ***	2.4725
$\Delta Profit_{i,t}$	0.0512	1.2546	0.0477	1.2146	0.0767 **	2.1438
$\Delta Liquidity_{i,t}$	0.0042	1.8384	0.0068 ***	2.4533	0.0053 **	2.0029
$\Delta Turnover_{i,t}$	−0.0011	−0.2480	0.0003	0.0852	0.0014	0.4091
$\Delta Idiosy_{i,t}$	0.0469	1.1866	0.0873 ***	2.4677	0.1235 ***	4.1172
$\Delta Performance_{i,t}$	−0.0591 **	−2.1625	−0.1238 ***	−3.5806	−0.0896 ***	−2.9993
$Month_m$	YES		YES		YES	
$Industry_k$	YES		YES		YES	
Adj. R^2	0.0446		0.0581		0.0592	
F-statstic	4.7977		6.0233		6.1230	
# of Obs.	4151		4151		4151	

Notes: This table presents the regression results for robustness. The dependent variables are estimated by the CAPM, Fama and French three-factor model and Carhart four-factor model, respectively. The main independent variable is change in CSR (CSiR) from time t − 1 to t, while the control variables are change in firm characteristics and cumulative abnormal return from time t − 1 to t. Following Petersen [53], the t-statistics are estimated corrections of standard errors for heteroscedasticity and autocorrelation. ***, ** and * indicate significance at the 1%, 5% and 10% levels, respectively.

4.3. Robustness Checks

Because the cumulative abnormal returns (CARs) overlap, following Gallant [70], this study employs a heteroskedasticity-and-autocorrelation-consistent (HAC) estimate of the variance, setting one-period lags equal to the number of overlapping months in the holding-period window (t + 2 to t + 12). After considering HAC effects, panel regression analysis was performed to test Hypotheses 1, 2, 3 and 4 using the cumulative abnormal returns obtained from the CAPM, Fama and French and Carhart's models (Table 7). We obtain similar results to those presented in Tables 4 and 5. Our findings indicate that firm $\Delta CSR_{i,t}$ is significantly positively related to firm performance in the CAPM and Fama and French models. Meanwhile, the relationship between the direct effect of $\Delta CSR_{i,t}$ and firm performance is insignificantly positive in Carhart model. Thus, Hypothesis 1 is partially supported. In all models, the direct effects of $\Delta CSiR_{i,t}$ on firm performance are significantly negative. Thus, Hypothesis 2 is supported. Table 7 details results similar to those in Table 4; Table 5, indicating that the interaction terms of $\Delta CSiR_{i,t} \times ACSI_{i,t}$ are positive and significant in pricing models. We have obtained supporting evidence: firms with a strong ACSI can undermine and reverse the negative relationship between $\Delta CSiR_{i,t}$ and stock return.

Table 7. Changes in cumulative abnormal returns without overlapping (t + 2 to t + 12).

	CAPM		Three-Factor		Four-Factor	
	Coef.	t-Stat	Coef.	t-Stat	Coef.	t-Stat
Intercept	0.0010	0.2551	0.0022	0.2092	−0.0028	−0.1943
$\Delta CSR_{i,t}$	0.0024 *	1.7407	0.0030 **	2.0076	0.0019	1.3760
$\Delta CSiR_{i,t}$	−0.0052 ***	−3.3970	−0.0049 ***	−3.0215	−0.0037 **	−2.2031
$ACSI_{i,t}$	0.0028 **	2.1006	0.0030 **	2.1607	0.0022 *	1.6708
$\Delta CSR_{i,t} \times ACSI_{i,t}$	−0.0025	−1.4287	−0.0027	−1.4191	−0.0022	−1.1604
$\Delta CSiR_{i,t} \times ACSI_{i,t}$	0.0041 *	1.8923	0.0058 **	2.6071	0.0042 *	1.8821
$\Delta LnSize_{i,t}$	−0.0259 ***	−4.7639	−0.0239 ***	−4.6751	−0.0174 ***	−3.5255
$\Delta Leverage_{i,t}$	0.0000 ***	2.4542	0.0000 ***	3.2565	0.0000 ***	2.6194
$\Delta Profit_{i,t}$	0.0251	0.6402	−0.0038	−0.1053	0.0474	1.4095
$\Delta Liquidity_{i,t}$	0.0029	1.2889	0.0054 **	2.2086	0.0047 **	1.9669
$\Delta Turnover_{i,t}$	−0.0005	−0.1177	0.0003	0.0933	0.0003	0.0953
$\Delta Idiosy_{i,t}$	0.0355	0.9798	0.0635 **	1.8721	0.1074 ***	3.7993
$Month_m$	YES		YES		YES	
$Industry_k$	YES		YES		YES	
Adj. R^2	0.0318		0.0309		0.0311	
F-statstic	3.8396		3.7608		3.7797	
# of Obs.	4328		4328		4328	

Notes: This table presents the regression results for robustness. The dependent variables are estimated by the CAPM, Fama and French three-factor model and Carhart four-factor model, respectively. The cumulative abnormal returns are set for one-period lags equal to the number of overlapping months in the holding-period window (t + 2 to t + 12). The main independent variables are change in CSR (CSiR) from time t − 1 to t and change in firm characteristics from time t − 1 to t. Following Petersen [53], the t-statistics are estimated corrections of standard errors for heteroscedasticity and autocorrelation. ***, ** and * indicate significance at the 1%, 5% and 10% levels, respectively.

This study also follows the literature [14,26] by excluding the product quality dimension, which represents a firm's efforts in extra quality control and product safety and the corporate governance dimension, which represents voluntary corporate activities for primary stakeholders. These two dimensions appear to contribute to the wellbeing of internal shareholders rather than society. The results are consistent with those reported in Tables 4–7.

5. Discussion and Conclusions

This study investigates whether CSR, CSiR, customer satisfaction and their interaction terms affect individual stock returns. Scholars have asserted that CSR helps a firm to acquire a competitive advantage over its competitors by building up its reputation and obtaining support from diverse stakeholders, thereby enhancing the firm's financial performance. According to the United Nations-supported Principles for Responsible Investment (PRI) survey (the PRI survey is a survey of 1100 financial professionals, predominantly CFA members, around the world), the size of assets managed by institutions incorporated into environment, social and governance (ESG) factors has exceeded US$86 trillion, and the number of institutions which had signed up to the PRI increased from 63 to more than 2370 companies between 2006 and 2018. Recent research has revealed that firms with higher CSR scores experienced less volatility [71], as well as higher profitability, growth and sales per employee [36], during the financial crisis. Despite the fact that an increasing number of studies have supported the positive effect on firms' performance in an investment perspective, more and more portfolio managers and analysts have selected firms on the basis of CSR criteria [72,73] but have rarely adjusted their models based on ESG information. (Brzeszczyński and McIntosh [10] and Statman, Fisher and Anginer [38] report that investors are willing to sacrifice their investment returns if social benefits can be achieved through their investments. Bollen [39] determines that investors have a multi-attribute utility function: they combine their investments' social responsibility and return characteristics during their investment decision making.) Only 20% and 17% of the respondents believed that CSR factors such as environmental and social issues would affect their stock returns. This study obtains statistical evidence that financial markets in the United States earn rewards for CSR and are penalized for CSiR. Managers of firms can consider the potential implications of the results of this research and maintain or increase their resources on CSR activities to enhance their firms' value.

CSR is a subject of increasing interest in business practice and marketing research, but we devote very little attention to the issue of corporate social irresponsibility [13]. CSiR is a phenomenon that is encountered time and again. CSiR may involve intentional or unintentional CSiR. Intentional CSiR indicates behavior which violates the law and legal but irresponsible behavior (potential lack of morality and opportunism) on the part of the firm. An example of violation of law like Enron is the extreme case of intentional CSiR that entails the demise of a company, while the case of a fast food manufacturer engaging in advertising near primary schools is a kind of legal but irresponsible behavior. An example like the explosion at the BP Deepwater Horizon oil rig, which released over 130 million gallons of crude oil into the Gulf of Mexico, constitutes unintentional CSiR but the pollution incident harmed wildlife and the marine environment and temporarily resulted in more than 50% loss in BP's stock price. In theory, public disclosure of CSiR may result in a variety of negative consequences for companies and attenuate firms' sustainable competitive advantages. However, the market may not systematically reward firms' actions that activate and advance social good, while it does consistently punish firms exposed to CSiR. Kim et al. [14] find that firms' CSiR improve firms' Tobin's Q when the competitive action level is low. In this study, we find that CSiR is significantly and negatively associated with firms' stock returns. Investors do not appreciate firms that engage in n corporate social irresponsibility activities.

Higher customer satisfaction should increase loyalty, insulate the current market share from competitors, help to build a firm's reputation, open the opportunity for new sources of revenue and increase investor recognition, and anticipated future cash flows should increase, boosting firm value and stock returns [27,47,74–76]. Previous research has presented the idea that customer satisfaction as an intangible asset works in achieving a sustainable competitive advantage. Regarding the direct effect of customer satisfaction, using Aksoy et al.'s [30] approach, the findings of this study are consistent with the marketing literature: higher customer satisfaction positively affects a firm's stock returns [20]. With regard to the interactive effects of CSR, CSiR and ACSI on a firm's financial performance, we do not find a significant synergistic effect of CSR and ACSI on firm performance. However, our research shows evidence that the relationship between the synergistic effect of CSiR and ACSI is positive.

Our results suggest that our understanding of the ACSI mechanism is strongly enriched when firms encounter difficulties in a series of unfortunate events not deliberately inflicted by a corporation. This study makes two key contributions. Firstly, our evidence offers a novel understanding of the stock market effects of CSR, CSiR and the interaction between CSR (CSiR) and customer satisfaction to the growing literature on CSR. This understanding is essential for researchers, practitioners and investors considering the ongoing debate regarding whether investors benefit from SRI. For instance, a firm's CSiR can be caused by unforeseen events such as an earthquake that could lead to the explosion of a power plant. This unintentional CSiR may entail a variety of negative consequence for the company value. Secondly, our results reveal that firms with higher customer satisfaction can undermine and reverse the negative effect of CSiR on their stock return. These findings are useful for management executives and investors. For firm managers, our findings can help them to allocate limited resources more efficiently to increase their customer satisfaction and then increase firm performance. From an investment perspective, investors can look to invest in firms with strong ACSI scores.

6. Limitations and Future Research Directions

Although the findings of this study are very encouraging, some limitations may pave new directions for future research. Firstly, by using firms' ACSI data to investigate the synergistic effects of CSR, CSiR and ACSI on firm performance, this study is limited to the sample of firms which have both ACSI and KLD scores. Secondly, the KLD data set has been elaborating over the years and variables have been modified, added or dropped. In addition, some firms have missed through mergers and acquisition and such changes have not been considered in the KLD database, therefore, the nominal firms' KLD scores at different periods are not directly compared across periods. Prior studies have reported that different independent effects of CSR, CSiR and ACSI on stock returns in different market states do exist. The results of this study thus call for future research to examine the effects of CSR, CSiR, ACSI and their interaction on firm performance under different market conditions.

Author Contributions: Conceptualization, A.-P.W. and C.-L.P.; methodology, A.-P.W. and C.-L.P.; software, A.-P.W.; validation, A.-P.W., C.-L.P., H.-C.H. and S.-P.Y.; formal analysis, A.-P.W. and C.-L.P.; investigation, A.-P.W. and C.-L.P.; resources, A.-P.W.; data curation A.-P.W.; writing—original draft preparation, A.-P.W. and C.-L.P.; writing—review and editing, H.-C.H. and S.-P.Y.; project administration, C.-L.P.; funding acquisition, A.-P.W. All authors have read and agreed to the published version of this manuscript.

References

1.   Chen, T.; Dong, H.; Lin, C. Institutional shareholders and corporate social responsibility. *J. Financ. Econ.* **2020**, *135*, 483–504. [CrossRef]

2.   Nguyen, P.-A.; Kecskés, A.; Mansi, S. Does corporate social responsibility create shareholder value? The importance of long-term investors. *J. Bank. Financ.* **2020**, *112*, 105217. [CrossRef]

3.   Oikonomou, I.; Yin, C.; Zhao, L. Investment horizon and corporate social performance: The virtuous circle of long-term institutional ownership and responsible firm conduct. *Eur. J. Financ.* **2019**, *26*, 14–40. [CrossRef]

4.   Jin, Y.; Cheng, C.; Zeng, H. Is evil rewarded with evil? The market penalty effect of corporate environmentally irresponsible events. *Bus. Strat. Environ.* **2019**, *29*, 846–871. [CrossRef]

5.   Marti, C.P.; Drescher, L.G.J.; Martí-Ballester, C.; Rovira-Val, M.R. Are Firms that Contribute to Sustainable Development Better Financially? *Corp. Soc. Responsib. Environ. Manag.* **2013**, *22*, 305–319. [CrossRef]

6.   Kiron, D. Sustainability nears a tipping point. *Strateg. Dir.* **2012**, *28*, 69–74. [CrossRef]

7.   Luo, X.; Bhattacharya, C. Corporate Social Responsibility, Customer Satisfaction, and Market Value. *J. Mark.* **2006**, *70*, 1–18. [CrossRef]

8.   Socoliuc, M.; Cosmulese, C.G.; Ciubotariu, M.-S.; Mihaila, S.; Gliga, I.D.; Grosu, V. Sustainability Reporting as a Mixture of CSR and Sustainable Development. A Model for Micro-Enterprises within the Romanian Forestry Sector. *Sustainability* **2020**, *12*, 603. [CrossRef]

9.   Yang, M.; Bento, P.; Akbar, A. Does CSR Influence Firm Performance Indicators? Evidence from Chinese Pharmaceutical Enterprises. *Sustainability* **2019**, *11*, 5656. [CrossRef]

10. Brzeszczynski, J.; McIntosh, G. Performance of Portfolios Composed of British SRI Stocks. *J. Bus. Ethics* **2013**, *120*, 335–362. [CrossRef]

11. McWilliams, A.; Siegel, D.S. Corporate social responsibility and financial performance: Correlation or misspecification? *Strateg. Manag. J.* **2000**, *21*, 603–609. [CrossRef]

12. McWilliams, A.; Siegel, D. Corporate Social Responsibility: A Theory of the Firm Perspective. *Acad. Manag. Rev.* **2001**, *26*, 117–127. [CrossRef]

13. Lenz, I.; Wetzel, H.A.; Hammerschmidt, M. Can doing good lead to doing poorly? Firm value implications of CSR in the face of CSI. *J. Acad. Mark. Sci.* **2017**, *45*, 677–697. [CrossRef]

14. Kim, K.-H.; Kim, M.; Qian, C. Effects of Corporate Social Responsibility on Corporate Financial Performance: A Competitive-Action Perspective. *J. Manag.* **2015**, *44*, 1097–1118. [CrossRef]

15. Korschun, D.; Bhattacharya, C.; Swain, S.D. Corporate Social Responsibility, Customer Orientation, and the Job Performance of Frontline Employees. *J. Mark.* **2014**, *78*, 20–37. [CrossRef]

16. Kang, C.; Germann, F.; Grewal, R. Washing Away Your Sins? Corporate Social Responsibility, Corporate Social Irresponsibility, and Firm Performance. *J. Mark.* **2016**, *80*, 59–79. [CrossRef]

17. Strike, V.M.; Gao, J.; Bansal, P. Being good while being bad: Social responsibility and the international diversification of US firms. *J. Int. Bus. Stud.* **2006**, *37*, 850–862. [CrossRef]

18. Lee, K.; Oh, W.-Y.; Kim, N. Social Media for Socially Responsible Firms: Analysis of Fortune 500's Twitter Profiles and their CSR/CSIR Ratings. *J. Bus. Ethics* **2013**, *118*, 791–806. [CrossRef]

19. Clifford, S. Wal-Mart Is Being Pressed to Disclose How Global Suppliers Treat Workers. Available online: https://www.nytimes.com/2011/05/31/business/31walmart.html (accessed on 20 May 2020).

20. Flammer, C. Does Corporate Social Responsibility Lead to Superior Financial Performance? A Regression Discontinuity Approach. *Manag. Sci.* **2015**, *61*, 2549–2568. [CrossRef]

21. Landsman, W.R.; Shapiror, A.C. Tobin's q and the Relation between Accounting ROI and Economic Return. *J. Account. Audit. Financ.* **1995**, *10*, 103–118. [CrossRef]

22. Grinblatt, M.; Keloharju, M.M. What Makes Investors Trade? *J. Financ.* **2001**, *56*, 589–616. [CrossRef]

23. Brønn, P.S.; Vrioni, A.B. Corporate social responsibility and cause-related marketing: An overview. *Int. J. Advert.* **2001**, *20*, 207–222. [CrossRef]

24. McWilliams, A.; Siegel, D.S.; Wright, P.M. Corporate Social Responsibility: Strategic Implications. *J. Manag. Stud.* **2006**, *43*, 1–18. [CrossRef]

25. McWilliams, A.; Siegel, D.S. Creating and Capturing Value. *J. Manag.* **2010**, *37*, 1480–1495. [CrossRef]

26. Servaes, H.; Tamayo, A. The Impact of Corporate Social Responsibility on Firm Value: The Role of Customer Awareness. *Manag. Sci.* **2013**, *59*, 1045–1061. [CrossRef]

27. Anderson, E.W.; Fornell, C.; Mazvancheryl, S.K. Customer Satisfaction and Shareholder Value. *J. Mark.* **2004**, *68*, 172–185. [CrossRef]

28. Rego, L.L.; Morgan, N.A.; Fornell, C. Reexamining the Market Share–Customer Satisfaction Relationship. *J. Mark.* **2013**, *77*, 1–20. [CrossRef]

29. Otto, A.S.; Szymanski, D.M.; Varadarajan, R. Customer satisfaction and firm performance: Insights from over a quarter century of empirical research. *J. Acad. Mark. Sci.* **2019**, *48*, 543–564. [CrossRef]

30. Aksoy, L.; Cooil, B.; Groening, C.; Keiningham, T.L.; Yalcin, A.; Yalçın, A. The Long-Term Stock Market Valuation of Customer Satisfaction. *J. Mark.* **2008**, *72*, 105–122. [CrossRef]

31. Surroca, J.; Tribó, J.A.; Waddock, S. Corporate responsibility and financial performance: The role of intangible resources. *Strateg. Manag. J.* **2009**, *31*, 463–490. [CrossRef]

32. Du, S.; Bhattacharya, C.B.; Sen, S. Maximizing Business Returns to Corporate Social Responsibility (CSR): The Role of CSR Communication. *Int. J. Manag. Rev.* **2010**, *12*, 8–19. [CrossRef]

33. Skroupa, C.P. CSR: How Fortune 500 Companies Measure up. Available online: https://skytopstrategies.com/csr-fortune-500-companies-measure/ (accessed on 20 May 2020).

34. Meier, S.; Cassar, L. Stop Talking about How CSR Helps Your Hottom Line. Harvard Business Review. Available online: https://hbr.org/2018/01/stop-talking-about-how-csr-helps-your-bottom-line (accessed on 20 May 2020).

35. Brière, M.; Peillex, J.; Ureche-Rangau, L. Do Social Responsibility Screens Matter When Assessing Mutual Fund Performance? *Financ. Anal. J.* **2017**, *73*, 53–66. [CrossRef]

36. Lins, K.V.; Servaes, H.; Tamayo, A. Social Capital, Trust, and Firm Performance: The Value of Corporate Social Responsibility during the Financial Crisis. *J. Financ.* **2017**, *72*, 1785–1824. [CrossRef]

37. Liu, Y.; Mantecon, T. Is sustainable competitive advantage an advantage for stock investors? *Q. Rev. Econ. Financ.* **2017**, *63*, 299–314. [CrossRef]

38. Statman, M.; Fisher, K.L.; Anginer, D. Affect in a Behavioral Asset-Pricing Model. *Financ. Anal. J.* **2008**, *64*, 20–29. [CrossRef]

39. Bollen, N.P.B. Mutual Fund Attributes and Investor Behavior. *J. Financ. Quant. Anal.* **2007**, *42*, 683–708. [CrossRef]

40. Oikonomou, I.; Brooks, C.; Pavelin, S. The Impact of Corporate Social Performance on Financial Risk and Utility: A Longitudinal Analysis. *Financ. Manag.* **2012**, *41*, 483–515. [CrossRef]

41. Massa, M. How do family strategies affect fund performance? When performance-maximization is not the only game in town. *J. Financ. Econ.* **2003**, *67*, 249–304. [CrossRef]

42. Bauer, R.; Derwall, J.; Otten, R. The Ethical Mutual Fund Performance Debate: New Evidence from Canada. *J. Bus. Ethics* **2006**, *70*, 111–124. [CrossRef]

43. Price, J.M.; Sun, W. Doing good and doing bad: The impact of corporate social responsibility and irresponsibility on firm performance. *J. Bus. Res.* **2017**, *80*, 82–97. [CrossRef]

44. Aboody, D.; Kasznik, R. CEO stock option awards and the timing of corporate voluntary disclosures. *J. Account. Econ.* **2000**, *29*, 73–100. [CrossRef]

45. Tench, R.; Bowd, R.; Jones, B. Perceptions and perspectives: Corporate social responsibility and the media. *J. Commun. Manag.* **2007**, *11*, 348–370. [CrossRef]

46. Jayachandran, S.; Kalaignanam, K.; Eilert, M. Product and environmental social performance: Varying effect on firm performance. *Strateg. Manag. J.* **2013**, *34*, 1255–1264. [CrossRef]

47. Peng, C.-L.; Lai, K.-L.; Chen, M.-L.; Wei, A.-P. Investor sentiment, customer satisfaction and stock returns. *Eur. J. Mark.* **2015**, *49*, 827–850. [CrossRef]

48. Huberman, G.; Regev, T. Contagious Speculation and a Cure for Cancer: A Nonevent that Made Stock Prices Soar. *J. Financ.* **2001**, *56*, 387–396. [CrossRef]

49. Cao, J.; Liang, H.; Zhan, X. Peer Effects of Corporate Social Responsibility. *Manag. Sci.* **2019**, *65*, 5487–5503. [CrossRef]

50. Cui, J.; Jo, H.; Na, H. Does Corporate Social Responsibility Affect Information Asymmetry? *J. Bus. Ethics* **2016**, *148*, 549–572. [CrossRef]

51. Hasan, I.; Kobeissi, N.; Liu, L.; Wang, H. Corporate Social Responsibility and Firm Financial Performance: The Mediating Role of Productivity. *J. Bus. Ethics* **2016**, *149*, 671–688. [CrossRef]

52. Deng, X.; Kang, J.-K.; Low, B.S. Corporate social responsibility and stakeholder value maximization: Evidence from mergers. *J. Financ. Econ.* **2013**, *110*, 87–109. [CrossRef]

53. Ivanov, V.; Joseph, K.; Wintoki, M.B. Disentangling the market value of customer satisfaction: Evidence from market reaction to the unanticipated component of ACSI announcements. *Int. J. Res. Mark.* **2013**, *30*, 168–178. [CrossRef]

54. Sorescu, A.B.; Sorescu, S. Customer Satisfaction and Long-Term Stock Returns. *J. Mark.* **2016**, *80*, 110–115. [CrossRef]

55. Huang, M.-H.; Trusov, M. Customer satisfaction underappreciation: The relation of customer satisfaction to CEO compensation. *Int. J. Res. Mark.* **2020**, *37*, 129–150. [CrossRef]

56. Lim, L.G.; Tuli, K.R.; Grewal, R. Customer Satisfaction and Its Impact on the Future Costs of Selling. *J. Mark.* **2020**, *84*, 23–44. [CrossRef]

57. Luo, X.; Zhang, R.; Zhang, W.; Aspara, J. Do institutional investors pay attention to customer satisfaction and why? *J. Acad. Mark. Sci.* **2013**, *42*, 119–136. [CrossRef]

58. Mittal, V.; Kamakura, W.A.; Govind, R. Geographic Patterns in Customer Service and Satisfaction: An Empirical Investigation. *J. Mark.* **2004**, *68*, 48–62. [CrossRef]

59. Fornell, C.; Morgeson, F.V.; Hult, G.T.M. Stock Returns on Customer Satisfaction Do Beat the Market: Gauging the Effect of a Marketing Intangible. *J. Mark.* **2016**, *80*, 92–107. [CrossRef]

60. Cai, Y.; Jo, H.; Pan, C. Doing Well While Doing Bad? CSR in Controversial Industry Sectors. *J. Bus. Ethics* **2011**, *108*, 467–480. [CrossRef]

61. Angulo-Ruiz, L.F.; Donthu, N.; Prior, D.; Rialp, J. How does marketing capability impact abnormal stock returns? The mediating role of growth. *J. Bus. Res.* **2018**, *82*, 19–30. [CrossRef]

62. Fama, E.F.; French, K.R. Common risk factors in the returns on stocks and bonds. *J. Financ. Econ.* **1993**, *33*, 3–56. [CrossRef]

63. Carhart, M.M. On Persistence in Mutual Fund Performance. *J. Financ.* **1997**, *52*, 57–82. [CrossRef]

64. Dyck, A.; Lins, K.V.; Roth, L.; Wagner, H.F. Do institutional investors drive corporate social responsibility? International evidence. *J. Financ. Econ.* **2019**, *131*, 693–714. [CrossRef]

65. Lin, Y.E.; Chu, C.C.; Omura, A.; Li, B.; Roca, E. Arbitrage risk and the cross-section of stock returns: Evidence from China. *Emerg. Mark. Rev.* **2020**, *43*, 100609. [CrossRef]

66. Brennan, M.J.; Chordia, T.; Subrahmanyam, A. Alternative factor specifications, security characteristics, and the cross-section of expected stock returns. *J. Financ. Econom.* **1998**, *49*, 345–373. [CrossRef]

67. Petersen, M.A. Estimating Standard Errors in Finance Panel Data Sets: Comparing Approaches. *Rev. Finance Stud.* **2008**, *22*, 435–480. [CrossRef]

68. Lehaney, B.; Mason, R.D.; Lind, D.A. Statistical Techniques in Business and Economics. *J. Oper. Res. Soc.* **1991**, *42*, 187. [CrossRef]

69. Kock, N. *Common Method Bias: A Full Collinearity Assessment Method for PLS-SEM*; Springer Science and Business Media LLC: Berlin, Germany, 2017; pp. 245–257.

70. Gallant, A.R. *Nonlinear Statistical Models*; John Wiley and Sons: New York, NY, USA, 2009.

71. Bouslah, K.; Kryzanowski, L.; M'Zali, B. Social Performance and Firm Risk: Impact of the Financial Crisis. *J. Bus. Ethics* **2016**, *149*, 643–669. [CrossRef] [PubMed]

72. Riedl, A.; Smeets, P. Why Do Investors Hold Socially Responsible Mutual Funds? *J. Financ.* **2017**, *72*, 2505–2550. [CrossRef]

73. Ammann, M.; Bauer, C.; Fischer, S.; Müller, P. The impact of the Morningstar Sustainability Rating on mutual fund flows. *Eur. Financ. Manag.* **2018**, *25*, 520–553. [CrossRef]

74. Gong, Y.; Ho, K.; Lo, C.; Karathanasopoulos, A.; Jiang, I.-M. Forecasting price delay and future stock returns: The role of corporate social responsibility. *J. Forecast.* **2019**, *38*, 354–373. [CrossRef]

75. Homburg, C.; Koschate, N.; Hoyer, W.D. Do Satisfied Customers Really Pay More? A Study of the Relationship between Customer Satisfaction and Willingness to Pay. *J. Mark.* **2005**, *69*, 84–96. [CrossRef]

76. Truong, C.; Nguyen, T.H.; Huynh, T. Customer satisfaction and the cost of capital. *Rev. Account. Stud.* **2020**, 1–50. [CrossRef]

9

The Role of CSR on Social Entrepreneurship: An International Analysis

Inmaculada Buendía-Martínez [1],*(iD) and Inmaculada Carrasco Monteagudo [2](iD)

[1]   Faculty of Social Sciences, University of Castilla-La Mancha, 16071 Cuenca, Spain
[2]   Faculty of Economics and Business, University of Castilla-La Mancha, Plaza de la Universidad, 02071 Albacete, Spain; Inmaculada.Carrasco@uclm.es
*   Correspondence: inmaculada.buendia@uclm.es

Abstract: The increase in the weight of social entrepreneurship (SE) in the economy has driven the increase in research on the subject. Within the set of approaches developed by scholars to analyse SE, the institutional approach has recently acquired greater relevance. Following this research trend, this article seeks to expand the empirical research on SE by focusing on the informal factors that are less studied in the literature and using a cross-national base. Using the New Institutional Economics and partial least squares–structural equation modelling (PLS-SEM), our findings show the influence of cultural context on the SE dimension. In addition, this influence occurs through two groups of variables led by social capital and corporate social responsibility, although their impacts show opposite signs. These factors have important implications for policy makers in charge of fostering SE development.

Keywords: culture; social entrepreneurship; corporate social responsibility; social justice; social capital; sustainable development

---

1. Introduction

The two crises of this century are currently having devastating effects on the economy and social structures of countries around the world. The 2007 crisis resulted in high levels of unemployment, and cutbacks in social policy have increased the vulnerability of many segments of the population [1]. Without consolidation of recovery, the new crisis caused by COVID-19 will lead to more negative economic and social scenarios, with a considerable increase in the magnitude of the vulnerable population [2]. In these crisis contexts, social entrepreneurship (SE) emerges as a powerful tool for civil society to meet the social needs and solve the problems that the public and private sectors are unable to address [3,4].

Although SE is far from a recent phenomenon, the 2007 crisis increased interest in SE, in both the public and academic spheres. In the first case, the increase in the contribution of the SE to the economic growth, competitiveness, and sustainable development of countries and regions [5–7], together with its role as a solution for state shortcomings in welfare provision [8], has led to SE assuming a more relevant position in public authorities' agendas. During the last decade, some supranational organisations, such as the World Bank, the Organisation for Economic Co-operation and Development (OECD), and the European Union, have developed different projects with the aim of advancing the construction of a favourable ecosystem where SE can flourish, develop, and consolidate [9–11].

From an academic perspective, studies on SE did not begin to appear in the literature until the end of the 1990s. Since then, research has increased considerably, and the related approaches and themes have evolved [12]. Hota, Subramanian, and Narayanamurthy [13] analysed the evolution of research on SE between 1996–2017, distinguishing two stages. In the first phase, which lasted until the first decade of the new century, the volume of contributions was limited. The authors focused on exploring the emergence of SE, its definitions, and its characteristics. In the second phase, the conceptual theoretical development of SE was produced, with a shift in focus from an idealistic position to a pragmatic one [14–26]. In recent years, scholars have focused on impact analyses of the social, cultural, political, and economic contexts of SE [27–33], as well as determining the societal values and individual attributes of SE [34–39]. Some authors claim to push SE research forward in two directions: understanding the specific contextual framework that promotes the rise of SE and the incorporation of cross-national empirical studies due to qualitative and case study methodologies dominating the research [13,40].

On this basis, this article aims to fill in the gap by enlarging empirical research on SE and analysing the contextual characteristics that favour SE's development on a cross-national base. Using the New Institutional Economics and partial least squares–structural equation modelling (PLS-SEM), we study whether the cultural environment defined by social capital, entrepreneurship capital, social justice, and corporate social responsibility (CSR) shape the size of SE. This conceptualization adds three contributions not previously considered by scholars:

(a) The few studies on SE from an institutional perspective are focused on formal factors [40,41], which are less difficult to measure than informal factors [42]. This issue is why social capital and entrepreneurship capital are the most commonly studied factors, although they represent only a small part of the global context that impacts SE. The inclusion of social justice and CSR fosters understanding of the institutional complexity that influences SE. Of particular relevance is the addition of CSR as a driver of SE, given that different authors have indicated a theoretical synergy between both concepts [43–48]. However, no empirical evidence has validated this relationship.

(b) The use of structural equation modelling that allows us not only to expand the number of variables but also to overcome the limitations of linear models that prevent us from considering the interdependence of the variables and their mutual reinforcement processes [49,50], leading us to consider the mediating role of some constructs.

(c) The use of a cross-country analysis, which represents an important advance due to the scarcity of data on the international stage.

This work is organised into six sections. The first section is this introduction; the second section analyses the current literature, which is used to propose the hypotheses on which the empirical study is founded; the third section consists of the methodology used, the description of the dataset used for the cross-country study, and the models developed; the results and the discussions are presented in the fourth and fifth sections, respectively; finally, the sixth section presents the conclusions of the study.

2. Literature Review

Of the various perspectives used to analyse the parameters impacting entrepreneurship, the institutional angle has recently emerged as the focus of a significant amount of studies [51–56]. Institutional analysis explores the link between institutions and organisational schemes and the resulting impacts on the economy, politics, and society in general [57]. Although there are several ways to handle the concept of "institution", the most standardised one is the method proposed by North, which defines institutions as norms that provide the motivational structure of an economy, thus reducing risk and providing stability by stipulating and determining the choices of individuals and shaping the gamut of prospects available to society. More concisely, institutions embody the foundation of the performance of economies, which is why certain economies establish institutions that result in growth, while others do not yield similar results [58,59].

To appreciate the effect of institutions on the business environment, it is critical to distinguish between formal and informal institutions: the former restrict individuals' behaviours to facilitate exchanges, while the latter relate to social norms and value systems, with a direct impact on the application, interpretation, and fulfilment of norms [58,59]. An important amount of research has established the relevance of informal factors on the business environment [60–66]; the impact of informal factors is more significant than that generated by formal factors [67]. The profile of SE based on project, objectives, mission, governability, income generation, and profit distribution is unlike that of other institutional forms [19,68–70], which suggests a specific combination of informal factors.

Although, conceptually, the nature of informal factors is delimited by formal factors, from an empirical perspective, their concretion is complex, fundamentally due to the difficulty in their observation, which is the main cause of their omission in many of the studies on the impact of institutions in the economy [71]. Since informal factors include the social and cultural norms embedded in society [72] from an aggregate perspective, the structure of the social values of a society defines the society's culture, and national culture is one of the antecedents of entrepreneurial activity [73]. Although many studies offer a definition of culture [50,74–76], for the purposes of this study, we draw on Inglehart [77], who proposes that culture is a set of basic, shared values that shape people's behaviour in society. These cultural values, which operate unconsciously, change depending on economic development. Indeed, Inglehart [77–79] suggests that, at a certain level of wealth, values tend to change from materialist to postmaterialist. Thus, the concept of postmaterialism refers to the extent to which the population of a society confers greater value to basic objectives, including personal growth, self-worth, and the need for important work, than to more materialistic objectives.

The literature is unclear regarding the impact of these postmaterialist values on entrepreneurship. Using linear models, some studies propose a negative relationship based on the fact that entrepreneurial activity is motivated by material objectives that are incompatible with the values of a postmaterialist society [80–82]. In addition, the empirical evidence presented in other works on SE shows a positive relationship based on the integration of a series of postmaterialist values (autonomy, concern for the welfare of others, and prosociality) in organizational dynamics [69,83,84]. To clarify these contradictory results, using four mediator variables, we propose a model in which postmaterialist values can impact SE.

2.1. Postmaterialist Values, Social Justice, and CSR

The change in values proposed by Inglehart [77–79,85] is associated with the economic development of nations. Consequently, postmaterialist values arise in societies that have passed beyond a certain threshold of economic development: once the basic needs of survival and safety have been met, individuals tend to focus on covering their higher needs related to self-expression and social justice. The latter value is regarded as a priority in society [86,87].

Social justice is not a new concept. Coined in the 18th century, Adam Smith defined social justice as the equal opportunities needed for all humans to prosper [88]. However, this concept did not fully crystallise in society until a century later because of economic, political, and social problems in the United States and the United Kingdom [89,90]. Presently, social justice is a key principle of society as a result of the cultural and economic evolution of relevant value systems [91,92]. On this basis, we propose the first hypothesis.

Hypothesis 1 (H1). *The greater the prevalence of postmaterialist values is in a country, the greater the level of social justice in that country.*

In recent years, the relationship between social justice and entrepreneurship has received great interest from researchers, practitioners, and policymakers. Some authors suggest that SE is rooted in social justice [93,94] and define it according to its final objective: the attainment of justice in society to ensure that all individuals have a decent quality of life [95]. Although from a theoretical perspective the relationship between social justice and SE has already been demonstrated, there are no empirical studies that support this. This leads us to consider social justice as an element of the institutional context with an indirect impact on SE.

Indeed, the emergence of social justice as a consequence of the negative impact of globalisation on the rights, opportunities, and living conditions of people leads us to consider it as a condition for the sustainability of a socially responsible market economy [96]—i.e., a regenerative factor of sustainable development [97]. Thus, as an underlying factor, social justice has an impact on CSR. The relevance of CSR has grown substantially over the last three decades due to the importance of sustainability and the key role of enterprises in the resolution of social and environmental issues [98]. Notwithstanding the large volume of research underwriting new theories, approaches, and terminology [99], the idea of CSR remains fairly obscure due to the duality of entrepreneurial strategies and ethical attitudes [100]. In the latter case, CSR is understood as compliance with certain ethical requirements that cement the relations between society and businesses. Hence, beyond any other consideration, CSR is an ethical obligation [99] (p. 53). On this basis, CSR is considered a country-wide tool for development [101], whose objective is to achieve sustainability. Sustainability, here, is understood as the process of achieving human development in an inclusive, connected, equiparable, prudent, and secure manner [102]. These arguments lead to the second hypothesis:

Hypothesis 2 (H2). *The higher the level of social justice is in a country, the greater the level of CSR in that country.*

However, CSR is also directly influenced by changes in values. Indeed, a wide swath of research has demonstrated that at an individual level, postmaterialism is related to attitudes favourable to the environment and volunteering [77,103,104]. In the space of a few years, this development has encouraged companies to include CSR in their business dynamics as a result of two axes of action: (1) The evolution in values, which has led to CSR being considered of global cultural value [105] and reflects the transformation of stakeholders' internal and external values; this, in turn, impacts the actions of the enterprises they are associated with. (2) The strategy by which companies commit to certain social and environmental behaviours to ensure continuity and growth [106–108]. Thus, the increase in CSR is not only explained by national inertias and trends (as economic globalisation is strongly linked to its emergence [109]) but is also derived from economic development and the ensuing changes in values. Consequently, we pose the third hypothesis:

Hypothesis 3 (H3). *The greater the prevalence of postmaterialist values is in a country, the greater the level of CSR in that country.*

Understanding CSR as a world cultural model, CSR has a direct impact on the socially responsible initiatives developed by companies [105]. Considering the institutional theory of CSR [110], firms will behave in a responsible way as a consequence of external pressures by confronting stakeholder groups—mainly investors, competitors, and the concerned public—due to their corporate visibility [111]. From an internal perspective, corporate governance plays an important role in determining CSR actions [112–115]. In this way, we can conceptualise CSR as a business driver to transfer cultural values from the macro-level and transform them into part of the corporate culture at the micro-level.

From this micro perspective, CSR can be considered as an outcome of the requirements of social environment, enacted by the institutional framework of business [116] (p. 341) and, consequently, includes a large variety of practices that go beyond a firm's typical activities that suggest engagement of the corporation in ecological and social issues [117]. Although this approach to CSR shares some aspects with SE, they are different concepts, which needs to be clarified to understand the relationship between them.

Taking CSR to be a concept whereby companies integrate social and environmental concerns into their business operations and their interactions with their stakeholders on a voluntary basis [118], many authors suggest that both concepts are synonymous since CSR projects are implemented by social entrepreneurs within companies, which is thus considered corporate social entrepreneurship [14,44,119–121]. In contrast, other authors consider CSR and SE to be different concepts, drawing on two criteria: objectives and the appropriation of profits [17]. CSR involves the integration of social factors in business dynamics to legitimise a company's existence with a proactive focus that goes beyond legal obligations. Conversely, the purpose of SE is to resolve a social problem with the objective of social value creation [18]. The second characteristic that differentiates the two concepts is the appropriation of the profit generated. In SE, which is defined as not-for-profit, profits are a tool to achieve a social mission and are reinvested in the project. In contrast, the final aim of socially responsible companies is the maximisation of profits directed towards shareholder value appropriation [23].

Despite these differences, the two concepts are interrelated, and SE can be regarded as a natural development of CSR [122]. However, this relationship is regarded as negative, given that the greater involvement of companies in socially responsible activities reduces market opportunities for the generation of SE. Furthermore, although an increase in donations, a fundamental tool in CSR, to a large number of non-governmental organisations can allow a company to be less dependent on public funding [123,124], it also prevents that company from evolving towards entrepreneurial initiatives, which requires independence from resource mobilization and sources of income [18]. Consequently, we put forth the fourth hypothesis:

Hypothesis 4 (H4). *The higher the level of CSR is in a country, the lower the size of SE in that country.*

2.2. Postmaterialist Values, Social Capital, and Entrepreneurship Capital

From an economic perspective, the construct of social capital has generated growing interest due to its contribution to economic development [125–129]. Despite the simplicity of its content, its multidimensional nature has led to the lack of a unifying definition [130]. Coleman [131,132] defines social capital against physical and labour force as a group of social resources with established interactions that can enhance the efficiency of society through the promotion of coordinated action. In this line, Putman [133] emphasises the importance of trust and social networks, defining social capital as a set of networks of interpersonal trust driven by norms of reciprocity and mutual assistance with strong links to social involvement and participation in community associations. The introduction of this construct suggests that social capital is a capability that arises from the prevalence of trust in a society [127]. Considering that postmaterialism includes a sense of community and the self-expression values that nurture social capital [85,134], we propose the fifth hypothesis:

Hypothesis 5 (H5). *The greater the prevalence of postmaterialist values is in a country, the greater the level of social capital in that country.*

At a high level, social capital can be interpreted as a philosophy of trust and tolerance [77] that results in the improved efficiency of society by enabling coordinated actions [133]. In this manner, social capital is viewed as a primary factor that encourages entrepreneurship as it promotes the flow and exchange of information, the coordination of activities, and communal decision-making schemes [135–138]. The idea of collectivism is a fundamental trait of social capital that provides a straight connection to SE. The research conducted by Ostrom [139–141] firmly established that social capital is a primary factor in local self-sufficient communities, implanting social norms between the contributing stakeholders to effectively manage collective resources. This behaviour is in line with SE as an initiator of joint action to transmute and assimilate individual needs to enable the empowerment of the community through the creation of communal wealth [70,95]. Consequently, SE cannot be generated without strong social involvement with the community. Considering the above, we put forth the sixth hypothesis:

Hypothesis 6 (H6). *The higher the level of social capital is in a country, the greater the size of SE in that country.*

Conversely, social capital also affects SE through entrepreneurship capital. In the last decades of the 20th century, studies on economic growth have focused on entrepreneurship capital as a parameter to demonstrate the impact of the capacity of economies to generate new ventures [135]. At a high level, entrepreneurship capital can be interpreted as a group of agents and institutions that enable the establishment of new ventures [142]. In other words, entrepreneurship capital is an amalgam of social, legal, and institutional forces that allow for entrepreneurial activity in each territory [143]. This is evidenced by the fact that strongly growing economies tend to draw more entrepreneurs [144].

Several researchers see social capital and entrepreneurship capital as equivalent concepts. Audretsch, Keilbach, and Lehmann [142] assert that entrepreneurship capital can be viewed as a subtype of social capital. Undoubtedly, the impact of social capital on economic growth is broadly acknowledged. However, there are numerous theories related to the impact on entrepreneurship. Nevertheless, entrepreneurship capital always has a positive impact on entrepreneurial activity. Therefore, we put forth the seventh hypothesis:

Hypothesis 7 (H7). *The higher the level of social capital is in a country, the greater the level of entrepreneurship capital in that country.*

Not only does entrepreneurship capital impact the generation of enterprises, it also fosters their variety in each economy [142]. In this sense, considering SE as a form of entrepreneurship [145], and thus complementary to other companies [16,146], we propose the final hypothesis:

Hypothesis 8 (H8). *The higher the level of entrepreneurship capital is in a country, the greater the size of SE in that country.*

Figure 1 summarizes the proposed hypotheses.

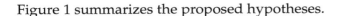
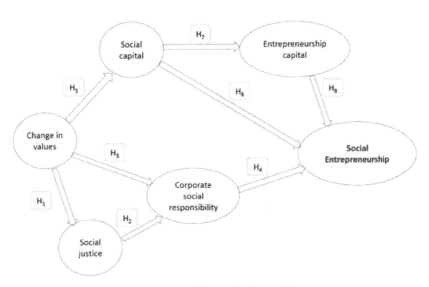

Figure 1. Theoretical model.

3. Model and Data

To verify the hypotheses, we developed a PLS-SEM. This method is adequate for causal–predictive analysis when there is a lack of theoretical information. It allows one to estimate non-observable latent variables when establishing dependent linear relationships (regressions) among them, thereby determining the paths between endogenous and exogenous constructs [147–149]. Then, PLS combines the predictive analysis of classic multivariate techniques with psychometric analysis. This model was chosen because it works adequately when the data sample is heterogeneous, small, and the theoretical model is causal and complex [148–150]. In addition, it is very flexible, as it admits both categorical and continuous scales [151]; it has no requirement for multivariate normality, generates consistent estimators without making any previous distributional assumptions, and does not have problems with multicollinearity [152–154]. The stability of the estimated parameters is calculated by means of a resampling method (bootstrapping or jack-knife), while the sample requirements (size and distribution) are lax because PLS-SEM divides the model into many segments as blocks of variables, analysing each one of them separately [152,155]. Nevertheless, the minimum size of the sample must be, at least, 10 times higher than the number of antecedents pointing to the more complex dependent structural variable [152,156,157].

PLS-SEM analysis requires the use of two sub-models: the measurement model and the structural model. Although PLS-SEM simultaneously calculates the parameters of the measurement and structural sub-models, it is, nevertheless, recommended to analyse them separately [158]. The first sub-model results from the application of a factor analysis to determine the loadings of the indicators and if they are properly placed in the corresponding construct. The latent variable condenses the information provided by the observable variables, and these indicators can be related to the construct in a reflective or formative way. We defined only the reflective indicators, so we must analyse only their loadings. The quality analysis establishes whether the indicators are correctly assigned to the construct and whether the theoretical conceptions defined in the constructs are adequately measured by the indicators assigned. If the indicators do not define the assigned construct or do not meet the standard criteria, they are removed.

The second model, the structural one, defines the paths or dependency relationships among latent variables based on the hypotheses of the theoretical model [152]. This sub-model permits one to establish dependency relationships among latent variables and allows one to evaluate the importance of the interactions between them by means of the structural (path) coefficients that are obtained from the regression of the formerly estimated non-observable variables.

Considering the above, PLS-SEM is a good methodology for our study. The proposed model was organised into 6 non-observed variables, fed by 27 indicators. A database for 52 countries was then built. Table 1 shows the specifications of the constructs and indicators along with their sources and countries.

Table 1. Constructs, indicators, sources, and countries.

Construct (Source)	Indicators (Code)
SE [25]	Traditional NGO (SE1) Not-for-profit (SE2) Economically oriented hybrid (SE3) Socially oriented hybrid (SE4)
Change in values [159,160]	Materialist/postmaterialist index (CHV1) Autonomy index (CHV2)
CSR [161]	Business actions (CSR1) Social enablers (CSR2)
Social justice [91]	Poverty prevention (SJ1) Access to education (SJ2) Labour market (SJ3) Social cohesion (SJ4) Health (SJ5) Inter-generational justice (SJ6)
Entrepreneurship capital [162]	Nascent entrepreneurship rate (EC1) New business ownership rate (EC2) Established business ownership rate (EC3) Improvement-driven opportunity entrepreneurship (EC4)
Social capital [159,160]	Active members of art, music, or educational organization (SC1) Active member of environmental organizations (SC2) Active member of charitable/humanitarian organizations (SC3) Active member of professional organizations (SC4) Active member of sports and recreations (SC5) Trust people of another nationality (SC6) Trust people you know personally (SC7) Trust people you meet first time (SC8) Trust in your neighbourhood (SC9)

Countries: Argentina, Australia, Austria, Belarus, Belgium, Bolivia, Brazil, Bulgaria, Canada, Chile, Colombia, Costa Rica, Croatia, Cyprus, Czech Republic, Denmark, Dominic Republic, Estonia, Finland, France, Germany, Greece, Guatemala, Honduras, Hungary, India, Ireland, Italy, Luxembourg, Lithuania, Latvia, Malta, Moldova, Netherlands, Norway, Paraguay, Peru, Poland, Portugal, Romania, Russia, Serbia, Slovakia, Slovenia, Spain, Sweden, Switzerland, Turkey, Ukraine, United Kingdom, Uruguay and USA.

4. Results

Figure 2 shows the resulting model, while Tables 2–5 contain the coefficients obtained for it. Assessing the quality of the model requires an analysis of each of its components. An analysis of the measurement model was conducted to confirm if the indicators could serve to symbolize the theoretical concepts and if they are unidimensional. The standard literature establishes the criteria that must be met [148,152,153,163–165] in terms of reliability and validity (see Figure 2 and Tables 2 and 3). First, individual reliability is measured by the factor loadings, which should be greater than 0.707. Graphically, the loadings are illustrated by the arrows between the latent variables and their indicators. Initially, there were 48 indicators used. However, 21 of them did not meet the criteria and were removed. Second, the internal consistency among the constructs and their items is measured by Cronbach's Alpha (values higher than 0.7 should be accepted) and by the Composite Reliability Index (which should be greater than 0.85). Third, to evaluate whether the sets of indicators represent the underlying latent variable, the convergent validity is analysed by means of the average variance extracted (AVE) from the constructs: the standard criterion is 0.5 or more. Lastly, the Fornell–Larker criterion serves to assess the discriminant validity; it indicates that each indicator has a stronger relation with its construct than with the others. The values of the cells on the diagonal must be greater than the values of the corresponding row [163].

Table 2. Measurement model: scale reliability and convergent validity.

Construct	AVE	Composite Reliability	Cronbach's Alpha
Change in values	0.823	0.903	0.786
CSR	0.792	0.884	0.738
Entrepreneurship Capital	0.651	0.881	0.822
Social Capital	0.685	0.951	0.942
SE	0.698	0.902	0.855
Social Justice	0.837	0.969	0.961

Table 3. Measurement model: discriminant validity Lornell–Larker criterion.

Construct	Change in Values	CSR	Entrepreneurship Capital	Social Capital	SE	Social Justice
Change in values	0.907					
CSR	0.444	0.890				
Entrepreneurship Capital	0.173	0.159	0.807			
Social Capital	0.885	0.375	0.162	0.828		
SE	0.120	−0.038	0.693	0.202	0.836	
Social Justice	0.472	0.566	−0.016	0.305	−0.055	0.915

After the measurement model is validated, we evaluate the explanatory capacity of the structural model. In this case, we use the R^2 and the path coefficients (see Table 5). The coefficient of R2 explains the quantity of variance of the endogenous latent variable explained by the exogenous constructs [151]. As in a linear regression, the higher the coefficients are, the better the model is [152], and no rejection limit is set [166]. In this case, the R^2 value, 0.527 for SE, indicates a good fit, considering a reduced number of independent constructs affecting it. The path coefficients show the strength of the relationship among constructs, and their algebraic signs indicate the nature (growing or decreasing) of their relationship.

This model supports the importance of cultural factors in SE, explaining slightly more than 50% of its variance. Notably, the R^2 (0.527) is markedly high if we consider that the endogenous construct is only explained by three latent variables: entrepreneurship capital, social capital, and CSR. Our results indicate that entrepreneurship capital has a very substantial influence on the existence of SE since the coefficient between both variables (0.700) is the most robust, and the correlation between them (0.693) is one of the highest that can explain SE.

Table 4. Structural model: quality criteria and correlation matrix.

	Change in Values	CSR	Entrepreneurship Capital	Social Capital	SE	Social Justice
R^2	—	0.361	0.026	0.784	0.527	0.222
Correlation among constructs						
	Change in values	CSR	Entrepreneurship Capital	Social Capital	SE	Social Justice
Change in values	1.000					
CSR	0.444	1.000				
Entrepreneurship Capital	0.173	0.159	1.000			
Social Capital	0.885	0.375	0.162	1.000		
SE	0.120	−0.038	0.693	0.202	1.000	
Social Justice	0.472	0.566	−0.016	0.305	−0.055	1.000
Path coefficients						
	Original Sample (O)	Sample Mean (M)		Standard Desviation (STDEV)	T Statistics (|O/STDEV|)	p Values
Change in values—>CSR	0.228	0.214		0.150	1690	**
Change in values—>Social Capital	0.885	0.888		0.029	30,480	***
Change in values—>Social Justice	0.472	0.473		0.121	3902	***
CSR—> SE	−0.212	−0.205		0.081	2630	***
Entrepreneurship Capital—>SE	0.700	0.704		0.068	10,293	***
Social Capital—>Entrepreneurship Capital	0.162	0.181		0.137	1680	**
Social Capital—>SE	0.168	0.158		0.102	1687	**
Social Justice—>CSR	0.459	0.481		0.163	2821	***

*** $p < 0.005$ ** $p < 0.05$.

Table 5. Hypothesis compliance.

Hypotheses	Accepted
H1. The greater the prevalence of postmaterialist values in a country, the greater the level of social justice in that country	✓
H2. The higher the level of social justice in a country, the greater the level of CSR in that country	✓
H3. The greater the prevalence of postmaterialist values in a country, the greater the level of CSR in that country	✓
H4. The higher the level of CSR in a country, the lower the size of SE in that country	✓
H5. The greater the prevalence of postmaterialist values in a country, the greater the level of social capital in that country	✓
H6. The higher the level of social capital in a country, the greater the size of SE in that country	✓
H7. The higher the level of social capital in a country, the greater the level of entrepreneurship capital in that country	✓
H8. The higher the level of entrepreneurship capital in a country, the greater the size of SE in that country	✓

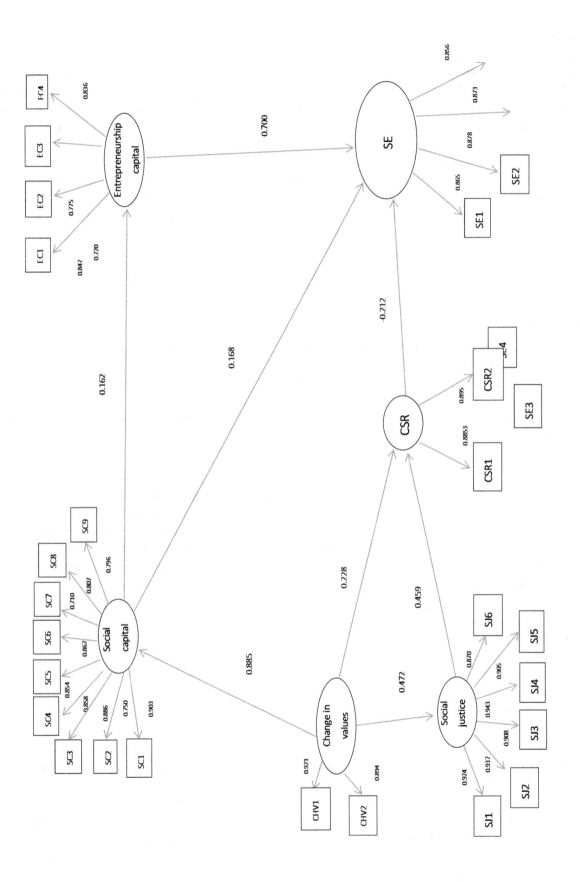

Figure 2. Model.

The second of the explanatory latent variables for SE in the model is social capital. In this case, although the relation between both variables is not as robust as that between social capital and entrepreneurship capital, it still shows the power of the construct in determining the size of SE. It should be noted here that the relevance of the coefficient of determination for entrepreneurship capital (0.026) is somewhat low, as this endogenous latent variable is explained by a single exogenous construct. This is because the examination of entrepreneurship capital is instrumental in this study, so it is reasonable that the explanation of this variable in the model is limited, as it depends on many factors not analysed here.

Lastly, the third construct explaining SE is CSR. In this case, CSR is presented in the model as an endogenous latent variable that depends on two new constructs: changes in values and social justice. These two constructs notably explain 36% of the CSR variance. The robust relationship among changes in values, social justice, and CSR notably has coefficients of correlation of 0.472, 0.444, and 0.566, respectively, as can be seen in Table 4. However, the correlation between CSR and SE (0.038) is much less substantial, suggesting a relationship that is weak but statistically significant within the model.

The quality criteria fulfilment of the measurement and structural models allows us to prove all the hypotheses proposed (see Table 5).

5. Discussion

From a global perspective, the results obtained confirm that institutional economics is an adequate theoretical approach to explain entrepreneurial activity, regardless of the different legal forms. In the case of SE, the creation of social value to trigger social change and address social needs as its main aim [14,18,21,24,26,70] suggests the need for a specific cultural context to flourish. Under the umbrella of cultural change, our work shows two specific combinations of informal factors that impact SE in opposite directions.

5.1. Social Capital, Entrepreneurship Capital, and SE

The first combination of informal factors that impact SE is composed of postmaterialist values, social capital, and entrepreneurship capital and allows us to prove Hypotheses 5–8.

Other studies established a negative relationship between post-materialistic values and entrepreneurial activity based on the fact that business activities are motivated by material objectives that are incompatibles with post-materialistic values [80–82]. However, the particularities of SE in its mission and project orientation allowed us to prove a positive relationship, albeit indirectly.

Indeed, the relationship between culture and SE involves social capital as its main driver. Our findings demonstrate that the sense of community and values of self-expression that comprise postmaterialism feed social capital, as suggested by Inglehart [85] and Welzel, Inglehart, and Deustch [134]. In this line, Putnam [133] established that a culture of trust facilitates the implementation of coordinated activities (in line with Putnam [133]), which shape a sense of community, thereby fostering the appearance of SE, which requires vigorous social connections with the community.

However social capital has a direct and indirect impact on SE, cementing its significance as an answer to difficulties in human interaction, engendering more and better cooperation among individuals than one would reasonably expect [57]. The direct effect on SE reaffirms the necessity of this core aspect in business development focused on the community or collectivistic groups, as the primary aim is to address social needs.

For indirect impact, the relationship confirms the approach of Audretsch, Keilbach, and Lehmann [142], which views entrepreneurship capital as a subtype of social capital. The impact of the former on SE is of great relevance, as it is the most robust of the three mediating variables, thereby confirming the key role of entrepreneurship capital in motivating business activities, regardless of the type of economic organisation generated. This indirect effect indicates that entrepreneurship capital has a very substantial influence on the existence of SE. Consequently, we can extend the ideas of Beugelsdijk and Noorderhaven [144] and state that if the highest-growing economies are those that attract the most entrepreneurs, then they will also be those where SE is the most likely to arise. However, entrepreneurship capital also acts as a moderating variable, expanding the positive influence of social capital into the dimension of SE. This suggests that the power of social capital, as an informal institutional factor for fostering SE, increases when there is a positive climate for business.

5.2. CSR and SE

The second group of informal factors that impact SE consists of postmaterialist values, social justice, and CSR; this group permits us to accept Hypotheses 1–4. Although these three constructs are interrelated, only the CSR has a direct effect on SE, highlighting the interrelation between both concepts.

Since the beginning of the new century, CSR has acquired remarkable relevance due to the great importance of sustainability. At the macro level, CSR is related to sustainable development [99] based on the integration of social, economic, and environmental considerations [167]. From this perspective, sustainable development is considered a process to achieve human development "in an inclusive, connected, equiparable, prudent and secure manner" [102] (p. 876).

Although CSR analysis is linked to its three dimensions, the results obtained in the model exclude the environmental dimension. As we explained in the methodology, the definition of each construct, the unobservable variable, is defined by a set of indicators, observable variables, which must meet certain reliability and validity criteria. Those that do not meet such criteria are removed, as was the case with the environmental indicators. This is why the analysis of the link between CSR and SE was carried out from social and economic perspectives.

5.2.1. Social Dimension of CSR

From a macro perspective, the conceptualization of CSR is shifting towards a broader concept that includes not only the aspects of corporate conduct that impinge on social, environmental, and economic issues but also the role of business in relation to sustainable development goals [168]. Using this global approach, CSR is presented in this study as an endogenous latent variable depending on two constructs: changes in values and social justice. This means that a socially responsible activity is substantially determined by contextual factors related to the shift of society towards postmaterialist values. In this way, we can consider CSR as an outcome of the obligations of [the] social environment, enacted by the institutional framework of business [116] that includes the business actions considered desirable for the social construction of values, beliefs, and norms [169].

In the relationship between culture and CSR, social justice has a fundamental role. Following Schraad–Tischler [91] and the United Nations [92], this model confirms that social justice is the result of the evolution of a value system towards postmaterialist values. In addition, social justice is part of the CSR and, therefore, affects CSR activities. This role of social justice as a mediating variable expands the impact of culture on CSR and SE. Consequently, this model also confirms that the shift of society towards postmaterialist values fosters the consolidation of CSR and allows us to conceptualise this latent variable, in line with Shamir [105], as a global cultural value reflecting stakeholders' changes in values and responding to their demands [116].

This approach to CSR as a global outcome is interconnected with SE. Both concepts are rooted in a social orientation that translates into an active commitment with the people that companies aim to support and with local communities. This link with local communities facilitates the development and maintenance of lasting relationships with local stakeholders, thereby ensuring the social impact of CSR through SE.

5.2.2. Economic Dimension of CSR

From an economic perspective, CSR and SE have much in common. At the macro level, economic sustainability refers to efficient and equitable economic development that generates an increase in the well-being of society. The translation of this concept to the corporate level determines the orientation of a company towards the generation of economic value with an impact on the communities in which that company operates. This refers to employment and the production of goods and services, which might involve sourcing from local suppliers and selling to local customers [170]. This approach is shared by SE, which seeks to generate a positive impact on society by offering innovative solutions to social changes. In addition, SE also contributes to economic growth, engaging job creation, revitalizing local economies, and boosting the potential for progress [7]. These two dimensions are interdependent since SE's ability to face social problems depends on its capacity to attract support from stakeholders and generate income [171].

Despite this shared orientation, CSR and SE have multiple differences in their purposes, structures, levels of profit generation, and stakeholder perspectives. CSR refers to business decisions to sustain social causes, while SE refers to a business that wants to provide solutions to social problems. Nevertheless, there is a complementary relationship between the two concepts. CSR indicates that a company interacts with its surrounding communities in several ways not directly related to the traditional operational aspects of running a business [170]. One of the main tools used is corporate philanthropy, defined as a direct contribution by a corporation to an organisation, cause, or project, most often in the form of cash grants, donations, and/or in-kind services [172].

In this way, corporate philanthropy, as an element of the economic dimension of CSR, can act as a key driver for SE creation. Note that financing represents one of the greatest challenges for SE. The attainment of the social mission also requires economic viability [173]. Although funding must be based on a portfolio of resources, private donations are an important source of funding and play a primary role in the financial leveraging of SE [174], but they cannot be the main source of financing over the long term.

This ability of the CSR to generate spin-offs will depend on the development of the relationship between the company and SE, since this relationship has a direct effect on SE's financial sustainability [175]. Thus, in the first phase, the philanthropic stage, this link is based exclusively on donations, which are considered to be the most passive form of CSR. As the CSR impact on core business operations increases, the relationships generate social share value for the two parties, eventually reaching the organizational stage with the development of new business opportunities [176–178]. This transition involves moving towards a more strategic approach for selecting social issues to support over the long-term based on partnerships.

These arguments confirm that CSR and SE are connected and oriented towards solving social problems, but they also highlight the trade-off between business and social imperatives in SE, justifying its negative and weak relationship with CSR. In situations of economic crisis, such as that in which this work is framed, the decrease in private CSR contributions to support social causes has a positive effect on the size of SE, which makes us think about other sources of financing, such as public support, thereby reducing SE's financial dependence on CSR.

Finally, although the data used in this work are from ten years ago, the results are still valid today. The data used to develop the model emerged from a context of economic crisis similar to that which is currently taking place as a result of the COVID-19 pandemic, according to the forecasts of international organizations [2]. This validity is supported by recent research affirming that crisis situations positively affect social capital to help individuals overcome social needs [179,180]. In the case of the CSR, periods of crisis represent a threat for companies [181,182], which might have a negative impact on support for SE. Furthermore, it is necessary to frame these trends within the institutional changes in which cultural values slowly evolve [183]; therefore, these results can be extrapolated to the present-day situation.

6. Conclusions, Limitations, and Further Research

Although the literature has extensively analysed SE from a sustainable development perspective, no studies have considered the impacts of cultural factors as part of the complex landscape to build a full map of SE. This work empirically confirms that postmaterialism is a valid tool to understand the culture of present-day societies and offers an explanation of its influence on SE through four mediating variables: social capital, entrepreneurship capital, social justice, and CSR.

Thus, using institutional economics as the theoretical framework, our work establishes two main drivers that impact SE. First, social capital is analysed from a top-down perspective as an endowed factor. Its impact on SE depends on the role of changes in values in shaping a culture of trust and tolerance. The positive direct impact of these changes on the size of SE confirms their importance in business projects aimed at meeting social needs from a community perspective. The indirect impact is channelled through capital that acts as a moderating variable expanding the positive influence of social capital when there is a positive climate for business.

The second informal factor that impacts SE is CSR. The change in values also affects the social involvement of companies and their commitment to solving problems in their environment in the form of socially responsible activities. This impact is reinforced by social justice due to society's shift in values towards postmaterialist ideas, which is also the main component of the social dimension of CSR. This produces a fairer and more egalitarian society with companies that are more committed to social responsibility. Furthermore, we were able to confirm that CSR and SE are connected concepts and that although SE may be considered a natural extension of CSR, the two concepts correlate negatively, as the greater involvement of companies in socially responsible activities reduces market opportunities for the generation of SE.

These results have implications for public policy. The importance of informal factors in the generation of SE requires their consideration as elements of the SE ecosystem and, therefore, as an object of public support. Cognitive measures are particularly important for raising the awareness and visibility of SE to deconstruct any misconceptions. To achieve this objective, actions to foster SE in the educational system and support for relevant researchers are required.

Notwithstanding the importance of our results, this study has several limitations that could become lines of future research. First, this model considers five informal factors that are rarely brought together in the literature. These factors, however, represent a small part of the institutional complexity that impacts SE. The inclusion of new constructs to add more formal and informal factors would be interesting to paint a global picture of SE's reality. Carrying out a study according to groups of countries with different levels of development would also allow us to assess the general validity of the model. In both cases, the development of these paths would be conditioned by an increase in sample countries since PLS-SEM requires that the sample size be at least ten times greater than the number of constructs. In addition, the empirical analysis was based on a single cross section of data. However, considering cultural context as dynamic concept requires a longitudinal approach to demonstrate the validity of the proposed relations over time. Using panel data can add value beyond the current empirical findings. The lack of standardised and normalised data for SE at the international level is also a significant limitation.

Another aspect that requires improvement is the search for more and better indicators to improve the quality of the latent variables and the structural relationships of the model. In particular, social capital is defined by the associative activity and trust variables, but it is also essential to include variables connected to civic norms. The improvement of this construct would have an impact on the construction of capital entrepreneurship, which would arguably help reflect their multifaceted and heterogeneous nature. CSR also requires additional research. The role of CSR as an interface between the macro and micro level must be developed, including the influence that greater visibility has on companies from both a communicational and a market penetration perspective, as well as the role that governance has in deciding the guidelines for CSR interventions. In addition, a new definition of CSR has to be investigated to include the environmental dimension excluded in this work. At this moment, the absence of adequate databases is also a significant limitation.

Author Contributions: Conceptualization, I.B.-M. and I.C.M.; methodology, I.B.-M. and I.C.M.; software, I.C.M.; validation, I.B.-M.; formal analysis, I.B.-M. and I.C.M.; investigation, I.B.-M. and I.C.M.; resources, I.B.-M. and I.C.M.; data curation, I.B.-M. and I.C.M.; writing—original draft preparation, I.B.-M. and I.C.M.; writing—review and editing, I.B.-M. and I.C.M.; visualization, I.B.-M. and I.C.M.; funding acquisition, I.B.-M. and I.C.M. All authors have read and agreed to the published version of the manuscript

References

1. Laparra, M.; Pérez Eransus, B. *Crisis y Fractura Social en Europa. Causas y Efectos en España*; Obra Social "La Caixa": Barcelona, Spain, 2012.
2. International Monetary Fund. *World Economic Outlook*; International Monetary Fund: Washington, DC, USA, 2020.
3. Kaufman, R.; Avgar, A.; Mirsky, J. Social Entrepreneurship in Crisis Situations. *Int. J. Divers. Organ. Communities Nations* **2007**, *7*, 227–232. [CrossRef]
4. Petrella, F.; Richez-Battesti, N. Social Entrepreneur, Social Entrepreneurship and Social Enterprise: Semantics and Controversies. *J. Innov. Econ. Manag.* **2014**, *14*, 143–156. [CrossRef]
5. Javed, A.; Yasir, M.; Majid, A. Is social entrepreneurship a panacea for sustainable enterprise development? *Pak. J. Commer. Soc. Sci.* **2019**, *13*, 1–29.
6. Organization for Economic Cooperation and Development (OECD). *Job Creation and Local Economic Development 2018: Preparing for the Future of Work*; OECD: Paris, France, 2018.
7. United Nations. *World Youth Report. Youth Social Entrepreneurship and the 2030 Agenda*; United Nations: New York, NY, USA, 2020.
8. Kliber, E.; Salmivaara, V.; Stenholm, P.; Terjesen, S. The evaluative legitimacy of social entrepreneurship in capitalist welfare systems. *J. World Bus.* **2018**, *53*, 944–957. [CrossRef]
9. Borzaga, C.; Galera, G.; Franchini, B.; Chiomento, S.; Nogales, R.; Carini, C. *Social Enterprises and Their Ecosystems in Europe. Comparative Synthesis Report*; Publications Office of the European Union: Luxembourg, 2020.
10. European Commission. Communication from the Commission to the European Parliament, the Council, the European Economic and Social Committee and the Committee of the Regions. Social Business Initiative creating a favorable climate for social enterprises, key stakeholders in the social economy and innovation. *COM/2011/0682 Final*. 2011. Available online: http://ec.europa.eu/internal_market/social_business/docs/COM2011_682_en.pdf (accessed on 14 January 2020).
11. European Commission. Commission Implementing Regulation (EU) No 593/2014 of 3 June 2014 laying down implementing technical standards with regard to the format of the notification according to Article 16(1) of Regulation (EU) No 345/2013 of the European Parliament and of the Council on European venture capital funds. *OJ L* **2014**, *165*, 41–43.
12. Rey-Martí, A.; Ribeiro-Soriano, D.; Palacios-Marqués, D. A bibliometric analysis of social entrepreneurship. *J. Bus. Res.* **2016**, *69*, 1651–1655. [CrossRef]
13. Hota, P.K.; Subramanian, B.; Narayanamurthy, G. Mapping the Intellectual Structure of Social Entrepreneurship Research: A Citation/Co-citation Analysis. *J. Bus. Ethics* **2019**. [CrossRef]
14. Austin, J.; Stevenson, H.; Wei-Skillern, J. Social and commercial entrepreneurship: Same, different, or both? *Entrep. Theory Pract.* **2006**, *30*, 1–22. [CrossRef]
15. Carraher, S.M.; Welsh, D.H.B.; Svilokos, A. Validation of a measure of social Entrepreneurship. *Eur. J. Int. Manag.* **2016**, *10*, 386–402. [CrossRef]
16. Dacin, P.A.; Dacin, M.T.; Matear, M. Social entrepreneurship: Why we don't need a new theory and how we move forward from here. *Acad. Manag. Perspect.* **2017**, *24*, 37–57. [CrossRef]
17. Huybrechts, B.; Nicholls, A. Social entrepreneurship: Definitions, drivers and challenges. In *Social Entrepreneurship and Social Business. An Introduction and Discussion with Case Studies*; Wolkmann, C.K., Tokarski, C.K., Ernst, K., Eds.; Springer Gabler: Wiesbaden, Switzerland, 2012; pp. 31–43.
18. Mair, J.; Marti, I. Social entrepreneurship research: A source of explanation, prediction, and delight. *J. World Bus.* **2006**, *41*, 36–44. [CrossRef]
19. Monzón Campos, J.L. Empresas sociales y Economía Social: Perímetro y propuestas metodológicas para la medición de su impacto socioeconómico en la UE. *Rev. Econ. Mund.* **2013**, *35*, 151–164.
20. Nicholls, A.; Cho, A. Social entrepreneurship: The structuration of a field. In *Social Entrepreneurship: New Models of Sustainable Social Change*; Nicholls, A., Ed.; Oxford University Press: Oxford, UK, 2006; pp. 99–118.
21. Peredo, A.M.; McLean, M. Social entrepreneurship: A critical review of the concept. *J. World Bus.* **2006**, *41*, 56–65. [CrossRef]
22. Peris-Ortiz, M.; Rueda-Armengot, C.; Palacios-Marqués, D. Is it possible to measure social entrepreneurship in firms? *Cuad. De Gest.* **2016**, *16*, 15–28. [CrossRef]
23. Santos, F. *A Positive Theory of Social Entrepreneurship*; Research Working Paper No. 2009/23/EFE/ISIC; INSEAD: Paris, France, 2009.

24. Short, J.; Moss, T.; Lumpkin, G. Research in social entrepreneurship: Past contributions and future opportunities. *Strateg. Entrep. J.* **2009**, *3*, 161–194. [CrossRef]

25. Terjesen, D.; Lepoutre, J.; Justo, R.; Bosma, N. *Report on Social Entrepreneurship*; Global Entrepreneurship Monitor: London, UK, 2012.

26. Weerawardena, J.; Mort, G.S. Investigating social entrepreneurship: A multidimensional model. *J. World Bus.* **2006**, *41*, 21–35. [CrossRef]

27. Bahena-Álvarez, I.L.; Cordón-Pozo, E.; Delgado-Cruz, A. Social entrepreneurship in the conduct of responsible innovation: Analysis cluster in Mexican SMEs. *Sustainability* **2019**, *11*, 3714. [CrossRef]

28. Felício, J.A.; Martins, H.M.; Gonçalves, V.C. Social value and organizational performance in non-profit social organizations: Social entrepreneurship, leadership, and socioeconomic context effects. *J. Bus. Res.* **2013**, *66*, 2139–2146. [CrossRef]

29. Fernández-Laviada, A.; López-Gutiérrez, C.; San-Martín, P. The Moderating Effect of Countries' Development on the Characterization of the Social Entrepreneur: An Empirical Analysis with GEM Data. *Voluntas* **2020**, *31*, 563–580. [CrossRef]

30. Fernández-Laviada, A.; López-Gutierrez, C.; Pérez, A. How does the development of the social Enterprise sector affect entrepreneurial behaviour? An empirical analysis. *Sustainability* **2020**, *12*, 826. [CrossRef]

31. García Alonso, R.; Thoene, U.; Figueroa, A.M.; Murillo Amaris, E. El Emprendimiento Social en el marco de la Alianza del Pacífico. *REVESCO Rev. Estud. Coop.* **2020**, *133*. [CrossRef]

32. Naderi, A.; Nasrolahi Vosta, L.; Ebrahimi, A.; Jalilvand, M.R. The contributions of social entrepreneurship and transformational leadership to performance: Insights from rural tourism in Iran. *Int. J. Sociol. Soc. Policy* **2019**, *39*, 719–737. [CrossRef]

33. Narangajavana, Y.; Gonzalez-Cruz, T.; Garrigos-Simon, F.J.; Cruz-Ros, S. Measuring social entrepreneurship and social value with leakage. Definition, analysis and policies for the hospitality industry. *Int. Entrep. Manag. J.* **2016**, *12*, 911–934. [CrossRef]

34. Dickel, P.; Sienknecht, M.; Hörisch, J. The early bird catches the worm: An empirical analysis of imprinting in social entrepreneurship. *J. Bus. Econ.* **2020**. [CrossRef]

35. García-Morales, V.J.; Martín-Rojas, R.; Garde-Sánchez, R. How to Encourage Social Entrepreneurship Action? Using Web 2.0 Technologies in Higher Education Institutions. *J. Bus. Ethics* **2020**, *161*, 329–350. [CrossRef]

36. Sahasranaman, S.; Nandakumar, M.K. Individual capital and social entrepreneurship: Role of formal institutions. *J. Bus. Res.* **2020**, *107*, 104–117. [CrossRef]

37. Sánchez Espada, J.; Martín López, S.; Bel Durán, P.; Lejarriaga Pérez de las Vacas, G. Educación y formación en emprendimiento social: Características y creación de valor social sostenible en proyectos de emprendimiento social. *REVESCO Rev. Estud. Coop.* **2018**, *129*, 16–38.

38. Solomon, G.T.; Alabduljader, N.; Ramani, R.S. Knowledge management and social entrepreneurship education: Lessons learned from an exploratory two-country study. *J. Knowl. Manag.* **2019**, *23*, 1984–2006. [CrossRef]

39. Zulfiqar, S.; Nadeem, M.A.; Khan, M.K.; Anwar, M.A.; Iqbal, M.B.; Asmi, F. Opportunity Recognition Behavior and Readiness of Youth for Social Entrepreneurship. *Entrep. Res. J.* **2019**. [CrossRef]

40. Hojnik, B.B.; Crnogaj, K. Social impact, innovations, and market activity of social enterprises: Comparison of European countries. *Sustainability* **2020**, *12*, 1915. [CrossRef]

41. Méndez-Picazo, M.-T.; Ribeiro-Soriano, D.; Galindo-Martín, M.-A. Drivers of social Entrepreneurship. *Eur. J. Int. Manag.* **2015**, *9*, 766–779. [CrossRef]

42. De Clercq, D.; Danis, W.M.; Dakhli, M. The moderating effect of institutional context on the relationship between associational activity and new business activity in emerging economies. *Int. Bus. Rev.* **2010**, *19*, 85–101. [CrossRef]

43. Acosta Veliz, M.M.; Coronel Perez, V.; Jimenez Cercado, M. Social entrepreneurship and its relationship with the base of the pyramid in Latin America. *3C Empresa* **2018**, *7*, 50–66. [CrossRef]

44. Baron, D.P. Corporate social responsibility and social entrepreneurship. *J. Econ. Manag. Strategy* **2007**, *16*, 683–717. [CrossRef]

45. Carvalho, L.C.; Verissimo, P. From social entrepreneurship to corporate social responsibility: A case study. *HOLOS* **2018**, *34*, 59–76. [CrossRef]

46. London, M. Understanding social advocacy. An integrative model of motivation, strategy, and persistence in support of corporate social responsibility and social entrepreneurship. *J. Manag. Dev.* **2010**, *29*, 224–245. [CrossRef]

47. Miragaia, D.A.M.; Ferreira, J.; Ratten, V. Corporate social responsibility and social entrepreneurship: Drivers of sports sponsorship policy. *Int. J. Sport Policy Politics* **2017**, *9*, 613–623. [CrossRef]

48. Mora Mayoral, M.J.; Martínez Martínez, F.R. Desarrollo local sostenible, responsabilidad social corporativa y emprendimiento social. *Equidad Y Desarro.* **2018**, *31*, 27–46. [CrossRef]

49. Pinillos, M.J.; Reyes, L. Relationship between individualist-collectivist culture and entrepreneurial activity: Evidence from Global Entrepreneurship Monitor data. *Small Bus. Econ.* **2011**, *37*, 23–37. [CrossRef]

50. Shwartz, S.H. A theory of cultural values and some implications for work. *Appl. Psychol. Int. Rev.* **1999**, *48*, 23–47. [CrossRef]

51. Bruton, G.D.; Ahlstrom, D.; Li, H.L. Institutional theory and entrepreneurship: Where are we now and where do we need to move in the future? *Entrep. Theory Pract.* **2010**, *34*, 421–440. [CrossRef]

52. Chen, H. A review of institutional theory and entrepreneurship. In Proceedings of the 19th International Conference on Industrial Engineering and Engineering Management; Qi, E., Shen, J., Dou, R., Eds.; Springer-Verlag: Berlin/Heidelberg, Germany, 2013; pp. 719–727.

53. Martinelli, A. The social and institutional context of entrepreneurship. In *Crossroads of Entrepreneurship*; Corbetta, G., Huse, M., Ravasi, D., Eds.; Kluwer Academic: New York, NY, USA, 2004; pp. 53–73.

54. Pacheco, D.F.; York, J.G.; Dean, T.J.; Sarasvathy, S.D. The coevolution of institutional entrepreneurship: A tale of two theories. *J. Manag.* **2010**, *36*, 974–1010. [CrossRef]

55. Simon-Moya, V.; Revuelto-Taboada, L.; Fernandez-Guerrero, R. Institutional and economic drivers of entrepreneurship: An international perspective. *J. Bus. Res.* **2014**, *67*, 715–721. [CrossRef]

56. Urbano, D.; Alvarez, C.P. Institutional dimensions and entrepreneurial activity: An international study. *Small Bus. Econ.* **2014**, *42*, 703–716. [CrossRef]

57. Caballero, G.; Arias, X.C. De la Nueva Economía Institucional al análisis institucional moderno de las ciencias sociales. In *Nuevo Institucionalismo: Gobernanza, Economía y Políticas Públicas*; Arias, X.C., Caballero, G., Eds.; Centro de Investigaciones Sociológicas: Madrid, Spain, 2013; pp. 17–40.

58. North, D.C. *Institutions, Institutional Change and Economic Performance*; Cambridge University Press: Cambridge, MA, USA, 1990.

59. North, D.C. Institutions. *J. Econ. Perspect.* **1991**, *5*, 97–112. [CrossRef]

60. Alvarez, C.; Urbano, D.; Corduras, A.; Navarro, J. Environmental conditions and entrepreneurial activity: A regional comparison in Spain. *J. Small Bus. Enterp. Dev.* **2001**, *18*, 120–140. [CrossRef]

61. Castaño, M.S.; Galindo, M.A.; Méndez-Picazo, M.T. The effect of social, cultural and economic factors on entrepreneurship. *J. Bus. Res.* **2015**, *68*, 1496–1500. [CrossRef]

62. Gimenez, D.; Peris-Ortiz, M.; Urbano, D. A cultural perspective on entrepreneurship and regional development. The case of the Bages (Catalonia). In *Entrepreneurship, Regional Development and Culture. An Institutional Perspective*; Peris-Ortiz, M., Merigó-Lindahl, J.M., Eds.; Springer: Geneva, Switzerland, 2015; pp. 1–21.

63. Nissan, E.; Galindo, M.A.; Méndez-Picazo, M.T. Innovation, progress, entrepreneurship and cultural aspects. *Int. Entrep. Manag. J.* **2012**, *8*, 411–420. [CrossRef]

64. Salimath, M.S.; Cullen, J.B. Formal and informal institutional effects on entrepreneurship: A synthesis of nation-level research. *Int. J. Organ. Anal.* **2010**, *18*, 358–385. [CrossRef]

65. Thornton, P.H.; Ribeiro-Soriano, D.; Urbano, D. Socio-cultural factors and entrepreneurial activity: An overview. *Int. Small Bus. J.* **2011**, *29*, 105–108. [CrossRef]

66. Veciana, J.M.; Urbano, D. The institutional approach to entrepreneurship research. Introduction. *Int. Entrep. Manag. J.* **2008**, *4*, 365–379. [CrossRef]

67. Engle, R.L.; Schlaegel, C.; Dimitriadi, N. Institutions and entrepreneurial intent: A cross-country study. *J. Dev. Entrep.* **2011**, *16*, 227–250. [CrossRef]

68. Dacin, M.T.; Dacin, P.; Tracey, P. Social entrepreneurship: A critique and future directions. *Organ. Sci.* **2011**, *22*, 1203–1213. [CrossRef]

69. Hoogendoorn, B.; Pennings, E.; Thurik, A.R. What do we know about social entrepreneurship: An analysis of empirical research. *Int. Rev. Entrep.* **2010**, *8*, 71–112.

70. Lévesque, B. *Entrepreneurship Collectif et Économie Sociale: Entreprendre Autrement*; Alliance de recherche universités-communautés en économie sociale (ARUC-ÉS): Montreal, Canada, 2002.

71. Voigt, S. How (not) to measure institutions. *J. Inst. Econ.* **2013**, *9*, 1–26. [CrossRef]

72. Hayton, J.C.; Cacciotti, G. Is there and entrepreneurial culture? A review of empirical research. *Entrep. Reg. Dev.* **2013**, *25*, 708–731. [CrossRef]

73. Alegre, I.; Berbegal-Mirabent, J. Entrepreneurship and the influence of history: How much impact do country-specific historical factors have on entrepreneurship initiatives? In *Entrepreneurship, Regional Development and Culture. An Institutional Perspective*; Peris-Ortiz, M., Merigó-Lindahl, J.M., Eds.; Springer: Geneva, Switzerland, 2015; pp. 35–52.

74. Hofstede, G. *Culture's Consequences: International Differences in Work-Related Values*; Sage Publications: Beverly Hills, CA, USA, 1980.

75. Mueller, S.L.; Thomas, A.S. Culture and entrepreneurial potential: A nine country study of locus of control and innovativeness. *J. Bus. Ventur.* **2001**, *16*, 51–75. [CrossRef]

76. Ulijn, J.; Weggeman, M. Toward an innovation culture: What are its national, corporate, marketing and engineering aspects, some experimental evidence. In *Handbook of Organisation Culture and Climate*; Cooper, C., Cartwright, S., Early, S., Eds.; Wiley: London, UK, 2001; pp. 487–517.

77. Inglehart, R. *Modernization and Postmodernization*; Princenton University Press: Princenton, NJ, USA, 1997.

78. Inglehart, R. Post-materialism in an environment of insecurity. *Am. Polit. Sci. Rev.* **1981**, *75*, 880–900. [CrossRef]

79. Inglehart, R. Globalization and postmodern values. *Wash Quart* **2000**, *23*, 215–228. [CrossRef]

80. Morales, C.E.; Holtschlag, C. Post materialist values and entrepreneurship: A multilevel approach. *Int. J. Entrep. Behav. Res.* **2013**, *19*, 266–282. [CrossRef]

81. Pinillos Costa, M.J. Cultura postmaterialista y variaciones en el espíritu emprendedor. *Investig. Eur. De Dir. Y Econ. De La Empresa* **2011**, *17*, 37–55. [CrossRef]

82. Uhlaner, L.; Thurik, R. Postmaterialism influencing total entrepreneurial activity across nations. *J. Evol. Econ.* **2007**, *17*, 161–185. [CrossRef]

83. Buendía-Martínez, I.; Carrasco-Monteagudo, I. El impacto de los actores institucionales en la actividad emprendedora: Un análisis del cooperativismo europeo. *Rev. Econ. Mund.* **2014**, *38*, 175–200.

84. Stephan, U.; Uhlaner, L.M.; Stride, C.B. Institutions and social entrepreneurship: The role of institutional voids, institutional support and institutional configurations. *J. Int. Bus. Stud.* **2015**, *46*, 308–331. [CrossRef]

85. Inglehart, R. *Culture Shift in Advanced Industrial Society*; Princeton University Press: Princeton, NJ, USA, 1990.

86. Andrain, C.F.; Smith, J.T. *Political Democracy, Trust, and Social Justice. A Comparative Overview*; Northeastern University Press: Lebanon, PA, USA, 2006.

87. Mau, S.; Veghte, B. (Eds.) *Social Justice, Legitimacy and the Welfare State*; Routledge: London, UK, 2007.

88. Ward, T.J. Adam Smith's views on religion and social justice. *Int. J. World Peace* **2004**, *21*, 43–62.

89. Fleischacker, S. *A Short History of Distributive Justice*; Harvard University Press: Cambridge, MA, USA, 2005.

90. Frohlich, N. A very short history of distributive justice. *Soc. Justice Res.* **2007**, *20*, 250–263. [CrossRef]

91. Schraad-Tischler, D. *Social Justice in the OECD. How Do the Member States Compare?* Sustainable governance indicators; Bertelsmann Stiftung: Gütersloh, Germany, 2011.

92. United Nations. *The International Forum for Social Development. Social Justice in an Open World. The Role of the United Nations*; Department of Economic and Social Affairs, United Nations: New York, NY, USA, 2006.

93. Caldwell, K.; Harris, S.P.; Renko, M. The potential of social entrepreneurship: Conceptual tools for applying citizenship theory to policy and practice. *Intellect. Dev. Disabil.* **2012**, *50*, 505–518. [CrossRef]

94. Cook, B.; Dodds, C.; Mitchell, W. Social entrepreneurship—False premises and dangerous forebodings. *Aust. J. Soc. Issues* **2003**, *38*, 57–72. [CrossRef]

95. Thake, D.; Zadek, S. *Practical People, Noble Causes. How to Support Community Based Social Entrepreneurs*; New Economic Foundation: London, UK, 1997.

96. Engle, E. A social-market economy for rapid sustainable development. *GNLU J. Law Dev. Politics* **2009**, *1*, 42–62.

97. Henrÿ, H. Superar la crisis del Estado de Bienestar: El rol de las empresas democráticas, una perspectiva jurídica. *Ciriec-España. Rev. Jurídica De Econ. Soc. Y Coop.* **2013**, *24*, 11–20.

98. Blowfield, M.; Murray, A. *Corporate Responsibility*; Oxford University Press: Oxford, UK, 2011.

99. Garriga, E.; Melé, D. Corporate social responsibility theories: Mapping the territory. *J. Bus. Ethics* **2004**, *53*, 51–71. [CrossRef]

100. Wan-Jan, W.S. Defining corporate social responsibility. *J. Public Aff.* **2006**, *6*, 176–184. [CrossRef]

101. Newell, P.; Frynas, J.G. Beyond CSR? Business, poverty and social justice: An introduction. *Third World Q* **2007**, *28*, 669–681. [CrossRef]

102. Gladwin, T.N.; Kennelly, J.J.; Krause, T.-S. Shifting paradigms for sustainable development: Implications for management theory and research. *Acad. Manag. Rev.* **1995**, *20*, 874–907. [CrossRef]

103. Bekkers, R. Participation in voluntary associations: Relations with resources, personality, and political values. *Political Psychol.* **2005**, *26*, 439–454. [CrossRef]

104. Frazen, A.; Meyer, R. Environmental attitudes in cross-national perspective: A multilevel analysis of the ISSP 1993 and 2000. *Eur. Sociol. Rev.* **2010**, *26*, 219–234. [CrossRef]

105. Shamir, R. Socially responsible private regulation: World-culture or world-capitalism? *Law Soc. Rev.* **2011**, *45*, 313–336. [CrossRef]

106. Dickson, M.; BeShears, R.; Gupta, V. The impact of societal culture and industry on organizational culture: Theoretical explanations. In *Culture, Leadership, and Organizations: The GLOBE Study of 62 Societies*; House, R.J., Hanges, P.J., Javidan, M., Dorfman, P.W., Gupta, V., Eds.; Sage: Thousand Oaks, CA, USA, 2004; pp. 4–93.

107. Lantos, G.P. The boundaries of strategic corporate social responsibility. *J. Consum. Mark.* **2002**, *18*, 595–630. [CrossRef]

108. Callado-Muñoz, F.J.; Utrero-González, N. Does it pay to be socially responsible? Evidence from Spain's retail banking sector. *Eur. Financ. Manag.* **2011**, *17*, 755–787. [CrossRef]

109. Gunther, M. Cops of the global village. *Fortune* **2005**, *151*, 158–166.

110. Campbell, J.L. Why would corporations behave in socially responsible ways? An institutional theory of corporate social responsibility. *Acad. Manag. Rev.* **2007**, *32*, 946–967. [CrossRef]

111. Li, F.; Morris, T.; Young, B. The Effect of Corporate Visibility on Corporate Social Responsibility. *Sustainability* **2019**, *11*, 3698. [CrossRef]

112. Endrikat, J.; de Villiers, C.; Guenther, T.W.; Guenther, E.M. Board Characteristics and Corporate Social Responsibility: A Meta-Analytic Investigation. *Bus. Soc.* **2020**. [CrossRef]

113. El Gammal, W.; Yassine, N.; Fakih, K.; El-Kassar, A.N. The relationship between CSR and corporate governance moderated by performance and board of directors' characteristics. *J. Manag. Gov.* **2020**, *24*, 411–430. [CrossRef]

114. Li, F. A survey of corporate social responsibility and corporate governance. In *Research Handbook of finance and Sustainability*; Boubaker, S., Cumming, D., Nguyen, D.K., Eds.; Edward Elgar: Cheltenham, UK, 2018; pp. 126–138.

115. Li, F.; Li, T.; Minor, D. A Test of Agency Theory: CEO Power, Firm Value, and Corporate Social Responsibility. *Int. J. Manag. Financ.* **2016**, *12*, 611–628. [CrossRef]

116. Matten, D.; Moon, J. A conceptual framework for CSR. In *Corporate Social Responsibility Across Europe*; Habisch, A., Jonker, J., Wegner, M., Schmidpeter, M., Eds.; Springer: Berlin, Germany, 2005; pp. 335–356.

117. Asslander, M.S. Corporate social responsibility as subsidiary co-responsibility: A macroeconomic perspective. *J. Bus. Ethics* **2011**, *99*, 115–128. [CrossRef]

118. European Commission. *Communication from the Commission to the European Parliament, the Council, the European Economic and Social Committee and the Committee of Regions: A Renewed EU Strategy for Corporate Social Responsibility (COM(2011)681 Final)*; European Commission: Brussels, Belgium, 2011.

119. Austin, J.; Reficco, E. *Corporate Social Entrepreneurship*; Working Paper No. 09-101; Harvard Business School: Boston, MA, USA, 2005.

120. Spitzeck, H.; Boechat, C.; Leão, S.F. Sustainability as a driver for innovation—Towards a model of corporate social entrepreneurship at Odebrecht in Brazil. *Corp. Gov.* **2013**, *13*, 613–625. [CrossRef]

121. Tasavori, M.; Ghauri, P.N.; Zaefarian, R. Entering the base of the pyramid market in India: A corporate social entrepreneurship perspective. *Int. Mark. Rev.* **2016**, *33*, 555–579. [CrossRef]

122. Freireich, J.; Fulton, K. *Investing for Social and Environmental Impact: A Design for Catalyzing an Emerging Industry*; Monitor Institute: Washington, DC, USA, 2009.

123. Dawkins, J. *The Expert Perspective: Views of Corporate Responsibility among NGOs and CSR Commentators*; MORI: London, UK, 2004.

124. Staples, C. What does corporate social responsibility mean for charitable fundraising in the UK? *Int. J. Nonprofit Volunt. Sect. Mark.* **2004**, *9*, 154–159. [CrossRef]

125. Doh, S.; Acs, Z.J. Innovation and social capital: A cross-country investigation. *Ind. Innov.* **2010**, *17*, 241–262. [CrossRef]

126. Doh, S.; McNeely, C.L. A multi-dimensional perspective on social capital and economic development: An exploratory analysis. *Ann. Reg. Sci.* **2012**, *49*, 821–843. [CrossRef]

127. Fukuyama, F. *Trust: The Social Virtues and the Creation of Prosperity*; Free Press: New York, NY, USA, 1995.

128. Westlund, H.; Adam, F. Social capital and economic performance: A meta-analysis of 65 studies. *Eur. Plan. Stud.* **2010**, *18*, 893–919. [CrossRef]

129. Woolcock, M. Social capital and economic development: Toward a theoretical synthesis and policy framework. *Theor. Soc.* **1998**, *27*, 151–208. [CrossRef]

130. Beugelsdijk, S.; Van Schaik, F.T. Social capital and growth in European regions: An empirical test. *Eur. J. Polit. Econ.* **2005**, *21*, 301–324. [CrossRef]

131. Coleman, J.S. Social capital in the creation of human capital. *Am. J. Sociol.* **1988**, *94*, S95–S120. [CrossRef]

132. Coleman, J.S. *Foundations of Social Theory*; Harvard University Press: Cambridge, MA, USA, 1990.

133. Putnam, R.D. The prosperous community: Social capital and public life. *Am. Prospect* **1993**, *13*, 35–42.

134. Welzel, C.; Inglehart, R.; Deutsch, F. Social capital, voluntary associations and collective action: Which aspects of social capital have the greatest civic payoff? *J. Civ. Soc.* **2005**, *1*, 121–146. [CrossRef]

135. Audretsch, D.B.; Keilbach, M.C. Entrepreneurship capital and economic performance. *Reg. Stud.* **2004**, *38*, 949–959. [CrossRef]

136. Aldrich, H.E.; Martinez, M. Entrepreneurship as social construction: A multi-level evolutionary approach. In *Handbook of Entrepreneurship Research: An Interdisciplinary Survey and Introduction*; Acs, Z.J., Audretsch, D.B., Eds.; Kluwer: London, UK, 2003; pp. 359–399.

137. Maskell, P. Social capital, innovation, and competitiveness. In *Social capital: Critical Perspectives*; Baron, S., Field, J., Schuller, T., Eds.; Oxford University Press: Oxford, UK, 2000; pp. 111–123.

138. Murphy, L.; Huggins, R.; Thompson, P. Social capital and innovation: A comparative analysis of regional policies. *Environ. Plan. C* **2016**, *34*. [CrossRef]

139. Ostrom, E. *Governing the Commons: The Evolution of Institutions for Collective Action*; Cambridge University: Cambridge, MA, USA, 1990.

140. Ostrom, E. Collective action and the evolution of social norms. *J. Econ. Perspect.* **2000**, *14*, 137–158. [CrossRef]

141. Ostrom, E. *Understanding Institutional Diversity*; Princeton University Press: New Jersey, NJ, USA, 2005.

142. Audretsch, D.B.; Keilbach, M.C.; Lehmann, E.E. *Entrepreneurship and Economic Growth*; Oxford University Press: New York, NY, USA, 2006.

143. Hofstede, G.; Hofstede, G.J.; Pedersen, P. *Exploring Culture, Exercise, Stories and Synthetic Cultures*; Intercultural Press: Yarmouth, ME, USA, 2002.

144. Beugelsdijk, S.; Noorderhaven, N. Entrepreneurial attitude and economic growth: A cross-section of 54 regions. *Ann. Reg. Sci.* **2004**, *38*, 199–218. [CrossRef]

145. Dees, J.G. Enterprising nonprofits. *Harv. Bus. Rev.* **1998**, *76*, 55–66.

146. Estrin, S.; Mickiewicz, T.; Stephan, U. Entrepreneurship, social capital, and institutions: Social and commercial entrepreneurship across nations. *Entrep. Theory Pract.* **2013**, *37*, 479–504. [CrossRef]

147. Felipe, C.; Roldán, J.; Leal-Rodríguez, A. Impact of organizational culture values on organizational agility. *Sustainability* **2017**, *9*, 23–54. [CrossRef]

148. Hair, J.; Hult, G.T.M.; Ringle, C.; Sarstedt, M. *A Primer on Partial Least Square Structural Equation Modelling (PLS-SEM)*; Sage Publications: Thousand Oaks, CA, USA, 2017.

149. Henseler, J.; Ringle, C.M.; Sinkovics, R.R. The use de partial least squares path modelling in international marketing. *Adv. Int. Mar.* **2009**, *20*, 277–320. [CrossRef]

150. Ringle, C.M.; Wende, S.; Becker, J.-M. *SmartPLS*; Version 3; SmartPLS GmbH: Boenningstedt, Germany, 2015.

151. Falk, R.F.; Miller, N.B. *A Primer for Soft Modeling*; University of Akron Press: Akron, OH, USA, 1992.

152. Barclay, D.; Higgins, C.; Thompson, R. The partial least squares (PLS) approach to causal modelling: Personal computer adoption and use as an illustration. *Technol. Stud.* **1995**, *2*, 285–309.

153. Fornell, C. *A Second Generation of Multivariate Analysis*; Praeger: New York, NY, USA, 1982; Volume 1.

154. Tenenhaus, M. *La Régression PLS: Théorie et Pratique*; Éditions Technip: Paris, France, 1998.

155. Gefen, D.; Straub, D.; Boudreau, M.C. Structural equation modelling and regression: Guidelines for research practice. *Commun. Assoc. Inf. Syst.* **2000**, *4*. [CrossRef]

156. Chin, W.W. Issues and opinion on structural equation modelling. *Manag. Inf. Syst. Q.* **1998**, *22*, 7–16.

157. Chin, W.W.; Newsted, P.R. Structural equation modeling analysis with small samples using partial least squares. In *Statistical Strategies for Small Sample Research*; Hoyle, R.H., Ed.; Sage Publications: Thousand Oaks, CA, USA, 1999; pp. 307–342.

158. Anderson, J.C.; Gerbing, D.W. Structural equation modeling in practice: A review and recommended two-step approach. *Psychol. Bull.* **1988**, *103*, 411. [CrossRef]

159. World Values Survey. World Values Survey wave 5 (2005–2009) [Data set]. 2010. Available online: http://www.worldvaluessurvey.org/ (accessed on 10 December 2019).

160. World Values Survey. World Values Survey wave 6 (2010–2014) [Data set]. 2015. Available online: http://www.worldvaluessurvey.org/ (accessed on 12 December 2019).

161. MacGillivray, A.; Begley, P.; Zadek, S. (Eds.) *The State of Responsible Competitiveness. Making Sustainable Development Count in Global Markets*; AccountAbility: London, UK, 2007.

162. Bosma, N.; Levie, J. *2009 Global Report. Global Entrepreneurship Monitor*; GEM: London, UK, 2010.

163. Fornell, C.; Larcker, D.F. Evaluating structural equation models with unobservable variables and measurement error. *J. Mark. Res.* **1981**, *18*, 39–50. [CrossRef]

164. Henseler, J.; Ringle, C.M.; Sarstedt, M. A new criterion for assessing discriminant validity in variance-based structural equation modeling. *J. Acad Mark. Sci.* **2015**, *43*, 115–135. [CrossRef]

165. Nunnally, J.C.; Bernstein, I.H. *Psychonnetric Theory*; McGraw-Hill: New York, NY, USA, 1994.

166. Ringle, C.M.; Sarstedt, M.; Mooi, E.A. Response-based segmentation using finite mixture partial least squares: Theoretical foundations and an application to American customer satisfaction index data. In *Data Mining. Special Issue in Annals of Information Systems*; Stahlbock, R., Crone, S.F., Lessman, S., Eds.; Springer: New York, NY, USA, 2010; pp. 19–49. [CrossRef]

167. World Business Council for Sustainable Development. *Corporate Social Responsibility: Making Good Business Sense*; World Business Council for Sustainable Development: Geneve, Switzerland, 2000.

168. Martinuzzi, A.; Schönherr, N.; Findler, F. Exploring the interface of CSR and the Sustainable Development Goals. *Transnatl. Corp.* **2017**, *24*, 33–47. [CrossRef]

169. Suchman, M.C. Managing Legitimacy: Strategic and Institutional Approaches. *Acad. Manag. Rev.* **1995**, *20*, 571–610. [CrossRef]

170. Bronchain, P. (Ed.) *Towards a Sustainable Corporate Social Responsibility*; European Foundation for the Improvement of Living and Working Conditions: Dublin, Ireland, 2003.

171. Bacq, S.; Eddleston, K.A. A Resource-Based View of Social Entrepreneurship: How Stewardship Culture Benefits Scale of Social Impact. *J. Bus. Ethics* **2018**, *152*, 589–611. [CrossRef]

172. Kotler, P.; Lee, N. *Corporate Social Responsibility. Doing the Most Good for Your Company and Your Cause*; John Wiley & Sons: Hoboken, NJ, USA, 2007.

173. Lückenbach, F.; Baumgarth, C.; Schmidt, H.J.; Henseler, J. To perform or not to perform? How strategic orientations influence the performance of Social Entrepreneurship Organizations. *Cogent Bus. Manag.* **2019**, *6*, 1647820. [CrossRef]

174. Organization for Economic Cooperation and Development (OECD); European Union. *Boosting Social Enterprise Development. Good Practice Compendium*; OECD: Paris, France, 2017.

175. Sepulveda, L.; Lyon, F.; Vickers, I. Social enterprise spin-outs': An institutional analysis of their emergence and potential. *Technol. Anal. Strateg. Manag.* **2018**, *30*, 967–979. [CrossRef]

176. Austin, J.E. *The Collaboration Challenge. How Nonprofit and Businesses Succeed through Strategic Alliances*; Jossey-Bass Publishers: San Francisco, CA, USA, 2000.

177. Kannampuzha, M.; Hockerts, K. Organizational social entrepreneurship: Scale development and validation. *Soc. Enterp. J.* **2019**, *15*, 290–319. [CrossRef]

178. Tracey, P.; Phillips, N.; Haugh, H. Beyond philanthropy: Community enterprise as a basis for corporate citizenship. *J. Bus. Ethics* **2005**, *58*, 327–344. [CrossRef]

179. Iglič, H.; Rözer, J.; Volker, B.G.M. Economic crisis and social capital in European societies: The role of politics in understanding short-term changes in social capital. *Eur. Soc.* **2020**. [CrossRef]

180. Ha, W. Social Capital and Crisis Coping in Indonesia. In *Risk, Shocks, and Human Development*; Fuentes-Nieva, R., Seck, P.A., Eds.; Palgrave Macmillan: London, UK, 2010; pp. 284–309. [CrossRef]

181. Fernández-Feijo Souto, B. Crisis and corporate social responsibility: Threat or opportunity? *Int. J. Econ. Sci. Appl. Res.* **2009**, *2*, 36–50.
182. Idowu, S.M.; Vertiganss, S.; Burlea, A.S. (Eds.) *Corporate Social Responsibility in Times of Crisis. Practices and Cases from Europe, Africa and the World*; Springer International Publishing: Wien, Austria, 2017.
183. Dacin, M.T.; Goodstein, J.; Scott, W.R. Institutional Theory and Institutional Change: Introduction to the Special Resea. *Acad. Manag. J.* **2002**, *45*, 45–57. [CrossRef]

10

CEO Pay Sensitivity (Delta and Vega) and Corporate Social Responsibility

Atif Ikram [1], Zhichuan (Frank) Li [2,*] and Travis MacDonald [3]

[1] Department of Finance, Arizona State University, Tempe, AZ 85281, USA; aikram@asu.edu
[2] Ivey Business School, University of Western Ontario, London, ON N6A 3K7, Canada
[3] Department of Economics, University of Western Ontario, London, ON N6A 3K7, Canada; tmacdo49@uwo.ca
[*] Correspondence: fli@ivey.ca

Abstract: We use CEO pay sensitivity to stock performance (delta) and stock volatility (vega) to provide empirical evidence that CEO compensation structure influences firm Corporate Social Responsibility (CSR) performance. We find that delta has no significant effect on CSR, while vega has a strong, causal relationship with CSR. Our findings suggest that CEOs do not view CSR as value enhancing, but as a way to increase their own compensation through vega. Firms that want to improve their social performance should consider vega as an important compensation incentive for executives.

Keywords: executive compensation; managerial incentives; corporate social responsibility; corporate social performance; firm risk; delta; vega; agency problem

JEL Classification: G32; M14; M22; J33

1. Introduction

This paper draws a causal relation between CEO compensation structure and firm corporate social responsibility (CSR). To draw our conclusions, we examine the sensitivity of CEO pay to both stock return volatility (vega) and stock returns (delta) using panel data spanning 1995–2013. CEO compensation has a profound influence on firm outcomes such as financial performance and investment and policy decisions; however, its effects on firm social performance are underexplored. The scarce literature examining the link between executive compensation and CSR has focused solely on the instruments of compensation as opposed to the underlying pay sensitivities that those instruments produce. Some use a lagged measure of long-term executive pay [1] or the percentage of salary from bonus and stock options [2]. McGuire et al. [3] use salary, bonus, and long-term incentives, while Deckop et al. [4] use percentage of short-term pay vs. long-term-pay to link CEO compensation with CSR levels. Although these studies address how CEO pay motivates CSR participation, they fail to address the reasons behind these investments. By using pay sensitivities, we can understand the underlying motivations behind CSR investment from the CEO's perspective, not just whether the investment is made. Higher vega incentivizes CEOs to pursue policies that will increase stock price volatility, whereas higher delta motivates the CEO to increase the stock price. Understanding how CEOs respond to incentives related to CSR is crucial to designing compensation policies that not only maximize shareholder value but also promote corporate citizenship in operating environments that are increasingly impacted by societal perceptions.

Employing fixed effects models and controlling for firm size, risk level, and industry, we find that CSR standing is significantly positively related to measures of vega but not significantly related to measures of delta. This suggests that CEOs view CSR investing as a risky policy, similar to what the previous literature concludes about R&D spending [5], financial leverage, and concentrated product lines [6–8]. That is, CEOs generally perceive CSR projects as riskier than the average projects they are running. It is plausible that CSR investments are usually for new innovative projects and, more importantly, impose enormous uncertainty to stock performance and shareholder value. Delta has no significant effect on CSR levels, which suggests that a CEO's decisions on CSR are independent of their pay sensitivity to the underlying stock price. Our findings indicate that stock option compensation significantly increases the likelihood of CSR initiatives, but only to the extent that the CEO's pay sensitivity to the underlying volatility of the stock price is increased. This paper links the existing CEO compensation literature with the CSR literature in a way that has not previously been explored.

In an ideal world, CEO and shareholder interests would perfectly align. Every decision a CEO makes would maximize shareholder value. However, managers solve their own maximization problem with the goal of increasing their own utility; this is known as the agency problem [9,10]. Corporate governance policies aim to ensure that managers act in a manner consistent with shareholder value maximization, and part of this goal is achieved through compensation policy [9,10]. An optimal compensation contract is one that promotes the managerial decision making that maximizes shareholder value. This involves exposing the CEO to varying risk/reward incentive combinations via cash, stock, and options payments in an effort to mitigate the agency problem [11]. Jenson and Murphy [12] argue that CEO pay should be substantially linked to shareholder welfare. This idea gained significant traction throughout the 1990s, and Hall and Liebman [13,14] document a dramatic increase in equity-based CEO compensation throughout this period. CEO compensation includes three components: cash, stock, and options. According to optimal contracting theory, when company boards determine CEO compensation, they target a compensation mix that they believe will maximize shareholder value by reducing agency costs [15]. This raises the question: how do CEOs respond to varying risk/reward combinations across compensation packages?

Naturally, CEO pay relating to the present cash component of compensation is independent of future stock price movements. However, equity-based compensation exhibits varying return characteristics depending on the instruments used. Stock-based compensation will move linearly with the stock price, resulting in a delta of 1; however, the sensitivity of options compensation depends entirely on the structure of the contracts. Given that CEOs are risk-averse and almost always highly exposed to firm specific risk, it is not enough to simply structure compensation policy to mimic the pay sensitivity of the shareholder. Even if managers are incentivized to take actions that increase shareholder wealth, they may still choose suboptimal policies that reduce personal portfolio risk [16]. Therefore, we need to understand the risks that the CEO faces, and how these risks influence decision making.

There is extensive literature examining the effect of delta and vega on CEO decision making [6,7,11]; however, the effect of delta and vega on CSR levels has not previously been explored. This shareholder value-maximization problem is further complicated by the issue of whether CSR is indeed a value-enhancing investment opportunity for a given firm. There is much debate surrounding this question in the existing literature [17–20]. Although it is beyond the scope of this paper to answer this question definitively, we contribute to the existing literature by identifying vega as an avenue that shareholders can use to encourage CEOs to alter CSR standings.

The remainder of this paper is organized as follows. In the following section, we review relevant literature and develop hypotheses. Section 3 introduces our data sample, and Section 4 presents empirical findings and discussion. Section 5 concludes.

2. Literature Review and Hypothesis Development

This section serves as a review of existing literature relating to the topics of both CEO compensation and corporate social responsibility. We will begin by surveying the existing literature regarding CEO compensation, followed by the CSR literature, and conclude with a brief discussion of how we plan to link these literatures in a unique way to gain insight into how CEOs alter CSR levels in response to compensation incentives.

As a means to mitigate costs arising from agency concerns, Jensen and Murphy [12] argue that CEO compensation should be substantially linked to shareholder value. They argue that since managerial actions and investment opportunities are not perfectly observable to shareholders, equity-based compensation encourages managerial actions that increase shareholder wealth. In accordance with this assertion, throughout the 1990s, there was a dramatic increase in both stock option compensation [21,22] and the sensitivity of CEO pay to the firm's stock price [14,23]. Perry and Zenner [22] raise the question of whether the increase in executive pay performance sensitivity is excessive, in that during bull markets (such as that of the 1990s), CEOs may be extracting excess rents from shareholders. This idea is built upon that by Bebchuk et al. [15], where the issue of CEO power is explored as a rationale for puzzling compensation practices, such as the lack of controls to filter out general market/sector factors influencing the share price when designing equity-based compensation packages. Bebchuk et al. [15] explore the idea that company boards are constrained when setting CEO compensation by CEO power. The argument is that powerful CEOs wield a degree of influence over the board and can use this influence to alter their own compensation structure, thereby extracting rents from shareholders. The CEO power approach to analyzing CEO compensation contracts contrasts the previous optimal contracting literature and has opened new avenues of study.

Much of the literature agrees that linking CEO compensation to shareholder wealth can reduce agency costs in many circumstances if implemented effectively. However, given the concerns surrounding imperfect information, ex-post contract enforcement feasibility, and the heterogeneity of both shareholders and CEOs, determining the appropriate compensation mix to maximize shareholder value is a contentious issue. A large problem with the idea of simply linking CEO compensation to shareholder wealth is that risk-averse CEOs are overly exposed to firm-specific risk because of equity-based compensation. This is a contrast to diversified shareholders who are owners of many firms and whose net worth is less sensitive to changes in the price of a given firm. Smith and Stulz [16] build on Ross [24] to demonstrate how risk-averse CEOs can be influenced to forgo positive NPV (net present value) projects when their total pay is linked to firm value. One solution to this problem is to mitigate the concavity of the utility of expected pay by using convex incentive schemes involving stock options. Guay [11] finds that providing managers with convex incentive schemes encourages managers to invest in risk-increasing, positive NPV projects. However, the question of how much convexity to provide to a given manager remains elusive. Indeed, Ross [25] proves that there exists no incentive schedule that renders all expected utility maximizers less risk averse.

There is a host of literature that details the responses of CEOs to the incentives created by options within a compensation structure. Defusco et al. [26] find that firms that approved executive stock options plans between 1978 and 1988 exhibited increased stock return variance. Ju et al. [27] show that usage of call options can induce either too much or too little risk-taking behavior. Jolls [28] shows that CEOs that are compensated with options are more likely to engage in stock repurchases rather than dividend issuance. Knopf et al. [8] show that the use of derivatives for hedging purposes within firms is negatively related to vega and positively related to delta. Ryan and Wiggins [5] find that stock option grants coincide with increases in R&D spending. The most intriguing findings are provided by Cohen et al. [6]. The authors augment the Hall–Liebman [13] database on executive options holdings and value the holdings using the Black–Scholes [29] method. They then compute the elasticity of CEO pay to changes in firm price volatility and find that executives respond to the incentives provided by options compensation. The authors further speculate, however, that as vega increases, CEOs may undertake negative NPV projects if they increase firm volatility. This is a key finding related to our paper because it raises the question of what CEOs may do in the face of uncertainty surrounding the profitability of investment projects.

Despite the extensive agreement in the literature that CEOs respond to the incentives created by compensation structure, there is often debate concerning the significance, magnitude and direction of various effects. There is a body of literature that takes advantage of the closed form solution of the Black–Scholes option-pricing model to take derivatives of option prices with respect to the underlying price (delta) and volatility (vega) [7,30–32]. However, how delta and vega fit into a given model has been interpreted in a wide variety of ways. Some studies try to use firm characteristics to estimate delta as a dependent variable [30,31], while others use delta as an independent variable [32]. Many studies omit vega altogether, partly because vega is difficult to compute and it is easier to find proxies for delta, such as number of options held, options granted, or the value of options at a point in time. To a large extent, this problem was remedied by Core and Guay [30] who developed a method to increase the accuracy of delta and vega estimates. Following this innovation, Coles et al. [7] reasoned that both vega and delta should be treated as independent variables that are chosen exogenously by shareholders to promote desired decision making in CEOs. They used the method of Core and Guay [30] to determine that higher vega results in the implementation of riskier firm policies, including higher R&D spending, less CAPEX, more concentrated product lines, and higher leverage. They also find that delta is generally inversely related to vega for these measures. From an optimal contracting perspective, the key point is that delta aligns the direction of managerial pay changes with that of the shareholders, while vega can be used to mitigate risk aversion.

All the above studies lead to a natural question: how is CSR as an investment perceived by CEOs? In order to answer this question, we need to obtain both an understanding of what CSR is and how to quantify it. Tsoutsoura [33] defines CSR as "a comprehensive set of policies, practices, and programs that are integrated into business operations, supply chains, and decision-making processes throughout the company and usually includes issues related to business ethics, community investment, environmental concerns, governance, human rights, the marketplace as well as the workplace". However, the question of how to quantify CSR has been approached from multiple angles. Some studies use subjective measures such as surveys [34–36], while others use Fortune rankings [17,37,38]. Waddock and Graves [39] recognized the need for a more objective way to quantify CSR. They made use of the Kinder Lydenberg Domini (KLD) corporate social performance (CSP) rating system, which draws upon a combination of financial statements, press articles, academic journals, and government reports to assess CSP along eight dimensions. The advantage of this approach is that KLD is an independent ratings service (since acquired by MSCI) that applies objective criteria consistently across time. Using this improved method, Waddock and Graves [39] find that CSP is initially driven by slackness in the budget constraints of firms that have high financial performance, but that CSP itself also creates positive financial performance. These findings concur with the positive relationship between firm performance and CSP found in the past [17,40,41]. However, it contrasted with both the negative relation hypothesized by Friedman [42] and the findings of a neutral relation by Ullmann [43]. Therefore, we have the alternative hypotheses based on the literature:

Hypothesis 1a (H1a). *CEOs with higher pay-performance sensitivity improve CSR if they view CSR as value enhancing.*

Hypothesis 1b (H1b). *CEOs with higher pay-performance sensitivity decrease CSR if they view CSR as value damaging.*

Hypothesis 2a (H2a). *CEOs with higher pay-risk sensitivity improve CSR if they view CSR as risk enhancing.*

Hypothesis 2b (H2b). *CEOs with higher pay-risk sensitivity decrease CSR if they view CSR as risk reducing.*

CSR affects firms through other avenues besides accounting profitability. Gregory et al. [44] look at the risk-reducing effects of CSR, and Albuquerque et al. [45] examine how CSR diversifies risk within firms. The relationship between CSR and better access to financing, along with lower financing costs, is also explored [46–48]. Attig et al. [49] find that CSR leads to higher credit ratings. Servaes and Tamayo [50] consider how CSR raises firm value through increased customer awareness. The effects of

CSR on corporate governance, firm value, and as a method of resolving conflicts between stakeholders is explored by Jo and Harjoto [51]. Jo and Harjoto [52] look at the causal effect of CSR on corporate governance. Hong et al. [53] and Ikram et al. [54] use hand collected compensation data to show that giving executives direct incentives related to CSR is effective at increasing CSP.

There is a wide body of literature indicating that CSR affects firms through a variety of channels. Part of this literature seeks to determine how executive compensation affects CSR [53,54]; however, this is performed by examining explicit incentives provided to executives. Our paper uses a new method to explore the relationship between CSR and compensation. Previous studies have focused on whether CEO compensation influences CSR ratings. Using pay sensitivities, we address the actual mechanism through which CEOs make their decision. We use the method of Coles et al. [7] to determine CEO delta and vega and then formulate a fixed effects model to estimate their effect on firm CSR ratings. As opposed to examining how CEOs respond to direct incentives, this approach examines how CEOs perceive CSR investment opportunities independent of other incentive frameworks.

3. Data

We created a panel dataset spanning 1995–2013 using firm fundamental data, executive compensation data, CSR ratings, and CEO pay sensitivity data. The firm fundamentals data were obtained using the Standard and Poor's COMPUSTAT North America database which covers all public firms listed in the U.S. across all industries. This database contains detailed, up-to-date firm fundamentals information for North American securities. The database uses SEC (the U.S. Securities and Exchange Commission) filings to track firm balance sheet, income statement, and cash flow statement entries on an annual, quarterly, and year-to-date basis. We used firms' unique identifier (GVKEY) to follow changes in firm fundamentals through time. We gather measures of Total Debt (DT), Total Assets (AT), Research and Development Expense (XRD), Total Sales (REVT), and Industry SIC Code (SIC). We then computed the variables Debt-to-Assets (DTA), LogAssets, LogSales, and LogR&D. These variables were later used as controls for firm size, firm risk, and industry when we constructed our model. For example, we used total sales and total assets as proxies for firm size in accordance with Tsoutsoura [33]; we controlled for R&D expenses following McWilliams and Siegel [55].

We obtained executive compensation data from the Standard and Poor's EXECUCOMP database. This database provides detailed compensation data for the highest paid executives at over 3462 firms that are part of the S&P 1500 index or were once part of the index and whose securities remain publicly traded. This database allows us to separate annual CEO compensation into its cash, stock, and options components. The data start in 1992, but the post-1994 data contain a much larger number of firms due to expansion of the database's mandate. The database also provides each executive with a permanent ID (EXECID), as well as each firm/executive combination with a unique identifier during their tenure (CO_PER_ROL). Data are reported on a fiscal year basis and contain information on cash awards, vested/unvested stock and options awards, deferred compensation, and pension awards. For a given year, a firm's CEO can be identified using the CEOANN flag variable.

CSR data were obtained using the MSCI ESG Stats Data Set. This is the same Kinder, Lydenberg, and Domini (KLD) data used in the previous literature [33,39,56,57], but the dataset is now managed by MSCI, who acquired KLD in 2010. The KLD data are collected by a global team of over 140 research analysts. They assess how well companies manage environmental, social, and governance (ESG) risks using macro data, company disclosures, government databases, news articles, and NGO data. Each company is then assigned a positive or negative indicator for ESG performance, and firms are invited to verify the findings. The dataset contains yearly ESG indicators for over 2600 firms. For the purposes of constructing the CSR rating, an ESG strength was assigned a score of +1, while a concern was given a score of −1. We used six different ESG strength/concern criteria in our analysis: company, diversity, employee, environmental, human rights, and product. We excluded the corporate governance category, following the literature. In our research setting, corporate governance measures may well be the determinants of CEO incentives, which defeats our attempt to study how incentives lead to social performance. We then summed the total strengths and concerns for firms to obtain our CSR rating variable.

Since Waddock and Graves [39], KLD data as a measure of corporate social responsibility have become increasingly popular [33]. Tsoutsoura [33] measures CSR using both the KLD ratings data for S&P 500 companies and the Domini 400 Social index (DSI 400). She follows the method of McWilliams and Siegel [55] by creating a dummy variable for CSP that is equal to 1 if a firm is included in the DSI 400 and 0 otherwise. She also uses COMPUSTAT to find measures of firm performance through accounting measures such as return on assets (ROA), return on equity (ROE), and return on sales (ROS). She then creates a panel dataset spanning 1996–2000 and adds control variables to account for firm risk, size, and industry. Previous studies [17,39,41] find that CSR is positively related to firm profitability.

Data on CEO pay sensitivity to the underlying stock price (delta) and stock volatility (vega) are obtained via the Core et al. [30] and Coles et al. [7] datasets. The authors use EXECUCOMP data to determine the number of vested and unvested stock and options holdings of each executive, as well as the expiration dates of the options. They then use the closed form solution of the Black–Sholes option-pricing model to compute delta and vega estimates for each individual CEO. We merged this CEO pay sensitivity data with our COMPUSTAT, EXECUCOMP, and KLD data using YEAR and GVKEY variables. This gave us a dataset that provides a complete picture of CEO pay sensitivity, firm characteristics, and CSR ratings over time.

4. Analysis and Discussion

4.1. Univariate Analysis

Tables 1–3 provide summary statistics for CSR ratings, delta sensitivities, and vega sensitivities across our sample over time. Figure 1 presents a graphic representation of Log(Delta), Log(Vega), and firm CSR rating over time. Table 4 provides a correlation matrix for these variables.

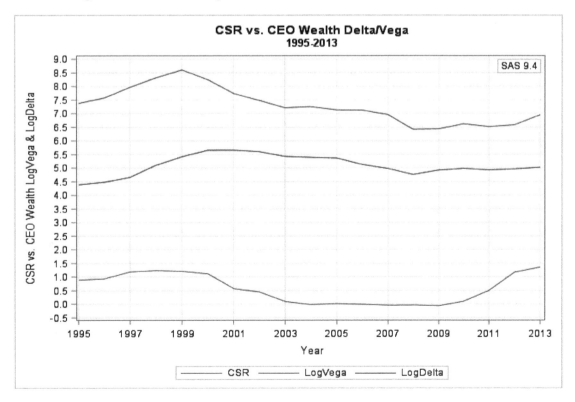

Figure 1. CSR vs. CEO Delta/Vega. This figure shows the relationship between CEO pay sensitivities and CSR over time. All variables are defined in the Appendices A and B.

Table 1. CSR over time. This table shows the summary statistics for the CSR variable over time. It contains the number of observations, the mean values, standard deviations, and min/max values of CSR for each year of our sample. All variables are defined in Appendix A.

Fiscal Year	N Obs	Analysis Variable: CSR N	Mean	Std Dev	Minimum	Maximum
1995	359	359.00	0.88	2.46	−6.00	9
1996	392	392.00	0.93	2.37	−8.00	9
1997	423	423.00	1.19	2.44	−6.00	8
1998	447	447.00	1.23	2.60	−7.00	9
1999	492	492.00	1.21	2.64	−7.00	11
2000	517	517.00	1.11	2.58	−8.00	11
2001	864	864.00	0.57	2.19	−9.00	9
2002	957	957.00	0.45	2.22	−9.00	9
2003	1577	1577.00	0.10	1.92	−9.00	8
2004	1627	1627.00	−0.02	2.12	−8.00	10
2005	1696	1696.00	0.02	2.26	−8.00	11
2006	1893	1893.00	−0.01	2.31	−8.00	15
2007	2155	2155.00	−0.05	2.28	−9.00	14
2008	2177	2177.00	−0.04	2.30	−9.00	13
2009	2176	2176.00	−0.06	2.30	−9.00	13
2010	2201	2201.00	0.10	2.95	−7.00	17
2011	2140	2140.00	0.50	3.27	−7.00	18
2012	2186	2186.00	1.17	2.47	−5.00	16
2013	2313	2313.00	1.35	3.02	−6.00	17.00

Table 2. Delta over time. This table shows the summary statistics for the Delta variable over time. It contains the number of observations, the mean values, standard deviations, and min/max values of Delta for each year of our sample. All variables are defined in Appendix A.

Fiscal Year	N Obs	Analysis Variable: Delta N	Mean	Std Dev	Minimum	Maximum
1995	359	344.00	1595.64	8108.59	2.11	127,526.64
1996	392	365.00	1945.68	10,685.86	2.25	169,506.27
1997	423	388.00	2890.48	18,284.74	1.73	342,219.71
1998	447	419.00	4098.10	29,621.63	2.18	558,974.19
1999	492	454.00	5458.15	42,013.39	3.94	709,829.7
2000	517	472.00	3821.29	15,309.13	6.95	213,589.37
2001	864	812.00	2305.58	9090.89	0.00	174,744.3
2002	957	915.00	1773.95	8467.23	0.39	181,294.18
2003	1577	1491.00	1354.17	6155.97	0.00	151,106.75
2004	1627	1542.00	1404.96	6444.14	0.00	163,382.82
2005	1696	1613.00	1251.78	4049.33	0.00	101,838.53
2006	1893	1721.00	1239.00	7222.91	0.00	247,452.89
2007	2155	2037.00	1050.79	6912.26	0.00	269,934.95
2008	2177	2070.00	613.21	5422.34	0.00	231,972.09
2009	2176	2066.00	623.04	6045.21	0.00	265,911.24
2010	2201	2102.00	749.70	8706.47	0.00	391,755.57
2011	2140	2062.00	676.82	7004.18	0.00	302,657.79
2012	2186	2096.00	722.55	8610.73	0.00	388,945.54
2013	2313	2206.00	1045.35	10,752.03	0.00	486,620.98

Table 3. Vega over time. This table shows the summary statistics for the Vega variable over time. It contains the number of observations, the mean values, standard deviations, and min/max values of vega for each year of our sample. All variables are defined in Appendix A.

			Analysis Variable: Vega			
Fiscal Year	**N Obs**	**N**	**Mean**	**Std Dev**	**Minimum**	**Maximum**
1995	359	356.00	80.27	116.50	0.00	902.91457
1996	392	377.00	87.78	205.58	0.00	3625.52
1997	423	407.00	105.35	218.37	0.00	3007.34
1998	447	439.00	164.35	274.08	0.00	3490.61
1999	492	482.00	225.65	306.73	0.00	3639.82
2000	517	501.00	286.13	650.70	0.00	11,261.69
2001	864	853.00	286.15	448.48	0.00	3768.64
2002	957	947.00	271.21	367.79	0.00	2992.8
2003	1577	1541.00	227.21	388.25	0.00	4536.19
2004	1627	1581.00	219.49	387.29	0.00	4196.82
2005	1696	1660.00	213.87	393.19	0.00	3670.8
2006	1893	1748.00	168.83	311.75	0.00	3984.76
2007	2155	2038.00	144.69	276.92	0.00	3098.71
2008	2177	2075.00	116.17	227.36	0.00	3841.35
2009	2176	2075.00	136.55	260.50	0.00	5041.26
2010	2201	2111.00	145.23	272.67	0.00	4446.21
2011	2140	2066.00	137.48	294.56	0.00	7885.78
2012	2186	2097.00	142.27	331.51	0.00	9442.93
2013	2313	2208.00	152.02	329.93	0.00	9389.01

Table 4. Correlations between variables. This table shows correlations, significance levels, and the number of observations for the variables: CSR, Delta, Vega, Delta_Lag, Vega_Lag, LogAssets, LogSales, and LogXRD. All variables are defined in Appendix A.

	Pearson Correlation Coefficients Prob > |r| under H0: Rho=0 Number of Observations								
	CSR	**Delta**	**Vega**	**Delta_Lag**	**Vega_Lag**	**LogAssets**	**LogSales**	**LogXRD**	**DTA**
CSR	1	0.0661	0.23985	0.06259	0.22734	0.2536	0.19616	0.03838	−0.09042
		<0.0001	<0.0001	<0.0001	<0.0001	<0.0001	<0.0001	<0.0001	<0.0001
	18,617	17,320	17,909	17,319	17,908	18,616	18,604	18,617	18,616
Delta	0.0661	1	0.28239	0.78326	0.24269	0.10456	0.12848	0.03599	−0.01331
	<0.0001		<0.0001	<0.0001	<0.0001	<0.0001	<0.0001	<0.0001	0.0798
	17,320	17,320	17,320	16,673	17,017	17,319	17,307	17,320	17,319
Vega	0.23985	0.28239	1	0.25464	0.80398	0.41042	0.44544	0.04997	0.01701
	<0.0001	<0.0001		<0.0001	<0.0001	<0.0001	<0.0001	<0.0001	0.0228
	17,909	17,320	17,909	17,020	17,592	17,908	17,896	17,909	17,908
Delta_Lag	0.06259	0.78326	0.25464	1	0.28238	0.1037	0.13001	0.03353	−0.01191
	<0.0001	<0.0001	<0.0001		<0.0001	<0.0001	<0.0001	<0.0001	0.1171
	17,319	16,673	17,020	17,319	17,319	17,318	17,306	17,319	17,318
Vega_Lag	0.22734	0.24269	0.80398	0.28238	1	0.38611	0.42025	0.04561	0.01619
	<0.0001	<0.0001	<0.0001	<0.0001		< 0.0001	<0.0001	<0.0001	0.0303
	17,908	17,017	17,592	17,319	17,908	17,907	17,895	17,908	17,907
LogAssets	0.2536	0.10456	0.41042	0.1037	0.38611	1	0.76525	−0.31739	−0.10975
	<0.0001	<0.0001	<0.0001	<0.0001	<0.0001		<0.0001	<0.0001	<0.0001
	18,616	17,319	17,908	17,318	17,907	18,616	18,604	18,616	18,616
LogSales	0.19616	0.12848	0.44544	0.13001	0.42025	0.76525	1	−0.02062	0.09239
	<0.0001	<0.0001	<0.0001	<0.0001	<0.0001	<0.0001		0.0049	<0.0001
	18,604	17,307	17,896	17,306	17,895	18,604	18,604	18,604	18,604
LogXRD	0.03838	0.03599	0.04997	0.03353	0.04561	−0.31739	−0.02062	1	0.20639
	<0.0001	<0.0001	<0.0001	<0.0001	<0.0001	<0.0001	0.0049		<0.0001
	18,617	17,320	17,909	17,319	17,908	18,616	18,604	18,617	18,616
DTA	−0.09042	−0.01331	0.01701	−0.01191	0.01619	−0.10975	0.09239	0.20639	1
	<0.0001	0.0798	0.0228	0.1171	0.0303	<0.0001	<0.0001	<0.0001	
	18,616	17,319	17,908	17,318	17,907	18,616	18,604	18,616	18,616

From the results of our correlation matrix in Table 4, we can see that CSR was positively correlated with delta and vega measures. We can also see that CSR was negatively correlated with financial leverage (DTA) and positively correlated with our proxies for firm size (LogAssets and LogSales) as well as R&D expense (LogXRD) which we used as a proxy for firm type. These univariate results present contrasting information on how to perceive CSR. On one hand, positive correlation with R&D expense points us in the direction that CSR is perceived as a risky investment policy. On the other hand, negative correlation with financial leverage leads us to the opposite conclusion. One potential explanation to this discrepancy is that many firms with high CSR ratings are in industries where equity plays a greater role in the capital structure, but R&D is a crucial part of the business. The technology sector is one such industry. Many technology companies do not have the cash flow necessary to sustain a leveraged capital structure, and therefore, rely heavily on equity for financing. However, these companies must also spend considerable funds on R&D to stay competitive. In order to fully understand this type of problem, we must turn to multivariate analysis.

4.2. Multivariate Analysis

We created a model to determine how CEO pay sensitivity is linked to firm CSR ratings. Using fixed effect estimation, we constructed a model to test the causal relationship between delta, vega, and CSR ratings. Our first hypothesis was that if CEOs view CSR as a positive NPV investment, they will invest resources into CSR initiatives, which should increase the firm's CSR rating. If CEOs view CSR as a nonpositive NPV investment, they will not invest resources into CSR initiatives, thereby decreasing or keeping constant the firm's CSR rating. In our fixed effects model, this should result in a positive sign on the coefficient of the delta parameter since higher delta incentivizes CEOs to pursue positive NPV projects. Our second hypothesis is that if CEOs view CSR as an investment that increases firm risk, then they will pursue more CSR projects as vega increases. This should lead to a positive coefficient estimate on the vega parameter. We also used control variables to remove firm size, risk, and industry effects from our estimates. We computed a variety of models to test our hypotheses for different combinations of both current period and lagged values of delta and vega. Each model that we tested follows this basic structure:

CSR Rating = f(Delta, Vega, Assets, Sales, R&D Expenses, Debt-to-Assets Ratio)

4.2.1. Dependent Variables

Consistent with the prior executive compensation literature, we sought to link firm policy choices to CEO pay sensitivity using delta [30,32] and/or vega [7,30]. The noncontrol variables that we used in our analysis are Delta and Vega, as well as Delta_Lag and Vega_Lag, which are one period lags of Delta and Vega, respectively. We formulated various combinations of the model using these variables in order to determine how CEO pay sensitivity to these factors influences CSR at a given firm.

4.2.2. Control Variables

Firm risk, size, and industry have all been identified as factors that affect CSR [33,43,55]. We drew upon Tsoutsoura [33] and McWilliams and Siegel [55] to determine appropriate control variables for our model. Tsoutsoura [33] uses Debt-to-Assets (DTA) as a proxy for firm risk. She tests separate models using LogAssets and LogSales to proxy firm size and then classifies firms by industry to remove industry effects. We used this method apart from her solution for industry effects. Classifying firms by industry can be challenging, and as the number of industry classifications decreases, the averaging across firms makes for a less accurate inference. McWilliams and Siegel [55] note that R&D expense is a useful proxy for industry (i.e., firm type) once firm risk and size have been accounted for. This method allows us to avoid the averaging effect that industry classifications cause, resulting in stronger correlations and more powerful inferences. Therefore, as control variables, we tested separate models using both LogAssets (Model A) or LogSales (Model B) as proxy for size and used DTA to account for risk and

R&D expense to account for firm type. In untabulated results, we controlled for a variety of additional firm, governance, and executive characteristics which we found did not change our main results.

4.3. Discussion

We computed 12 separate fixed effects models to properly understand the relationship between CSR and CEO pay sensitivity. Since the link between these two variables has not previously been studied, we felt it important to run several different models to properly determine the direction of the effects provided by delta and vega. The first point to note is that all 12 models were statistically significant at the 99% level as indicated by the F-test results. We ran each combination of Delta, Vega, Delta_Lag, and Vega_Lag using both LogAssets and LogSales as control variables for size. This is consistent with the method of Tsoutsoura [33]. We denoted the LogAssets models with an "A" and the LogSales models with a "B". As per Table 5, Model A consistently outperformed Model B on an R-squared basis. For this reason, we viewed LogAssets as a superior proxy for size to LogSales for our purposes.

Table 5. Model comparison. This table compares the various models that we constructed to explain CSR scores using CEO pay sensitivities. For each model that we constructed, Model A used LogAssets as a proxy for firm size, while Model B used LogSales as a proxy for firm size. Further details on each model are contained within Appendix B. All variables are defined in Appendix A.

Model	Adj R-Sq	Pr > F	Key Variables	Estimate	Pr > |t|
Model 1A	0.104	<0.0001	Delta	0.00000	0.64570
			Vega	0.00102	<0.0001
Model 1B	0.082	<0.0001	Delta	0.00000	0.46030
			Vega	0.00131	<0.0001
Model 2A	0.104	<0.0001	Vega	0.00102	<0.0001
Model 2B	0.081	<0.0001	Vega	0.00130	<0.0001
Model 3A	0.089	<0.0001	Delta	0.00001	<0.0001
Model 3B	0.056	<0.0001	Delta	0.00001	<0.0001
Model 4A	0.103	<0.0001	Delta_Lag,	0.00000	0.54390
			Vega_Lag	0.00094	<0.0001
Model 4B	0.079	<0.0001	Delta_Lag,	0.00000	0.38530
			Vega_Lag	0.00121	<0.0001
Model 5A	0.089	<0.0001	Delta_Lag	0.00001	0.00030
Model 5B	0.056	<0.0001	Delta_Lag	0.00001	<0.0001
Model 6A	0.103	<0.0001	Vega_Lag	0.00095	<0.0001
Model 6B	0.078	<0.0001	Vega_Lag	0.00121	<0.0001

Note: Model A uses LogAssets and Model B uses LogSales as proxy for firm size. All Models use DTA and LogR&D to control for firm risk and type, respectively.

Both the Vega and Vega_Lag parameters were significant beyond the 99.99% level in every model in which they appeared. On the other hand, Delta was insignificant in every model in which it appeared with either Vega or Vega_Lag. Delta parameters were only ever significant in models in which they appeared alone without Vega parameters. From this, we conclude that CSR is primarily driven by Vega related parameters. Model 6A was the strongest of the 12 we produced. It used Vega_Lag as the noncontrol dependent variable and had an R-squared value of 0.103. The 12 models can be examined in further detail in Appendix B. In untabulated results, we also studied different CSR categories and CSR strength/concern separately. We found that the effects of CEO incentives were generally similar and consistent across different categories. We also found consistent results for CSR strength and concern; vega was positively related to strength and negatively to concern.

In summary, we found that Vega and Vega_Lag parameters are significant drivers of firm CSR ratings. Therefore, we conclude that vega related parameters belong in the true model. As delta related parameters only ever demonstrate significance when vega related parameters are removed, we believe that Delta and Delta_Lag do not belong in the model. Furthermore, as Delta and Delta_Lag are never significantly different than zero at higher confidence levels, it suggests that CEOs do not act as if investing in a higher CSR rating is a positive NPV project. From the CEO standpoint, a decision made independently of delta could be consistent with the neutral present value proposition from Ullmann [43]. However, it could also be reconciled with the viewpoint that CSR increases financial performance [17,40,41], because it could be argued that CEOs implement CSR measures when there is a clear benefit to the firm, regardless of delta exposure.

Most importantly, our findings draw a causal relation between CEOs' pay sensitivity to vega and CSR ratings. This could indicate that CEOs perceive that CSR projects increase firm risk, which would be inconsistent with Attig et al. [49] and Albuquerque et al. [45]. This may be because CSR performance is difficult to quantify, and hence justify, to shareholders. It may also be due to the fact that the benefits of CSR are perceived as too distant to be of concern today. The other explanation is that CEOs simply do not know what the effects of CSR ratings will be on their firm's value. This leads us to the most interesting conclusion of this paper: CEOs are motivated to invest in CSR through vega. CEOs may be unsure of the effect of CSR on shareholder wealth; however, they pursue CSR ratings as a way of increasing firm risk when incentivized by higher vega.

4.4. Endogeneity Issues

We adopted a variety of control variables and fixed effects models to address the omitted variable problem. The results are robust after controlling for observable firm and managerial characteristics, as well as for various unobservable characteristics such as time, industry, and firm fixed effects. Furthermore, we control for instances of lagged dependent variables for robustness checks. Lagged CSR is important because it contains all the information that determines CSR until the point of year t. Even after controlling for CSR at year t, CSR at t still provides incremental explanatory power to explain CSR at year t+1. This suggests that vega has explanatory power to predict future CSR even after controlling for current CSR level.

5. Conclusions

We developed a model to estimate CSR ratings as a function of CEO pay sensitivity to delta and vega. We used panel data spanning 1995–2013 to construct yearly firm CSR ratings and estimates of CEO pay sensitivity to firm stock price (delta) and volatility (vega). This was the longest sample period we were able to collect. The nineteen years were long enough for the statistically significant tests we conducted. In addition, to capture macro shocks in the sample period, we controlled for year fixed effects. We found that CSR ratings increased as CEOs were exposed to higher levels of vega, but not delta. This leads us to conclude that CEOs make CSR related decisions independent of their pay sensitivity to the underlying stock price, but that CEOs view CSR projects as a way of promoting stock volatility. Given that we should expect CSR ratings to have a positive relationship with delta if it is viewed as a value-enhancing policy, these results suggest that CEOs may be pursuing CSR projects simply to increase their own compensation through vega by increasing stock price volatility.

When interpreting these results, it is imperative not to infer conclusions regarding the actual effect of CSR on firm value. Our analysis only indicates how CEOs perceive CSR standings, not the actual effect these investments have on a firm's financial performance. CEO actions are not always value maximizing from the shareholder's perspective. Sometimes, this manifests itself through agency problems, but sometimes it is because CEOs do not have the necessary information to make ex-post value-maximizing decisions. The effects of CSR on financial performance are a major source of debate in the literature. Therefore, it is reasonable to assume that CEOs may also be unsure of how to make value-maximizing CSR investments. If we infer that CEOs are acting in the best interest of shareholders, then a decision made independently of delta could be consistent with the neutral present value proposition from Ullmann [43]. However, it could also be reconciled with the viewpoint that CSR increases financial performance [17,40,41], since it could be argued that CEOs implement CSR measures when there is a clear benefit to the firm, regardless of delta exposure.

Most importantly, our findings on the relation between CEOs' pay sensitivity to vega and CSR ratings indicate that CEOs make CSR investments to increase firm risk, which would be inconsistent with [45,49]. One plausible explanation is that CEOs may simply view CSR as a way of increasing stock price volatility without having adverse effects on operational risk. For example, this could be achieved if many market participants have diverging views on the correct valuation methods to apply to CSR projects. Under these assumptions, a situation could be constructed where the expectation of the stock price remains unchanged with an increase in CSR standing while volatility of the stock price increases. Another potential explanation is that CEOs with higher vega exposure choose riskier CSR projects than other CEOs. Further research needs to be performed in this area in order to properly identify the source of this relationship. These findings have implications for both the executive compensation literature and the CSR literature. By understanding how CEOs respond to various compensation incentives, we can begin to formulate better compensation structures that minimize agency costs and simultaneously maximize shareholder and stakeholder value.

To better address the omitted variable bias that likely exists in this paper and any studies alike, future research should focus on better empirical proxies and theoretical frameworks for managerial risk aversion and talent. Empiricists should collect more detailed information, for instance, on CEOs' background and personal experience. For theorists, it is important to model other forces aside from those in the agency framework. Developing new theories of how managerial attributes affect firm policy and outcomes and the contractual structure of managerial compensation can contribute to our understanding of the relationships between executive compensation and CSR.

Author Contributions: Methodology, T.M.; formal analysis, T.M.; resources, Z.L.; writing—original draft preparation, T.M.; writing—review and editing, A.I.; supervision, A.I. and Z.L. All authors have read and agreed to the published version of the manuscript.

Appendix A. Variable Definitions

Variable	Description
CSR	KLD scores for Corporate Social Responsibility (CSR); total strengths minus total concerns, aggregated across the categories of community, diversity, employee relations, environment, human rights, and product.
Delta	The CEO's pay sensitivity to the underlying stock price
Vega	The CEO's pay sensitivity to the volatility of the underlying stock price
Delta_Lag	A 1-year lag of the Delta variable from our sample.
Vega_Lag	A 1-year lag of the Vega variable from our sample.
LogAssets	A control variable which takes the natural logarithm of total firm assets.
LogSales	A control variable which takes the natural logarithm of total firm sales.
LogXRD	A control variable which takes the natural logarithm of firm research and development expense.
DTA	The debt-to-assets ratio of the firm.

Appendix B. Additional Tests for Robustness Check

Model 2 uses alternative firm size measures to check robustness of the relationship between Vega and CSR. Model 3 checks robustness of the relationship between Delta and CSR. Model 4 uses both Delta and Vega with one-year lag. Models 5 and 6 study lagged Delta and Vega, respectively.

Model 2

Independent Variable: Vega

Model 2A

Firm Size Control: LogAssets

Source	DF	Sum of Squares	Mean Square	F Value	Pr > F
Model	4.00	10,690.25	2672.56	520.22	<0.0001
Error	17,903	91,975.17	5.14		
Corrected Total	17,907	102,665.41			

R-Square	Coeff Var	Root MSE	CSR Mean
0.10	1370.82	2.27	0.17

Parameter	Estimate	Standard	t Value	Pr > |t|
Intercept	-2.02796	0.08571	-23.66	<0.0001
vega	0.00102	0.00006	18.05	<0.0001
LogAssets	0.28862	0.01080	26.73	<0.0001
LogXRD	0.03023	0.00193	15.67	<0.0001
DTA	-1.32407	0.10296	-12.86	<0.0001

Model 2B

Firm Size Control: LogSales

Source	DF	Sum of Squares	Mean Square	F Value	Pr > F
Model	4.00	8350.51	2087.63	396.71	<0.0001
Error	17,891	94,148.45	5.26		
Corrected Total	17,895	102,498.96			

R-Square	Coeff Var	Root MSE	CSR Mean
0.08	1400.65	2.29	0.16

Parameter	Estimate	Standard	t Value	Pr > |t|
Intercept	-1.20187	0.09023	-13.32	<0.0001
vega	0.00130	0.00006	22.85	<0.0001
LogSales	0.19086	0.01222	15.62	<0.0001
LogXRD	0.01392	0.00183	7.63	< 0.0001
DTA	-1.67248	0.10481	-15.96	< 0.0001

Model 3

Independent Variable: Delta

Model 3A

Firm Size Control: LogAssets

Source	DF	Sum of Squares	Mean Square	F Value	Pr > F
Model	4.00	8869.00	2217.25	423.82	<0.0001
Error	17,314	90,580.47	5.23		
Corrected Total	17,318	99,449.47			

R-Square	Coeff Var	Root MSE	CSR Mean
0.09	1340.10	2.29	0.17

Parameter	Estimate	Standard	t Value	Pr > |t|
Intercept	-2.52989	0.08347	-30.31	<0.0001
delta	0.00001	0.00000	4.02	<0.0001
LogAssets	0.37392	0.00996	37.53	<0.0001
LogXRD	0.03540	0.00195	18.18	<0.0001
DTA	-1.26982	0.10532	-12.06	<0.0001

Model 3B

Firm Size Control: LogSales

Source	DF	Sum of Squares	Mean Square	F Value	Pr > F
Model	4.00	5565.92	1391.48	256.89	<0.0001
Error	17,302	93,717.39	5.42		
Corrected Total	17,306	99,283.32			

R-Square	Coeff Var	Root MSE	CSR Mean
0.06	1376.61	2.33	0.17

Parameter	Estimate	Standard	t Value	Pr > |t|
Intercept	-1.85823	0.08830	-21.05	<0.0001
delta	0.00001	0.00000	4.84	<0.0001
LogSales	0.31029	0.01136	27.30	<0.0001
LogXRD	0.01518	0.00188	8.06	<0.0001
DTA	-1.76972	0.10777	-16.42	<0.0001

Model 4

Independent Variables: Lag(1) delta and Lag(1) Vega

Model 4A

Firm Size Control: LogAssets

Source	DF	Sum of Squares	Mean Square	F Value	Pr > F
Model	5.00	10,202.11	2040.42	397.53	<0.0001
Error	17,312	88,858.23	5.13		
Corrected Total	17,317	99,060.34			

R-Square	Coeff Var	Root MSE	CSR Mean
0.10	1345.97	2.27	0.17

Parameter	Estimate	Standard	t Value	Pr > |t|
Intercept	-2.11504	0.08631	-24.51	<0.0001
delta_lag	0.00000	0.00000	-0.61	0.54390
vega_lag	0.00094	0.00006	16.20	<0.0001
LogAssets	0.30090	0.01081	27.82	<0.0001
LogXRD	0.02975	0.00196	15.21	<0.0001
DTA	-1.33713	0.10409	-12.85	<0.0001

Model 4B

Firm Size Control: LogSales

Source	DF	Sum of Squares	Mean Square	F Value	Pr > F
Model	5.00	7769.69	1553.94	295.02	<0.0001
Error	17,300	91,124.37	5.27		
Corrected Total	17,305	98,894.06			

R-Square	Coeff Var	Root MSE	CSR Mean
0.08	1376.72	2.30	0.17

Parameter	Estimate	Standard	t Value	Pr > |t|
Intercept	-1.30703	0.09107	-14.35	<0.0001
delta_lag	0.00000	0.00000	-0.87	0.38530
vega_lag	0.00121	0.00006	20.54	<0.0001
LogSales	0.20713	0.01227	16.88	<0.0001
LogXRD	0.01293	0.00186	6.95	<0.0001
DTA	-1.70928	0.10600	-16.13	<0.0001

Model 5

Independent Variable: Lag (1) Delta

Model 5A

Firm Size Control: LogAssets

Source	DF	Sum of Squares	Mean Square	F Value	Pr > F
Model	4.00	8855.74	2213.93	424.92	<0.0001
Error	17,313	90,204.61	5.21		
Corrected Total	17,317	99,060.34			

R-Square	Coeff Var	Root MSE	CSR Mean
0.09	1356.09	2.28	0.17

Parameter	Estimate	Standard	t Value	Pr > |t|
Intercept	−2.52370	0.08316	−30.35	<0.0001
delta_lag	0.00001	0.00000	3.64	0.00030
LogAssets	0.37322	0.00992	37.61	<0.0001
LogXRD	0.03523	0.00194	18.15	<0.0001
DTA	−1.28132	0.10481	−12.22	<0.0001

Model 5B

Firm Size Control: LogSales

Source	DF	Sum of Squares	Mean Square	F Value	Pr > F
Model	4.00	5547.51	1386.88	257.05	<0.0001
Error	17,301	93,346.54	5.40		
Corrected Total	17,305	98,894.06			

R-Square	Coeff Var	Root MSE	CSR Mean
0.06	1393.36	2.32	0.17

Parameter	Estimate	Standard	t Value	Pr > |t|
Intercept	−1.85595	0.08812	−21.06	<0.0001
delta_lag	0.00001	0.00000	4.37	<0.0001
LogSales	0.31002	0.01134	27.34	<0.0001
LogXRD	0.01508	0.00188	8.03	<0.0001
DTA	−1.78167	0.10722	−16.62	<0.0001

Model 6

Independent Variable: Lag (1) Vega

Model 6A

Firm Size Control: LogAssets

Source	DF	Sum of Squares	Mean Square	F Value	Pr > F
Model	4.00	10,543.26	2635.82	511.32	<0.0001
Error	17,902	92,282.63	5.15		
Corrected Total	17,906	102,825.89			

R-Square	Coeff Var	Root MSE	CSR Mean
0.10	1389.50	2.27	0.16

Parameter	Estimate	Standard	t Value	Pr > |t|
Intercept	-2.09684	0.08493	-24.69	<0.0001
vega_lag	0.00095	0.00006	17.04	<0.0001
LogAssets	0.29916	0.01064	28.11	<0.0001
LogXRD	0.03119	0.00192	16.21	<0.0001
DTA	-1.32449	0.10259	-12.91	<0.0001

Model 6B

Firm Size Control: LogSales

Source	DF	Sum of Squares	Mean Square	F Value	Pr > F
Model	4.00	8048.23	2012.06	380.46	< 0.0001
Error	17,890	94,611.10	5.29		
Corrected Total	17,894	102,659.33			

R-Square	Coeff Var	Root MSE	CSR Mean
0.08	1421.02	2.30	0.16

Parameter	Estimate	Standard	t Value	Pr > |t|
Intercept	-1.29368	0.08965	-14.43	<0.0001
vega_lag	0.00121	0.00006	21.44	<0.0001
LogSales	0.20596	0.01208	17.05	<0.0001
LogXRD	0.01448	0.00183	7.92	<0.0001
DTA	-1.69264	0.10447	-16.20	<0.0001

References

1. Mahoney, L.S.; Thorn, L. Corporate social responsibility and long-term compensation: Evidence from Canada. *J. Bus. Ethics* **2005**, *57*, 241–253. [CrossRef]
2. Mahoney, L.S.; Thorn, L. An examination of the structure of executive compensation and corporate social responsibility: A Canadian investigation. *J. Bus. Ethics* **2006**, *69*, 149–162. [CrossRef]
3. McGuire, J.; Dow, S.; Argheyd, K. CEO incentives and corporate social performance. *J. Bus. Ethics* **2003**, *45*, 341–359. [CrossRef]
4. Deckop, J.R.; Merriman, K.K.; Gupta, S. The effects of CEO pay structure on corporate social performance. *J. Manag.* **2006**, *32*, 329–342. [CrossRef]
5. Ryan, H.E., Jr.; Wiggins, R.A., III. The interactions between R&D investment decisions and compensation policy. *Financ. Manag.* **2002**, *31*, 5–29.
6. Cohen, R.B.; Hall, B.J.; Viceira, L.M. *Do Executive Stock Options Encourage Risk-Taking*; Harvard University: Cambridge, MA, USA, 2000; unpublished manuscript.
7. Coles, J.L.; Daniel, N.D.; Naveen, L. Managerial incentives and risk-taking. *J. Financ. Econ.* **2006**, *79*, 431–468. [CrossRef]
8. Knopf, J.D.; Nam, J.; Thornton, J.H., Jr. The volatility and price sensitivities of managerial stock option portfolios and corporate hedging. *J. Financ.* **2002**, *57*, 801–813. [CrossRef]
9. Jensen, M.C.; Meckling, W.H. Theory of the firm: Managerial behavior, agency costs and ownership structure. *J. Financ. Econ.* **1976**, *3*, 305–360. [CrossRef]
10. Fama, E.F. Agency Problems and the Theory of the Firm. *J. Polit. Econ.* **1980**, *88*, 288–307. [CrossRef]
11. Guay, W.R. The sensitivity of CEO pay to equity risk: An analysis of the magnitude and determinants. *J. Financ. Econ.* **1999**, *53*, 43–71. [CrossRef]
12. Jensen, M.C.; Murphy, K.J. Performance pay and top-management incentives. *J. Polit. Econ.* **1990**, *98*, 225–264. [CrossRef]
13. Hall, B.J.; Liebman, J.B. Are CEOs really paid like bureaucrats? *Q. J. Econ.* **1998**, *113*, 653–691. [CrossRef]
14. Hall, B.J.; Liebman, J.B. The taxation of executive compensation. *Tax Policy Econ.* **2000**, *14*, 1–44. [CrossRef]
15. Bebchuk, L.A.; Fried, J.M.; Walker, D.I. *Managerial Power and Rent Extraction in the Design of Executive Compensation*; No. w9068; National Bureau of Economic Research: Cambridge, MA, USA, 2002.
16. Smith, C.W.; Stulz, R.M. The determinants of firms' hedging policies. *J. Financ. Quant. Anal.* **1985**, *20*, 391–405. [CrossRef]
17. McGuire, J.B.; Sundgren, A.; Schneeweis, T. Corporate social responsibility and firm financial performance. *Acad. Manag. J.* **1988**, *31*, 854–872.
18. Graves, S.B.; Waddock, S.A. Institutional ownership and control: Implications for long-term corporate strategy. *Acad. Manag. Perspect.* **1990**, *4*, 75–83. [CrossRef]
19. Hillman, A.J.; Keim, G.D. Shareholder value, stakeholder management, and social issues: What's the bottom line? *Strat. Manag. J.* **2001**, *22*, 125–139. [CrossRef]
20. Mackey, A.; Mackey, T.B.; Barney, J.B. Corporate social responsibility and firm performance: Investor preferences and corporate strategies. *Acad. Manag. Rev.* **2007**, *32*, 817–835. [CrossRef]
21. Murphy, K.J. Executive compensation. In *Handbook of Labor Economics*; Elsevier: Amsterdam, The Netherlands, 1999; pp. 2485–2563.
22. Perry, T.; Zenner, M. CEO compensation in the 1990's: Shareholder alignment or shareholder expropriation. *Wake For. L. Rev.* **2000**, *35*, 123.
23. Hall, B.J. *The Pay to Performance Incentives of Executive Stock Options*; No. w6674; National Bureau of Economic Research: Cambridge, MA, USA, 1998.
24. Ross, S.A. The economic theory of agency: The principal's problem. *Am. Econ. Rev.* **1973**, *63*, 134–139.
25. Ross, S.A. Compensation, incentives, and the duality of risk aversion and riskiness. *J. Financ.* **2004**, *59*, 207–225. [CrossRef]
26. DeFusco, R.A.; Johnson, R.R.; Zorn, T.S. The effect of executive stock option plans on stockholders and bondholders. *J. Financ.* **1990**, *45*, 617–627. [CrossRef]
27. Ju, N.; Leland, H.; Senbet, L.W. Options, option repricing in managerial compensation: Their effects on corporate investment risk. *J. Corp. Financ.* **2014**, *29*, 628–643. [CrossRef]

28. Jolls, C. *Stock Repurchases and Incentive Compensation*; No. w6467; National Bureau of Economic Research: Cambridge, MA, USA, 1998.

29. Black, F.; Scholes, M. The pricing of options and corporate liabilities. *J. Polit. Econ.* **1973**, *81*, 637–654. [CrossRef]

30. Core, J.; Guay, W. Estimating the value of employee stock option portfolios and their sensitivities to price and volatility. *J. Account. Res.* **2002**, *40*, 613–630. [CrossRef]

31. Bizjak, J.M.; Brickley, J.A.; Coles, J.L. Stock-based incentive compensation and investment behavior. *J. Account. Econ.* **1993**, *16*, 349–372. [CrossRef]

32. Aggarwal, R.K.; Samwick, A.A. The other side of the tradeoff: The impact of risk on executive compensation-A reply. *SSRN Electron. J.* **2002**. [CrossRef]

33. Tsoutsoura, M. *Corporate Social Responsibility and Financial Performance*; Center for Responsible Business: Berkeley, CA, USA, 2004.

34. Heinze, D.C. Financial correlates of a social involvement measure. *Akron Bus. Econ. Rev.* **1976**, *7*, 48–51.

35. Moskowitz, M. Choosing socially responsible stocks. *Bus. Soc. Rev.* **1972**, *1*, 71–75.

36. Aupperle, K.E. The use of forced-choice survey procedures in assessing corporate social orientation. *Res. Corp. Soc. Perform. Policy* **1991**, *12*, 479–486.

37. Herremans, I.M.; Akathaporn, P.; McInnes, M. An investigation of corporate social responsibility reputation and economic performance. *Account. Organ. Soc.* **1993**, *18*, 587–604. [CrossRef]

38. Preston, L.E.; O'Bannon, D.P. The corporate social-financial performance relationship. *Bus. Soc. Rev.* **1997**, *36*, 419. [CrossRef]

39. Waddock, S.A.; Graves, S.B. The corporate social performance-financial performance link. *Strat. Manag. J.* **1997**, *18*, 303–319. [CrossRef]

40. Cochran, P.L.; Wood, R.A. Corporate social responsibility and financial performance. *Acad. Manag. J.* **1984**, *27*, 42–56.

41. Aupperle, K.E.; Carroll, A.B.; Hatfield, J.D. An empirical examination of the relationship between corporate social responsibility and profitability. *Acad. Manag. J.* **1985**, *28*, 446–463.

42. Friedman, M. The social responsibility of business is to increase its profits. *New York Times Magazine*, 13 September 1970; pp. 32–33, 122, 124, 126.

43. Ullmann, A.A. Data in search of a theory: A critical examination of the relationships among social performance, social disclosure, and economic performance of US firms. *Acad. Manag. Rev.* **1985**, *10*, 540–557.

44. Gregory, A.; Tharyan, R.; Whittaker, J. Corporate social responsibility and firm value: Disaggregating the effects on cash flow, risk and growth. *J. Bus. Ethics* **2014**, *124*, 633–657. [CrossRef]

45. Albuquerque, R.A.; Durnev, A.; Koskinen, Y. Corporate social responsibility and firm risk: Theory and empirical evidence. *Manag. Sci.* **2019**, *65*, 4451–4469. [CrossRef]

46. Chava, S. Socially responsible investing and expected stock returns. *SSRN Electron. J.* **2010**. [CrossRef]

47. El Ghoul, S.; Guedhami, O.; Kwok, C.C.; Mishra, D.R. Does corporate social responsibility affect the cost of capital? *J. Bank. Financ.* **2011**, *35*, 2388–2406. [CrossRef]

48. Cheng, B.; Ioannou, I.; Serafeim, G. Corporate social responsibility and access to finance. *Strat. Manag. J.* **2014**, *35*, 1–23. [CrossRef]

49. Attig, N.; El Ghoul, S.; Guedhami, O.; Suh, J. Corporate social responsibility and credit ratings. *J. Bus. Ethics* **2013**, *117*, 679–694. [CrossRef]

50. Servaes, H.; Tamayo, A. The impact of corporate social responsibility on firm value: The role of customer awareness. *Manag. Sci.* **2013**, *59*, 1045–1061. [CrossRef]

51. Jo, H.; Harjoto, M.A. Corporate governance and firm value: The impact of corporate social responsibility. *J. Bus. Ethics* **2011**, *103*, 351–383. [CrossRef]

52. Jo, H.; Harjoto, M.A. The causal effect of corporate governance on corporate social responsibility. *J. Bus. Ethics* **2012**, *106*, 53–72. [CrossRef]

53. Hong, B.; Li, Z.; Minor, D. Corporate Governance and Executive Compensation for Corporate Social Responsibility. *J. Bus. Ethics* **2015**, *136*, 199–213. [CrossRef]

54. Ikram, A.; Li, Z.; Minor, D. CSR-Contingent Executive Compensation Contracts. *J. Bank. Financ.* **2019**. [CrossRef]

55. McWilliams, A.; Siegel, D. Corporate Social Responsibility: A Theory of the Firm Perspective. *Acad. Manag. Rev.* **2001**, *26*, 117–127. [CrossRef]

56. Berman, S.L.; Wicks, A.C.; Kotha, S.; Jones, T.M. Does stakeholder orientation matter? The relationship between stakeholder management models and firm financial performance. *Acad. Manag. J.* **1999**, *42*, 488–506.
57. Chatterji, A.K.; Levine, D.I.; Toffel, M.W. How well do social ratings actually measure corporate social responsibility? *J. Econ. Manag. Strat.* **2009**, *18*, 125–169. [CrossRef]

Permissions

List of Contributors

Thorey S Thorisdottir
Faculty of Business, University of Iceland, 101 Reykjavik, Iceland

Lara Johannsdottir
Environment and Natural Resources, Faculty of Business, University of Iceland, 101 Reykjavik, Iceland

Yi-Bin Li and Gui-Qing Zhang
School of Business Administration, Huaqiao University, Quanzhou 362021, China

Tung-Ju Wu
School of Management, Harbin Institute of Technology, Harbin 150001, China

Chi-Lu Peng
Business Intelligence School, National Kaohsiung University of Science and Technology, Kaohsiung 824303, Taiwan

Haywantee Ramkissoon
College of Business, Law & Social Sciences, Derby Business School, University of Derby, Derby DE22 1GB, UK
School of Business & Economics, UiT, The Arctic University of Norway, 1621 Alta, Norway
College of Business & Economics, Johannesburg Business School, University of Johannesburg, APB 17011 Johannesburg, South Africa

Felix Mavondo and Vishnee Sowamber
Department of Marketing, Monash Business School, Clayton Campus, Monash University, Melbourne, VIC 3000, Australia
Faculty Research Centre for Financial and Corporate Integrity, Coventry University, Coventry CV1 2TU, UK

An-An Chiu
Department of International Business, College of Business, Feng Chia University, Taichung 40724, Taiwan

Ling-Na Chen and Jiun-Chen Hu
Department of Accounting and Information Technology, College of Management, National Chung-Cheng University, Chiayi 621301, Taiwan

Feifei Zhang and Jin-young Jung
College of Business Administration, Inha University, Incheon 22212, Korea

Istianingsih
Economics and Business Faculty, Universitas Bhayangkara Jakarta Raya, Kota Jakarta Selatan, Daerah Khusus Ibukota Jakarta 12550, Indonesia

Terri Trireksani
Murdoch Business School, Murdoch University, Murdoch 6150, Australia

Daniel T. H. Manurung
STIE Widya Gama Lumajang, Jawa Timur 67352, Indonesia

Eneko Ibarnia
Tourism Department, Deusto University, Universities Avenue, 24, 48007 Bilbao, Spain

Lluís Garay
Economics and Management Department, Open University of Catalonia (UOC), Avinguda Tibidabo, 39, 08035 Barcelona, Spain

Antonio Guevara
Faculty of Tourism, Málaga University, León Tolstoy St., Campus de Teatinos, 29071 Malaga, Spain

An-Pin Wei
International School of Business and Finance, Sun Yat-sen University, Zhuhai 519082, China

Hao-Chen Huang
Department of Public Finance and Taxation, National Kaohsiung University of Science and Technology, Kaohsiung 82445, Taiwan

Shang-Pao Yeh
Department of Hospitality and M.I.C.E. Marketing Management, National Kaohsiung University of Hospitality and Tourism, Kaohsiung 812301, Taiwan

Inmaculada Buendía-Martínez
Faculty of Social Sciences, University of Castilla-La Mancha, 16071 Cuenca, Spain

Inmaculada Carrasco Monteagudo
Faculty of Economics and Business, University of
Castilla-La Mancha, Plaza de la Universidad, 02071
Albacete, Spain

Atif Ikram
Department of Finance, Arizona State University,
Tempe, AZ 85281, USA

Zhichuan (Frank) Li
Ivey Business School, University of Western Ontario,
London, ON N6A 3K7, Canada

Travis MacDonald
Department of Economics, University of Western
Ontario, London, ON N6A 3K7, Canada

Index

Printed in the USA
CPSIA information can be obtained
at www.ICGtesting.com
JSHW051405091023
49903JS00006B/290